MANAGING THE GLOBAL NETWORK
CORPORATION

As barriers to international trade and investment have fallen worldwide, the multi-national enterprise has become the leading engine of economic integration and growth. To implement global strategies in an increasingly complex environment, MNEs are adopting novel forms of organization. This book examines in detail the structures, strategies and processes employed in a variety of international corporations, offering insight into the demands placed on international managers at every level.

Based on the findings of a research project sponsored by the Carnegie Bosch Institute, this is an in-depth study of the topics most relevant to international management, with each chapter covering a specific issue that confronts the leaders of major corporations. Topics include:

- strategic integration and decision-making
- structuring of joint ventures
- headquarters–subsidiary relations
- international adaptation of Human Resource Management.

With contributors from the USA, Europe and Asia, this is a vital overview of the contemporary multinational enterprise in its global context.

Bruce McKern is a faculty member at the Stanford Graduate School of Business and is Director of the Stanford Sloan Masters Program.

MANAGING THE GLOBAL NETWORK CORPORATION

Edited by Bruce McKern

Routledge
Taylor & Francis Group

LONDON AND NEW YORK

First published 2003
by Routledge
11 New Fetter Lane, London EC4P 4EE

Simultaneously published in the USA and Canada
by Routledge
29 West 35th Street, New York, NY 10001

Routledge is an imprint of the Taylor & Francis Group

Typeset in Baskerville by Wearset Ltd, Boldon, Tyne and Wear
Printed and bound in Great Britain by TJ International Ltd, Padstow, Cornwall

British Library Cataloguing in Publication Data
A catalogue record for this book is available from the British Library

Library of Congress Cataloging in Publication Data
A catalog record for this book has been requested

ISBN 0-415-29706-0 (hbk)
ISBN 0-415-29705-2 (pbk)

CONTENTS

CONTENTS

ILLUSTRATIONS

Figures

ILLUSTRATIONS

Tables

NOTES ON CONTRIBUTORS

Bruce McKern is Director of the Stanford Sloan Program and teaches in the field of International Business in the Graduate School of Business at Stanford University. McKern gained a BE at the University of Sydney and a Ph.D. in International Business at Harvard University, was Dean of two Australian business schools and President of the Carnegie Bosch Institute. He is the author or editor of eight books, including *Multinational Enterprise and Natural Resources* and *Transnational Corporations in the Exploitation of Natural Resources* (United Nations and Routledge, 1993) and has published numerous papers in academic and professional journals on multinational enterprise, industrial development and international business. He is a consultant to multinational enterprises in the fields of strategy and international management.

Brent B. Allred is an Assistant Professor of Business Administration in the School of Business at the College of William and Mary in Williamsburg, Virginia. He specializes in global competitive strategy and organization structure, gaining and sustaining competitive advantages in emerging markets, and the management of technology and innovation.

Christopher A. Bartlett is the Thomas D. Casserly, Jr. Professor of Business Administration at the Harvard Graduate School of Business Administration. He has published eight books, including (co-authored with Sumantra Ghoshal) *Managing Across Borders: The Transnational Solution*, named by the *Financial Times* as one of the 50 most influential business books of the century; and *The Individualized Corporation*, winner of the Igor Ansoff Award for the best new work in strategic management. In 2001 he received the Academy of Management's International Division Distinguished Scholar Award.

Manuel Becerra is Professor of Strategy and International Management at the Instituto de Empresa (Madrid). He holds a Ph.D. in Strategic Management from the Smith School of Business (University of Maryland, College Park) and an M.Sc. from the Marshall School of Business (University of Southern California, Los Angeles).

Roland Calori died on July 14 2002, the day his school, EM-Lyon, had celebrated his twenty-year tenure as a Professor of Strategic Management. He was visiting professor at universities in Japan, China and the USA and an active member of the editorial boards of the *British Journal of Management, Journal of World Business, Long Range Planning, Management, Management International, Metamorphosis,*

Strategic Organization. At the time of his death he was President-Elect of the International Association of Strategic Management.

Sea Jin Chang is a Professor at Korea University. He received his BA and MA in economics from Seoul National University, and Ph.D. in strategic management from the Wharton School of the University of Pennsylvania, where he was a Dean's Fellow.

John Child is Chair of Commerce at the Birmingham Business School, University of Birmingham. He consults for major corporations in the fields of strategic alliances, organization, organizational learning and business operations in China.

Richard Florida is the H. John Heinz III Professor of Regional Economic Development at Carnegie Mellon University's Heinz School of Public Policy and Management. He has served as an advisor to US government agencies, the Canadian government, the European Union, the Japanese government, and multinational corporations.

Sumantra Ghoshal is Professor of Strategic and International Management at London Business School. He earned the degrees of MS and Ph.D. at MIT and DBA at Harvard Business School. His research interests are in the fields of international management, global strategy, strategic management, corporate entrepreneurship, and corporate renewal.

Anil K. Gupta is the Ralph J. Tyser Professor of Strategy and Organization at the Robert H. Smith School of Business, The University of Maryland at College Park. Professor Gupta consults with international corporations in the fields of strategy and international management.

The late **Professor Gunnar Hedlund** was Professor of International Business at the Institute of International Business at the Stockholm School of Economics. He wrote extensively about the management of multinational corporations, entry strategies in foreign markets, and global innovation processes. His work is commemorated in an annual doctoral prize in the field of international management.

Dr Gary Katzenstein is an Assistant Professor in the School of Business and Management at the Hong Kong University of Science and Technology. He graduated with a Ph.D. in Organizational Behavior from the Graduate School of Industrial Administration, Carnegie Mellon University and an MBA from the Anderson School at the University of California at Los Angeles.

Dr F. Javier Lerch is Senior Research Scientist and Director of the Center for Interactive Simulations in the Graduate School of Industrial Administration, Carnegie Mellon University. He earned the degrees of M.Sc. at the University of Sussex, and the MBA and Ph.D. at the University of Michigan.

Raymond E. Miles is Professor Emeritus and former Dean at the Haas School of Business, University of California, Berkeley. He is the author of over 50 articles and four books, which have included editions in other languages, including Japanese and German. He has consulted with business and government agencies in the US and abroad and is a Fellow of the Academy of Management.

John Naman is Program Director of the Innovation and Organizational Change Program at the National Science Foundation. He gained his Ph.D. at the University of Pittsburgh and taught management in leading business schools, including Carnegie Mellon and the University of Maryland. Dr Naman has been a consultant to over 50 organizations, including: American General Corp., Boeing, the Department of Defense, IBM, and the US International Trade Commission.

Jonas Ridderstråle is Assistant Professor at the Centre for Advanced Studies in Leadership at the Stockholm School of Economics. He is the author of *Global Innovation: Managing International Innovation Projects at ABB and Electrolux* and co-author of an international bestseller *Funky Business: Talent Makes Capital Dance.*

Philip Rosenzweig is Professor of Management at IMD in Lausanne, Switzerland. His research and teaching center on the challenges of managing multinational firms. Fields of interest include global strategy, foreign investment, multinational organization design, and international staffing and career management. He is co-author of *International Management, Text and Cases.*

Kendall Roth holds the J. Willis Cantey Chair of International Business and Economics at the University of South Carolina and serves as the Director of the Ph.D. program in International Business. He teaches in USC's international masters and doctoral programs, predominantly in the areas of global strategic management, international management, and international management theory and research.

Charles C. Snow is the Mellon Foundation Professor of Business Administration in the Smeal College of Business Administration at Penn State University. He teaches in the areas of Strategic Management and International Business, and has recently taught courses in Executive MBA programs in Australia, New Zealand, Turkey, France, and Norway.

Sharon Watson is Assistant Professor of Management in the College of Business and Economics, University of Delaware. She received the Ph.D. from the University of South Carolina and the MBA from the State University of New York at Buffalo. She teaches in the areas of Corporate Strategy and International Business Management. Professor Watson has received numerous awards for academic achievement and is active as a reviewer for several academic journals, including *Academy of Management Journal, Journal of International Management* and *Management International Review.*

Jeffrey R. Williams is Professor of Business Strategy in the Graduate School of Industrial Administration, Carnegie Mellon University. He has authored 40 studies on strategy, as well as articles in *The Journal of Law and Economics, The Journal of Economic Behavior and Organization, Fundamental Issues in Strategy, Industrial and Corporate Change,* the Federal Trade Commission, the Sloan Foundation and the National Science Foundation. He is on the editorial board of the *Strategic Management Journal* and has received the *California Management Review* Pacific Telesis Award for best contribution to new thinking in management. Professor Williams is the highest-ranked teacher at the Carnegie Mellon business school and has twice been awarded the George Leland Bach Prize for excellence in education. He is an adviser to policy makers on competitive advantage in the new economy.

FOREWORD

Drawing together the contributions of a distinguished group of scholars, each of whom is working at the frontiers of research on multinational enterprises (MNEs), Professor McKern has produced an intellectually robust and forward-looking volume. As he states in his introduction, the research which led to this monograph was commissioned by him during his tenure as the first President of the Carnegie Bosch Institute in the early 1990s. As a member of his Research Advisory Council during this time I was privileged to experience, at first hand, some of Professor McKern's vision, ideas and imaginative leadership; and to share with him some of his pride and pleasure (not to mention relief!) as the fruits of the early research projects he commissioned began to come on-stream. By the time he left Carnegie Bosch in 1996 for a post in Australia, the Institute had gained high acclaim among both practitioners and scholars of international business; and much of the credit for this lies in Professor McKern's scholarly acumen, creative entrepreneurship and fine administrative qualities.

This volume contains the results of some of the early research projects. It focuses on one – albeit a critical – aspect of the impact of globalization and the advent of the knowledge-based economy on the organization of value-added activities, both within and between firms. It is a subject which, over the last decade, has gained the increasing attention of scholars from a variety of disciplines; and it embraces a host of issues ranging from the governance and organizational structure of firms to the changing strategy and locus of decision taking, and their implications for human-resource management.

At the core of the subject matter of this book is the growing role intra- and inter-firm networks play as organizational and decision-influencing entities. Why is this? Why are networks now centre stage in the international business (IB) scholarly research? Let me suggest five reasons; there are no doubt several others.

The first has to do with the emergence of alliance or collective capitalism, in which, in order to attain their economic objectives, firms are increasingly needing to cooperate with each other. Sometimes this cooperation is dyadic; sometimes it is between groups of firms. Sometimes this is along, and sometimes between, value chains. Often it is made possible or enhanced by networks. *Inter alia*, it is demonstrated by the explosion of cross-border strategic alliances, joint ventures, and mergers and acquisitions over the last two decades.

The second reason is that, to be properly understood, networks need to be both multi-faceted in the issues they explore, and interdisciplinary in their scholarly input. Even a cursory glance at the burgeoning literature on networks reveals that geographers, economists, sociologists, management strategists and political scientists, as well as organizational and behavioural scholars, are making an important contribution to our understanding of the *raison d'être*, and the nature and consequences of, multiple and integrated inter-firm relationships.

Third, I find network analysis important in that it is rehabilitating the dimension of human resource management into mainstream IB scholarship. Too often, in recent years, purely technology-related issues have claimed most of the attention of academic researchers interested in the competitive enhancing strategies of firms. If nothing else, the emergence of networks is telling us that the success of the constituent enterprises critically rests on harmonious interactive personal relationships, which, in turn, are based on such attributes as mutual trust, forbearance, reciprocity and good will.

Fourth, recent events – and especially innovatory imperatives and competitive pressures – are encouraging or forcing firms to develop new forms of coalitions along and between value chains in order to capture the benefits of scale and scope economies. Such affiliations, which again may be dyadic or multilateral, may then be vertical, horizontal or functional. In our contemporary global economy, for example, cross-border networks are an essential component of the upgrading of organizational expertise of firms in sectors such as autos, textiles, computer software, banking and biotechnology.

And, lastly, aligned with the fourth reason, there is the increasing tendency for spatially confined networks or clusters of related activities to be formed – a subject that has so much engaged the scholars such as Michael Porter and Michael Enright in recent years.

This volume offers the reader a tantalising glimpse into several of the organizational issues that are now at the forefront of IB research. These include the locus of decision-taking within firms; the changing nature of managerial competencies and competitive advantages; the reorientation of business process engineering; the relationship between ownership and access strategies of firms; and the implication of networks for human-resource management, transaction costs, spatial product diversity and the organization of cross-border research and development.

In short, this is a volume to be highly commended. It is rich in analytical insights. It is bold in its attempt to tackle unfamiliar areas of research. It is visionary in its attempt to identify an agenda for IB scholars for several years to come. Professor McKern is to be congratulated for assembling such a rich array of talent and commissioning research on so many interrelated and overlapping topics. This volume is not only an excellent example of the whole being greater than the sum of the parts; it is also a fitting tribute to the leadership and scholarship he brought to the early years of the Carnegie Bosch Foundation.

John H. Dunning
Reading and Rutgers Universities

PREFACE

This book reports the findings of a series of research projects commissioned during my tenure as President of the Carnegie Bosch Institute. The Carnegie Bosch Institute is a research and teaching institution of Carnegie Mellon University, focused on the study of international management. It is housed within the Graduate School of Industrial Administration, and funded by a major endowment provided by the Bosch Group. In keeping with its mission to improve the understanding and practice of international management, the Institute commissioned a series of research projects on the strategies, organizational structures and processes of international "network" corporations.

Preliminary findings from this project were discussed at an International Conference on High-Performance Global Corporations sponsored by the Institute in Boca Raton in 1995, which brought together senior business executives and researchers to exchange views on issues of international management. As is evident from their emphasis on managerial issues, the chapters of this book benefited greatly from that exchange of ideas between seasoned practitioners and researchers of business practice.

Both Gunnar Hedlund and Roland Calori, contributors to Chapters 3 and 6 respectively, were greatly esteemed by their colleagues and known worldwide for their work in international management. Their bright intelligence and strong contributions to the field of international business are greatly missed and I am saddened by the loss of two friends.

This book would not have been possible without the international vision of the Bosch Group in establishing the Institute and supporting its research efforts. I would like to take this opportunity to acknowledge the company's support, both in funding the Institute and supporting its many activities and in providing access to its executives for research purposes. I should also like to acknowledge the support of the members of the Institute's Advisory Committee who provided constructive criticism and support for the research program. Richard Cyert, Herbert Simon, Allan Meltzer, John Dunning, Michael Kutschker, Yuji Ijiri, and Robert Mehrabian were particularly generous in advice and encouragement.

A number of people assisted in bringing this book to fruition. They include Cathy Burstein, who provided the administrative backbone to the Boca Raton Conference, the business executives who gave their time to many projects, Jamie Anderson, Margaret Nash, and Lan Hoang, who cheerfully undertook editorial work, and the academic colleagues who contributed to this volume. Their patience during the gestation period of the book is greatly appreciated and will, I trust, be in some measure justified by its publication.

Bruce McKern, Stanford, September, 2002

1

ORGANIZATIONAL INNOVATION IN MULTINATIONAL CORPORATIONS

Bruce McKern

Introduction[1]

In the early years of the post-war development of the modern international corporation, organizational structures evolved slowly in response to geographical and market diversity. It was possible for corporate management to change organization structure incrementally, beginning with an international division to handle the international activities of the company, shifting over time to a product-based or geographic divisional structure. The important determining variables were the importance of international business relative to the company's total business, on the one hand, and the diversity of products sold abroad, on the other (Stopford and Wells, 1972). However, today it is clear that the adoption of global strategies by many corporations has been accompanied by a significant increase in environmental complexity. In response, organization structures are changing more rapidly and there is a heightened degree of experimentation with innovative structures and processes.

Given the fluidity of organization structures and management processes within multinational corporations, the Carnegie Bosch Institute decided in 1994 to commission studies on international "network" corporations. These were viewed as international corporations in which there was an emphasis on the autonomy of subsidiaries, lateral communication flows and the cross-border generation and transmission of knowledge.

The intentions of the project were to understand the theoretical and operational factors that contribute to superior business performance. The intention was to focus on firms whose structures were close to that described by Nohria and Ghoshal (1997) as a "differentiated network." In this chapter I summarize briefly their view of these structures, then outline the main themes that emerged from the CBI research program, which are presented in the chapters of this book. As it turned out, not every research project focused exclusively on corporations that fitted the network definition. In many cases, the research was broader in scope and the coverage broader than firms with such specific attributes. Nevertheless, we believe the findings have application to most corporations operating internationally.

Nohria and Ghoshal view the modern international corporation as evolving toward a network of related affiliates, rather than a hierarchical structure. They take a contingency perspective, emphasizing the importance of *fit* between the structure of the corporation, its strategy and the environmental forces it faces.

Fit between the environmental demands and the choice of corporate structure should have a strong impact on firm performance. This is a complex question, because the typical multinational corporation operates in a variety of industries and business environments, in addition to the diversity of its geographic spread. The traditional view of the international environments in which MNCs operate is based on the opposing forces of *national responsiveness* and *global integration*. This leads to four potential environments, which have been characterized as:

- *international* (in which neither force is particularly strong, as for example in the metals, machinery, paper, and textiles industries);
- *multinational* (in which the forces for responsiveness are strong and the integration forces weak, as in packaged goods, household appliances, and beverages);
- *global* (strong integration forces, weak responsiveness, as in chemicals, construction equipment, and credit card services);
- *transnational* (in which both forces are strong, such as pharmaceuticals, computers, and automobiles).

Corporations respond to their environments by adjusting the relative weight given to "differentiation" and "integration," as described by Lawrence and Lorsch (1967). The complexity of the environment of multi-business corporations implies that organization structures and processes need to respond to the special circumstances of each business and region. This imperative suggests an organizational response that is highly differentiated across the corporation's disparate activities. On the other hand, the need for control and economies of scale requires a degree of integration across those activities. In attempting to reconcile these contradictory demands, modern corporations have adopted a variety of approaches.

In describing the structure of multinational corporations, Nohria and Ghoshal (1997) discerned four forms, based on the degree of integration and differentiation of subsidiary roles:

- *structural uniformity* (in which there is high integration and low differentiation of subsidiary roles);
- a *differentiated network* (high integration with high differentiation);
- *differentiated fit* (low integration and high differentiation); and
- ad hoc *variation* (low integration and low differentiation).

Many of today's multinational corporations face considerable diversity of businesses, yet are driven by competitive pressures to achieve system-wide economies and control. The particular structural form identified as the differentiated network is an emerging response to this complex environment.

In the view of Nohria and Ghoshal, the appropriateness of the fit in a differentiated network needs to be considered in terms of four major features. First, there is a differentiated distribution of resources and roles among the various subsidiaries in the network. Subsidiaries differ considerably in size, internal structure, and managerial competencies.

Second, there are different forms of relationship between the headquarters and the subsidiaries (a relationship studied in depth by McKern and Naman in Chapter 12). It is important to consider the full range of responsibilities controlled by all parties, and the allocation of these responsibilities differs systematically among subsidiaries and corporations.

Third, network organizations employ a variety of socialization mechanisms designed to ensure a degree of normative integration. In addition to the intellectual capital of individual managers, each possesses social capital, which can be directed toward integration by the incentives and human resource practices of the company.

Finally, communication flows between and within subsidiaries, between them and the headquarters, and outside the corporation, are a critical feature of the modern international firm. Managers are much more concerned today with communications laterally, across functions and across national boundaries, than with the vertical flows associated with the traditional hierarchy. Managers have to deal with far greater complexity in the management of the business than in the past, arising from the more rapid pace of change, the density of communication linkages and greater diversity in business lines, geography, personnel, and business partners.

For most industries and for most firms, it is no longer possible to depend on a competitive position arising from monopoly, location, protection or privileged access to resources or markets. This is not to imply that companies can ignore strategy or strategic positioning, which constitute the plan of campaign for the firm in its struggle for supremacy against competitors, an important goal of which is to gain a preferred position. The point is that competitive positions that are not supported by the core competences of a company are likely to be transitory. As is commonly argued, it is intellectual capital that is now the basis of enduring competitive advantage. Intellectual capital is an intangible resource residing primarily within the minds of the firm's people. It is intimately linked to the organization's internal culture, management processes and incentives, and its nurturing is a critical leadership task.

Developing structures and processes that stimulate individual responsibility and innovation has long been a concern for the top managements of international companies. Innovation in multinational enterprises in the past has followed a variety of patterns, paralleling the historical development of international strategies. Innovation can be center-for-global, in which innovation is created at the center and implemented by subsidiaries worldwide; local-for-local, in which a national subsidiary innovates for its own market; local-for-global, where a national subsidiary provides innovations to the firm's global market; and global-for-global, where many of the subsidiaries provide innovations for the firm which are exploited worldwide (Nohria and Ghoshal, 1997).

In a network form of organization, the distributed resources and competences of managers make it increasingly less efficient to focus solely on global-for-local forms of innovation. Capitalizing on the distributed knowledge of the firm worldwide requires matching the patterns of innovation to all the environmental opportunities, be they local or global. In promoting worldwide innovation in a differentiated network, firms need to pay attention not only to the distribution of resources and the headquarters–subsidiary relationships, but also to patterns of socialization and communication between and among subsidiaries and headquarters. Success in integrating across the network will depend at least as much on these processes as on the structure and resource distribution.

The chapters that follow explore the organization structure and processes of multinational corporations, with emphasis on the differentiated network form. The process of innovation and the transfer of knowledge across international networks is the first theme. Four chapters consider the dynamics of knowledge transfer, the management of international innovation projects, international joint ventures, and the globalization of R&D.

As noted earlier, a variety of integrative processes is employed by firms to develop a common understanding of strategy and to align employee behavior and business functions toward corporate goals. Most international corporations, and the differentiated network in particular, rely on processes of socialization to a greater or lesser degree to help achieve integration. This is the theme of the second section of the book, in which we first explore mechanisms for developing a common perception of strategic reality through the use of cognitive mapping. We then look specifically at a key force in environmental complexity, the pace of change, and its impact on the strategic possibilities or management styles open to the firm, which are strong integrating mechanisms.

Remuneration systems are also an important mechanism for integration and differentiation in global corporations. Even in highly integrated corporations, remuneration systems differ according to the degree of structural differentiation in branches and subsidiaries. By comparing two different international structures, which Nohria and Ghoshal would characterize as structural uniformity, on the one hand, and differentiated networks, on the other, Chapter 8 provides an explanation for patterns of remuneration that are designed to fit differing environmental contexts. The final chapter in this section takes a broader view of organizational processes within international companies, focusing on the failures of business process re-engineering. This chapter demonstrates that effective transformation in an international corporation must be undertaken at the deep level of organizational processes, rather than at the more superficial level of structure or rules.

A key characteristic of global competition, as discussed earlier, is the rapid evolution of organizational forms and managerial roles. This constitutes the third theme of the book, which deals with structural evolution, the devolution of responsibilities between the center and the business units, and changes in the roles and personal competences needed by managers in the international network corporation.

We now consider each of these three themes in more detail, as an introduction to the subsequent chapters.

Innovation and knowledge transfer

The pioneering work of Nonaka and Takeuchi (1995) provided a view of corporate innovation as involving the alternation of knowledge between tacit and explicit forms. In the virtuous circle of knowledge creation proposed by them, the tacit knowledge possessed by individual managers or product developers needs to take explicit form before it can be properly incorporated into innovation. Likewise, explicit knowledge is built on by individuals and becomes tacit in the process of further development. While this circle of knowledge creation is helpful to understanding the innovation process within a particular business unit, the relationships and roles of business units within a corporate structure are equally important in promoting innovation worldwide. The roles of subsidiaries within a differentiated network in relation to innovation are three-fold: adoption of innovations created at the center; creation of innovations suited to the local environment; and diffusion of their innovations to the headquarters and other business units (Nohria and Ghoshal, 1997). Their abilities to fulfill these roles are a function of the availability of "slack" resources in the unit, the degree of local autonomy, communication patterns within the network, and the extent of normative integration across the network.

Trust and internal markets for innovation

According to Anil Gupta and Manuel Becerra (Chapter 2), knowledge transfer can be either centrally managed by the corporate hierarchy or through an internal market for knowledge. Under a hierarchical approach, it is the center's role to identify the knowledge to be transferred and to make the transfer happen. The internal market approach, which is consonant with our view of the differentiated network, depends on choices for knowledge acquisition or transfer made by individual managers across the network. Gupta and Becerra argue that an internal market is able to foster a much greater transfer of knowledge because of its multiple connections, and there is less likelihood of knowledge loss. It is also much more likely to produce serendipitous innovations than a hierarchically controlled process, due to stronger motivation coupled with diffused resources and opportunities. This conclusion is consistent with that of Nohria and Ghoshal (1997).

Gupta and Becerra argue that the effectiveness of an internal market for innovation depends on creating the impetus among units to learn from each other; a willingness to share knowledge; mechanisms for subsidiaries to learn about and contact each other; and mechanisms for the actual transfer of knowledge. Success in this endeavor depends primarily on trust.

In their view, trust is the most important variable, apart from the distribution of knowledge across the corporation, in facilitating the knowledge flow process. What determines a high level of trust? Since trust is based on judgments about others, Gupta and Becerra argue that socialization is the most important influence. Managers who know each other well, or come from similar backgrounds, are more likely to trust each other and to share knowledge across the corporation.

By studying knowledge flows in a multinational enterprise structured to include both strategic business units and geographical marketing units, they conclude that the level of trust is influenced by the strategic context, managerial systems and policies, and the social context. It can be improved through a number of managerial actions. First, a more cooperative relationship can be created between autonomous units by reducing the degree of overlap between them, thus decreasing the degree of competition. Managerial policies that can have a positive influence on trust include regular meetings, transfer pricing policies, incentive payments, and rotation of employment. Finally, the social context can be modified by providing extensive opportunities for informal personal contact, by leaders whose behavior demonstrates a culture that values trust, and by attention to coaching of individual managers.

Effective international innovation teams

One of the most common means of developing new knowledge in a corporation is the use of project teams. Such teams are frequently composed of individuals from different cultural backgrounds and there is evidence from work on cultural difference that diversity enhances the productivity of a team.

As the late Gunnar Hedlund and Jonas Ridderstråle argue in their study of international innovation projects (Chapter 3), such projects can result in the development of products or services of high quality and performance. They can also contribute to their acceptance within the international network and promote opportunities for learning across national boundaries. However, there are detractions in terms of the time and cost of managing projects across borders. In their study, based on intensive research in ABB and Electrolux, together with surveys of 12 other Swedish multinational companies, they found a number of impediments to successful international research projects. Interestingly, most of these had little to do with the international nature of the teams or the companies; rather, they were problems that are encountered more generally in project management.

One of the most serious (and surprising) problems observed in their study was lack of integration between the R&D projects and the strategy of the firm. This was due to lack of communication of the strategy across the corporate network, perhaps because of the lack of a common culture, which was exacerbated as a result of acquisitions. This finding reinforces the often-expressed desirability of sharing the corporate vision widely and ensuring that strategic actions are fully understood and accepted.

Other problems faced in many international innovation projects include insufficient resources (in terms of money and people), lack of full commitment at critical phases of the project, and lack of integration between the various functions. Again, this is a surprising finding given the wealth of evidence on the importance of parallel development and functional integration in project development.

A further issue identified by Hedlund and Ridderstråle is that of communication. It is clear that face-to-face communication is critical and that this must include lower levels of the organization as well as project leaders. Communication can be enhanced by a strong information infrastructure and shared strategic "maps" and "vocabulary" (echoing the findings of Calori in Chapter 6).

Not surprisingly, leadership was a critical issue in international project development. Hedlund and Ridderstråle call for "sumo" leaders, who have both situational power as well as strong personal competences. A project not guided by a strong leader, with corporate support, is unlikely to be successful. A number of useful and practical solutions are offered to the problem of why managers do not do what it appears obvious to do in international projects.

Innovation and control in joint ventures

Developing and transferring knowledge effectively in a diversified network is made more difficult when the subsidiary is a joint venture and the environment is that of a developing country. Foreign corporations operating in China face both of these problems. How they resolve the competing pressures for global integration and local responsiveness is an interesting question, addressed by John Child in a study of MNC joint ventures in China.

Child found that the structures adopted by the sample of companies he studied generally conformed to the conventional wisdom regarding multinational organizational design. There was a stronger orientation toward global integration for those firms operating in the electronics sector, where structural uniformity might be expected, than in the fast-moving consumer goods sector which exhibited characteristics closer to differentiated fit. However, there were variations driven by the peculiar circumstances of operations in China, where relations with Chinese partners and government authorities force firms do be more locally responsive. This imperative makes it less possible for the corporate headquarters to exercise as much control as it might wish for its global strategy. As a result, a regional or China office takes more responsibility than would be the case in other countries, where a global strategy would call for centralized responsibility for each business at the headquarters of the SBU.

Child makes it clear that a corporation intending to establish a serious strategic position in China must grant the local subsidiary a higher degree of initiative and resources than would be customary elsewhere in the world. In his words, "a significant capacity for intelligent local response has to be built into the organization." For a corporation operating multiple joint ventures, there will be a need to decide whether each venture should be managed by the relevant global business unit or whether a Chinese regional company should be established with responsibility for all the SBUs' operations in that country.

His research indicates that the latter is the preferred strategy. In terms of socialization of local management, this is a much more difficult undertaking in a culture that is very different from the experience of most Western corporations. As a result, there is a need not only for majority equity holding but also for substantial expatriate staffing and efforts to develop and train local managers.

Globally diffused R&D centers

The adoption of the differentiated network by multinational enterprises has led to the development of foreign R&D centers. Most frequently these are located in the United States, which has attracted the largest amount of foreign R&D spending and the largest number of R&D laboratories affiliated with foreign companies. A handful of countries accounts for the parent companies of these R&D subsidiaries in the US, led by Britain, followed by Japan, France, Germany, and Switzerland.

The primary motivation for the establishment of these offshore laboratories, according to Richard Florida's study of foreign affiliated R&D laboratories in the USA (Chapter 5), has been the desire to acquire and develop technology. This technology-seeking motivation is in sharp contrast to the conventional market-seeking view of foreign direct investment.

The principal factor driving these technology-seeking investments has been the search for intellectual capital, embodied in personnel at certain locations in the United States close to centers of innovation (for example, NEC's information technology research near Princeton, Canon's center in Palo Alto, Mitsubishi's software laboratory near MIT, and the car makers' design centers in Southern

California). The main reason for this choice has been to recruit and retain research staff who are attracted to such locations.

Florida also concludes that the management processes and policies employed in foreign R&D laboratories in the United States reflect the need to retain scientific and technical talent of the highest quality. The subsidiaries operate with a significant degree of autonomy and encourage their staff to publish in scientific journals. The management style in the subsidiaries reflects the local environment far more than parent company cultures and policies.

A related difference is the extent to which local R&D affiliates are permitted to develop and manage their technical agendas. While there is a significant degree of communication with corporate headquarters and other R&D affiliates globally, there is surprisingly little direct central control of the research agenda. In this respect, the R&D units operate as decentralized and differentiated elements in a network with a considerable degree of slack, which places the necessity of processes for diffusion of knowledge throughout the network on the parent company. While it is clear that the foreign R&D labs in the US are successful innovators, exhibiting rates of patenting and publication in excess of the US norm, it is not clear from Florida's research that the full value of the innovations is captured and exploited by the parent companies. Further research on the processes and structures that stimulate adoption, perhaps along the lines of Nonaka and Takeuchi, would be an interesting line of enquiry.

Integrative processes, differentiation, and strategy

Cognitive schema

An important dimension of the socialization of individuals is the extent to which there is commonality in their representations of reality. Normative socialization mechanisms used within corporations help to create, if not uniformity, at least awareness and legitimation of differences. This is particularly important in relation to a common understanding of the strategic context of the business. Since managers differ in the experiences and preconceptions they bring to their views of the business context, which are often exacerbated by differences in culture and the role of the subsidiary, there can be substantial differences in the assumptions on which they operate. Strategic views are seldom totally objective or rigorous, but they constitute a basis for managerial actions. Clarifying assumptions and perceptions is a valuable adjunct to formulating strategy and undertaking strategic actions.

A useful technique for representing strategic views of reality, as well as for making tacit knowledge explicit, is the use of cognitive mapping. Cognitive maps, or cognitive schema, according to Calori (Chapter 6), can be used to make explicit different views of the strategic environment held by managers from diverse backgrounds. In a study of the use of cognitive mapping within firms in the automobile and brewing industries in Europe, he shows that there were considerable differences between managers from differing cultural backgrounds regarding the competitive positions of individual firms, the competitive factors they regarded as important, and the relationships between important strategic variables.

Calori concludes that exposing managers to the cognitive schema of others in the explicit form of a map improves their understanding of complex environments in two key areas: competitive analysis and scenario planning. In addition to the exchange of explicit knowledge, managers learn from exposure to the diversity of individual viewpoints and the recognition of boundaries to their own cognitive structures. The network organization requires an openness of mind and willingness to learn from others, both within and beyond the business unit. As Calori argues, cognitive analysis can improve the learning process and help managers to be more effective in the complex environment of the network organization.

Strategy and pace of change

One of the environmental pressures with which firms have to cope is differing rates of change across SBUs in the network. Rate of change is one of the dimensions of complexity which, along with diversity and dense communication linkages, exacerbates the difficulties of managing internationally (as discussed further in Chapter 12). Williams, in his analysis of international strategies, draws attention to the importance of understanding the speed of innovation in an industry, and its impact on the industry's pace of change. Williams focuses on "economic time," the rate at which a key dynamic indicator such as price changes over time. He argues that the dynamics of different industries can be grouped into three different strategic types or styles: slow-, standard-, and fast-cycle styles, and that SBU strategies and capabilities must fit the pace of change in each environment.

Specifically in relation to international corporations, Williams argues that the different strategy styles required by the pace of change add a further dimension of complexity to the traditional dimensions of national difference and distance. In respect of a contingency approach to the fit between strategy and environment, Williams follows a well-established path. By considering examples of three companies whose industry environments differ substantially according to cycle time, he demonstrates the diversity of strategies and management styles adopted to cope with cycle time differences.

It is not clear to what extent corporations recognize the issue of cycle time explicitly as a problem and, if they do, how they respond to it in terms of structure and processes. Of course, many firms are concerned about rapid change and attempt to organize for it. However, we have little evidence to guide managers on how internal processes should differ due to cycle time differences, from those observed in differentiated networks. Although the issue of international structure is not explicitly addressed in this chapter, each of the three firms described is relatively undiversified, with a global focus. It seems likely that structural uniformity would describe the organization of a global company in a monopolistic, slow cycle environment, such as Mattel. But Williams sees the management style of Mattel as more like that of an artisan organization, which suggests lesser centralization and strong socialization. For a global firm in a fast-cycle or Schumpeterian environment, such as Compaq, we would expect a lower degree of centralization and higher socialization. His description of the management style at Compaq, with its emphasis on entrepreneurship, is consistent with this expectation. American Airlines, operating in a standard cycle, oligopolistic environment, is described as having a managerial style of command and control, with high formalization.

Williams suggests that the ability to manage a corporation of such diversity effectively may itself be a core competence. Many MNCs are diversified by product line and geography and their SBUs often differ along the dimension of pace of change or "cycle time" as well, so managers have to be particularly flexible in devising structures and processes to deal with this degree of complexity. This competence may well be a differentiator.

The introduction of cycle time as an environmental variable influencing organization design raises a number of interesting questions, which deserve further consideration. More work needs to be done to establish the impact of cycle time on the processes of integration and innovation within the differentiated network, and this could be a useful line of research. (The issue of competencies and roles in "transnational" corporations, or differentiated networks, is discussed in depth by Bartlett and Ghoshal in Chapter 13.)

Remuneration of international personnel

Much of the discussion concerning the socialization of executives in an international network assumes alignment between the incentives provided to executives and the goals of the subsidiary. Watson and Roth (Chapter 8) investigate this question by examining the compensation and reward systems in a number of multinational enterprises differing in the extent to which the subsidiary role is integrated with that of the headquarters (which they describe as "global rationalization") or strategically independent ("lateral centralization").

Watson and Roth do not make clear the distinction between the nature of the environment and the structure of the international firm, as do Nohria and Ghoshal in their contingency view of network structures. However, the structures of subsidiaries they regard as involved in global rationalization are similar to what Nohria and Ghoshal describe as structural uniformity. The subsidiaries are contributors to the global value chain but have responsibility for only part of it and little slack for autonomous innovation.

By contrast, subsidiaries following a strategy of lateral centralization are closer to the differentiated network, operating in a transnational environment, in which the subsidiary has full strategic and operational responsibility for a product line delivered through the worldwide network. Such subsidiaries may innovate for the local market and the corporation's challenge is to diffuse these innovations system-wide.

Watson and Roth characterize the subsidiaries involved in a strategy of lateral centralization as having low proportions of purchases from, and sales to, the corporation, as well as a high proportion of international sales by the subsidiary. In the subsidiaries concerned with global rationalization, these characteristics are the opposite: high connections within the corporation for both purchases and sales, and low international sales from the subsidiary.

The relations with the parent company also differ considerably between these two strategic forms. The lateral centralizing subsidiaries display higher decision-making autonomy, and low commitment to (and conflict with) the parent as well as low cultural distance, whereas the global rationalizers have low autonomy but rank high on the other dimensions.

Compensation policy reflects the relative importance of a long-term and strategic approach on the part of subsidiary top management. It is difficult to implement a compensation program that pays attention to both corporate objectives and regional performance, so there is a tendency to focus on one of these dimensions or the other. Where the subsidiary is an implementer of strategy determined elsewhere, incentives play a smaller part in compensation. On the other hand, subsidiaries pursuing a more independent and strategic role typically employ a high proportion of incentive compensation, as might be expected from agency theory.

It is also interesting that most of the companies studied base their financial incentives primarily on numeric targets, rather than the more diverse range of performance variables employed in such systems as the Balanced Score Card. Clearly, an important variable in developing the social capital of executives in the network organization is the degree of congruence between the reward system and the strategy of the organizational unit. A broader definition of desired objectives would appear to be necessary, along the lines of the Balanced Score Card: more short-term in the case of the global rationalizer and more long-term for the more independent subsidiaries.

Business process re-engineering in multinational companies

Multinational enterprises, like many corporations, have attempted to implement an integrated process view of their operations to ensure the delivery of greater value to customers. Many of them have implemented approaches such as business process re-engineering and quality management systems as a means of reducing unnecessary activities and focusing processes on value creation. However, quite often these have failed to deliver the benefits hoped for. The reported failure rate of such innovations has been in the range of 40 percent to 70 percent.

Javier Lerch and Gary Katzenstein (Chapter 9) believe that a number of factors contribute to these failures, including resistance to radical change, failure to understand the impact of BPR on human issues and, despite growing experience with BPR, a misunderstanding of the way BPR works and what factors are critical to its success.

To remedy these problems, the authors propose that business processes be viewed at both surface and "deep" levels. The surface level of a process includes its daily operations, the visible activities, and the flow of physical objects and information. Deep-level structures are less tangible organizational context elements, such as goals, expertise, accountability, and power, which help determine and constrain the surface level operations. (The authors use the term "structures" to describe these elements, whereas other writers might consider them to include roles and competencies, as elaborated by Bartlett and Ghoshal in Chapter 13.) Traditional BPR process analysis focuses only on surface or logistic features. Although more accessible than deep structures, these are inadequate because they describe "what" is happening, but not "why." Lerch and Katzenstein argue that for process analysis to be successful it must tap the deep structure level in the firm's organizational processes. BPR, they argue, should be a task of first co-ordinating deep-level structures and then generating suitable surface-level operations.

To analyze processes in a way that helps reveal deep structures, the authors propose a Goal–Exception–Dependency model of BPR. The goals of the various actors in a business process are achieved through the creation of dependencies with other actors, which become established as standard operating procedure. When dependencies are congruent with goals, the standard operating procedure achieves a satisfactory outcome, in terms of satisfying the accountability goals of the various actors. When there is misalignment, actors seek to attain their goals by creating new dependency relationships, which the authors call "exceptions."

They argue that failures in processes can be understood better by mapping dependency relationships using two diagrams or conceptual maps, of which the first is a Goal/Exception Diagram. This has three elements: the actors or roles in the process; their respective goals; and exceptions, which are anomalies or aberrant actions that bypass the standard procedure in order to achieve individual goals. Goals include the overall goals the process is set up to achieve and the subordinate goals of each actor. Mapping the network by which goals are linked and grouped around actors is a valuable step in making explicit any pathologies in the process. The exceptions are pointers to inherent problems in the process, caused by conflicting goals or other reasons, and mapping them helps find remedies to the problem.

A second tool is a Dependency Diagram. This has three elements: the dependency relationships between individuals (for example, the Purchasing Department relying on engineer A for the specifications of an order); the extent to which each dependency is fulfilled; and the enforcement strength or likelihood of a dependency being fulfilled. The diagram makes explicit the dependency relationships between all the actors and quantifies their effectiveness and probability of success. Using both diagrams helps in creating new processes or alternative pathways to existing ones.

While the focus of this work is internal to the firm and not specifically addressed to the network corporation, their view of BPR has interesting implications for the study of international corporations because differences in culture and business unit roles affect dependencies. One example is the prevalence of parallel product development processes earlier in Japanese companies as compared to the sequential approach of US firms. Lerch and Katzenstein attribute this difference to the more communitarian and interdependent culture of Japan as compared to the individualistic, independent culture of America. In rationalizing processes that span divisions of a business across international borders, a BPR approach that fails to take account of these deep-seated differences is likely to fail.

Another implication flows from the difference between societies in respect of tacit versus explicit understanding. The high-context culture of Japan enables dependencies to be less explicit, requiring fewer written rules and procedures; whereas in low-context cultures such as Germany, dependencies need to be more explicitly revealed. In a high-context culture exceptions may be fewer, since those that arise may be resolved by accommodation.

For MNCs spanning several cultures, and international joint ventures, these cultural differences need be recognized, as there will be difficulties in transferring processes between nations with differing views of dependencies and procedural explicitness. Leaders of international corporations have long been aware of the need to take account of cultural differences, but in the specific context of process re-engineering, explicit recognition of these differences would appear critical for success. Mapping dependencies and exceptions should be helpful in communicating and improving processes between the subsidiaries and affiliates in a differentiated network.

Structural evolution, management roles, and competences

Firm evolution

Another issue, not hitherto greatly explored, is the evolution of structure and processes within a firm as it expands internationally. Whereas a great deal is known about the motivations and strategies of a firm's initial foreign direct investment, little attention has been paid to the pattern of growth of international firms and the changes in management required (although the evolution of organization structure has been thoroughly explored). Philip Rosenzweig and Sea Jin Chang address this question by considering the evolution of a firm after the entry phase. Based on a detailed case study of Sony Corporation's entry to the United States, they propose a model of firm growth in terms of two processes of capability development. The first of these is the development of country-specific capabilities, which allow the firm to diversify into new fields within the country. The second is a process of deepening capabilities within a business, so as to evolve from the "implementer" role identified by Bartlett and Ghoshal (1989), concerned only with the marketing of imported products, to being a "strategic leader" with a fully integrated manufacturing and product development role.

Their conclusions are that development of the firm after its initial entry takes place along three discrete dimensions: functional migration, diversification by line of business, and geographic expansion. Each step requires the development of specific capabilities. They also conclude that there are important interactions between these dimensions which need to be managed, as a series of impediments develop along the way, which vary according to the depth of functional migration. A consequence of this is that firms need a variety of skills, including abilities to transfer technology successfully, sourcing of local resources, and political skills in the host country.

The authors point out that their conclusions are based on a single case and may not generalize to a variety of different starting points. In particular, Sony's approach was one of gradual development and learning along the way, whereas many firms today take a bolder approach, often through acquisition. It might be argued that Sony could afford to take a cautious approach at the time, given that it was a pioneer in the USA, whereas in the highly contested markets of today a firm needs to act quickly and boldly in order to secure a market position.

This work could be expanded with a larger sample and with a more substantial theoretical framework, which could give sharper definition to the development of core competencies. There would also be value in relating subsidiary evolution to the broader work on the development of international structures and processes sketched earlier.

Emerging organizational forms in the Knowledge Age

Is the differentiated network the final flower of mankind's genius for organization or just a step in the path of evolution? Charles Snow, Raymond Miles, and Brent

Allred address this question by providing a general if simplified historical context for the evolution of corporate structures. They associate the hierarchical M-form corporation with the Industrial Age (1860–1970), vertical integration, and the human relations school of management. They label the years 1975 to 1995 as the Information Age, characterized by a focus on core competences, network structures, and the human resources school of management. The year 1995 ushered in the Knowledge Age, focused on providing customers with instant gratification worldwide, a philosophy of management they describe as "human investment" and a new "cellular" organization structure.

Snow, Miles, and Allred provide an alternative view of the network structure, seeing it as the concomitant of the contemporary emphasis on core competencies, which results in outsourcing of non-core activities from a network of arm's-length suppliers. They observe the shift in large firms to closer supplier relationships, in a hybrid of market and hierarchy based on inter-company trust. While their interests are not restricted to MNCs, they do see international outsourcing and joint ventures as further developments of the network form, as suggested by Nohria and Ghoshal (1997). They do not explore the internal structures and processes of the differentiated network, which are the main concerns of Bartlett and Ghoshal, but they stress the importance of trust and collaboration as key elements of the managerial culture, as do Gupta and Becerra in Chapter 2.

Their description of the cellular organization as the appropriate structure for the Knowledge Age is provocative. In the Knowledge Age, they argue, the key strategic imperatives will be innovation and entrepreneurship, to satisfy consumer demands for delivery of products and services "anytime, anywhere." Achieving this degree of responsiveness means openness to ideas, entrepreneurship at many levels, and structures that can quickly change to meet new needs. They see this as requiring a form of organization close to a group of "cells" that can act alone or together in various combinations, responding quickly to diverse opportunities.

In corporate terms, their cellular organization combines entrepreneurship, self-organization, and member ownership to search for opportunities and grasp them quickly. Their ideal cellular form would be composed of extraordinary individuals possessing "a combination of technical, entrepreneurial, leadership and self-governing skills." The authors acknowledge the scarcity of such people and the difficulties of managing such an organization. They quote the example of a consulting firm, TCG, whose members take responsibility for acquiring new business and forming appropriate teams. The authors also regard Acer Inc. as another example, citing its vision of a "federation" of relatively independent companies linked by minority shareholdings and product and knowledge transactions.

In my view, neither of these examples makes a convincing case for the cellular structure as a common future organization form. TCG is a grouping of specialized consulting firms, probably organized as partnerships, in which issues of asset specificity (the specialized knowledge of individual members) and moral hazard (potential shirking and free riders) are less likely to be the major concerns they are in most companies that separate ownership and management.

Acer's international structure resembles the cellular form, as individual company members appear to have a high degree of entrepreneurial autonomy. But it is not clear to what extent the subsidiaries in fact behave flexibly, nor whether their internal processes fit the cellular model. (An alternative view of Acer's structure, in terms of a market failure approach to the headquarters–subsidiary relationship, is provided in Chapter 12.)

Perhaps the cellular form will be a good description of the consulting and professional services firms of the future, in which the majority of employees are qualified professionals with a personal stake in the business. Where there is a need for specialized skills which are difficult or costly to broaden, in great variety and located in many countries, there will be a need to co-ordinate and share knowledge, bringing with it attendant issues of moral hazard. These features will, I expect, characterize the majority of industries and corporations for some time to come and the network organization will continue to be relevant.

Notwithstanding these reservations, the cellular structure exemplifies many of the characteristics sought by corporations today: encouragement of entrepreneurship, development and sharing of knowledge, sharing of risks and rewards, and flexibility. By projecting forward the environment of firms in the Knowledge Age and drawing implications for structure and management, Snow, Miles, and Allred provoke a rethink of assumptions about the nature of the firm in a new environment and about the network corporation in particular.

The role of the corporate center in diversified international corporations

Deciding the role of the corporate headquarters relative to the other administrative units in a corporation is a major task for top management. In the past, the decision as to how much responsibility to delegate has been made arbitrarily, based on prevailing views about appropriate decision-making structures. The bureaucratic model common to the age of the large industrial corporation placed top management at the apex of a chain of information with little devolution to staff at lower levels. As the single-product company evolved into the M-form corporation, responsibilities were devolved to SBUs according to top management's preferences for power and control, but without a clear logic. At the opposite extreme, conglomerates devolved most arenas of responsibility except for shareholder and capital market relations, with questionable results.

As is now well accepted, the competitive advantages of firms have come to be based far more than in the past on competences, captured in operating routines and knowledge. In seeking to manage this precious and intangible resource, corporate managers rely far more on the knowledge, skills, and initiative of executives throughout their enterprises, and this entails a greater reliance on decentralization. The wave of interest in tapping the individual well-springs of knowledge is not transient. It reflects both a rational response to the management of complexity and a more enlightened, if self-interested, view of human nature and the potential of motivated people. This is the "human investment" approach of Snow, Miles, and Allred (Chapter 11) and the positive view of organization man espoused by Bartlett and Ghoshal in Chapter 13.

Important as these trends are in promoting the shift toward greater devolution, they provide no guide to the question of which functions should be devolved in the complex environment of the differentiated network corporation, and to what degree. The market failure approach developed by Bruce McKern and John Naman (Chapter 12) provides guidance on this issue.

The research focused on a set of arenas of activity that must be managed in respect of any business unit. The authors identify three forces of complexity (diversity; pace of change; and density of linkages), which have a powerful influence on the ability of corporate headquarters to control the far-flung operations of the typical multinational network. The consequence is that headquarters is forced to allocate greater responsibility for the key arenas to the management of the business units.

However, the degree of delegation has limits. Corporate headquarters reserves to itself certain functions over which it exercises responsibility. The authors propose that the rationale for corporate headquarters intervention is to compensate for "market failure" at the SBU level. They view market failure more broadly than does Williamson (1975) who saw the role of corporate headquarters in diversified firms primarily as providing an internal market for capital for which SBUs compete. They argue that the center's role is to consider all the resources that can be exploited across the corporation and to intervene wherever market pressures are insufficient. By examining a sample of international corporations pursuing global strategies, the authors draw conclusions regarding the optimal set of activities that should be controlled centrally.

The critical arenas of activity that need to be controlled by any corporation include six externally focused arenas and six internally focused ones, and in a single-business firm all of these are centralized. In a diversified firm, in order to justify a degree of centralized responsibility over these 12 key arenas, the corporate center must be able to add shareholder value beyond what could be achieved by a portfolio of commonly owned businesses. Which arenas are most likely to add value when managed centrally, and under what circumstances, are the central questions of this chapter.

The authors argue that top management should devolve to SBUs those arenas of responsibility in which market forces exist to promote efficiency. These are predominantly in customer and supplier relations, relations with government, the community, and local stakeholders and internal transfers of components, products or services.

Where there is market failure, because of "externalities" (such as customers common to more than one SBU, or relations with government that affect more than one SBU) or moral hazard, there may be benefits in co-ordinating administratively. This can be done by central authority or by consultation between SBUs.

In the arenas of relations with shareholders and the capital markets, as well as the strategic process and performance measurement and incentive system, the role of the headquarters, as the only interface under market pressure, is clear. But the example of Acer, which has set up regional business units with considerable autonomy, many arenas, including capital structure, shows that even this assumption may change over time.

In some arenas, such as technology and human resources management, the research indicates that, for the most part, competitive pressures on SBUs push firms to devolve responsibility. But there are possibilities of externalities across SBUs and moral hazard in SBU management, where pay-offs are long-term, that justify a measure of corporate intervention.

The research is inconclusive on the financial benefits of adopting this approach, as the sample is too small to provide reliable conclusions. However, on theoretical grounds, the authors argue that a centralized, administrative solution should be seen as appropriate only when there is evidence of market failure. Corporate headquarters cannot centrally manage the enormous complexity of the modern multinational corporation and the concept of market pressure provides necessary guidance in devolving arenas of responsibility to SBUs.

Management roles and competencies in a network

Amongst the papers resulting from the CBI program and other research on network corporations, the work of Ghoshal and Bartlett, since published in *The Individualized Corporation*, has probably been the most successful in describing the complexity of the MNC and the changes in structures, processes, and managerial competencies over recent years.

In further developing their model of the "transnational" corporation as a differentiated network, Ghoshal and Bartlett called upon detailed studies of a group of major corporations from three regions of the developed world, observed over several years. These included AT&T, Komatsu, ABB, Corning, 3M, Kao, ISS, and Intel.

They view these transnational corporations as distinguished by three characteristics:

1   multidimensional perspectives, gained from the complementary resources of:

   * national subsidiary management focused on local markets;
   * global or regional business management concerned with worldwide rationalization of assets, products, and strategies; and
   * strong functional management, consolidating corporate expertise and transferring it across the network.

2   distributed interdependent capabilities, in which assets and knowledge are dispersed across the network, with a variety of subsidiary roles in initiating, developing, transferring, and exploiting intellectual capital and other assets.
3   flexible, integrative processes, to manage the diversity of interests and capabilities optimally for the corporation.

As described in the introduction to this chapter, three well-established processes are important in balancing flexibility and integration: centralization, formalization, and socialization.

Each of these is used in a restrained manner: centralization to resolve tensions between subsidiaries; formalization to define roles and systems for reaching decisions; and socialization to provide a culture to support delegation and strategic coherence.

Bartlett and Ghoshal observed three additional characteristics of these companies. First was a belief in pushing responsibility down to relatively small profit centers (ABB's 1,300 operating companies, and 3M's 3,900 profit centres, for example). The second feature was the widespread use of project teams, business boards, regional meetings, training and development activities, and other forms of communication, designed to promote lateral knowledge transfer and cross-unit integration. These were complemented by a third characteristic: empowerment of managers through a combination of delegation and accountability.

These structures and processes are powerful forces in the effectiveness of the transnational network, but they are not sufficient. Ghoshal and Bartlett place great emphasis on changes in managerial roles at each level of the company. These roles, they argue, are very different from those associated with the hierarchical model.

At the front-line manager level, for example, the manager's role is changing from that of an implementer of operations to that of entrepreneur. This development is consistent with the belated acknowledgment in Western corporations of the importance of knowledge residing at the organizational front-line, so ably tapped by Japanese corporations in the 1970s and 1980s. The benefit of this view of the front-line manager role is found in greater productivity, innovation, and growth.

At the level of senior managers, the shift identified by Ghoshal and Bartlett is from the "administrative controller" to the supportive "coach," and the benefits are the resource support they can bring to front-line activities.

At the top level of the corporation, the shift is from resource allocation to institutional leadership, or the "strategic visionary" role. The benefit is the creation and sustaining of direction and commitment across the organization.

Of course, changes in roles to the degree experienced by these transnational companies also demand a great deal in the competencies of managers in each role. Ghoshal and Bartlett identify competencies of three kinds: individual attitudes or traits (inherent and acquired); knowledge and experience (acquired through education and career); and skills and abilities (linked to work requirements and building on abilities and knowledge). Avoiding the temptation to search for universal leadership traits, they discuss the relative importance of each of these competencies at the three levels of managerial role. They put strongest emphasis on personal attributes, differentiating the desirable features from role to role. Likewise, desirable knowledge and experience vary from role to role, as do skills and abilities.

For example, the role of top-level leader requires traits of challenging and stretching; open-mindedness and fairness; and insight and inspiration. The knowledge and experience competence includes understanding of the company and its business; the organization, its processes and cultures; and different industries, companies, and societies. The leader's skills and abilities include the ability to create an exciting and demanding work environment; to inspire confidence and belief in the company; and to combine insight with motivational challenges.

Ghoshal and Bartlett conclude that the hierarchical model of the corporation, with its "organization man," is no longer relevant to the knowledge age and must be replaced by the "individualized corporation," in which managers' roles and competences are differentiated extensively, as they describe. Although their conclusions derive from a study of transnationals, the contribution of Ghoshal and Bartlett is more general than their MNC sample would imply. The processes, roles, and competences they describe are consistent with other work on leadership in the modern corporation and relevant to any corporation faced with complexity and a dynamic environment. Their identification of these three specific classes of competencies sheds a useful light on key questions of organization structure and process, both for managers and for researchers interested in the resource-based view of the firm.

A challenging conclusion that emerges from this work and the chapters that precede it, is the power of the intellectual capital of the corporation and the difficulty of capturing its essence, embedded as it is in the hearts and minds of a company's people. The systemic nature of the structures, processes, roles, and competencies as unveiled by Ghoshal and Bartlett reminds one of recent progress in the elucidation of the human genome. The expansion of understanding is considerable, yet we are still a long way from understanding how the variables interact to produce the dynamic, living organism that is the modern corporation. There is room for more work in this direction.

References

Bartlett, C. and S. Ghoshal (1989) *Managing Across Borders: the Transnational Solution*, Boston: Harvard Business School Press.

Lawrence, P.R. and J.W. Lorsch (1967) *Organization and Environment: Managing Differentiation and Integration*, Boston, MA: Harvard Business School.

Nohria, N. and S. Ghoshal (1997) *The Differentiated Network*, San Francisco, CA: Jossey-Bass.

Nonaka, I. and H. Takeuchi (1995) *The Knowledge-Creating Company*, New York, NY and Oxford: Oxford University Press.

Stopford, J.M. and L.T. Wells, Jr. (1972) *Managing the Multinational Enterprise*, New York, NY: Basic Books.

Williamson, O. (1975) *Markets and Hierarchies: Analysis and Antitrust Implications: A Study in the Economics of Internal Organization*, New York, NY: Free Press.

Part 1

INNOVATION AND KNOWLEDGE TRANSFER IN INTERNATIONAL NETWORKS

2

IMPACT OF STRATEGIC CONTEXT AND INTER-UNIT TRUST ON KNOWLEDGE FLOWS WITHIN THE MULTINATIONAL CORPORATION

Anil K. Gupta and Manuel Becerra

Introduction

In the 1990s, the concepts of organizational competence, knowledge, and learning have acquired a prominent place in the strategic management literature. In many industries characterized by rapid technological development and intense competition, superior knowledge, rather than market power and positioning, is the key to long-term success. Though companies that actually isolate themselves from the pressure of competitors may enjoy above-average returns (Porter, 1980), it has become clear that unique internal capabilities and resources lie behind above-average performance (Barney, 1991; Prahalad and Hamel, 1990). Broadly defined, knowledge and, more specifically, core competencies, are some of these critical internal resources. From this standpoint, strategic management requires the development, storage, and actual use of carefully chosen competencies.

New knowledge and competencies are created by combining existing capabilities into new ideas, products, and procedures. This creative process is facilitated by sharing expertise among the units of an organization. Innovations would be much more difficult to produce in isolated units. Thus, fluid transfer of knowledge within the organization is necessary for fast and effective innovation. A famous case in point is the collaborative effort and combination of knowledge of the research units of Procter and Gamble worldwide in order to develop the liquid detergent Tide, based on locally-developed product characteristics merged into an advanced winning formula.

But the benefits of effective transfer of knowledge within the organization go beyond product and process innovation into its use across the different products and locations of the multinational enterprise (MNE). Transfer of core competencies makes it possible to engage in synergistic diversification across related industries, as Corning has done from a basis of glass technology. On the other hand, competencies owned by the organization may also be used across borders in other markets. It has long been argued that MNEs exist primarily because they are usually the best mechanisms to transfer proprietary knowledge across geographical locations (Hymer, 1960; Kogut and Zander, 1992). Alternative governance mechanisms, such as exporting and licensing, would either have higher costs or higher risks, including the risk that leakage of knowledge may end up generating a strong foreign competitor. Once they become global, MNEs enjoy the benefits of the worldwide generation, storage, and rapid deployment of relevant knowledge in markets with different needs and characteristics. This constitutes a substantial advantage over domestic firms with more limited locally derived knowledge (Ghoshal, 1987). For instance, engineering and consulting MNEs have this clear advantage over domestic competitors, which have a smaller pool of knowledge with less varied customer base. The internal strategic context and management systems within the MNE can be designed to allow different types of knowledge to flow throughout the organization as needed.

Strategic context and management systems

Transfer of knowledge is therefore a critical activity within the MNE. Until recently, the analysis of knowledge flows has relied on the study of the strategic context within the organization, such as structure, management systems, unit goals, and policies. In one of the more influential books on organization theory, Thompson (1967) analyzed how workflow interdependence determines different types of departmentalization and co-ordination, such as standardization, planning, and mutual adjustment. Units that need each other for their daily routines within the MNE have greater co-ordination and continuous transfer of information between them. Different mechanisms of co-ordination can be designed to process the information flow among these units, including reports, teams, liaisons, and co-ordination through hierarchical supervisors (Galbraith, 1973).

However, simple information and data are only part of the knowledge base of any organization. Such "declarative knowledge" is relatively easy to codify and transfer. Organizational arrangements can be used to manage and even guarantee that the necessary transfer of this type of knowledge will take place within the organization rapidly and without overloads and bottlenecks. In contrast, "procedural knowledge" that deals with skills and competencies is usually tacit, often impossible to codify, and much more difficult to transfer. It frequently involves different managers and/or units interconnected through complex processes and procedures. It is this type of knowledge that may be the source of competitive advantage and which constitutes the core competence of an organization. Interestingly, to remain competitive, organizations have the need to facilitate this transfer of knowledge inside the organization, while making the process difficult to replicate outside the organization (Kogut and Zander, 1992).

The transfer of procedural knowledge presents a much more important challenge for the MNE. Certainly, management systems can be designed to facilitate this type of transfer of knowledge, but their effectiveness is more limited in comparison to their effectiveness in transferring simple information. In addition, since this knowledge constitutes the essence of competitive advantage, its transfer entails some risk. Even within the organization, the transfer of strategic resources from one unit to another may have important consequences for the functioning and future of these units, of which their managers are fully aware. In certain cases, some units may be reluctant to transfer strategic knowledge elsewhere within the organization, when there is some risk involved in it from the unit's point of view. The problem becomes significant when, given the type of knowledge, its actual transfer cannot be forced by organizational policies. In these situations when the units perceive some risk, trust is essential for fluid transfer of knowledge to take place.

Trust within the organization

Trust has been defined as the willingness to become vulnerable to the actions of another party (Mayer, Davis, and Schoorman, 1995). In general, when individuals and organizations have trust in their partners, they become willing to engage in collaborative action with them despite the presence of risk that is contingent on the other party's less than fully controllable behavior. The need for risk-taking and trust are central to all business activities. Since there is always some level of risk in any business relationship, a certain amount of trust is necessary for the economic system to function (Arrow, 1974). After all, we are willing to accept some degree of economic and even physical vulnerability when we buy, say, a TV or a toothpaste. Thus, it is not surprising that the concept of trust has a central role in management theory.

According to transaction–costs economics, the possibility of a partner's opportunistic behavior (and the impossibility to write a contract that fully avoids such behavior in all unpredictable future scenarios) induces exchange partners to form a combined organization (Williamson, 1985). In this newly created organization, common interests should prevail over selfish opportunism of the previously independent partners. In terms of trust, managers place greater trust in other units or managers within their own organization than in those of other organizations, particularly if they are competitors. That is, they are willing to accept much more vulnerability in their exchanges with other managers within their organization than in any interaction with other organizations. Trust is a traditional element of business relations that becomes critical when risk is high. Only if there were sufficient trust would managers voluntarily engage in exchanges with risk and vulnerability.

But the organization does not generate an environment where every unit and manager will fully trust his or her peers. Organization members will not accept total vulnerability in their relations with other members. In particular, we are concerned in our analysis with the risk that arises from other members' benevolent attitude and intentions (as opposed to their competence or the risk caused by the environment). Sociologists have warned us against "over-socialized" views of the organization as a monolithic entity where everyone has totally overlapping and coherent goals (Granovetter, 1985). In fact, organization theorists often consider the top management of an organization to be a dominant "coalition" of individuals with somewhat divergent, though usually compatible, interests. Recently, a number of articles and books have been published on how trust varies across and within organizations (Kramer and Tyler, 1996). Divergence is more likely in a firm that operates in more than one culture.

Thus, trust is not distributed homogeneously throughout the organization. Trust or, equivalently, the willingness to become vulnerable to the actions of other units, will vary within the organization. Since the transfer of strategic resources, such as knowledge, carries some risk, the level of trust should play a role in how much and how easily knowledge actually flows within the organization. This impact of trust on knowledge transfers constitutes the core of this chapter. In the next section, we analyze how the strategic and social contexts between the units of an MNE determine the amount of knowledge transferred between them, mediated partially by inter-unit trust. Later, we investigate in greater detail the level of trust and knowledge flows in different strategic contexts within the MNE, using as an illustration one MNE and its units worldwide. Finally, we discuss the implications for management and provide some recommendations on how MNEs can ensure that appropriate knowledge flows will take place.

Impact of strategic context and trust on knowledge flows: a conceptual framework

In this section, we develop a model of inter-unit trust and its effects on the transfer of knowledge within the MNE. Below, we briefly analyze the key drivers of knowledge flows, particularly inter-unit trust. The model is presented in Figure 2.1.

Drivers of inter-unit transfer of knowledge

Strategic context

Though transfer of knowledge is critical for MNEs, not every unit needs to exchange a similar amount of knowledge with all others. There are systematic differences within the MNE with regard to which units possess what type of knowledge and how they exchange it with the rest of the organization. These differences underlie the strategic role of the units within the MNE. For instance, Gupta and Govindarajan (1991) have classified subsidiaries on a two-by-two matrix in terms of how much knowledge they contribute to the MNE and how much knowledge they obtain from it. This classification results in four strategic roles that the subsidiaries may take within the MNE: global innovator, integrated player, local innovator, and

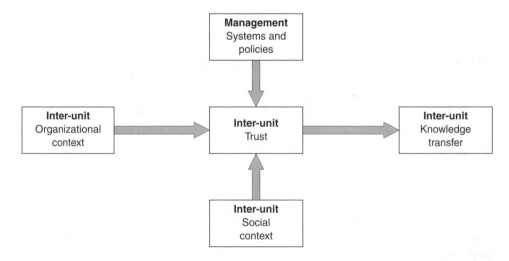

Figure 2.1 The impact of context and trust on knowledge transfer.

implementer. Their strategic role reflects how these units are managed and their relationships with others within the MNE.

The relationship between any two specific units can also be analyzed in terms of their mutual strategic context within the MNE's configuration. Certain units, depending on their specific characteristics, responsibilities, and roles within the organization, will have a more collaborative relationship between them than with other units. In turn, the strategic context of these relationships is intimately associated with the amount and type of knowledge flows between them. For example, the transfer of knowledge between autonomous sales subsidiaries is typically less critical than the transfer of knowledge between production and sales units, which have a much more interdependent strategic context.

Management systems and policies

Given the need to transfer knowledge within the MNE, management systems allow the flow of knowledge to take place across different types of strategic contexts. Management systems and policies are designed to channel inter-unit knowledge flows and to regulate the relationships between the units of the MNE and their different strategic contexts. Obviously, the effectiveness of these organizational mechanisms varies. Not all co-ordination mechanisms are equally effective, nor can all types of knowledge be transferred through the same type of mechanisms. Therefore, the extent of knowledge transfer is partially determined by the choice of management systems and their actual effectiveness. Without the appropriate channels of communication, only casual knowledge flows can occur.

Inter-unit trust

In addition to the influence of strategic context and management systems, the units' disposition to transfer knowledge is also an important element to be considered, as we discussed earlier. When there is greater trust, managers will be more willing to transfer critical knowledge to other units, whose future use could potentially have a negative impact on the contributing unit.

Thus, there are different factors that drive knowledge flows. On one side, the strategic context of relationships and the management systems allows certain knowledge flows to occur between the units of an MNE, regardless of the level of trust. On the other side, trust between the units facilitates knowledge transfer, since higher trust reflects greater willingness to accept risks and, therefore, the disposition to transfer critical knowledge.

Drivers of inter-unit trust

Strategic context

To a large extent, the level of inter-unit trust also depends on the strategic context and the management systems within the MNE. Units with more divergent interests within the organization would trust each other less. Their interests are heavily determined by the strategic roles of the units within the MNE and the existing management systems.

In other words, different strategic contexts produce different levels of trust, which ultimately are closely associated with the amount of knowledge flows between the units. For example, as we discuss later in greater detail, units operating in a complementary strategic context (for example, a production and a sales unit) typically enjoy greater mutual trust than two units, which operate in a more competitive strategic context (for example, production units making similar or substitute products).

Management systems and policies

Mechanisms such as incentives, teams, and formal reports also have an important effect on the level of inter-unit trust. These mechanisms lie on top of the strategic context of relationships, but directly affect the perspectives of the units and their managers. For instance, mechanisms for frequent co-ordination with substantial direct contact between managers from different units are more likely to generate trust than formal reports. Similarly, individual incentives may have important consequences in how managers perceive their relationships with others within the MNE.

Social context

Inter-unit trust is not determined exclusively by strategic context and management systems and policies. Even within the same strategic context, such as hierarchical relations, the level of trust between the regional office or headquarters and the sales subsidiaries varies across specific relationships. Some subsidiaries will trust their regional office more than other subsidiaries (and vice versa), to a large extent because there may be differing social contexts across headquarters–subsidiary relationships. Factors apart from strategic context and management systems may affect how much trust exists between any two units. These social context factors – such as culture distance, length and history of the relationship, mutual knowledge, and so forth – are specific to each relationship.

The model shown in Figure 2.1 summarizes the impact of strategic context and trust on inter-unit knowledge flows. On one side, the level of trust is driven by the strategic context of the relationship, the management systems within the MNE, and the social context between the two units. These three sets of factors either produce or destroy inter-unit trust, which ultimately affects the disposition to transfer knowledge. On the other side, the strategic context and the management systems also act as substitutes for trust and have a direct impact on the amount of transferred knowledge. Thus, strategic context and management systems are not sufficient to explain trust levels and, ultimately, knowledge transfers within the MNE, despite their effects on both.

Trust is a lubricant of relationships that facilitates knowledge flows. We would expect there to exist a positive, although not perfect, association between inter-unit trust and transfer of knowledge. A certain amount of knowledge is transferred within the organization through formal mechanisms and systems even if trust is low. On the contrary, high trust is not sufficient to allow a fluid transfer of knowledge without the existence of effective and efficient transmission channels. The best combination is obviously having an MNE configuration and management systems, which facilitate the transfer of knowledge, combined with high levels of trust to improve the disposition to transfer it. The following analysis of inter-unit trust within an MNE illustrates the instrumentality of inter-unit trust in facilitating knowledge flows.

Context, trust, and knowledge flows: a field study

To examine further the role of trust within organizations, we report the results of a field study within one highly globalized MNE. The company, which we will call by the pseudonym "SAF," had sales in 1997 close to $1 billion in the construction equipment industry and forms part of a larger profitable diversified corporation listed on several European and American stock exchanges. The firm has facilities in France, the USA, Brazil, Scandinavia, and South Africa, and it directly employs about 4,000 individuals worldwide. The MNE was formed in the late 1980s after the merger of three equal-sized companies within the industry: one Scandinavian, one American, and one French.

As Figure 2.2 shows, the organization is divided into three main product-based units (Global Product Centers or GPCs) with worldwide responsibilities for R&D, production, and basic strategy for their respective lines of products, and three geographic Marketing Areas (MAs) with sales and service responsibilities (Europe, the USA, and Asia-Pacific). Thus, there are six basic units within the MNE. Though the structure within each unit is quite complex, we will concentrate on a reduced set of top managers from these units, mainly presidents of Local Sales Units (LSUs) and worldwide product managers (PMs), from the MAs and GPCs respectively.

We conducted a total of 26 one-hour long interviews within the six units of

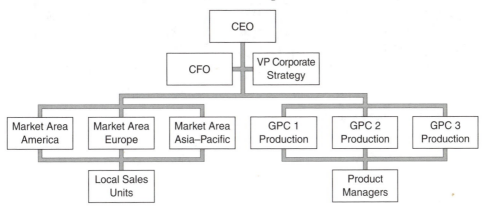

Notes

Top Management Team – CEO, CFO, VP Corporate Strategy, 3 GPC VPs, and 3 MA VPs.

Global Product Center (GPC) – Worldwide responsibilities for R&D, production, and broad marketing strategy for their respective lines of products.

Market Areas (MA) – Sales, marketing, and service responsibilities for their geographical continental areas.

Product Managers – Responsibilities for one type of product worldwide: engineering, development, sales support, and training.

Local Sales Units – Sales and customer service responsibilities within one geographical area, usually a country, led by one LSU president.

Figure 2.2 SAF organizational structure.

the MNE, including the entire top management team, product managers, foreign subsidiary presidents, and other top managers. In addition, a survey of the top 59 managers assessed the level of mutual trust and the amount of knowledge flows between them. The responses were aggregated for the managers within the same unit providing the average measures of trust and knowledge flows shown in Figures 2.3 and 2.4.

Strategic context and trust

For this manufacturing MNE, we can group the six units into the three GPCs with product-related responsibilities and the three MAs with sales responsibilities, which have the national subsidiaries (Local Sales Units or LSUs) reporting to them. Other MNEs would have a different strategic context, which could be analyzed in a similar

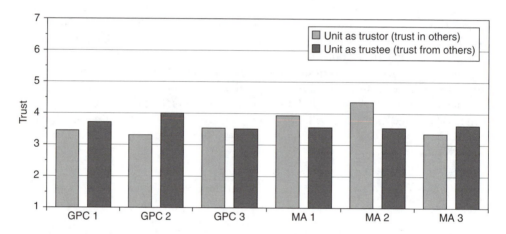

Figure 2.3 Trust among units.

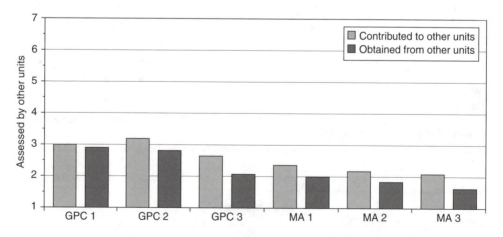

Figure 2.4 Transfer of knowledge with other units.

Table 2.1 Trust and knowledge flows across strategic contexts

Relationship	1 GPC/GPC (Production)	2 MA/MA (Sales)	3 GPC/MA (Production/Sales)	4 MA/LSU (Sales/ Subsidiaries)
Context	Competitive	Autonomous	Collaborative	Hierarchical
Transfer of knowledge[a]	2.56	1.35	2.96 (average) GPC to MA = 3.21 MA to GPC = 2.76	3.46 (average) MA to LSU = 3.17 LSU to MA = 3.75
Trust level[b]	3.29	3.75	3.72 (average) GPC to MA = 3.46 MA to GPC = 3.98	4.51 (average) MA to LSU = 4.87 LSU to MA = 4.15

Notes

a Knowledge contributed to other units as assessed by the receiving unit (e.g. 3.21 knowledge transferred from GPC to MA, as assessed by MA).

b Self-assessed trust in other unit (e.g. 3.46 = GPCs trust in MAs, as assessed by GPCs).

fashion as we do below. In this case, we can analyze four types of relationships separately: among production units (GPCs), among sales units (MAs), between GPCs and MAs, and between LSUs and MAs. The levels of trust and knowledge flows in these four contexts are summarized in Table 2.1.

Relations among GPCs: A "Competitive" Relationship Context

The three GPCs manufacture specialized large machines to be used in the construction and mining industries. These units have virtually exclusive responsibility for their own lines of products, which are usually targeted to different types of customers who need machines of somewhat different specifications. However, some of these products are possible substitutes for each other, mainly because two smaller machines may substitute for a larger one. In fact, before the MNE was formed, the three merged companies considered themselves competitors.

After the merger, the need for efficiency has induced some restructuring aimed at reducing duplication. These changes caused GPC2 to be downsized and to report to GPC1 for many decisions, which has resulted in a quite low level of trust between GPC2 managers and GPC1 managers. However, to a large extent each GPC conducts its own R&D, and over the years each GPC has also established special relations and co-ordination mechanisms with some selected LSUs.

Overall, the relations between the three GPCs can be considered competitive. There are still clear signs of internal competition since many of their products compete in the market for the final customer, channeled through the LSUs. The future may bring further restructuring and concentration of responsibilities, of which managers in the three GPCs are fully aware. It is viewed as likely that the ongoing search for cost efficiencies may result in greater consolidation of the GPCs or their relocation. Given this context, trust among the three GPCs is relatively low within the organization. As one product manager openly indicated, they could not trust other GPCs since the situation was a zero-sum game, where one would win what the other would lose. According to top executives, the transfer of best practices among these units has been below expectations. In fact, many managers

31

believe that transferring their competencies to other GPCs puts them in some jeopardy about the future use of such knowledge and the possible consequences for their own unit.

Relations among MAs: an "autonomous" relationship context

In contrast to the relationship among the GPCs, the marketing units focus on different geographical locations and can be described as largely autonomous. An MA cannot take over the sales units of another MA or compete for the same customer with another MA. In these circumstances, MAs do not pose a threat to each other and they do not need to avoid situations of vulnerability. Consequently, trust among these units is greater than that among GPCs. They can transfer information and trade secrets without being afraid of negative consequences for their own units.

Relations between GPCs and MAs: a "collaborative" relationship context

GPCs and MAs have a traditional supplier–buyer relationship. Based on the needs of their customers, MAs may acquire products from any of the three GPCs. There is continuous daily interdependence within a collaborative context that requires substantial mutual transfer of knowledge. However, there is some degree of tension in this relationship – particularly with regard to transfer prices. GPCs sell their production at certain transfer prices to the MA. These transfer prices are supposed to be determined on the basis of a targeted discount from the expected local market price. Given that both units are profit centers, a higher transfer price obviously benefits the GPC and hurts the MA; the reverse holds true in the case of lower transfer prices. Thus, there is constant tension over what the transfer prices should be as each side tries to hide their unique knowledge (that is, costs and local market prices) in order to gain an advantage in their negotiations.

In contrast to the previous two relationships, the directionality of trust and knowledge flows has an important meaning between GPCs and MAs. These relations are not symmetrical in terms of knowledge flows from one side to the other. With regard to knowledge flows, MAs provide market data information about actual sales and forecasts necessary for production, whereas GPCs provide a substantial amount of technical support and product training, among other knowledge flows.

Importantly, the sales units control the critical interface with the customer, the market, and the local competition. In the last few years, the company has become more customer-driven as opposed to production-driven. Thus, MAs have been gaining more responsibilities and have been transformed from a distribution channel reporting to the GPCs into independent units reporting directly to the CEO. The greater power that MAs are accumulating is necessarily associated with the reduced responsibilities and growing vulnerability of the GPCs toward the MAs, which can be observed in the moderately high, but not very high, level of trust between GPCs and MAs.

Relations between MAs and LSUs: a "hierarchical" relationship context

As opposed to the lateral relationships analyzed above, the relations between the three MNE regional sales headquarters (MAs) and their subsidiaries (LSUs) represent classical reporting lines within the hierarchy. The performance of each MA results from the aggregation of the performance of their LSUs. Their interests are, therefore, very much aligned. In this hierarchical context, trust is substantially higher than in any other lateral context within the organization. As one top executive indicated, if he did not have reasonably high trust in one of his subordinates, he could and would replace him. The LSUs can also expect that their interests will be taken into consideration to a much greater extent by their bosses at the MA level than by managers in other units within the MNE.

This type of relationship is also not symmetric. LSUs report formally to the MA. An important responsibility of the MA is the control of the LSUs, which need to provide information about their performance in their local markets to the regional office. Despite continuous knowledge flows and very similar interests within the MNE, there is a clear difference in power and perspective. Typically, what is good for an LSU is also good for the MA; but not every decision of the MA is well received by every LSU. Thus, we can see greater top-down trust from the MA in the LSU than vice versa, always within an overall context of high mutual trust.

In summary, we can see in Table 2.1 how strategic context has an important effect on the amount (and type) of knowledge transferred among the units of the MNE. Very little knowledge is transferred among the sales units, some is transferred among the production units, more is transferred between MAs and the GPCs, and much more between the MAs and their subsidiaries. But there are also systematic differences across these contexts regarding trust levels. The lowest level of trust occurs in the competitive context between GPCs, greater trust exists between the autonomous MAs, somewhat higher trust in the collaborative GPC–MA context, and it reaches its highest level in the hierarchical MA–LSU relationships.

Trust and knowledge flows

Neither knowledge nor trust is homogeneously distributed within the MNE. We can see how both – knowledge transfers and trust levels – vary across different strategic contexts. But does trust actually affect knowledge transfers? The answer is a clear "Yes," based on interviews with the managers within the MNE as well as statistical analysis of the survey data.

"When there is trust, I can give all the information I have," said one of the interviewed managers. "With higher trust, it would be easier to transfer best practices between production units and much easier to make certain decisions, like combination of manufacturing," claimed a GPC manager. Another manager reflected on his reluctance to seek support from a less-trusted unit: "Even if I knew that it might help me, I would never go to him. It is very bad for the company that, because of trust problems, we cannot count on everyone's ability and skills."

These quotations illustrate how managers' behavior depends to some extent on how much they trust their peers in other units. When trust is high, there is more open communication and transfer of knowledge between units. This idea can be tested statistically on the data from the survey that includes each unit's evaluation of the level of trust and knowledge flows with each of the other five units within the MNE. The correlation between how much a unit is trusted within the MNE and the amount of knowledge that the unit contributes to the rest of the MNE is positive and statistically significant.[1] More trusted units actually contribute more knowledge to the organization, as assessed by the other MNE units.

We can go further and investigate whether, within each of the strategic contexts, higher trust is also associated with greater transfer of knowledge. ANCOVA analysis of the dyadic relations among the six units shows that, even after controlling for the different strategic contexts, higher trust is positively and significantly associated with greater knowledge flows.[2] Within the hierarchical relationship context (MA–LSU) also, we obtained a similar positive correlation coefficient of 0.30.[3]

Social context and trust

To summarize so far, the extent of knowledge transfers is determined by both trust and strategic context. There is greater transfer of knowledge, for instance, between MAs and their subsidiaries in comparison to the flows among the GPCs, because of the specific characteristics of these relationships. This level of trust is caused by strategic context so that, for instance, competitive intra-MNE relations have less mutual trust than hierarchical relationships.

Thus, strategic context and management systems and policies have important influences on trust levels and knowledge transfers. But, even on top of the effect of context, trust affects the transfer of knowledge. For any type of relationship, there is greater transfer of knowledge when there is higher trust between the units. What else, besides context, can be driving trust within the organization? To address this question, we turn to the effects of social interaction.

Trust is, after all, a cognitive assessment about others. Managers decide whether they want to share knowledge with other managers based on their perceptions of the other managers' benevolence toward them. If they think that the other managers will not use the transferred knowledge in ways that will damage them, then they will be willing to accept the risk and transfer to them such a precious resource. Otherwise, they will act in a defensive manner, sharing only the barest minimum amount of knowledge that they can possibly get away with. Since the transfer of certain types of knowledge cannot be forced, trust becomes critical.

Certainly, their respective roles within the MNE is an important factor that will affect managers' perceptions about other managers' future use of the transferred knowledge. But people rely on many other factors to evaluate whether they should or should not trust specific managers from other units. These factors include individual characteristics of the managers as well as the nature of their social interaction. People have different personalities. Some individuals are more trusting and/or trusted than others. Also, each relationship has a history that affects the ongoing level of trust. All these individual-level factors pertaining to the social context of relations also affect how much managers trust each other. In a comprehensive study of the dyadic relationships between specific managers within this MNE, the statistical analysis showed that individual characteristics, such as attitudinal predisposition toward peers, significantly affect the level of trust between managers – over and beyond the impact of strategic context (Becerra and Gupta, forthcoming).

In addition, virtually all interviewed managers indicated that they placed greater trust in those colleagues with whom they shared some individual characteristics, such as nationality, age, and functional background. Also, greater contact tends to increase trust. As one manager put it, "To have trust, you have to know the other person." In short, the human side of business also has an important effect on the level of trust between managers.

Conclusions

As the model in Figure 2.1 shows, there are three basic antecedents of trust within the organization. These routes can be used to manipulate the level of trust among the units of a MNE. Let us analyze to what extent organizations can manage their strategic and social context to improve or at least to deal with their current inter-unit trust, so that the necessary transfer of knowledge will actually happen.

Designing the strategic context

The context in which relationships take place (for example, a competitive versus a collaborative context) has a strong impact on the amount of trust among units. Notwithstanding exogenous imperatives (for example, locational advantages or disadvantages, transportation costs, and so on), it is sometimes possible to shape the context partially in order to increase the likelihood of greater trust. An organization may alter the responsibilities and the interdependence among its units by manipulating its formal organizational structure. The structure may prevent the occurrence of dysfunctional competitive relations within the organization, in which low levels of trust would inhibit desirable transfer of knowledge. This can be done in two basic ways.

First, a competitive context can be converted into a cooperative relationship between autonomous units by restructuring the degree of overlap between them. This is typically done, for example, after a merger or an acquisition, when the value-chain activities are reconfigured in search of greater efficiency. Besides the clear benefits in tangible economies of scale and in knowledge management provided by centers of excellence, greater specialization has clear effects on trust levels. The transfer of knowledge between two centers of excellence dedicated to very similar products or customer needs is not likely to be fluid because of low trust. For SAF, the level of trust among production centers and consequently their willingness to transfer knowledge seems to have increased after the reconfiguration among the different production centers and the creation of the three GPCs with less overlapping strategic responsibilities. Nonetheless, the GPCs still suffer from product overlaps and the level of mutual trust among them is clearly lower than that among the virtually fully independent MAs.

Second, if the structure cannot be reconfigured into autonomous units because of the intrinsic similarities of their activities, the hierarchy becomes the logical alternative path. Similar units can be grouped under the same hierarchical umbrella, which will eventually develop higher levels of vertical trust, as we could observe between subsidiaries and the regional sales headquarters (MAs).

Thus, either specialization or combination of activities would increase trust among competing units by altering the strategic context. Unfortunately, this is more difficult to do in an intermediate situation with some similarity of resources, but not enough to warrant the hierarchical solution. In these cases, and also when the activities are necessarily complementary (for example, buyer–supplier relations within the MNE), a collaborative relationship is preferable to a hierarchical or an autonomous context and, even more so, to a competitive one. Over the last decade, it has become clear in the international management literature that formal structural solutions are not sufficient to induce appropriate collaboration among units (Martinez and Jarillo, 1989). A variety of formal and informal processes and systems within the MNE structure can be designed to manage these types of collaborative contexts and the level of trust among units. These systems should preferably create or otherwise substitute for inter-unit trust in order to ensure that the flow of knowledge will take place.

Setting management systems and policies

Organizations establish different systems and policies to produce and to manage collaborative relationships. For instance, periodic meetings can be set to facilitate some degree of collaboration among otherwise autonomous units, and planning processes can be used to control the product flow through the stages of the value chain. The level of trust will affect the fluidity of knowledge transfers among these collaborating units. To analyze the impact that management systems and policies have on the level of trust within the organization, it is useful to distinguish between different effects that systems and policies may have on either a manager's attitude or his/her behavior.

On one side, organizational processes affect the managers' behavior with regard to other units. These processes encourage, discourage, and regulate certain behaviors in the MNE. For instance, incentives have a direct impact on behavior by directing attention to a reduced number of observable variables, which will drive the incentive payouts. Similarly, transfer pricing has an important effect on the relationships between production and sales units. These systems guide managers' behavior and their interaction with other units within the MNE, by forcing certain types of objectives, interdependence, collaboration, and even transfer of knowledge among units.

However, their impact on the attitudes of managers is not always as intended. One top executive claimed: "Though our systems are as good as anybody else's, some of our systems have created mistrust." Since every unit is a profit center, their relationships are sometimes affected by conflicting interests. Some of these systems make managers distrust the use of the information and knowledge they transfer to other units, and even question the motivation and the truthfulness of the received information. For instance, one manager commented: "Since we are all making a profit from each other, we are reluctant to share information."

Thus, though management systems are carefully designed to guide the behavior of managers and their relations with other units, they also have important effects on the managers' attitudes with respect to other units. On many occasions, management systems designed to regulate observed behavior may substitute for trust. In fact, they may be the only short-term option when trust levels are very low. For instance, group-based incentives may achieve the necessary transfer of knowledge between low-trust units, at least for certain types of knowledge.

However, since not every aspect of behavior can be regulated and enforced by management policies and incentives, the complete and accurate transfer of sensitive knowledge cannot be fully guaranteed by management systems. Then, inter-unit trust becomes essential. Managers will be willing to transfer strategic knowledge if they have (and perceive) a positive attitude in their relationships with other units. The attitudes are driven to a large extent by the systems in place, which, unintentionally, often destroy rather than create trust. Therefore, to create trust rather than substitute for it, it is essential to investigate the impact that management systems may have on the actual and perceived attitudes of managers with respect to other units within the MNE.

Influencing the social context

Management systems guide behavior, but also have a less obvious effect on managers' attitudes, which constitute the basis of trust. When the systems are discontinued, their impact on relationships and trust levels disappears immediately. In contrast, the social context within organizations is more difficult to change and it has a longer lasting impact on intra-MNE trust.

The different elements of the social context are usually considered part of the organization's climate. Some of these elements are, for instance, the characteristics of the individuals that the company attracts and keeps, the acceptable norms for interaction with others, and the history of the company. These can be influenced over the long term by the symbolic and exemplary conduct of top executives and by certain actions that affect the degree and type of socialization within the MNE, such as rotation of managers.

Like most other organizational attributes, trust can be measured and tracked across organizational and geographic space as well as across time. For instance, we can measure a particular manager's propensity to trust, the specific directional trust from one unit to another, and the average amount of trust within the entire organization. Trust at all of these levels is affected by the specific social context operative within the organization. Thus, how much trust exists between two specific units is determined in part by how much contact exists between them, their interaction history, and the similarity between their managers, as well as by the overall culture of the organization. To improve trust within certain specific relationships, MNEs can intervene in the social context of those specific relations exclusively.

Given a reasonable time horizon, it is possible to create a more trusting climate within the whole MNE that facilitates internal transfers of knowledge. There are three types of actions that organizations might consider:

- *increase personal contact among managers.* Trust is substantially easier to develop when there is direct contact. Though reports, telephones, and email are good means of communication for basic data, they do not promote the emergence of personal ties that allow managers to raise positive attitudes and mutual trust. Any policies that boost direct contact, such as cross-unit teams, transfer of managers, and periodic company meetings, are instrumental in reducing barriers among managers and improving the social context within the MNE.
- *cultivate a culture that places high value on trust within the organization.* A community's culture refers to the shared values, norms, and assumptions of its members. Further, culture is always a product of history. In order to cultivate a culture that values trust, senior managers would need to begin by "walking the talk." Beyond

the signaling value of leaders' own behavior, another prime determinant of culture change would be the "engineering" of experiences that demonstrate that cultivating mutual trust creates both personal as well as organizational success.

- *coach managers in building high-trust relationships.* At the individual level, once managers come to believe that trust is an asset of any relationship that increases its effectiveness, they may need to be coached on how to improve trust within their own relations. The goal here would be to build a cognitive mind-set with a higher propensity to trust and behavioral skills that foster a self-reinforcing cycle of greater trust rather than greater distrust.

Whether higher levels of trust develop through inter-unit contact, organizational culture, or individual actions, a high-trust social context will have a positive effect on the transfer of knowledge within the MNE. However, strategic context and management systems also have important effects on both trust and knowledge transfers. To this effect, it is essential as well to analyze the intended and unintended consequences that the strategic configuration and policies may have on trust levels.

It is obvious that the goal of organizations is not to maximize internal trust. Certain levels of task-related conflict and less-than-full trust will always exist among specific units of an organization. Management systems that substitute for trust may be sufficient in many cases. However, to the extent that trust has important consequences for the transfer of certain types of knowledge, it is worthwhile for MNEs to investigate the levels of trust among their different units and whether it should be improved. As an essential ingredient of business transactions, including those inside the organization, intra-MNE relationships need to be well lubricated with a sufficient amount of trust, particularly from their social context.

Notes

1 The Pearson correlation coefficient is 0.28, significant at 0.05 level. This coefficient was computed for the 30 dyadic unidirectional evaluations among the six units. Even after considering the dependence among the observations using the regression permutation MRQAP procedure suggested by Krackhardt (1988), the correlation remained significant.
2 The ANCOVA table is the following:

	df	F
Intercept	1	2.72
Trust	1	5.03*
Strategic context	3	17.18**
Error	25	
Model	30	15.00**

Notes
*Significant at 5% confidence level.
**Significant at 1% confidence level.

Trust is also significant ($\beta = 0.39$, significant at 0.05 level) even when MRQAP regression (Krackhardt, 1988) is used to account for the dependence of the 30 dyadic observations, using dummy variables for the organizational contexts (GPC/GPC, MA/MA, GPC/MA, and MA/GPC).

3 Though this coefficient is actually greater than the correlation observed among lateral units, it does not achieve significance at the 0.05 level because of the lower number of observations ($n = 21$).

References

Arrow, K.J. (1974) *The Limits of Organization*, New York, NY: Norton

Barney, J.B. (1991) "Firm resources and sustained competitive advantage," *Journal of Management*, 17: 99–120.

Becerra, M. and A.K. Gupta (forthcoming 2003) "Perceived trustworthiness within the organization: the moderating impact of communication frequency on trustor and trustee effects," *Organization Science*.

Galbraith, J. (1973) *Designing Complex Organizations*, Reading, MA: Addison-Wesley.

Ghoshal, S. (1987) "Global strategy: an organizing framework," *Strategic Management Journal*, 8: 425–440.

Granovetter, M. (1985) "Economic action and social structure: the problem of embeddedness," *American Journal of Sociology*, 91: 481–510.

Gupta, A. and V. Govindarajan (1991) "Knowledge flows and the structure of control within multinational corporations," *Academy of Management Review*, 16: 768–792.

Hymer, S.H. (1960) The international operations of national firms: a study of foreign direct investment, Ph.D. dissertation, Massachusetts Institute of Technology.

Kogut, B. and U. Zander (1992) "Knowledge of the firm, combinative capabilities, and the replication of technology," *Organization Science*, 3: 383–397.

Krackhardt, D. (1988) "Predicting with networks: a multiple regression approach to analyzing dyadic data," *Social Networks*, 10: 359–381.

Kramer, R.M. and T.R. Tyler (eds) (1996) *Trust in Organizations: Frontiers of Theory and Research*, Thousand Oaks, CA: Sage Publications.

Martinez, J. and J.C. Jarillo (1989) "The evolution of research on coordination mechanisms in multinational corporations," *Journal of International Business Studies*, 20: 489–514.

Mayer, R.C., J.H. Davis, and F.D. Schoorman (1995) "An integrative model of organizational trust," *Academy of Management Review*, 20: 709–734.

Porter, M.E. (1980) *Competitive Strategy*, New York, NY: Free Press.

Prahalad, C.K. and G. Hamel (1990) "The core competence of the corporation," *Harvard Business Review*, May–June, 79–93.

Thompson, J.D. (1967) *Organizations in Action*, New York, NY: McGraw-Hill.

Williamson, O.E. (1985) *The Economic Institutions of Capitalism*, New York, NY: Free Press.

3

MANAGING INTERNATIONAL INNOVATION PROJECTS

Why firms do not do the obvious

Gunnar Hedlund and Jonas Ridderstråle

Introduction[1]

In recent discussions of the modern multinational corporation (MNC), the increased competence of foreign subsidiaries and the need for close and increasingly sophisticated collaboration between units in the global corporate network are emphasized. The international dispersion of research and development (R&D) units is integral to this development, often reinforced by the dominance of acquisitions as a global expansion strategy. In this view of the MNC the effective management of an international network of innovative, or potentially innovative, units within a firm becomes an important determinant of competitiveness. Representative contributions in academic research are Doz (1986), Hedlund (1986), Bartlett and Ghoshal (1989), and White and Poynter (1990). However, few of these more speculative contributions have investigated in depth how these transnational or heterarchical processes work and the difficulties involved. Thus, there is a call for studies with a more explicit focus on a phenomenon that captures real action rather than a dream.

This chapter is an effort to contribute to the meager empirical knowledge of how MNCs handle the task of managing international innovation projects (IIPs). An IIP is a project that aims at an international market, utilizes human resources from many countries, and constitutes an organized effort rather than spontaneous, internal collaboration. The focus on projects avoids the danger of confusing proclaimed intentions with real processes and results. It also naturally lends itself to consider relevant factors at many levels: the individual (for example, the characteristics of the project leader), the project (for example, the spread of resources over phases of the project), the total organization (for example, the systems for assigning priority to projects), and the inter-organizational (for example, the relationships with suppliers).

In an age of ever-shorter product life-cycles and increasing development costs, combined with the globalization of technology and markets, it becomes essential for the modern multinational to use the best units anywhere in the network to respond to problems worldwide. Some companies may even actively seek to rejuvenate their industries by creating new and powerful international combinations, using the full potential of the international network. The IIP can be regarded as a prime vehicle in leveraging knowledge assets across borders, and in creating competitive advantages by combining internationally dispersed needs and resources.

Without a doubt, global innovation presents many challenges. In these processes, product development is no longer only a question of integrating and co-ordinating activities across functions and over time, a task demanding in itself, but also across geographical and cultural borders. An additional problem is that structures and systems at an organizational level often interfere with the intentions and actions of the people in the projects. Time after time in our research, we witnessed IIP managers not getting the obvious things right because the overall organizational architecture of the company suppressed rather than supported global knowledge-creation processes.

The goal of this chapter is threefold. First, we will discuss the factors that seem to constitute the most serious obstacles for the effective management of IIPs. Second, we will make recommendations on how management can overcome these difficulties. Third, given that structures and systems beyond the control of the global product development team appear to have a strong impact on project performance, we will elaborate on the question of why managers do not always do the obvious. It is also our aim to suggest remedies for this problem.

Research design

The empirical basis for this chapter consists of two parts: in-depth case studies of two IIPs in both ASEA Brown Boveri (ABB) (electrical engineering) and Electrolux (home appliances),[2] and a study of 32 IIPs in 12 Swedish MNCs through a mail survey to the project leaders.[3] Appendices 3.1 and 3.2 provide lists of firms and projects. We sent the survey to 20 of the largest Swedish MNCs to get complementary data, and to develop our thoughts on questions such as project characteristics, perceived problems, advantages and disadvantages, and perceived success.

ABB and Electrolux were chosen since both firms can be described as truly "international" in at least three respects:

a   asset dispersion, with some 80 percent of the employees located outside the home country;
b   market dispersion, with approximately 85 percent of sales outside the home country, and
c   administratively international, in that we knew from previous research that both companies were moving toward globally integrated organizational networks.

Thus, we expected IIPs to be quite common in these firms, and anticipated that their approaches would represent the forefront of modern multinational management. In all, we undertook close to 100 interviews in more than ten countries at the project and organizational levels. The main objective was to get the respondents to describe how the projects were organized and managed, and to elaborate on problems, new organizational solutions, and other general points of learning.

How international participation affects IIP performance

Before identifying the main factors that seem to inhibit successful execution of IIPs, and suggesting possible remedies for such deficiencies, one may rightly ask oneself whether IIPs are a good idea at all. Table 3.1 provides the survey respondents' views on how successful their projects had been in relation to goals defined initially.

Although a reference point is not available, the scores appear rather high. Perhaps more interestingly, they vary over performance dimensions. Generally, the more "technical" dimensions, such as product performance and quality, score higher than those dealing with process efficiency and market aspects. The project leader can, of course, be suspected of seeing their projects in a more favorable light than is justified. A more neutral question is what advantages and disadvantages they see in the internationalism of the IIP.

Figure 3.1 provides a summary of the project leaders' views. IIPs, in comparison with purely national projects, are seen to increase the creativity of the process and the competence of those involved and their organizational units. This benefits the

Table 3.1 Average performance in relation to goals (1–7 scale, 1 = very low, 7 = very high)

Goals	Mean	Minimum	Maximum	(n)
Time	4.40	2	7	30
Budget	4.61	2	7	28
Product performance	5.29	3	7	31
Quality	5.00	3	7	30
Manufacturing cost	4.41	2	7	27
Consumer price	4.59	3	7	17
Market share	4.62	1	6	13

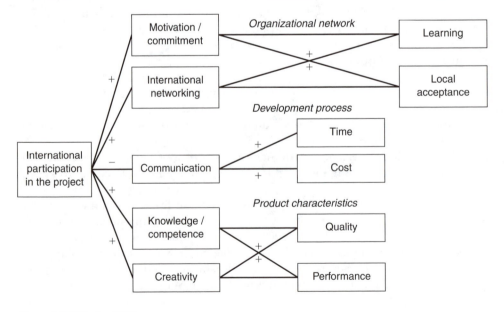

Figure 3.1 Effects of IIPs.

quality and performance of the product developed in the project. Also, the increased motivation and commitment provided by the challenge of working across borders, and the formation of new contacts within the firm, make for learning within the entire organization. It also helps local acceptance of the product, both within the subsidiary and, indirectly, on the market. On the negative side, communication and co-ordination problems increase costs and time to complete the project.

In summary, these firms engage in IIPs successfully, but there are identifiable advantages and costs associated with them. What then distinguishes a good from a bad IIP? We have elected to discuss the factors that seem to constitute obstacles for the effective management of IIPs. This is because success seems to be more a matter of avoiding rather obvious, but common, pitfalls than of implementing some surprising miracle formulae. Below is a list of the most critical problems. We will discuss each of these factors in turn.

1   Lack of strategic and individual significance of the project.
2   Resource deficiencies and process imbalance.
3   Functionally fragmented process.
4   Poor communication.
5   Lack of continuity.
6   Weak and unclear project leadership.
7   Weak project location.
8   Weak development architecture.

Lack of significance

A lack of links to the overall strategy and R&D plans of the company characterizes the unsuccessful projects. They may be launched as a pet idea of a top manager, or as a way to find something useful for a factory to do (common when global manufacturing rationalization projects are going on). They may be outside the real core of corporate priorities; the important stuff is kept centrally. Or, they may be the result of well-intended efforts to improve international contacts more generally. Successful projects, on the other hand, are firmly and visibly tied to the key strategic thrust of the corporation. The "ownership" is broadly shared, and projects are priority items rather than marginal endeavors. This also strengthens a sense of urgency about and in the project, easily lost in marginalized action not clearly consistent with the company's strategic direction.

A particular issue, related to the organizational structure of the firm, is how IIPs fare in a geographically oriented structure, such as the mother/daughter (headquarters/subsidiary) one, in comparison with a product-centered one. It seems that the problems of lacking strategic significance are higher in the geographically organized firms, particularly if they have emerged through acquisitions. Strong national units do not necessarily share the same strategic consensus, and systems for aligning overall organizational issues with those at the level of the project may not exist. The most effective basic structure seems to be one of fairly narrow and small global product divisions. Almost by definition, everybody is then "in the same boat," and it is easier to communicate strategic development priorities worldwide, since their scope is narrower in terms of products and technologies. This is true as long as the project does not involve several such global product divisions. Although we do not have any such cases in our research, it seems difficult to have any definite view of the relative merits of basic international structures in such cases.

The question of project significance is also a matter of stakes and incentives, for individuals as well as organizational units. In none of the 36 cases we studied was the salary of the project leader determined primarily by how well the project went. In none of the four in-depth studies could the project leader set the salary of project members. If such were the case, local and short-term tasks could naturally take precedence over complex and long-term international ones. Evaluation could easily becomes a process of apportioning blame for why things did not work rather than one of giving credit for things that did work.

Thus, it appears critical to establish clear priorities and strategic consistency before launching international projects. All parties and all levels, that is, the local units, individuals, and so on, taking part in the venture must have stakes and incentives to contribute to the success of the IIP. These links must be designed in a way that minimizes the risk for local mutiny or ignorance. It is critical for the top-management team to actively promote a sense of urgency and commitment. Unless the entire organization believes that senior management is serious in its aspiration to undertake global projects, the units may easily decide to put more priority on local ventures more directly linked to their own performance. A final warning is related to the tendency to launch too many projects. It was our impression that most companies tended to underestimate the resources needed to develop and commercialize new products, particularly international ones. Since strong systems for screening potential projects were lacking, the firms launched new ventures on a "try and see if it works out" basis. In our minds, it is critical not only to ensure that the projects match the strategy of the firm, but also to align them to the capabilities and capacity of the firm. Here, a much more systematic approach is called for.

Resource deficiencies and process imbalance

Partly because of the marginalism inherent in projects of low or unknown strategic significance, and the more general tendency to launch too many projects, several IIPs suffer from chronic resource problems, of both a financial and, particularly, a human kind. If the project organization is not strong and supported continuously by top management (more on this later), it will lose struggles for resources with the various line organizations. A case for providing central, corporate money, even if the project is basically financed by the contributing parties, can be made. The difficulties are even greater when it comes to access to critical individuals. Such "core competents" in firms are extremely busy and sought after for many tasks. For an IIP to lay its hands on them, it takes strong backing from corporate management. One strong conclusion from our case studies is that the success of an IIP is critically dependent on one or a few key people. If and when these disappear from the project, things almost invariably go wrong, even if everything else is fine (money, project organization, management backing, systems, communications, and so on). Thus, there is an issue of the *quantity* and *quality* of resources at the IIP's disposal.

There is also an issue of the degree of *commitment* of human resources, which partly has to do with incentives, as already discussed. However, it is also related to the intensity of involvement, in terms of whether people work full-time or part-time on the project. The importance of "100 percent-ers" is stressed in the literature on project management. However, our IIPs seem not to have heeded such advice. Figure 3.2 shows that the proportion of people in the project groups included in the survey varied considerably. Of course, there may be good reasons not to have everybody at 100 percent all the time. However, we observed cases of severe delay when people were not working full-time on the IIP even at moments when their individual input was critical. Thus, it would seem beneficial to encourage fully committed spurts of activity, and mistrust averaging of labor over long periods.

The imbalance in the distribution of resources and commitment over the phases of the project is, in our view, the most serious shortcoming in the IIPs studied. Most people and other resources are involved in the engineering phase of a project, whereas the earlier ones of conception and planning, and the later ones of production and market launch, receive less attention (see Figure 3.3).

This technical orientation is also reflected in goal setting for the projects. Only 13 of the 32 IIPs had goals for market share or sales and just 17 for consumer price, whereas 30 and 31, respectively, had goals for product quality and product performance. The consequences of not considering the later phases right from the start were late and slow commercialization and uncertainties about whether the team had developed a product the market would really accept and buy.

In all, the consequences of not investing in preparatory phases were that important design issues were forgotten, problems crept in later in the process (when they were much harder to solve), and communication difficulties were guaranteed, since people had not got to know and trust each other. "Front-loading" an IIP builds commitment and a shared interpretation of the task, surfaces assumptions about things taken for granted, and solves or avoids problems at inception. Therefore, the understandable pressure to move on and get something done should be resisted, and time and resources for considering the fundamentals of the project as well as

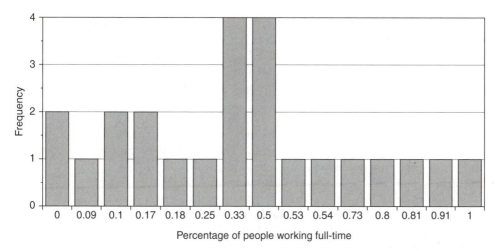

Figure 3.2 Frequency distribution of people working full-time on the IIPs (mean = 0.405; median = 0.333; $n = 24$).

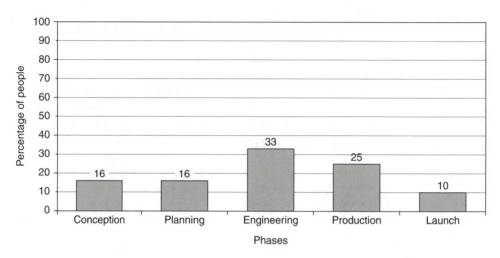

Figure 3.3 Relative number of people involved in the different phases.

building a cohesive project group should be reserved. It is critical to establish a core team of 100 percent-ers early on. Senior management must also be prepared to set aside corporate money to further sponsor the venture. This is particularly so in the case of IIPs since local managers outside the IIP may find it difficult to understand why they should invest in a project that develops a product for "someone else" in a global network.

Functionally fragmented process

In much of the recent research and managerial practice concerning product development, there have been calls for multi-functional groups, where different tasks are pursued in parallel rather than sequentially (see, for example, Takeuchi and Nonaka, 1986; Wheelwright and Clark, 1992). However, we find rather little evidence of this in our cases. We have already mentioned the lack of market-related goals. The projects were seen as technical tasks, where commercialization was seen as another and later matter. Figure 3.4 shows the proportion of people involved over the five phases of the projects. Marketing is conspicuously under-represented in the first four.

There is simultaneous involvement of manufacturing and R&D, strengthening the impression that the projects are treated as technical matters. However, Figure 3.4 may suggest an exaggerated degree of even such engineering related cooperation. Even when functional tasks proceeded in parallel, in our in-depth cases, where it was possible to study the degree of interaction directly, they did so in separation from each other. Thus, preparation for manufacturing was handled as a separate concern. In some cases, issues of spreading production tasks fairly over the globe, or of compensating countries for the loss of manufacturing mandates, or of politicized power struggles, overrode the logic of the project. Late assignment of manufacturing tasks, or sudden changes in location, spelled trouble and delays in several cases. Even more noticeably in the in-depth cases was the isolation from the rest of the

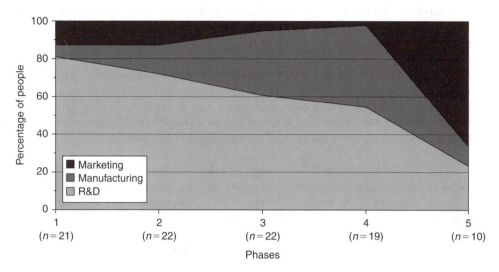

Figure 3.4 Percentage of people from different functions involved in the different phases of the innovation process.

project of the marketing function. Input in the initial phases was weak and scattered, and marketing people did not seem to be seen as really belonging to the project.

Conflicts between functions were also seen as more serious than conflicts between units of different nationality (see Table 3.2). This was something of a surprise to us, since so much of the critique of the heterarchical/transnational hypothesis builds on the presumed complexity of inter*national* collaboration.

It is interesting that some of the most intense conflicts we observed were between functional units *in the same country*. Intra-functional collaboration, even across national borders, on the other hand, mostly went smoothly. Since our projects were predominantly seen as technical affairs, the conclusion has to be tempered by the proviso that little marketing globalism was even attempted.

The remedies for lack of successful inter-functional collaboration are largely the same as for correcting the imbalance of resource input over time: early investment in dialog over fundamental issues and in forming a cohesive team. It was also apparent in our in-depth cases that the absence of marketing people, held responsible for the fate of the project in the market, contributed to delays and expensive engin-

Table 3.2 Severity of conflicts between different organizational entities (1–7 scale, 1 = not at all serious, 7 = very serious), *n* = 29–31

Conflicts	Mean	Minimum	Maximum
Countries	3.21	1	7
Functions	4.00	1	7
Business areas	3.76	1	7
Project/line	3.26	1	6
Phases	2.97	1	7

eering solutions. Deficient or non-existent incentive structures conspired against successful project completion.

The difficulties associated with multi-functional teams are well known. Educational background, professional norms, vocabulary, and sense of belonging are often shared more easily with foreign colleagues of the same functional group than with compatriots from other functional camps. Dougherty (1992) discusses a similar phenomenon when talking about "functional thoughtworlds." To illustrate our point, let us use a few examples from one of our in-depth cases where representatives of different departments within an international project claimed:

> We do not have any guys from marketing in our development teams. They can only indicate problems and not come up with any solutions – you just cannot communicate ideas to them, they only understand a finished product.

> Keep production people away from the market. They think that marketing is something trivial that anyone can do.

> Marketing people cannot foresee anything but general trends and cannot help us in product development.

> The product developers do not listen to the marketing people with the brightest ideas – they listen to the guys with the biggest order blocks.

The international context adds to the inter-functional problems. A simple point, very hard to address in a practical manner, is the differing function-specific locational logics. Mostly, and for quite clear reasons, R&D is the least dispersed function, and marketing the most dispersed one, with manufacturing somewhere in between. In one of our case companies, an IIP was launched to merge six traditional product designs into a new and common generation. Three R&D centers, six manufacturing units, and some fifteen marketing units participated. In this case, the problem was not so much if marketing should be involved, but *which* units to involve, and *how*.

Accordingly, it is vital to include commercialization and market launch in the definition of the projects, not only formally but also mentally. To improve inter-functional co-ordination it may be necessary to co-locate people from the various departments, at least temporarily, and primarily at the beginning of the process. Particularly, in projects marked by global "hand-overs" from one function to another, the need for early interaction and co-ordination is strong.

Poor communication

A general problem is the tendency to confine co-ordination and communication to channels already existing for the normal operations of the firm. The much higher frequency and interactivity required for simultaneously cross-national and cross-functional work was thus often inadvertently neglected. For example, project reviews took place on those rare occasions when top managers could meet at one location, rather than according to the needs of the project.

Specifically, four aspects of communication seem critical:

* focus on face-to-face communication;
* attention to lower and middle hierarchical levels;
* letting problems rather than plans guide;
* determined investment in information technology.

The need for face-to-face contact, particularly early in the project, is easily compromised because of the cost and logistical difficulties involved. The need is partly a matter of getting to know and trust each other and build a committed team. It is also, however, a matter of articulating hidden and possibly mutually conflicting assumptions and of arriving at an effective distribution of tasks. The high interactivity and flexibility of direct personal communication cannot be replaced by technical means, but the latter can support the former.

At the time of the survey, a minority of projects used various IT-based communication solutions (see Table 3.3). Those that did use them generally saw great value in them. Today, no doubt, such methods figure even more prominently. Indeed, the advent of technologies for interactive, joint work over distances has probably revolutionized the prospects for making IIPs more effective, and also cut communication cost.

Many problems seemed to be caused by the lack of interaction at the level where real work went on. Issues were dealt with at high levels, with consequent lack of detailed knowledge and time to really penetrate the questions. Matters could be left unresolved just because there was not time to discuss them given the hectic travel schedules of top decision-makers. Related to this, personal communication in particular seemed to follow a predetermined plan, with meetings at regular intervals, rather than in response to problems occurring during the process. In this way, some meetings were unnecessary, whereas others never took place, although they could have been crucial.

Consequently, to handle the problems referred to, a much stronger information infrastructure for securing communication across functions and countries is necessary. If the company is not willing to invest heavily in traveling and co-location, it may well be better to abort the entire idea of running international projects. The people that need to interact on a continuous basis are mostly those directly involved in the development effort, not only those senior executives occupying seats in the

Table 3.3 Perceived importance of different communication methods used (scale 1–7, 1 = very low, 7 = very high)

Communication method	Mean	Minimum	Maximum	(n)
Face-to-face	6.23	4	7	26
Phone	5.85	4	7	27
Fax	5.30	2	7	27
Letter	4.19	2	6	16
Electronic mail	6.09	4	7	12
Common database	5.66	5	7	6
Common CAD/CAM	5.77	4	7	14

steering committee. Moreover, the former group of people does not constitute much of a bottle-neck. By using these people, the company can ensure that meetings take place when implied by the natural activities and problems of the innovation process, rather than by the time available of those in charge of the operating organization.

Lack of continuity

IIPs risk being fragmented due to resource imbalances between phases, and inter-functional conflicts. However, there is also an additional danger of breaking continuity over time. Three frequent and serious sources of discontinuity have to do with:

- top management involvement;
- team composition and project leadership;
- instability in the basic organizational structure of the corporation.

Top management is mostly active during the launch of an IIP. The global project is seen as a challenging and interesting task, and mobilizes and ties together resources from many corners of the firm. This is the kind of process that engages top managers. However, when the project gets to real work, top management support risks dwindling. This is not usually because of a change of priorities, but simply because of lack of time and ability to master the details of the project, and perhaps also of simply forgetting about it. The consequence is that the project is put even more at the mercy of the various units from which it has to continuously procure resources and moral support. In the worst case, this can force top management to cancel the project altogether, even if it was their personal "pet project." "Go–Forget–Stop" involvement from the top should be replaced by more continuous and patient support. Such sponsoring and championing is recognized as important in the general debate on product development (see Roberts and Fusfeld, 1981). It becomes even more so in the IIP, since the potential for local obstruction is so much greater.

Continuity should also apply to the composition of the core group of people and the project leader. Co-ordination and the securing of commitment become almost impossible if the project crew changes frequently. Transferring information to new members is costly, at best. Also, much of the experience of a well-knit team is only tacitly understood. For example, knowledge of what did not work in earlier phases is very valuable but not naturally documented and transferred to new members. Changes of project leadership, in addition to generating information and incentive problems, risks destroying hard-won, mutually agreed ways of working together and shared conceptions of the distribution of authority.

Finally, IIPs need to be protected against reorganizations at the level of the line organization. In several of our in-depth cases, the IIPs were almost killed by the turmoil surrounding large corporate restructuring initiatives. First, the general commotion and uncertainty associated with such processes seriously disturb potentially fragile initiatives such as IIPs. Second, the re-manning of important positions easily robs projects of critical individuals who may be anxious to secure interesting and more permanent operations positions but may also fear that the impermanence of a project role could become a personal liability. The best way to counter such tendencies is to make IIP success truly rewarding both in the pecuniary and career sense. Communicated commitment, and commitment in action, on the part of top management is necessary for this to be credible.

Therefore, to ensure continuity, we believe it is vital for senior management to take on the task of continuously supporting product development projects in general, and international ones in particular. The task of exploiting previous innovations should mostly be left to functional and/or country management. However, the creation of new competitive advantages is a much more demanding task, infected with high levels of uncertainty and in need of continuous sponsoring from the top. A serious approach to innovation management also means not promoting people away from critical positions in the projects to, apparently more important, jobs in the operating organization. As much as the project needs to be linked to the overall strategic intentions of the firm and the continuous interest of senior executives, it must be protected against formal reorganizations. Rearranging the boxes and arrows of the positional structure should not be confused with or left to affect the fate of action-oriented processes such as new product development.

Weak and unclear leadership

Project leadership was often weak, in several senses. It was split into technical and managerial parts in several cases, each part having its own so-called project manager. It was impotent in that real power was nested with supervising bodies, sometimes several of them. It was vague, for example when project leaders were called "co-ordinators." It was junior, in that sometimes young and inexperienced people were appointed as project leaders. In the most extreme case, project leadership came to be seen as somewhat of a curse. At least five "leaders" had been involved with the project before the product had even been brought to the commercialization phase.

Current research emphasizes the importance of "heavyweight" project leaders (see Wheelwright and Clark, 1992). In IIPs, strong project leadership is even more essential. Perhaps one could call for "sumo" project leaders, since the challenges of defending project integrity against both local and functional management, as well as that of instilling energy and "soul" to the international project, are so much greater.

Thus, "sumo" IIP leaders should be given a broad mandate and much power over firmly dedicated resources; they should be respected across national and functional borders; they should exude a certain seniority even if young; they should possess both know-how about the tasks to be completed and "know-who" about people in the corporation and its environment; they should motivate and inspire people; they should have the power to recruit, sack, reward, and punish project members; and they should captain during the entire voyage.

Weak project location

It seems crucial that project leadership is given a strong locational base. This may seem a contradiction in terms, as an IIP is by definition footloose. However, it is quite feasible to locate the project manager and critical resources consciously. We saw several IIPs face difficulties because of a weak "base." The distance to top managers weakened the critical continued support of the project. Legitimacy is hard to uphold if you come from a place obviously technically inferior to those you are supposed to co-ordinate. Again, the IIP must be, and be seen as, an important and strategically significant initiative and not as a marginal one, which is easily the impression conveyed by a marginal location.

Less obvious is an idea that we admittedly cannot claim strong empirical support for, or against. Nevertheless, there is an argument for locating project leadership in "Tacitland." The strong base should be where the least codifiable type of knowledge is located. In many cases, this means locating leadership in important markets rather than technical centers, since often market knowledge is hard to articulate, compare, and transfer between locales. Such reasoning also supports determined investments in temporarily locating engineering talent in important markets. The reverse does not hold the same promise, although this would also contribute to the sharing of knowledge and help to form a cohesive team.

Accordingly, it seems that the core of an IIP should be located either where there is some corporate clout or where there is critical competence, or preferably both. Surprisingly often, decisions on where to locate leadership appeared more contingent on commitment, or as compensation for decisions affecting the operating organization. For example, in one case, project leadership was awarded as compensation for the transfer of a product mandate to another country. Weak units will almost by definition fail in bringing any innovation to the market. This fact is even more true in the case of IIPs since they will have to rely on the benevolence of other, more powerful units. As a rule, these units will put more priority on their "own" projects. This also implies that the sheer size of the unit in charge, and of its local market, may matter. Our advice is thus to locate leadership of international projects at large and resourceful subsidiaries, with direct access to the final customer.

Weak development architecture

We have argued against the establishment of IIPs that are not firmly linked to the strategic priorities of a corporation. One reason for the creation of such freely floating projects is the absence of systems for assigning priorities, starting and closing projects, and allocating resources in the development work of most firms. There are accepted techniques for the management of routine tasks. However, when it comes to innovation, sometimes there are not even simple lists of projects going on, much less a focused attention to them. Systems are built for the exploitation of resources and existing and known opportunities, less for creation or experimentation. For a discussion of this point in the context of the MNC see Hedlund and Rolander, 1990; Hedlund and Ridderstråle, 1993.

Thus, effective management of IIPs is not only a matter of positive factors such as strong individuals, energy, and commitment. It is also a matter of systems and procedures – a "development architecture" supporting individual projects and setting them in the context of the entire development thrust of the corporation. Such systems are needed at several levels.

Implicit in the earlier discussion is a plea for systems for setting and communicating development philosophies, strategies, and priorities, as a whole. There is also a need for set procedures of project management and tracking. Such systems abounded in our case firms. The problem was that they were complicated, idiosyncratic, and weak – in the sense of not really being adhered to – rather than being simple, shared, and strong. In one instance, we were shown a "development map," 2×3 meters in size. This is not "simple." It had been developed in a large subsidiary, and was very different from corresponding process maps at HQ and at the other subsidiary critical to the project in question. This map was not "shared." Systems of this kind are particularly important in an MNC, since in their absence nobody knows what is meant by terms such as "product plan," "design," "pilot," "market launch," and so on. Simple and shared systems are needed not so much in order to direct the process in a strongly controlled fashion. Rather, they serve as a corporate grammar and vocabulary, allowing for intelligible communication and countering the natural "Tower of Babel" tendencies inherent in international communication.

A final aspect concerning development architecture is the need for, and seeming absence of, systematic efforts to learn within, between, and beyond projects. The absence is a natural consequence of the slightly *ad hoc* approach to innovation in general and IIPs in particular. Again, what seems to be needed are fairly simple things, such as: project log books and final project reports specifying what went well and what went wrong; the dissemination of such pieces; the rotation of people to new projects (for example, not "rewarding" successful project leaders by taking the person permanently off such responsibilities into the "bosom" of corporate management); formal project reviews with top management on completion (makes noncompletion very embarrassing!). The problem is not so much one of analysis as of determination to speed up the transfer of lessons hard learned.

Improving IIP performance: why managers do not always do the obvious

Considering the list of problems and our tentative approaches to them in their totality (see Table 3.4), one is struck by their almost simple nature. Who would argue: against having clear priorities; for fragmentation between functions; against communication; for unclear leadership? One is also reminded of similar lists in many books on project management and product development.

The international dimension appears to add surprisingly little to the problematique. Increased geographical scope probably implies that it is more difficult to establish clear stakes and incentives for all, and it does take more time to develop a shared interpretation and conception, thus prolonging the initial phases. It may also be more problematic to secure involvement of marketing, since the question of which, out of all the marketing units, to listen to is added. The greater physical distances complicate co-ordination and communication, and the sometimes simultaneous hand-over across functional and national borders obstructs continuity and opens up the opportunity for the same mistakes being made twice. The requirements on the project leader and the location in charge are much tougher, and the demands for a more systemic approach to innovation management are brought to an extreme. However, one is still surprised by how similar the challenges seem to those present in more local ventures.

Table 3.4 Problems in IIPs and approaches to handle them

Common problems	*Suggested approaches*
Lack of significance	Establish clear priorities Ensure strategic consistency Promote a sense of urgency and commitment Establish stakes and incentives for all parties and at all levels
Resource deficiencies and process imbalance	Front-load projects in terms of time and resources Develop shared interpretation of task Be prepared to set aside corporate money Use 100 percent members when possible
Functionally fragmented process	Include market launch in project definition Decide early on manufacturing site(s) Co-locate different functions temporarily
Poor communication	Spend more time and resources on establishing face-to-face communication Co-ordinate also at low and middle levels Ensure that the meeting schedule is driven by problems, not plans Utilize information technology as a complement to personal interaction
Lack of continuity	Ensure continuous commitment from top management A core team should remain on board throughout the entire process Stick to one project leader throughout the process Protect the project against reorganizations
Weak and unclear leadership	Appoint leaders with "sumo" characteristics and extensive responsibilities
Weak project location	Locate leadership where there is clout or competence Locate leadership in "Tacitland"
Weak development architecture	Develop systems that are strong, shared, and simple Ensure learning within, between, and beyond projects

So, the conclusions seem to be: first, that IIPs are best approached in a common sense way; and, second, that they do not differ that much from national projects. However, both of these "conclusions" are interesting. The second one implies that IIPs are indeed possible to manage and not an exotic luxury that firms should avoid. The general point seems to be that the international dimension adds to the difficulties of finding appropriate solutions, but does not pose qualitatively new problems.

The first point is more intricate. Why, if the correct approaches are so obvious, do firms not adopt them? One possible explanation is inexperience. Indeed, in our in-depth cases, we observe rapid progress in adhering to the dicta summarized in Table 3.4. Another possibility is, of course, that firms are either irrational or incompetent, or both. Although we do not want to exclude these possibilities, we would like to suggest a more insidious reason.

Repeatedly, we find that difficulties on the surface, seemingly to do with project management, originate in the tensions between the organizational structures and routines, on the one hand, and the project logic, on the other. Unless this tension is directly addressed, non-compliance with the received wisdom of project management will continue. It is all very well to argue for full-timers in IIPs, but the problem is the reluctance on part of the line organization to allow this. Also, as long as careers are based on hierarchical ascent, there are only slim chances that the real talent will engage in project leadership, at least more than a few times. If you have sumo qualities, you want to hang around with the other sumo wrestlers, not with the featherweights.

No doubt, tightening the ship in terms of project discipline can make some improvements. However, the real obstacle to really significant progress is the nature of the large, bureaucratic organization itself. We are not thinking here primarily of the inertia and slow reaction time often characteristic of large corporations. Instead, the real problem is the construction of the firm as a set of hierarchically related and specialized units. We have earlier argued that the modern MNC is a complex blend of three different structuring principles: administrative position, knowledge, and action (Hedlund, 1993; Hedlund and Ridderstråle, 1995, 1997; Hagström and Hedlund, 1998).

The problem of the MNC, or of any large organization in a complex and changing environment, is that these three structures, and the systems supporting them, are increasingly decoupled. High position does not necessarily imply specialized or even strategically encompassing knowledge, at least not knowledge pertaining to all the different activities of the firm. Neither does a high position necessarily imply the locus of strategic action and initiative. In the classical hierarchical bureaucracy, the three systems coincide: senior people with great knowledge and strategic decision-making power at the top; junior people with limited and given knowledge and implementation at the bottom. As long as knowledge is not complex, does not change very rapidly, and is not highly dispersed geographically and functionally – and, in no need of transfer and combination over such borders – it is also possible to use the positional structure for knowledge creation. However, our research indicates that the knowledge landscape facing many firms today is more characterized by its depth, dispersion, diversity, and decreasing durability.

Since knowledge develops quickly over time and the creation of novelty and competitive advantage rests with (re-)combining diverse skills, dispersed throughout the international network, action has to be organized in ever-new constellations. The required composition of resources is not easily extracted from a "line organization" where naturally complementary competencies are close organizational neighbors. So far, the temptation often succumbed to by organizational designers, both in theory and in practice, has been to mirror an ever-increasing complexity of environment and task by even more elaborate and sophisticated formal structures. But there is an alternative, suggested by the triad nature of organization.

In our minds, the managers of successful international network corporations will let the positional structure be a simple and straightforward hierarchy. They will add structures and systems for knowledge management that are fluid, dispersed, interactive, and catalytic. It is critical to mobilize knowledge through an action structure built on temporary projects and teams (see Hedlund, 1993, for a more detailed argument). Nonaka and Takeuchi (1995), have proposed an almost identical conception in their study of Japanese corporations, mostly at work in Japan. Thus, again, the international aspect does not seem to be the main factor.

This argument holds, we believe, the explanation for why the obvious is not done and why the most important problems of IIPs appear trivial. The positional structure gets in the way of action and does not effectively mobilize the knowledge structure of the firm. To address this "meta-problem" requires a fundamental overhaul of the way of organizing, managing, and leading the MNC. The issue is not qualitatively different for the MNC than for any organization facing demands for rapid change and utilization of complex and dispersed competencies. However, the MNC faces the problems in a starker form and earlier than national firms. The MNC here joins ranks with organizations such as professional service firms and universities in developing approaches to effective global knowledge management.

Conclusions

In this chapter, we have discussed the recent phenomenon of international innovation projects. We have identified eight areas that are perceived as problematic by firms trying to engage in global processes of knowledge creation. To summarize, successful international innovation projects are regarded as significant and critical by the entire organization, and they are given sufficient resources. A large proportion of these resources needs to be spent at the beginning of the process to secure the development of a shared interpretation of what to do, as well as the articulation of the underlying assumptions of those taking part. The innovation process is both conceived of and designed as a functionally integrated venture, where much effort is put into co-ordinating activities at those levels at which real work gets carried out. The prime mechanisms for establishing appropriate degrees of integration are intense traveling and co-location, complemented with extensive use of information technology. Continuity is secured by top management proving its commitment in action, and by, as early as possible, establishing a core team that will follow the product from beginning to end, including successful initial marketing activities. The project is given a strong geographical location, and a project manager with "sumo" qualities is appointed. Consistency in performance and learning is attained by introducing a development architecture that is strong, simple, and shared across geographical and functional borders.

Many of the critical issues and remedies are well known to most managers and academics. Still, the problems prevail. We attribute this situation to a more general intricacy. Any company is a blend of three structures: administrative positions, knowledge, and actions. In the classical bureaucratic firm, these structures coincide. However, given that knowledge critical to the development of competitive advantage in the global firm is becoming increasingly dispersed, organizationally as well as geographically, and that the rate of change is constantly on the rise, these three structures should also become more and more decoupled. Unless we treat these structures separately, they will inevitably collide. In the practice of IIPs, this is exactly what we see. Repeatedly, the dominating and rigid positional structure interferes with the more dynamic activities of the project. Instead of mirroring increased complexity by adding more boxes and arrows to the organizational chart, we propose that the positional structure should be kept simple. Focus the efforts on strengthening the power of the action structures by creating "real" projects with "real" project managers who can take the critical decisions. Then add mechanisms to manage knowledge as a strategic resource. The resulting architecture is flatter and more temporary. A modern firm also relies heavily on shared values, identities, rewards, visions, and so on, following a horizontal rather than a vertical logic.

To conclude, despite a number of identifiable problems, some general to all innovation processes and some more specific to international projects, our research suggests that for many international firms the only alternative more difficult than learning to manage cross-border projects, is learning to operate without them. Solutions for handling the difficulties can be developed and implemented. One could even say that, on the project level, managing IIPs is very much about getting the obvious things right. However, securing a steady stream of successful projects is far more than a question of improving project management. Without also changing individuals' mind-sets and the overall organizational architecture of the internationally networked firm, the critical problems may be reduced, but probably not resolved.

Appendix 3.1: companies included in the survey

AGA
Alfa Laval[a]
Eka Nobel
Ericsson
Gambro
Pharmacia
SCA
SKF
Tarkett
Telia
Tetra Pak[a]
Volvo

Note
[a]After the IIPs were initiated, Tetra Pak and Alfa Laval merged to form Tetra Laval.

Appendix 3.2: products

Base-station for GSM
Advanced personal communication system
A series of medium-size trucks for North America
New dashboard for car
New generation of spherical roller bearing
Drug for use in hospitals
Interior items of a car (rear-seats, dashboard, etc.)
Market adaptations of a new vehicle
(No description given)
Base-station and switch for cellular system in North America
Truck
Telephone system for local exchange applications
New heavy vehicle family
New paper product for packaging industry
Process to improve productivity in glass melting furnaces
Process for production of cast iron already supplied by competitors
New seal type on standard ball bearings
Wood laminated floor-product family
On-line safety system for chemical process
Housed rolling bearing unit
Centrifugal separator based on existing product
Hub unit with ABS-sensor, for cars
Tunnel freezer for cryogenic freezing
High-flux dialyzer
Car radios
Plant for recycling of dissolvers
A sizing agent for cellulose fibers
A wood floor with thicker surface layer
Membrane for hemodialysis
New intravenous nutritional support for critically ill patients
Packaging system for milk and juice
Fat soluble anaesthetic agent

Notes

1 The authors gratefully acknowledge financial support from the Carnegie Bosch Institute, Handelsbanken Research Foundations and the assistance of Mr. Stefan Löhr and Mr. Martin Zetterström in conducting the research.
2 The case studies are reported in summary in Hedlund, G. and Ridderstråle, J. (1995) "International Development Projects – Key to Competitiveness, Impossible or Mismanaged?," *International Studies of Management and Organization*, 25, 1–2, Spring/Summer, and in Ridderstråle (1996).
3 The firms were asked to provide information for two to six projects each. Most of the non-response was due to "lack of time" and the firm claiming not to be engaged in IIPs. The sample is biased in favor of successful IIPs.

References

Bartlett, C.A. and S. Ghoshal (1989) *Managing Across Borders: The Transnational Solution,* Cambridge, MA: Harvard Business School Press.

Dougherty, D. (1992) "Interpretive barriers to successful product innovations in large firms," *Organization Science,* 3, 2: 179–202.

Doz, Y.L. (1986) *Strategic Management in Multinational Companies,* Oxford: Pergamon Press.

Hagström, P. and G. Hedlund (1998) "A three-dimensional model of changing internal structures in the firm," in Chandler, A.D., P. Hagström, and Ö. Sölvell (eds) *The Dynamic Firm: The Role of Technology, Strategy, Organization and Regions,* Oxford: Oxford University Press, pp. 329–354.

Hedlund, G. (1986) "The Hypermodern MNC – a heterarchy?," *Human Resource Management,* Spring, 9–35.

Hedlund, G. (1993) "Assumptions of hierarchy and heterarchy: an application to multinational corporations," in Ghoshal, S. and E. Westney (eds) *Organization Theory and the Multinational Corporation,* London: Macmillan.

Hedlund, G. and J. Ridderstråle (1995) "International development projects – key to competitiveness, impossible, or mismanaged?," *International Studies of Management & Organization,* 25, 1–2, Spring/Summer, Special Issue.

Hedlund, G. and J. Ridderstråle (1997) "Toward the N-form corporation: exploitation and creation in the MNC," in Toyne, B. and D. Nigh (eds) *International Business Inquiry: An Emerging Vision,* Charleston, SC: University of South Carolina Press, pp. 166–191.

Hedlund, G. and D. Rolander (1990) "Action in heterarchies: new approaches to managing the MNC," in Bartlett, C.A., Y.L. Doz, and G. Hedlund (eds) *Managing the Global Firm,* London: Routledge.

Nonaka, I. and H. Takeuchi (1995) *The Knowledge-Creating Company,* New York and Oxford: Oxford University Press.

Ridderstråle, J. (1996) *Global Innovation: Managing International Innovation Projects at ABB and Electrolux* (published doctoral dissertation).

Roberts, E.B. and A.R. Fusfeld (1981) "Staffing the innovative technology-base organization," *Sloan Management Review,* Spring, 19–34.

Takeuchi, H. and I. Nonaka (1986) "The New Product Development Game," *Harvard Business Review,* Jan.–Feb., 137–146.

Wheelwright, S.C. and K.B. Clark (1992) *Revolutionizing Product Development,* New York, NY: The Free Press.

White, R.E. and T.A. Poynter (1990) "Organizing for world-wide advantage," in Bartlett, C.A., Y.L. Doz, and G. Hedlund (eds) *Managing the Global Firm,* London: Routledge.

4

THE MANAGEMENT OF JOINT VENTURES WITHIN INTERNATIONAL BUSINESS NETWORKS

US companies in China[1]

John Child

Introduction[1]

Diversified multinational corporations (MNCs) have to manage a high level of complexity which, as Doz and Prahalad (1993) have argued, stems from a combination of heterogeneity and multidimensionality. Heterogeneity results primarily from the particular trade-offs between businesses, countries, functions, and tasks that best suit the economic and political circumstances of different countries. Multidimensionality reflects the range of products or services, geographical regions, and supporting functions which diversified MNCs encompass. The need to articulate forms of organization that can cope with growing MNC complexity has been increasingly recognized in recent years (cf. Bartlett *et al.*, 1990; Ghoshal and Westney, 1993), and the "network" form is a possible response.

The entry of numerous MNCs into China since the beginning of that country's "open door policy" in 1979 has added to their heterogeneity because of China's special circumstances. Chinese government policy, expressed in regulations and economic incentives, has tended to favor equity joint ventures between foreign-investing firms and local partners. Most foreign production operations in China have been joint ventures in which one or more local partners are involved with ownership rights.

China's business environment is one in which central and local government authorities exercise considerable influence on foreign joint ventures. This takes a direct form through their interpretation of legal provisions, structuring of taxes, and approval of expansion plans. It takes an indirect form in that most Chinese joint venture partners report to higher governmental authorities. As Nolan (1995: 9) comments with reference to one of Coca-Cola's joint ventures in China, the state is "an important shadow figure" on the Board of Directors. The management of external relations therefore assumes a special importance.

In view of these complications, the question arises as to whether to treat China as just another country or to give it greater than usual prominence within an MNC's organization, thereby adding to heterogeneity. There are several considerations which favor the latter view. For instance, China is a huge potential market, sustaining a high rate of growth. It is, at the same time, a developing country in which joint ventures will normally be dependent upon their foreign parents for substantial technology transfer, managerial inputs, and assistance in supplier and market development in attaining international standards.

The particular characteristics of China as a business environment also impinge on the product, regional, and functional aspects of MNC multidimensionality in three ways. First, there is a need to assist and monitor technology transfer for which the relevant expertise is likely to be located within an MNC's product groups or businesses. Second, an MNC has to view China as consisting of several internal markets because of its scale, infrastructural limitations, and regional differences in economic development. This requires a regional organization with the sensitivity to manage the differentiation and heterogeneity of its markets. Because of the country's size and regional diversity, many MNCs now have multiple joint ventures in China. They may have to co-ordinate the relations between these joint ventures and the central authorities, as well as exploiting marketing and supply economies among them. Third, there is a need to provide functional support which is not always available from local partners, in areas such as finance and accounting, HRM, and legal affairs.

China is therefore a unique business environment, creating complications for MNCs that attempt to integrate local operations into wider organizational systems. The problem is heightened by the fact that Chinese partners often supply the bulk of the ventures' managers and staff, who are normally not used to, and will not necessarily identify with, the norms and procedures of the MNC without foreign managerial guidance. Joint ventures in China may require an unusually heavy managerial investment by foreign partners, at least in the early years of their life, drawing heavily on the different dimensions of MNC organizational expertise.

This chapter first addresses the ways in which nine prominent American MNCs have linked the management of their China joint ventures into their global structures. These structures have provided the multidimensional frameworks for intra-organizational managerial networking, concerned with decision-making and information exchange (Boyer, 1989). For such networking to extend effectively to joint ventures in China, it has been essential for US parent companies to exercise effective control and influence over management. The question then arises of where to locate decisions relevant to the joint ventures within the overall managerial network, bearing in mind the problem of reconciling the conflicting criteria of global integration and local differentiation. These three issues – linkage, control, and decision levels – are the main subjects of this chapter. The chapter poses a number of important questions which, while focused on China, also have a much wider relevance within global management:

1 how do MNCs link the management of China ventures into their corporate structures?
2 how do MNCs exercise and sustain control over these ventures?
3 how do MNCs locate decision-making relevant to their China business?

This chapter focuses on the structural aspects of managing China joint ventures in relation to parent MNCs. The full investigation from which it draws also examined certain processual aspects of the corporate networks operating within the structures. Indeed, a number of senior MNC managers both at corporate and regional levels emphasized that structure alone would not provide an adequate understanding of how their management systems operate with respect to, for example, the integrative functions performed by information exchange and the fostering of shared norms and values. This supports the view advanced by Doz and Prahalad (1993: 26) that, for diversified MNCs, "one needs a theory that transcends the structural dimensions and focuses on underlying processes." Nonetheless, as the theory of "structuration" would suggest (Giddens, 1984), action and structure have a symbiotic relationship in organizations such that, while action can modify structure, it is also shaped and constrained by it. The structural dimensions do constitute a significant design challenge for MNC managers, and need to be considered.

Scope and method of the inquiry

The investigation from which this chapter draws covers nine multinational enterprises whose headquarters are located in the United States. The companies are situated in the non-consumer electronics and fast-moving consumer goods [FMCG] sectors – four in the former and five in the latter. The non-consumer electronics companies manufactured telecommunication, process control, and office equipment. The FMCG companies produced branded foods, beverages, and household products. The choice of these two sectors was informed by the desire to contrast companies possessing a strong technological core competence in product design (electronics) with those possessing a strong consumer marketing core competence linked to the promotion of international brands (FMCG). Technological competence is likely to favor a logic of organization by product group, whereas a strong marketing orientation is likely to favor a logic according to geography.

Nine joint ventures were visited in order to collect information on their internal management and links with parent companies – that is, one joint venture established by each US corporation in China. Expatriate general managers, and in one case the American head of operations, were the informants for material presented in this chapter. Interviews were subsequently conducted in the USA with 12 senior corporate executives who had responsibility for China or who were otherwise closely involved with the corporation's policy toward its China ventures. A further six persons in the Hong Kong regional offices of five of the companies, who had a responsibility for their China ventures, were also interviewed. The procedure adopted for each interview was to ask open-ended questions based on standardized checklists. All the corporate and regional level interviews were tape-recorded, as were some in the joint ventures, depending on the acceptability of this procedure to the interviewee. In the following text and tables, the electronics companies are identified by the prefix "E" and FMCG companies by the prefix "F".

The location of China joint ventures in global management structures

It is useful to distinguish between the *transactional* (input/output) and *managerial* links of the China joint ventures into their foreign parents' multinational networks. They were, in fact, considerably less integrated into global transactional networks than they were into the foreign parents' international management systems.

Only one of the joint ventures was selling any outputs to its MNC parent. The exception was Corporation E4, which had allocated the worldwide production of an older electronic process control system to its China joint venture. This corporation was therefore selling 25 percent of its output value to other parts of its MNC parent's network. Rather more joint ventures were integrated with their MNC parents on the supply side. Three of the four electronics joint ventures purchased components from their MNCs. E3 took 80 percent by value, E4 took 45 percent, while E2 took 30 percent. Among the fast-moving consumer goods joint ventures, only F2 received an appreciable amount of its process inputs from its MNC parent, at 40 percent by value. The other FMCG joint ventures received under 5 percent of their inputs from the American parents.

This low level of transactional integration is explained largely by the fact that all the MNCs had the establishment of a strategic position vis-à-vis competitors and access to the market as their over-riding priorities for establishing joint ventures in China. They were not primarily motivated by supply-side factors such as the availability of low-cost materials or labor. Their intention, at least initially, was to produce for the Chinese market rather than to integrate China into their international production networks.

The relatively limited transactional integration of these China joint ventures justifies focusing on managerial integration. The points at which China joint ventures are linked into the wider corporate structure of MNCs depends on how the issue of multidimensionality is resolved. This is clearly easier in the case of a single joint venture producing one product than that of several joint ventures producing different products, possibly destined for different segments of the Chinese market. In the former case, a straightforward product divisional line linkage down to the China joint venture, through one or more regional levels and supported by functional services, will be appropriate (Stopford and Wells, 1972). In the latter case, with diversified product categories, the regional and/or China level office has co-ordinating and representative roles to play, and probably responsibility for new business development in China as well.

Meier, Perez, and Woetzel (1995) note that many MNCs have established "China corporate centers" to assist business development and corporate positioning in China by co-ordinating and supporting business units in negotiating and establishing new ventures. They distinguish two main ways in which these centers can achieve effective co-ordination between product businesses or divisions active in China. One is the "team approach" where "the China center comprises senior representatives or heads of the local business units, plus a senior country representative" (1995: 25). It can, however, be difficult to achieve collaboration in this way between the business managers and the country manager. An alternative approach is therefore to have "focused leadership" with the China center "led by a China

CEO with country P&L responsibility to whom the China business units report" (ibid.).

A further consideration which bears on the role performed by the regional or country office is the operational status given to the China joint venture(s). There are several options relating to the level of local initiative that is favored. Joint ventures can, for example, be defined as business units, with their own technological and functional resources and the autonomy to undertake their own commercial initiatives. Another option is to locate the formation of their strategy and most of their support at a China country or Asia–Pacific regional level, and to run the joint ventures primarily as manufacturing and sales branch units with perhaps the additional responsibility for relations with local governmental authorities. The issue of how much decentralization is accorded to the joint ventures is thus bound up with the role that is given to the country or regional office. It is part of the wider issue of how decision-making autonomy for China is distributed through the MNC structure and how responsibilities are allocated to different levels and groups within that structure.

The nine corporations investigated attached great importance to the design of their global structures. These corporations found the question of how such design should map onto their joint ventures in China a significant challenge. Two important design decisions concerned the main lines of control and co-ordination relating to the joint ventures, and the autonomy they were accorded within the MNC framework. Five of the companies were actively experimenting with their structures for China. All were continuing to explore issues of balance and co-ordination between vertically and horizontally differentiated units within the overall matrix. As one corporate FMCG senior director commented on proposals to reorganize within China into business units:

> This calls the China structure into question again. We've argued the functional structure versus the autonomous business unit structure ad infinitum ... It has been the most difficult challenge that we have had [in the corporation globally] and it has been ugly, it really has been ugly.
>
> (Corporation F3)

The corporate strategy director of an electronics corporation indicated that his company faced similar uncertainties over appropriate reporting lines for its China joint ventures:

> That's switched back and forth a few times: whether it's a solid line into the product divisions, which figure out the products the market needs during engineering, design and delivery, and dotted line into the geographic structure – or solid into the geographic and dotted into the divisions.
>
> (Corporation E2)

Table 4.1 summarizes how the nine MNCs were structured globally, the roles of their regional and China offices, the number of joint ventures they had in China, and how these formally linked into their structures. Four of the nine corporations were organized on the basis of global product businesses: three in electronics and

Table 4.1 The location of China joint ventures in MNE structures

Company	Global structure	Role of regional office	Role of China company	Number of JVs, reporting to
E1	Product based	Primary role is as regional offices for product divisions. Also new territory development; functional support including IT and legal; government relations.	*Holding company (limited team approach).* Government relations; profit consolidation; secure potential inter-JV synergies; functional support including quality.	6 JVs, reporting to region-based product division managers.
E2	Product based	Product marketing, sales and service; functional support. Also regional offices of product divisions.	*Team approach.* Consolidating China market strategy; co-ordinating JVs and field operations; functional support.	3 JVs, reporting primarily to China company JV manager.
E3	Matrix	Business development; marketing; functional support.	*Focused leadership. Reports directly to corporate CEO.* Government relations; co-ordinate business units in China for market advantage; functional support, including operations and legal.	9 JVs, reporting to CEO of China company.
E4	Product based	Assist business units (JVs, subsidiaries) in market development, co-ordination of marketing and technology transfer.	*No China company.*	1 JV, reporting to regional manager.
F1	Product based	Policy and consolidation for regional group of countries within product business; functional support.	*China office for each product business. Line responsibility for JVs.* Central government relations; functional support (including marketing and operations).	13 JVs in main product sector, reporting to VP Sales Operations in China office.

continued

Table 4.1 continued

Company	Global structure	Role of regional office	Role of China company	Number of JVs, reporting to
F2	Geographical	*Limited team approach at this level.* Overseeing businesses in Asia–Pacific region with functional support. Also product category officers to disseminate and oversee product strategy.	*Line responsibility for JVs.* Central Asia office with Country Manager overseeing China businesses; functional support (including marketing, government relations, China information).	4 JVs, reporting to Country Manager, China.
F3	Geographical	Overseeing country units; functional support.	*Line responsibility for China businesses* especially marketing; functional support (including R&D).	3 JVs, reporting to Managing Director for China.
F4	Geographical	Overseeing country units; functional support (HR is at this level). Also product category managers.	*Primarily line responsibility for JVs with limited team approach.* Functional support (including marketing).	3 JVs (plus 3 wholly-owned subsidiaries) reporting to Regional VP for China.
F5	Geographical	General overseeing of geographical divisions within regional groups; functional support.	*Line responsibility for JVs.* Functional support (including legal, marketing, IS, PR).	17 JVs, reporting to Executive VP in China company.

Note
Unless otherwise mentioned, functional support in all cases includes finance, HR/personnel, and technical.

one in FMCG. These businesses normally had worldwide responsibility for R&D, manufacturing and, in some cases, marketing. They carried profit responsibility and were the main investment arms of their corporations. Their regional offices had responsibilities primarily for business development, market co-ordination, and functional support. One electronics corporation (E3) operated a balanced matrix of product and geographical units. The remaining four FMCG corporations were organized primarily on a geographical basis. As expected, the product dimension tended to be more prominent in the electronics sector and the geographical dimension in the FMCG sector.

Multiple-product business MNCs faced a greater challenge in how to organize for China than those which had all their products falling within the same category, especially when, at the same time, there are potential synergies in China between the product groups. The status and role of the unit dealing with China varies between the six MNCs (E1, E2, E3, F1, F2, and F4) with diversified products. The organization of their China centers varied from few links between product personnel at the China level (F1), through a limited team approach, to a highly focused leadership. The organization of China activities was more uniform and straightforward in the remaining MNCs that had products with relatively homogeneous technologies and markets. Every corporation, except for E4, however, had a China company or office, and each one had recently created or was developing the role of a China CEO.

Those companies which pursued a dominant dimensional logic nonetheless endeavored to build in other dimensions in a complementary manner. As is well appreciated from experience with multidimensional structures (cf. Davis and Lawrence, 1977; Knight, 1977), this is liable to generate friction, and several of the MNCs had experienced resistance over attempts to reinforce non-dominant structural dimensions.[2] It is therefore instructive to examine some examples of corporate–joint venture structures in more detail, with particular reference to the role of the regional and China levels. These are the three electronics MNCs with multiple product operations in China, and one of the geographical-line organizations which was quite highly diversified into different categories of food and beverages.

Example E1 was organized on the basis of global vertical product businesses which had worldwide responsibility for R&D, manufacturing, marketing, and sales. Its six joint ventures in China were integrated into the worldwide organization of their respective product lines, with products assigned to each as a result of global planning by one of the product businesses. Their general managers reported to business managers located at the Asia–Pacific level.

The geographical arm of the organization subdivided below the corporate level into three regions, of which one was Asia–Pacific. The Asia–Pacific region had, in turn, a China country general manager reporting to it. The Asia–Pacific regional office provided what it termed "the horizontal infrastructure" for the businesses, and this involved a complete range of functions such as financial, accounting, corporate treasury, information systems, human resources, legal, and facilities. The role of the geographical dimension was, according to its Senior Vice-President:

> to do with delivering common shared corporate services in support of the [vertical] businesses. It also includes things like government and public affairs, new market development and new territory development – not necessarily what a business might do once we, in a sense, create a presence in that particular territory.

Its geographical organization was also intended to present a unified corporate face, both internally to its employees, administering, for instance, a common benefits policy, and externally to customer and governments. To quote the same SVP:

> We have very focused, aggressive businesses that can basically compete with any niche competitor, yet have the ability to look and act like one extremely large corporation when we want to.

The corporation had recently extended its geographical dimension within China with the establishment of a holding company as an umbrella over all the corporation's joint ventures in that country. In addition to the taxation and foreign exchange management advantages this offered, the major organizational benefit was seen to be better positioning for the corporation vis-à-vis the central government. Relationships with ministries relevant to its various products were vital for the continued development of its business, as were those with the municipal government of Shanghai, where three of its joint ventures are located. Nonetheless, the corporation saw its China holding company as performing a supportive role to the product-based businesses that remained the focus of its organization. This exemplifies a relatively weak team approach. In fact, the regional CEO described it as "really more like a paper corporation."

Example E2 had recently enhanced its China company and was intending this to operate in a stronger team mode. It had felt the need to develop a comprehensive strategy for China which was not forthcoming from the previous arrangement whereby self-contained joint ventures, with their own engineering, manufacturing, selling, and service facilities, reported to separate business divisions. There had indeed been considerable conflict between the joint ventures and the China office, which tried to co-ordinate the product divisions and to orient them more toward the market. According to the CEO of the China company:

> Instead of worrying about the customer or competition, there were a lot of inter-murals going on and because of that ... we really have not invested what we feel now is necessary to go into the market ... When I came here, one of the jobs that I was given was to get ourselves into a dominant position in the market, and to try to get some better focus on the customer. That clearly requires a distribution system and a field system that is more co-ordinated among all of the divisions than we had.

The corporation had reorganized its China company to contain four business division directors, a consolidated marketing function in charge of China field operations, and an executive in charge of the joint ventures which it intended to expand beyond the existing number of three. While all of these key positions reported to the CEO of the China company, the intention was to generate a team approach rather than one of focused leadership. That is, to bring strategic and market development perspectives alongside those of product "push" which were already influential. To quote the China CEO again:

> The intention really is to try to get a more focused strategy on China, and not necessarily just from the products that we make over there but from the strength that the corporation can bring to the market because it clearly has a lot of strength that we have not capitalized on for this market. To try to get a strategy put together is probably one of the biggest issues we had in that ours was a product, dealer-driven strategy rather than what the end-customers may need ... [Also] not to worry too much about what you can make right now, but trying to judge a little bit as to which way the market will go.

Example E3 is pursuing business opportunities in China on the basis of a Memorandum of Understanding with the central government. Subsequent to the Memorandum, the corporation established a China company intended to present a single face to the Chinese government and to co-ordinate the hitherto separate initiatives of its product businesses. It exemplified the focused approach and has been regarded by some as pioneering a new structure for China. The China CEO enjoyed considerable personal respect within the corporation, and unusual status, since he was the only country head to report directly to the corporate CEO alongside the heads of the five global product groups and four regions. He claimed that this arrangement signified the first time his corporation had applied a combined global and local strategy.

The corporation's international operations were organized as a balanced matrix. Its "shared accountability model" stated that product groups and regions share responsibility for its business in China. The product groups had responsibility for the products that were available, the kinds of services the corporation was willing to offer, linkages to other (telecommunications) operations, and the sourcing of products that were not built locally. The regions had the main say on decisions which were customer-facing in terms of sales and project-bidding. However, the China company constituted something of an exception to this balance. It shared responsibility with the product groups for the China income statement and it jointly signed up the plans that were drawn up for China along with the product groups. The China company did, however, co-ordinate the various product groups in order to offer complete solutions to Chinese customers, and it showed the corporation's face to the Chinese government. It is also reported to have taken the lead in formulating the corporation's strategy for China. According to the VP of Strategic Planning for the China company who, significantly, was located at corporate head office:

> Increasingly, [the China company] will be speaking with a voice of its own. It says that it has a strategy and the groups have to bring themselves into conformity with that strategy as they operate in China. That's developing as time goes on.

An example of this developing role concerned a major initiative with the Chinese civil aeronautics administration. The project was not sufficiently attractive to win the enthusiasm of any individual product group, but taken as a whole it could do a great deal to enhance the reputation of the corporation in China as a total solutions vendor in the information technology field. The CEO of the China company pushed the project through, even though none of the product groups thought it was worth their time.

Example F2 had four China joint ventures which were responsible for different products that, collectively, fell into its three main food processing categories. While organized on the basis of geographic line responsibilities, F2 has addressed the question of how to build into its structure the specific strategic considerations of each product category. In addition to its geographical structure, it had established a "category management system" at the global and regional levels of its organization. Each of the corporation's three main product categories had a manager located at the Asia–Pacific regional office. This arrangement was intended to ensure that the relevant joint ventures in China were sufficiently briefed on corporate thinking for the product category. In the regional office, which physically contained the subsidiary area office for China, Hong Kong, and Taiwan, the corporation pursued a limited team approach:

> [The regional category manager] might be lending help to Japan or Australia or Singapore, but would also be providing similar assistance to the PRC joint ventures. For example, joint venture A would be getting the latest thinking on our coffee strategy and our coffee label ... So there is a pan-Asia category manager system that works with the marketing and development lady who is in charge of PRC.
>
> (Corporate President F2)

At a corporate level, the global product categories were linked together through "worldwide category councils" which met to review progress and strategy. Although the issue had been debated within the corporation, and remained highly sensitive, the regional organization retained the line responsibility and was the stronger dimension. This was illustrated by its regional and country level organization. Each of the corporation's four joint ventures in China reported to a country manager for China who also had two other managers under him with responsibilities for PRC sales and marketing/strategy across all three product categories. The sub-regional Area Office for Central Asia (PRC, Hong Kong, and Taiwan), to which the country manager reported, had no product category representatives either. It provided functional support in the areas of finance, human resources, technical, PRC information, and government relations areas. The product category managers were located at the next level up, namely Asia–Pacific, from which they performed the largely advisory roles already mentioned.

In short, senior executives in each of the MNCs were exploring how best to locate China joint ventures within their global structures. This was a significant issue within the wider problem of how best to organize the management of worldwide activities. When their structures reflected the primacy of one dimension, such as differentiated product businesses, they endeavored to incorporate other complementary dimensions. China's huge size, and the unusual significance of governmental authorities in its business environment, obliged MNCs to pay particular attention to the co-ordination of their China policies.

Joint venture ownership, management, and MNC control

All nine corporations held at least a fifty percent equity share in the joint ventures (Table 4.2). In five cases, they had increased their share of equity since the joint venture was formed. One of the objectives of majority equity holding was to secure the right to manage the joint venture and in this way to incorporate it within the wider management structure and systems of the MNC. In the words of one regional manager "a majority holding is the only way you can control, that you can manage" (Corporation F1).

Majority equity share by itself, however, does not guarantee management control in China (Child *et al.*, 1997). There was only a modest association between the level of equity share the nine companies hold in the joint ventures and a measure of their influence in joint venture management relative to that of the Chinese partner.[3] One

Table 4.2 Control of China joint ventures

Company	US equity share at formation (%)	US equity share in 1994–1995 (%)	Representation on JV board (US/Chinese)	Expatriate JV managers
E1	50	57.5	6/6	GM, Personnel, Marketing, Business Development, Finance, Technical, Product Units, Branches, Customer Support.
E2	51	51	3/3	GM, Operations, Technical, Finance.
E3	50	50	3/3	GM, Operations, Technical, After-Sales Service, Purchasing.
E4	49	51.5	4/3	GM, Marketing, Technical.
F1	10	50	3/3	GM.
F2	50	60	3/3	GM, Operations, Finance.
F3	51	51	2/2	GM, Marketing.
F4	55[a]	65[a]	4/2	GM, Marketing, Finance, HRM, Operations, Technical, Quality, Purchasing, Management Systems.
F5	60	60	5/5	GM, DGM (one of two), Finance

Note [a] Plus 10 percent other foreign equity holding.

of the reasons for this is that the Chinese partner had rather greater power on the joint venture's board of directors than was indicated by its equity share. There is usually considerable pressure from the Chinese side in negotiations to form joint ventures to be granted enhanced representation on their boards. Table 4.2 indicates that six of the US parent corporations with majority equity shares had equal representation on their joint venture boards. At the time of writing, Chinese equity joint venture regulations specify, moreover, that a joint venture's business plan, including the use of any surplus, has to be approved unanimously by its board.

Even when the joint venture board could decide through a simple majority, several of the corporations endeavored to achieve consensus. One consideration is that Chinese board members often include one or more government officials and, as an expatriate board chairperson put it, "it is definitely not wise to bulldoze things through and find later that you have got yourself a lot of unnecessary trouble that eats up a lot of your managerial time" (Corporation F2). Foreign companies therefore seek to persuade Chinese members of the joint venture boards. According to the Senior VP of Corporation E1:

> Because it's a joint venture, and because we respect our other partners, we go through the process of having the board approve an annual financial plan and an annual capital budget. If they objected to either of those, we would probably push it through them, through persuasion ... we have our own ideas about what's right ... [and] in China we have a board consisting of [PRC] people who actually don't understand our business.

While the board can somewhat constrain the exercise of ownership rights by MNCs, at least on matters of overall joint venture planning, a majority equity share also provides justification for the determination of key appointments and the direction of joint venture management. This may be deemed necessary for a joint venture's successful development, because managers recruited from the Chinese parent corporation may lack experience and a sense of personal identity with the managerial norms and standards of the foreign joint venture parent corporation. The senior joint venture appointments made by the corporations examined in this study were mainly expatriates from within the corporation, but they also included some mainland Chinese.

While there was disagreement among the MNCs over the desirability of having joint ventures managed by expatriates, they agreed as to its necessity at least in the short term. Each of them had appointed its own expatriate JV general manager. As Table 4.2 indicates, all the electronics companies had expatriates heading the joint venture operational and/or technical functions as well. On the whole, the number of senior expatriate managers was larger in the electronics companies compared to those in FMCG. Among the latter, somewhat greater reliance was placed exclusively on the general manager. In two FMCG joint ventures, expatriate functional heads had only been appointed to complement the foreign general manager shortly before the time of study. The distribution of expatriate appointments bore out the expectation that technical management was a vital competence to locate within the electronics joint ventures, and a key link to higher levels in the MNCs. It was likewise anticipated that the marketing function would be headed by expatriates within the FMCG joint ventures, though in three cases it was located one level up in the China company/office.

Most, but not all, of the MNCs had an explicit policy on senior joint venture appointments. Half of them identified the general manager and chief financial officer as the two key appointments that need to be in their hands in order to ensure joint venture control and to provide the key links to its higher management on operational and financial matters respectively. For example:

> We send in our own people. Basically in all the joint ventures that's the general manager and the financial manager. They will be sent from Hong Kong ... [The policy] will come from head office to here, and here we dictate it.
>
> (Regional manager, Corporation F5)

There was, in fact, a strong correlation among the nine joint ventures between the number of key functions held by non-PRC managers and assessments made by senior managers of overall foreign influence in joint venture management.[4] Since all the joint venture general managers were expatriates, it is not possible to test for the impact of that appointment, but the other element in the regional manager's statement just quoted was borne out by the consistent association between appointing expatriate financial officers and MNC influence within the joint ventures. The significance of appointing finance managers from the US parent corporation was not so much to apply corporate accounting standards, which was not regarded as a major problem, as to enhance the management of the joint venture's funds and to ensure financial probity. Some, but not all, of the expected associations between expatriate appointments to specific functions and the US corporation's influence in those areas of management were also apparent, especially for the operations and technical functions.

Expatriates were, on average, appointed to over half of the six key positions, namely joint venture general manager and the core functional headships of finance, HRM, marketing, operations, and technical. This quite costly investment was regarded as necessary to ensure control and to support the ventures' development. One regional CEO likened it to providing scaffolding while constructing a new building, which the builder expects to take down once it is firmly established. The involvement of expatriate managers and the training of Chinese managers and staff promote the introduction of the US parent's management systems.

In every case but one, the joint venture's management procedures and systems for items such as accounting, sales and operational information, and quality control, were imported from the US parent. In seven of the nine cases, the US parent corporation provided complementary training over and above that conducted by the joint venture. These provisions enhanced the joint venture's operational competence in a context where local Chinese management had not been strongly oriented to either market or profit criteria. At the same time, and very importantly, they established channels for the regular reporting of performance data to higher levels in the US corporation, and in a form that was standardized to the global systems of the corporation. The one instance where the US parent's procedures and systems had not been introduced was F3's only operational joint venture, which, at the time it was visited, had no clear reporting lines to its parent. This was because, as a corporate executive put it, "it was such a small thing that we really paid no attention to it whatsoever" and because of the corporation's own lack of a clear regional organization. During the period of study, a new organization was introduced to conform to the level of managerial involvement and reporting which was the norm among the other US corporations.

These generally strong linkages into the management of China joint ventures reflect the relatively wide range of resource inputs provided by US parent corporations. All of the MNCs studied had transferred product as well as production technology, usually on the basis both of formal technology contracts and ongoing support. Contracts provided conditions under which know-how, as well as brands or trademarks, could be used by the joint venture, but they did not carry very significant implications for internal management. Indeed, there is some indication that those MNCs with less influence over internal joint venture management tended to use contractual resource provision more, thereby securing a guarantee of returns through fees and royalties. This applied particularly in the case of contracts for the supply of product know-how.

All but one of the nine MNCs were providing support on a non-contractual basis, which signifies a more open-ended commitment to their joint ventures. MNC management and technical systems were transferred to joint ventures through this route. Implementation required ongoing links between corporate managers and staff, and their counterparts in the joint venture, thereby providing channels for exercising influence over joint venture operations. This complemented the influence derived from control of managerial appointments (Child *et al.*, 1997). The provision of management systems support on this basis was particularly associated with the perceived influence of the MNC parent on joint venture management. The only instance where management systems support was not being provided at the time of study was F3, which as noted was a special case.

In short, the formal links between MNCs' China joint ventures and their wider global structural networks are heavily reinforced by the investment of ownership, resourcing, and management. This investment provides the legal and moral right to link local joint venture management strongly with that of higher corporate levels. It also provides the operational foundation for so doing, in terms of systems and technologies. Further insight into how these links function is provided by the distribution of decision-making within these corporations.

Distribution of decision-making authority within the joint venture–corporate network

The distribution of decision-making authority was in each of the MNCs investigated in terms of seven issues relevant to its China joint ventures, namely:

- capital expenditure for the joint venture;
- policy on allocation of joint venture profit;
- product modification;
- choice of joint venture suppliers;
- choice of the joint venture's markets;
- appointment of a joint venture general manager;
- remuneration policy for joint venture managers of PRC nationality.

Table 4.3 outlines the extent to which authority for these decisions was decentralized down the MNC global structure at four levels: corporate, sub-corporate (that is, product division or region), China corporation or office, and joint venture.

The distribution of decision autonomy within the MNC's corporate networks differed according to the type of decision and was also variable between the companies themselves. In the main, their China joint ventures could choose which suppliers to use, though this was often subject to certain restrictions. For instance, the supplier typically had to meet technical specifications for a global product or international brand. In the case of four FMCG companies, the corporate level placed pressure on the joint ventures to secure some supply from within the MNC or from its preferred global sources. The choice of markets to serve was also largely left to the joint venture in five of the companies, though in the FMCG sector the issue was of less significance, either because the joint ventures could not meet existing demand in China or because their overall territories were already defined. Two MNCs were exceptional to the localization of market choice. E1 had a strongly defined corporate policy on the areas of business in which its subsidiary units could compete. It did not, for example, offer system solutions to some sectors. F4 centralized its marketing policies and decided annually on every marketing territory. This particular corporation was, overall, the most centralized among those studied.

Approval to spend against capital expenditure budgets tended to be distributed

Table 4.3 Distribution of decision autonomy within MNE corporate networks

Decision	Organizational level			
	US/corporate	Sub-corporate: region or product division	China	Joint venture
Approval for capital expenditure			E3 F2 F3 F4 F5	E1 E2 E4 F1
Policy on allocation of JV profit	E1 E4 F3	F1 F2	E2 E3 F4 F5	
Product modification	E4 F1 F3 F4 F5	E1 F2	E2 E3	
Choice of suppliers			F4	E1 E2^a E3^a E4 F1 F2^b F3 F5
Choice of markets	F4	E1	E2^c E3	E4 F1 F2 F3 F5
Appointing JV GM	E1 E4 F3 F4	F1 F2	E2^d E3 F5	
JV remuneration policy (Chinese managers)	E4	E1 F2 F3	E3 F1 F4 F5	E2

Notes
a For locally built and distributed products.
b For non-globally-sourced supplies.
c At regional level if choice affects a global customer.
d Decision goes to corporate level if appointee is an expatriate.

across the levels of MNC structure according to the amount of expenditure involved and depending on whether the capital project has strategic implications. Four MNCs, three of them in electronics, decentralized capital expenditure approvals to their China joint ventures within specified financial limits. The other five, four of them in the FMCG sector, did not decentralize these decisions below their China company or office. This apparent difference between the two sectors may be due to the less integrated nature of production technology in electronics, where much capital expenditure can be made in smaller, discrete "chunks." It is also an important indicator of the extent to which the joint ventures were run as full-blown business units.

Policy on the remuneration packages offered to the local PRC managers of joint ventures was decided at various levels within the MNCs. (The equivalent for expatriate managers was in all cases determined in the USA as part of a corporate HRM policy.) This reflected a wide variation in the levels at which HRM policy was determined within the international operations of the MNCs. The difficulty of striking the right balance between maintaining corporation-wide norms and accommodating to local labor markets is particularly marked with respect to PRC managers' remuneration. The acute shortage of local Chinese managers with the levels of training and types of experience sought by MNCs had resulted in some companies bidding up levels of compensation. In China, these local circumstances can threaten to dictate terms to international corporations which do not conform to the regional or global policies they seek to maintain.

Two other decisions could not, by definition, be taken within the joint ventures. These concerned the allocation of joint venture surpluses, particularly whether to distribute or re-invest, and the appointment of a new joint venture general manager. Both decisions tended to be taken either by the China company or at the corporate level. Even when decisions on the allocation of joint venture surpluses were taken by the former, there was usually a general corporate policy framework which served as a guide. The MNCs looked on China as a location for business development, and they preferred to re-invest surpluses within the country, whereas their local partners were generally looking for any profits to be distributed.

Product modification was, overall, the most centralized decision among those investigated. It was not an area for joint venture discretion. Indeed, product modifications could be decided at the China company level in just two of the MNCs, and only then if they did not involve the introduction of a new product and did not have any wider global implications. The centralization of product modification reflected the vital necessity for MNCs to safeguard the integrity of their corporate names or their brands in the world marketplace.

The distribution of decision-making autonomy within the MNC managerial structures indicates that some areas were more tightly coupled to the corporate level, and hence within the MNC network as a whole, than others. Capital expenditure was tightly coupled. In all the MNCs, capital budgets for China had to receive corporate approval and this was accompanied by personal presentations which informed corporate officers of the relevant background. Expenditure within approved capital expenditure budgets was decentralized, but only within the limits and specifications approved at a higher level. Product technology was another tightly coupled area. Each corporation held strictly to centrally determined technical standards for the global products allocated to the China joint ventures, though discretion to modify purely local Chinese products was in some cases decentralized.

Decisions on human resource issues were rather less consistently located within MNC structures. The terms and conditions of expatriate managerial appointments and, in several cases, the specific appointments themselves, were generally approved at corporate level. This ensured the consistency of treatment which underpins the identity of such managers with the MNC's culture, which, in turn, was an important integrating force within the MNC as a whole. On the other hand, decisions on remuneration policy for local PRC managers were in most cases made at regional or China company level, reflecting the desire of corporate policy-makers to combine, in this instance, general principles and standards with the flexibility to respond to local circumstances. Decisions concerning joint venture transactions were generally localized. They were left to the discretion of the joint venture more than the other areas investigated, and were loosely coupled both with the center and with other MNC affiliates.[5] This was consistent with the generally low intensity of transactional networking between the China joint ventures and other parts of the MNCs.

While decision-making autonomy varied among the MNCs according to the areas of decision concerned, there were also considerable differences between the MNCs themselves in the overall level of decentralization they displayed, as judged by the seven types of decision investigated.[6] Two electronics companies (E2 and E3) were, on this basis, the most decentralized, followed by the two beverage companies (F1 and F5) within the FMCG sector. Companies E1, E4, and F4 were the most central-ized, though for different reasons. E1 and F4 are noted for their strongly developed corporate cultures and accompanying policies which consequently placed con-straints on initiative lower down their managerial networks. E4 is a rather different case, since it operated with a regional office of quite limited scope. As a result decisions tended to pass up to the corporate level. Although it ran its joint ventures as business units, they were in fact tightly monitored by the corporate President, who claimed to spend three weeks out of four traveling to different geographical areas of his corporation's operations, primarily to review their performance.

In short, the management networks of the MNCs had to cope with variation in the distribution of decision-making autonomy as between areas in which their China joint ventures were closely coupled to the corporate level and other areas where there was local autonomy. In effect, they operated dual network systems, the one being oriented toward control and risk minimization, as in the areas of finance and product integrity, the other being oriented toward local adaptation, as in the area of HRM, and devolved initiative, as in marketing. This dualism is a response to the contingencies bearing upon different areas of decision-making. Contrasts between the MNCs themselves appeared to reflect not only their distinctive corpor-ate cultures, but contingent factors as well, such as the nature of the technology employed in the two sectors. The cases examined indicate that MNC executives have to work out their own patterns of decision-making within corporate networks, and have to accept that solutions will be complex and evolutionary.

Conclusion

This chapter has posed three questions:

1 how do MNCs link the management of China ventures into their corporate structures?
2 how do MNCs exercise and sustain control over these ventures?
3 how do MNCs locate decision-making relevant to their China business?

The ways that MNCs linked their China joint ventures into their corporate struc-tures reflected the balance between forces for global integration and those for local responsiveness. This was weighed somewhat more toward global integration in the case of the electronics MNCs and toward local circumstances in the case of the FMCG corporations. Although the FMCG corporations had introduced their global brands into China, some were modified to suit the Chinese market and their promotion had to be sensitive to local culture and taste. Moreover, their production chains were more locally self-contained. The electronics corporations were required to be responsive to the local, often governmental, organizations who were their main customers in China, and also to government policy toward the high techno-logy sector; but, at the same time, they exhibited a higher level of global transac-tional integration on the supply side. The power and role of worldwide product businesses were correspondingly greater in the electronics MNCs and they were the channels through which joint ventures reported into their multinational structures.

The limited density of transactions that most of the joint ventures had with other MNC subsidiaries or affiliates should have permitted the corporate headquarters to play a central role, according to the argument advanced by Ghoshal and Bartlett (1990). Any such tendency was, however, offset by the special features of operating in China. The close support in technology transfer, marketing and functional activities which joint ventures require there, and the necessity of managing relations both with Chinese partners and with government authorities, greatly enhanced the role that the regional or China office had to play. All the corporations, except E1 and E4, had established or were building up China offices or companies to perform a substantial managerial role in what was seen to be a particularly important and challenging business environment. They were moving toward more focused leadership for their China operations, even in cases where, in other parts of the world, managerial responsibilities were differentiated according to product business. This is witnessed by the recent creation, and/or enhancement, of China company CEO roles in all but one of the MNCs.

With regard to the question of control, it is clear that the active management of China operations has to extend down into the joint ventures themselves if they are to be integrated into MNC structures and systems. The formal links between MNCs' China joint ventures and their wider global structural networks can be heavily reinforced by the investment of ownership, resourcing, and management. This investment provides legal, technological, and moral rights to link local joint venture management strongly with higher corporate levels. It also provides the operational foundation for so doing, in terms of systems and technologies. In this respect, majority equity holding proves to be a necessary but not sufficient basis for exercising direction over joint venture management. The continued commitment of support over and above that which is formally contracted is important. It probably requires the quite heavy level of expatriate staffing which characterized several of the joint ventures, including the appointment of expatriate general managers. This support, of which a transfer to joint ventures of management systems and training is a major component, both enhances efficiency in the short term and provides the opportunity to develop local managers to assume responsibility in the longer term.

With regard to the location of decision-making, one of the implications of this study is that a serious intention to establish a strong strategic position in China requires that the country company be granted a level of initiative and of managerial resource that is unusual within MNC structures. In this sense, a significant capacity for intelligent local response has to be built into the organization. It is necessary then to decide whether the China company or individual joint ventures should be the primary business units. Where there are significant synergies to be secured between multiple joint ventures, the advantage lies in recognizing the China company as the business unit with full profit and loss responsibility.

Moreover, the management networks of the MNCs had to cope with variation in the distribution of decision-making autonomy as between areas in which their China joint ventures were closely coupled to the corporate level and other areas where there was local autonomy. They were learning how to operate multidimensional network systems, with a duality between centralization and autonomy, and a relationship between product, regional, and functional decision involvement appropriate to the circumstances. When top MNC executives state that finding the right structure for global management is the most difficult problem they face, as did the CEO of F4, they have the tensions between these different criteria primarily in mind.

Notes

1 This investigation was funded by the Carnegie Bosch Institute. The Institute's support is gratefully acknowledged. Part of the research findings of the project were published in John Child and Sally Heavens (1999) "Managing corporate networks from America to China," *Asia Pacific Business Review*, 5, 3–4: 147–180.
2 Such attempts are not always successful. The corporate director of strategic planning for F1 stated that "we are very much in silos, if you will, by business sector." He said that the corporation was moving toward inter-product business co-ordination, but that this had so far generated so much conflict as to be "counter-productive." It is "almost de-leverage, as opposed to a leverage effect. And that may partly be because of [F1]'s culture, and the tradition of having these very autonomous business units."
3 The coefficient of correlation (r) was 0.58, with $p = 0.05$. The measure of influence covered 13 areas of joint venture activity and decision-making: use of profit, re-investment policy, allocating senior managerial positions, setting strategic priorities, product pricing, training and development policies, reward and incentive policies, financial control, purchasing policies, production planning, sales and distribution, technological development, and quality control. The subjective assessments of senior joint venture managers were obtained as to the influence of the foreign and Chinese partners (or their representatives) on each of these areas. With such a low number of cases, statistical associations should only be regarded as suggestive.
4 The coefficient of correlation (r) was 0.77, with p less than 0.01. The "key functions" were considered to be finance, HRM, marketing, operations, and technical. The post of Deputy General Manager was held in eight of the joint ventures by a PRC national and in the ninth there were two DGMs: one PRC and one expatriate. This appointment was usually regarded as complementary, if not compensatory, for the Chinese partner vis-à-vis that of General Manager, and it appeared to carry little influence.
5 On the concept of organizational coupling, see Peters and Waterman (1982) who popularized it, and Weick (1976) who first wrote of organizations as "loosely coupled systems."
6 An indicator of overall autonomy was constructed by scoring each decision by its level of decentralization as follows, and then aggregating the scores for each MNC: Corporate = 1; Region/product division = 2; China company/office = 3; Joint venture = 4.

References

Bartlett, Christopher A., Yves Doz and Gunnar Hedlund (eds) (1990) *Managing the Global Firm*, London: Routledge.
Boyer, Robert (1989) *New Directions in Management Practices and Work Organization: General Principles and National Trajectories*, Paris: OECD.
Child, John, Yanni Yan and Yuan Lu (1997) "Ownership and control in Sino-foreign joint ventures," in Beamish, Paul W. and J. Peter Killing (eds) *Cooperative Strategies: Asian Pacific Perspectives*, San Francisco, CA: New Lexington Press.
Davis, Stanley M. and Paul R. Lawrence (eds) (1977) *Matrix*, Reading, MA: Addison-Wesley.
Doz, Yves and C.K. Prahalad (1993) "Managing DMNCs: a search for a new paradigm," in Ghoshal, Sumantra and D. Eleanor Westney (eds) *Organization Theory and the Multinational Corporation*, New York, NY: St. Martin's Press.
Ghoshal, Sumantra and Christopher A. Bartlett (1990) "The multinational corporation as an interorganizational network," *Academy of Management Review*, 15: 603–625.

Ghoshal, Sumantra and D. Eleanor Westncy (eds) (1993) *Organization Theory and the Multinational Corporation*, New York, NY: St. Martin's Press.

Giddens, Anthony (1984) *The Constitution of Society*, Cambridge: Polity Press.

Knight, Kenneth (ed.) (1977) *Matrix Management*, Aldershot: Gower Press.

Meier, Johannes, Javier Perez, and Jonathan R. Woetzel (1995) "Solving the puzzle: MNCs in China," *The McKinsey Quarterly*, 2: 20–33.

Nolan, Peter (1995) "Joint ventures and economic reform in China: a case study of the Coca-Cola business system, with particular reference to the Tianjin Coca-Cola plant," ESRC Centre for Business Research Working Paper Series, WP 24, University of Cambridge, December.

Peters, Tom J. and Robert H. Waterman, Jr. (1982) *In Search of Excellence*, New York, NY: Warner Books.

Stopford, John M. and Louis T. Wells, Jr. (1972) *Managing the Multinational Enterprise: Organization of the Firm and Ownership of Subsidiaries*, New York, NY: Basic Books.

Weick, Karl E. (1976) "Educational organizations as loosely coupled systems," *Administrative Science Quarterly*, 21 (1): 1–19.

5

INNOVATION GOES GLOBAL

A study of foreign-affiliated R&D laboratories in the USA

Richard Florida

Introduction[1]

IBM conducts its research on superconductors in Switzerland and its personal computer research in Japan. NEC operates a basic research institute for information technology near Princeton University. Mitsubishi conducts software research in a laboratory across the street from MIT. Canon develops new technology in Palo Alto in close proximity to Stanford University and Xerox Palo Alto Research Center. Mercedes, BMW, Toyota, Nissan, and virtually ever other major car maker operates state-of-the-art vehicle design centers in Southern California. Innovation has become global in nature, as multinational enterprises establish a growing number of research and development (R&D) laboratories in offshore locations.

What is powering this globalization of innovation? What are the central forces and factors involved? What is motivating firms to establish networks of R&D laboratives abroad? How do they operate and manage these far-flung facilities? What do foreign R&D subsidiaries do? How well do they perform? What are the emerging best practices? This chapter takes up these important questions.

A growing number of studies have examined foreign direct investment (FDI) in research and development (Cantwell, 1989; Casson, 1991; Dalton and Serapio, 1993; Dunning and Narula, 1995; Florida and Kenney, 1994; Howells, 1990; Mansfield, Teece, and Romeo, 1979; Mowery and Teece, 1992, 1993; Ronstadt, 1977, 1978; Westney, 1992). Generally speaking, these studies suggest that foreign direct R&D investment is a relatively small component of all R&D and that it tends to be oriented to foreign markets and support offshore manufacturing investments. Several recent studies, however, suggest that the rapid growth of foreign direct R&D investment, particularly in the United States, reflects corporate efforts to harness external scientific and technological capabilities and generate new technological assets (see Dunning and Narula, 1995). The establishment of foreign R&D facilities is clearly an important development in the acquisition and generation of knowledge in multinational enterprises.

Despite the rapid growth of foreign direct R&D investment, little is known about the activities, organization, and performance of foreign-affiliated R&D laboratories. Several studies have examined the motivations of foreign-affiliated research facilities in the United States, mainly through interviews and case studies of small samples of firms (see Angel and Savage, 1994; Dalton and Serapio, 1993, 1995; Florida and Kenney, 1994; Herbert, 1989). For the most part, however, existing studies rely heavily on government statistics which provide useful data on foreign R&D spending but do not cover other aspects of foreign-affiliated laboratories, or on case studies of small numbers of foreign-owned laboratories from which it is hard to generalize.

This chapter explores the globalization of innovation, reporting the findings of a major research study and several reports on foreign-affiliated R&D laboratories in the USA (see Florida, 1996, 1997, 1998). The United States is a particularly interesting case from which to examine the phenomenon of globalization of innovation, since it has attracted a large amount of foreign R&D spending and a considerable number of R&D laboratories affiliated with foreign parent companies. The survey used in this research identified more than 200 foreign-affiliated R&D laboratories. Foreign corporations spent nearly $15 billion on research and development (R&D) in the United States in 1994, accounting for more than 15 percent of total US industrial R&D expenditures.

This chapter seeks to cover four related issues. First, it examines the motivations for firms to invest in R&D activities abroad, distinguishing between two principal types of foreign direct R&D investment – market-seeking and technology- or capability-seeking. A key argument is that technology-seeking behavior is increasing in importance as a principal force motivating firms to invest in R&D abroad. Studies of foreign direct investment have long noted the role of demand-side factors in motivating FDI in R&D, particularly to support offshore markets and manufacturing (Abernathy and Utterback, 1978; Utterback, 1989; Vernon, 1966, 1977). According to this conventional view, FDI in R&D is motivated principally to adapt and tailor products for foreign markets and provide technical support to offshore manufacturing operations. More recent studies note the pursuit of so-called "global localization" strategies for manufacturing and product development by multinational corporations (Porter, 1986, 1990). Several other studies note the importance of science and technology or supply-side factors in motivating FDI in R&D. Several studies note that foreign R&D investment represents a strategy to maintain competitive advantage by generating new technological assets and capabilities (see, particularly, Cantwell, 1989; Casson, 1991; Dunning and Narula, 1995; Howells and Wood, 1993). This study finds that technology-seeking or supply-side factors are increasingly important in motivating and shaping foreign direct investment in R&D.

Second, this chapter finds that firms are principally motivated by the desire to gain access to intellectual capital embodied in people and institutions, specifically scientific and technical talent. Furthermore, the findings suggest that the organization and management of offshore R&D laboratories is in large measure shaped by the need to harness these intellectual assets embodied in human capital. In order to attract talented people, firms have to establish foreign R&D affiliates which are relatively autonomous and have the freedom to develop research initiatives, engage in highly innovative activities, and allow their staffs to interact with outside scientists and technical staff and to publish their findings in the scientific literature. In other words, foreign R&D affiliates in the USA are managed and organized like basic research centers or to some degree like university-based research laboratories.

The reason is not due to some sort of corporate altruism – the reason is that such organizational structures and practices are required to attract top scientific and technical talent.

Third and related to this, this chapter submits that a key task of international R&D management involves balancing central corporate co-ordination with the autonomy required to attract and retain talent. The findings indicate that the foreign-affiliated laboratories in our sample possess considerable autonomy in developing and managing their scientific and technical agendas. Studies of international R&D management note the difficulties associated with co-ordinating offshore R&D subsidiaries (see Bartlett and Ghoshal, 1989; Florida and Kenney, 1994; Howells and Wood, 1993; Kenney and Florida, 1993). While foreign R&D subsidiaries require linkages to other corporate units to co-ordinate their activities, complex reporting requirements and the perception of external control can have negative impacts both on innovative performance and on the ability to recruit and attract high-quality scientific and technical human capital.

Fourth, this chapter finds that foreign R&D affiliates in the USA are far more likely to emulate prevailing R&D management practice of the sort found in basic research centers or university research laboratories in the United States. In sharp contrast to the experience in manufacturing (for example the so-called Japanese manufacturing transplants in the USA, discussed in Kenney and Florida, 1993) the foreign-affiliated R&D laboratories in this study make little apparent effort to transfer the management and organizational systems associated with R&D laboratories in their home country. Instead, sample laboratories tend to emulate and attempt to learn from prevailing US approaches to R&D organization and management. This again is required to attract and retain top quality scientific and technical talent.

Research design

The study is based on a national survey of foreign-affiliated R&D laboratories in the United States. The sample was limited to independent or stand-alone foreign-affiliated laboratories in the United States, engaged principally in research, development, and design activities and, as such, does not include research, development, and design activities conducted by other organizational units, such as corporate divisions or manufacturing plants. The initial sample of 393 foreign-affiliated R&D laboratories was compiled from government sources, including a 1993 study by the Department of Commerce (Dalton and Serapio, 1993), and directories of R&D facilities such as the *Directory of American Research and Technology*. The sample was checked against other available lists of foreign-affiliated R&D laboratories available at the time, and appeared to be the most comprehensive listing available. Compare, for example, the 393 listings in the sample to the 255 listings in the 1993 US Department of Commerce study (Dalton and Serapio, 1993).[2]

Screening interviews eliminated 153 establishments from the survey: 88 were not involved in any research, development or design activities; another 33 were duplicate listings; and 32 could not be located. The screening phase resulted in an overall response rate of 91.9 percent, including establishments that could not be located. Only one of the 361 contacted units refused to participate in the screening phase.

The survey was administered by telephone by the Center for Survey Research at the University of Massachusetts–Boston. The survey produced a total of 186 completed interviews. The survey identified 33 additional establishments which were ineligible either because they were duplicates ($n = 4$), not foreign-owned ($n = 4$), or were not engaged in research, development, or design ($n = 21$). This resulted in a response rate of nearly 90 percent of those eligible. In the following analysis, the survey data are arrayed according to 13 specific technology fields and a broader grouping of four technology sectors (electronics, automotive technology, chemicals and materials, and biotechnology and pharmaceuticals).[3]

Foreign R&D laboratories in the USA: scope, magnitude, and activities

A useful place to begin is by reviewing some of the key characteristics of the R&D laboratories in this study (see Table 5.1). Foreign-affiliated R&D laboratories ($n = 207$) spent $5.14 billion on R&D in 1994.[4] This is equivalent to roughly 7 percent of US company-financed industrial R&D ($76.9 billion as of 1993) (National Science Board, 1993: 371), and more than one-third (35.2 percent) of the $14.6 billion in total R&D carried out by foreign corporations in the United States (Dalton and Serapio, 1995: 7).[5] Foreign-affiliated R&D laboratories in the United States employed an estimated 65,800 workers, 25,000 scientists and engineers, and 7,400 doctoral level researchers in 1994, equivalent to roughly two-thirds of all R&D workers (105,200) employed by foreign companies in the United States (Dalton and Serapio, 1995: 8).[6] The respondents averaged $26.6 million in total R&D spending, or roughly $100,000 in R&D spending per employee, and employed an average of 286 people, including 181 scientists and engineers, and 33 doctoral researchers.

The foreign-affiliated R&D laboratories in the sample devoted $396 million (8 percent) to basic research, $1.8 billion (36 percent) to applied research, and $3 billion (58 percent) to product development. Thus, these foreign-affiliated R&D laboratories appear to be slightly more research-intensive than US industrial R&D as a whole, which devoted 4.2 percent of total R&D effort to basic research, 23.5 percent to applied research, and 72.2 percent to product development in 1993 (National Science Board, 1993: 333–336). This is not surprising since the US figure includes the R&D resources of manufacturing plants and corporate administrative units, while the foreign-affiliated figure is limited to stand-alone R&D laboratories.

Table 5.1 Characteristics of sample laboratories

Number of laboratories	207
R&D spending (millions)	$5,140
Basic research (millions)	$396
Applied research (millions)	$1,830
Product development (millions)	$2,976
Total employment	65,800
Scientists and engineers	25,000
Doctoral level researchers	7,400

Source: Richard Florida (1995) *Survey of Foreign-Affiliated R&D Laboratories in the United States*, Pittsburgh, PA: Center for Economic Development, Carnegie Mellon University.

A handful of technologically advanced nations account for the overwhelming bulk of foreign R&D spending in the USA (Dalton and Serapio, 1995: 11–12). More than half of respondents ($n = 100$) had European parents, while 45.2 percent ($n = 84$) were affiliated with Asian parents. The only respondents outside these two regions were two Canadian affiliates. R&D laboratories affiliated with European parent companies accounted for more than three-quarters of R&D spending and two-thirds of employees.[7] R&D laboratories with British parents ranked first in R&D spending ($1.03 billion), followed by Japan ($737 million), France ($708 million), Germany ($699 million), and Switzerland ($656 million).

Foreign-affiliated R&D laboratories in the sample are concentrated in four broad fields of science and technology (biotechnology and pharmaceuticals, chemicals and materials, electronics, and automotive technology) and 13 sub-fields. The biotechnology and pharmaceutical sector is the largest of the four broad fields, with more than 60 percent of reported R&D spending ($2.5 billion), as Table 5.2 shows. Pharmaceuticals is the largest of the 13 sub-fields ($1.44 billion) followed by biotechnology ($851 million), telecommunications ($420 million), chemicals ($399 million), audio–video equipment ($257 million), and biomedical technology ($193 million).

The foreign laboratories in the sample are reasonably innovative. The findings indicate that foreign-affiliated laboratories in the United States produced 2,469 patent applications, 1,068 patents, 669 copyrights, and 1,812 published articles in 1994. The 1,068 patents reported by foreign-affiliated R&D laboratories in the

Table 5.2 Sample laboratories by technology field

Technology	Number	R&D spending (millions of dollars)	Employment	R&D spending per employee ($)
Biotechnology/drugs	57	2,488	19,465	110,371
Biotechnology	30	851	6,630	120,010
Pharmaceuticals	14	1,444	7,320	150,713
Biomedical	13	193	5,515	46,373
Electronics	63	936	17,874	115,535
Computer and peripherals	8	74	2,378	87,875
Computer software	11	50	920	112,314
Audio–video equipment	9	257	4,071	315,543
Telecommunications	15	420	6,635	101,644
Semiconductors	13	97	3,200	80,705
Instruments	6	37	670	44,933
Chemical/materials	42	407	11,092	60,077
Chemical	37	399	10,150	67,914
Materials	5	8	942	9,921
Automotive	24	262	3,964	138,433
Manufacturing	18	151	3,218	107,961
Design	6	111	746	270,476

Source: Richard Florida (1995) *Survey of Foreign-Affiliated R&D Laboratories in the United States,* Pittsburgh, PA: Center for Economic Development, Carnegie Mellon University.

Note
$n = 186.$

United States are but a small fraction of the more than 30,000 US patents granted to foreign corporations (National Science Board, 1993).[8] It is important, however, to control for differences in size when analyzing innovation outputs. This can be done by using performance measures which normalize output by the level of spending and/or employment.[9] When this is done, foreign-affiliated R&D laboratories appear to be more innovative than US industrial R&D. Foreign-affiliated R&D laboratories in the United States generated 7.3 patents per $10 million in R&D spending compared to 4.7 patents per $10 million of company-financed industrial R&D for the USA as a whole.[10] Foreign-affiliated R&D laboratories produced 12.8 patents per 100 scientists and engineers – more than double the rate of 4.9 patents per 100 scientists and engineers for US industrial R&D.[11]

There are considerable differences in innovative performance by industry and technological field. Chemicals ranked first in patent performance (14.2 patents per $10 million in R&D spending), followed by instruments (10.5 patents), computer software (10.1 patents), audio–video equipment (7.8 patents), automotive manufacturing (7.6 patents), semiconductors (6.2 patents), and biotechnology (6.2 patents). Many of the same fields led in patent performance per employee, although their order was somewhat changed.

Motivations for offshore R&D: technology and markets

Both technology and markets play a role in motivating foreign investment in research and development. The literature to date has stressed the role of market or demand-side factors in motivating foreign direct investment in R&D. It is our contention that technology or supply-side factors are increasingly important in motivating and shaping the activities of foreign-affiliated R&D laboratories. To shed light on this issue, we distinguish between two principal types of foreign direct investment in R&D: market- and technology-seeking. Several studies note the increasing dependence of firms on external sources of technology (Roberts, 1994) and the development of global networks for both technology acquisition and monitoring (Bartlett and Ghoshal, 1989; Cantwell, 1989; Casson, 1991; Howells and Wood, 1993). Graham (1992) further distinguishes between two types of technology-driven strategies: "listening post" whose primary function is to monitor the scientific and technical capabilities of US firms and universities, and "generating station" which generates new scientific and technical knowledge. Some, however, continue to argue that offshore R&D investment accounts for a small share of total industrial innovation and that multinational corporations tend to retain advanced research and development capabilities in the home country (see Porter, 1986, 1990; Patel and Pavitt, 1991).

We begin by using the survey data to look at the relative importance of technology- versus market-seeking activities among sample laboratories (see Table 5.3). The survey asked a series of questions about the activities of sample laboratories. Respondents were asked to rate the importance of various activities on a three-point scale where 1 is "not important" and 3 is "very important." The survey obtained information on five technology-seeking activities:

1 developing new product ideas;
2 developing new science and technology;

3   gaining access to technical talent;
4   obtaining information on US science and technology; and
5   developing links to the US scientific and technical community.

Data were also sought on two market-seeking activities:

1   customizing products for the US market; and
2   working with the US manufacturing facilities of the parent company.

Generally speaking, the findings from the survey data indicate that both market- and technology-oriented activities are important, but, that the technology-oriented ones are, on balance, more important.

The three highest ranked activities were technology-seeking in nature. The respondents rated "developing new product ideas" as the highest ranked activity (2.84 score, 86.8 percent of respondents reporting "very important"). The second highest ranked activity was "obtaining information on scientific and technological developments in the United States" (2.70 score, 71.5 percent "very important"). This was followed closely by "obtaining access to high-quality scientists, engineers and designers in the United States" (2.69 score, 73.7 percent "very important"). In addition, only very small percentages of respondents (less than 5 percent) rated any of these three activities as "not important."

Two technology-seeking activities ranked somewhat lower: "developing links to the scientific and technological community in the United States" (2.48) and "developing new science and technology" (2.36). It should be noted, however, that more than 90 percent of respondents listed the latter as somewhat important. These

Table 5.3 Motivations and activities of sample laboratories

Activity	Score	Very important	Somewhat important	Not important	N
Developing new product ideas	2.84	86.8% (161)	11.3% (21)	2.2% (4)	186
Obtaining information on US scientific and technical developments	2.70	71.5% (133)	26.9% (50)	1.6% (3)	186
Access to scientific and technical talent	2.69	73.7% (137)	22.0% (41)	4.3% (8)	186
Customize products for US market	2.56	67.6% (125)	20.5% (38)	11.9% (22)	185
Establish links to the US scientific and technical community	2.48	53.2% (99)	41.4% (77)	5.4% (10)	186
Work with manufacturing facility in USA	2.40	59.4% (107)	21.1% (38)	19.4% (35)	180
Develop new science and technology	2.36	44.1% (82)	47.8% (89)	8.1% (15)	186

Source: Richard Florida (1995) *Survey of Foreign-Affiliated R&D Laboratories in the United States*, Pittsburgh, PA: Center for Economic Development, Carnegie Mellon University.

Note
Number of respondents in parentheses.

results suggest that foreign-affiliated R&D laboratories are involved in both technology monitoring and technology development. Furthermore, technology development activities appear to revolve more around commercial technology rather than contributing to scientific and technical knowledge.

Interestingly, market-seeking activities were somewhat less important to the overall activities of foreign-affiliated R&D laboratories. "Customizing products for the US market" ranked fourth (2.56 score, 67.6 percent "very important"). In addition, nearly 12 percent of respondents listed this as not important. Furthermore, respondents rated working with US manufacturing facilities of the parent company quite low, with nearly one-fifth of respondents reporting "not important." This is so even though eight in ten respondents report that their parent companies have manufacturing plants in the United States. The survey data thus provide only limited support for the notion that firms seek to link offshore R&D and manufacturing in accordance with a global localization strategy.

The findings thus indicate that technology-seeking activities are relatively more important in motivating the behavior of multinational enterprises establishing offshore R&D subsidiaries in the USA.

Capabilities, intellectual capital, and the role of talent

The increase in technology-seeking behavior witnessed in offshore R&D can be traced to one principal factor: the critical importance of intellectual capital embodied in scientific and technical talent. The role of talent in driving this process cannot be over-emphasized. This was confirmed time and time again in the field research and site visits conducted during the course of this study. Foreign-owned companies repeatedly reported that they opened laboratories in the United States to gain access to world-class scientific and technical talent. One strategy for doing so was to locate US R&D subsidiaries in close proximity to major research universities. The NEC Research Institute, for example, was able to recruit renowned computer scientists partly because it is adjacent to Princeton University. When Canon established a research center for work on optical character recognition, image compression, and network systems, the company chose Palo Alto to be close to Stanford University and Xerox's Palo Alto Research Center (PARC). Mitsubishi Electric Research Laboratory, which conducts R&D on a range of information technologies including computer vision, is located within walking distance of MIT.

Other companies have formed agreements with leading US universities and research institutes to reach their talent. Ciba Geigy, for example, sponsors research at the University of San Diego, and the Swiss company Sandoz Pharma funds basic science at the Scripps Research Institute in San Diego. Shiseido, the Japanese cosmetics company, invested $90 million in the Harvard Medical School for skin research. In the automotive industry, foreign R&D laboratories have geared their work to supporting US manufacturing plants and customizing products for the American market. Nissan Design International's close ties to the US market enabled them to realize that Nissan could attract American car buyers by adding a stylish body to a pickup truck platform, leading to the development of the Pathfinder, which launched the sport utility craze and transformed the automotive market.

While funding for these laboratories comes from abroad, their organization and management style is very much "American." Multinational firms generally recognize that, to recruit and retain American researchers, an American style of management needs to be adopted. In this respect, these laboratories differ markedly from foreign-owned manufacturing facilities. Japanese companies that run US factories, for example, typically seek to transfer and transplant manufacturing practices honed at home into the USA.

The literature on multinational management notes that, at times, corporations seek to transfer certain manufacturing management practices abroad. Studies of Japanese manufacturing in the United States provide evidence of the ability of Japanese automotive producers to transplant key aspects of their work and production organization (see Kenney and Florida, 1993). There is interest among organizational researchers in the ability of multinational corporations to transplant and replicate aspects of their organizational systems to overseas locations. However, foreign-affiliated R&D laboratories may seek to fit into the immediate environment or to learn from and emulate existing US approaches to managing innovation. Indeed, it is widely believed that the United States possesses a general climate which fosters creativity, and that US organizations – both firms and universities – have developed management and organizational strategies which facilitate innovation.

The survey collected information on whether foreign-affiliated R&D laboratories seek to transfer management systems and practices associated with parent company R&D laboratories in the home country, or, conversely, whether they aim to emulate the innovation management systems of US R&D laboratories, firms, and universities. The findings indicate that foreign-affiliated R&D laboratories primarily seek to emulate and learn from prevailing US practices. Nearly 40 percent of respondents (39.5 percent, $n = 73$) reported that their management system is "American-style." More than half (52.4 percent, $n = 97$) of respondents reported their management system as "hybrid," combining elements of the management system used by their corporate parent and American-style innovation management.

This stands in contrast to the pattern in manufacturing, where studies note transfer and replication of home-country practices. This difference should come as little surprise, given the underlying differences between manufacturing and R&D. Manufacturing is a highly standardized activity, while R&D is, by definition, concerned with non-routine activities of the sort involved in knowledge generation, much of which is tacit (see Nonaka and Takeuchi, 1995). In this respect, foreign direct R&D investment in the USA appears, at least in part, to represent a strategy for learning about R&D management and organization as practiced in leading US organizations.

There is very little evidence to support the notion that foreign-affiliated R&D laboratories aim to transfer and replicate the management practices of their corporate parent. Just 1.6 percent of respondents reported that they actively seek to replicate a research management system which is similar to that used by R&D facilities at home. There is little variation in this pattern, either by technology field or country of ownership. The one exception, however, is the automotive sector. Respondents in this sector are considerably less likely than those in other sectors to adopt American-style innovation management and are considerably more likely to prefer hybrid approaches.

Generally speaking, foreign laboratories in America are organized much like leading research centers of American universities. These laboratories encourage scientific and technical staff to work autonomously and publish widely, as we will further document later in this chapter. They sponsor visiting scholars and host seminars and symposia – practices that are less familiar in Japanese corporate laboratories. The manager of one foreign laboratory noted in an interview: "Everyone comes in and talks with us, individual researchers can invite their peers for discussion." Another senior R&D manager produced a company memorandum outlining the mission as building a laboratory where scientists "do their basic research, regardless of whether or not it produces a saleable product, or any product at all."

By setting themselves up this way, companies can attract top-class scientific and technical talent and build important connections to leading scientists and researchers at other institutions. The reason for this lies in the nature of the market for scientific and technical talent. Scientific labor markets differ from other labor markets in that they are driven to a large degree by reputation and prestige. This is why universities with leading scientists and departments are able to recruit the top new researchers and graduate students. These lessons are not lost on foreign corporations, which organize themselves like American R&D centers and universities to attract the top scientists, who, in turn, attract other scientists, bolstering the overall reputation of the organization.

Mitsubishi's Electric Research Laboratories, for example, organized its Cambridge Research Center so that computer scientists, artificial intelligence experts, and software developers can explore how people work with computers and modern technology. In an interview, the founder of the laboratory reported that the facility was established in part to learn about the ability of American organizations to spur innovation. "We can be much more creative over here," he said, largely due to the synergies between the laboratory's scientists and the rich university community of Cambridge.

Having laboratories in the United States also makes it easier to recruit top people back home and in other nations around the world. The founder of NEC Research Institute in Princeton, NJ, reported that the biggest dividend of operating the laboratory was that it increased the company's ability to attract the best Japanese scientific and technical talent by showcasing the organization's award-winning scientists.

Sources of innovation

Another way to gauge the importance of scientific and technical talent is to look closely at where foreign R&D labs get their ideas. The short answer is predominantly from the people who work there.

There is a large and very useful literature on the sources of innovation. The most important of these studies (Von Hippel, 1988) notes the importance of customers and end-users as sources of innovation. Recent studies suggest that corporate R&D laboratories may be declining as a source of innovation, as the importance of external sources (for example, joint venture partners, suppliers, and universities) grows (see Roberts, 1994).

To shed light on this issue, the survey collected detailed data on the sources of innovation for foreign-affiliated R&D laboratories, including: in-house research staff, corporate executives, manufacturing plants, customers, suppliers, universities, joint venture partners, competitors, and consultants. Respondents were asked to rate the

Table 5.4 Sources of innovation for sample laboratories

Source of new project ideas	Score	Very important	Somewhat important	Not important	N
In-house research staff	2.72	73.1% (136)	25.8% (48)	1.1% (2)	186
Customers	2.54	64.5% (120)	25.3% (47)	10.2% (19)	186
Other R&D laboratories	2.12	29.6% (55)	53.2% (99)	17.2% (32)	186
Competitors	2.08	29.0% (54)	50.5% (84)	19.9% (37)	185
Joint ventures	2.01	23.1% (43)	54.8% (102)	22.0% (41)	186
Universities	1.81	16.1% (30)	48.9% (91)	34.9% (65)	186
Corporate executives in home country	1.71	13.5% (25)	43.8% (81)	42.7% (79)	185
US manufacturing plants of parent company	1.66	15.2% (28)	34.8% (64)	49.5% (91)	183
Suppliers	1.61	9.7% (18)	41.9% (78)	48.4% (90)	186
Consultants	1.54	8.6% (16)	37.1% (69)	54.3% (101)	186

Source: Richard Florida (1995) *Survey of Foreign-Affiliated R&D Laboratories in the United States*, Pittsburgh, PA: Center for Economic Development, Carnegie Mellon University.

Note
Number of respondents in parentheses.

importance of each as a source of new project ideas on a three-point scale. The sources of innovation for foreign-affiliated laboratories are presented in Table 5.4.

The leading source of project ideas is in-house research staff (score = 2.72), with nearly three-quarters of respondents rating this as very important. Respondents ranked customers as the second most important source of project ideas (2.54 score, 64.5 "very important"). Three additional groups were rated as "somewhat important": other R&D laboratories of the parent company (2.12), competitors (2.08), and joint venture partners (2.01). However, less than one-third of respondents rated each of these sources as "very important." Other sources ranked considerably lower as sources of new project ideas.

The findings further indicate that both parent manufacturing plants in the USA and suppliers are relatively unimportant sources of innovation. Survey respondents ranked manufacturing plants of the parent company as the third least important source of new project ideas (1.66 score, 15 percent "very important"). Respondents rated suppliers even lower, with an overall score of 1.61. Nearly 50 percent (48.4 percent) of respondents rated suppliers as "not important"; and, conversely, just 9.7 percent of respondents rated suppliers as a very important source of new project ideas. These findings suggest that, even though a considerable fraction of foreign R&D activity appears to be related to supporting US manufacturing, such activity primarily takes the form of technical support rather than developing new technological assets.

The findings also suggest that universities are a relatively unimportant source of project ideas (score = 1.81). More than one-third of respondents reported that universities were "not important" as a source of new project ideas, and only 16 percent of respondents listed universities as "very important." This is so even though more than two-thirds of respondents (67.6 percent, *n* = 125) report that they engage in cooperative research with US universities, and roughly half of respondents report that they recruit senior technical staff from US universities "frequently" (22 percent) or "sometime" (26 percent).

As noted earlier, the literature on technical change notes that the sources of innovation differ substantially by industry and technical field, with some sectors drawing heavily from basic science and others linked quite closely to more applied activities (Nelson, 1986, 1993; Rosenberg, 1982; Rosenberg and Nelson, 1994). Nelson (1986) notes that the process of technological change is distinguished by a division of innovative labor, wherein the relationships among innovating institutions (for example, universities, R&D laboratories, and manufacturing plants) varies across technological fields. A study of industrial R&D laboratories (Klevorick *et al.*, 1993; Levin *et al.*, 1987), for example, found considerable variation in the role and importance of university research and academic science across a large number of technology fields.

The survey findings indicate that there is considerable variation in the sources of new project ideas by technology field. On the one hand, respondents in the biotechnology sector were more than three times as likely to rate universities as a very important source of new project ideas. This reflects the close connection between commercial biotechnology and advances in basic science, particularly university science, as noted above. Furthermore, nearly nine out of ten foreign-affiliated biotechnology laboratories reported that they engage in cooperative research with US universities, compared to an average of between half and two-thirds of laboratories in the three other sectors. On the other hand, respondents in the automotive sector were two to three times more likely to rate suppliers and manufacturing plants as very important sources of project ideas.

Managing the laboratories: strategies for scientific labor markets

Foreign R&D units face a host of management challenges, some of them rather unique. As noted above, the market for scientific and technical talent is different from other labor markets. Scientists are principally concerned about prestige and reputation as well as having the ability to work in environments where they can pursue autonomous research and publish their work. Moreover, it is fairly clear that excellent scientists attract good scientists and so on down the line, so that having such an organizational environment is required not only to attract distinguished senior scientists and engineers but also to attract better people in other technical positions throughout the organization.

The ability to initiate new projects and hire new scientific and technical staff is an indicator of the autonomy of foreign R&D subsidiaries. Respondents were asked to indicate how frequently various groups initiate new research projects on a 1 to 4 point scale (see Table 5.5). The findings indicate that foreign-affiliated R&D laboratories possess considerable autonomy in initiating new projects and in hiring new scientific and technical staff. Survey respondents reported that in-house research scientists are the most frequent initiators of new research projects. Corporate executives and R&D managers in the home country were less frequently involved in initiating new projects. In fact, more than half of the respondents reported that these two groups were rarely or never involved in initiating new projects. More than 90 percent of respondents reported that in-house research scientists have significant responsibility for new hiring decisions. Less than 40 percent of respondents

Table 5.5 Sources of research projects for sample laboratories

Source	Score	Often	Sometimes	Rarely	Never	N
In-house research scientists	3.59	68.1% (126)	23.8% (44)	7.0% (13)	1.1% (2)	185
In-house R&D managers	2.73	22.7% (42)	37.6% (70)	29.2% (54)	10.3% (19)	185
R&D managers at home	2.52	18.5% (32)	37.0% (64)	22.5% (39)	22.0% (38)	173
Corporate executives at home	2.42	15.7% (29)	29.2% (54)	36.2% (67)	18.9% (35)	185

Source: Richard Florida (1995) *Survey of Foreign-Affiliated R&D Laboratories in the United States*, Pittsburgh, PA: Center for Economic Development, Carnegie Mellon University.

Note
Number of respondents in parentheses.

reported that parent company managers have significant responsibility for new hiring decisions.

The ability to publish the results of scientific research is a key dimension of scientific and technical labor markets. The foreign laboratories in the sample report that they allowed their staffs to publish freely and widely. Foreign-affiliated laboratories produced an average of 16 articles in the open scientific literature per $10 million in R&D expenditures. This is nearly ten times the rate of 1.65 articles per $10 million of company-financed industrial R&D for the USA as a whole.[12] The rate of article production was 10.3 articles per 100 employees, 25.7 articles per 100 scientists and engineers, and 95.5 articles per 100 doctoral-level researchers, nearly one article per doctoral-level researcher per year. The rate of 10.1 articles per 100 scientists and engineers for foreign-affiliated R&D laboratories is significantly higher than the rate of 1.65 articles per 100 scientists and engineers for US industrial R&D.[13] This is understandable, however, given that the US industrial total is not limited to scientists and engineers working in R&D laboratories but also includes those working in manufacturing units and other corporate activities as well as those working in R&D laboratories.

Management challenges: balancing autonomy and co-ordination

Autonomy can pose management challenges of its own. Studies of international R&D management document the difficulties associated with co-ordinating offshore R&D subsidiaries (see Bartlett and Ghoshal, 1989; Florida and Kenney, 1994; Howells and Wood, 1993; Kenney and Florida, 1993). Offshore R&D facilities may report to related "sister" R&D facilities in the home country, to corporate headquarters, or to other business units of the corporation. Reporting requirements also reflect the nature of R&D activities to some degree. Reporting to sister R&D facilities tends to reflect technology activities, while reporting to corporate headquarters or to manufacturing units is more likely to concern manufacturing support. While foreign R&D subsidiaries require linkages to other corporate units and to the home base to co-ordinate their activities, complex reporting requirements and the perception of external control can have negative impacts on organizational performance. Furthermore, a number of studies highlight the tension between the autonomous pursuit of research and innovation and the need to channel and direct R&D

activities toward areas of strategic interest (see Florida and Kenney, 1991; Gomory, 1989; MIT Commission on Industrial Productivity, 1989). Balancing these objectives is a central element of the management of R&D subsidiaries.

The survey explored the reporting requirements of foreign-affiliated R&D laboratories with regard to sister R&D facilities and corporate headquarters. More than three-quarters ($n = 144$) of respondents report to a sister R&D facility and nearly two-thirds report to a corporate headquarters. Furthermore, more than 40 percent of respondents indicated that they report to a sister R&D facility on a daily basis and 30 percent do so on a weekly basis. Roughly 35 percent of respondents indicated that they report to corporate headquarters on a daily basis and 30 percent do so weekly. Close links to, and regular communication with, sister R&D facilities provide additional indications of the technology-driven nature of foreign R&D investment in the United States.

There are numerous dimensions to reporting and external communication, such as financial reporting, corporate co-ordination, general technical direction, and providing information on technological or market trends. These have different implications for the management of offshore R&D subsidiaries. There is considerable difference, for example, between providing regular financial reports and requiring external approval for new research projects. The largest percentage of respondents (84.7 percent) reported co-ordination with other corporate activities as an important purpose of communication with the home base, followed by overall technical direction (78.0 percent), information on technical trends (73.7 percent), financial reporting (72.6 percent), and information on market trends (70.9 percent). Interestingly, "new project ideas" was cited by the lowest percentage of respondents as an important purpose of reporting and external communication (69.5 percent).[14]

The frequency with which R&D subsidiaries are required to obtain spending authorization from their corporate parents is an indicator of the level and extent of external corporate control. Respondents were asked to indicate how frequently their facility is required to obtain spending authorization from the parent company. More than one-third of respondents indicated that they were required to obtain spending authorization "often" and another third were required to do so "sometimes." However, slightly more than 30 percent reported that they were "rarely" (19.8 percent) or "never" (11.6 percent) required to obtain spending authorization from the parent company.

In short, the findings indicate that foreign-affiliated R&D laboratories possess considerable autonomy in proposing projects, setting technical agendas, and hiring new staff, with these functions being the primary responsibility of in-house technical staff. While foreign-affiliated R&D laboratories regularly report both to sister facilities and to corporate headquarters in the home country, such communication is principally concerned with administrative and co-ordination functions. While this communication does involve the overall technical direction of foreign R&D laboratories, it does not appear to impinge upon the design of new projects and the direct organization, nor on the performance of research and development activities.

Conclusions

What have we learned from our look into the motivations, operation, and management of foreign R&D laboratories? Clearly, innovation has become global, as foreign direct R&D investment has grown rapidly over the past decade. The United States has attracted a considerable amount of foreign R&D spending and a large number of R&D laboratories affiliated with foreign companies. The findings of this study lead us to four basic conclusions.

First, firms are increasingly motivated by the need to acquire and develop technology in establishing offshore R&D laboratories. In fact, this sort of technology-seeking behavior is becoming more prevalent than traditional market-seeking behavior, though market-seeking remains important as well. This stands in contrast to the conventional view, which has tended to emphasize market-seeking investment.

Second, the principal factor underlying technology-seeking investments appears to be the constant search for capabilities, that is, intellectual capital embodied in people, institutions, and places. The most important source of innovation for foreign-affiliated R&D laboratories is their own in-house research staff. Foreign investment in R&D is a management strategy designed to tap that pool of intellectual capital. For managers, then, attention is being – and should continue to be – shifted from offshore R&D as a strategy developed principally to promote market access, toward a strategy designed to harness capabilities where they exist around the globe. This may also entail some shifts in internal R&D strategy, particularly in the role and function of the central R&D laboratory.

Under this emerging model of global innovation, the role of the central R&D laboratory is shifting from developing new ideas and products inside to absorbing new ideas and capabilities from the external environment, increasingly via the conduit of offshore R&D affiliates. Managers must consider how to optimize a network of R&D institutions inside and outside the firm which is oriented to harnessing, absorbing, and utilizing scientific and technical capabilities on a global basis. This entails designing R&D organizations which can attract the best and the brightest scientific and technical talent on a worldwide basis. It may inevitably mean a reduction in the relative importance of central R&D facilities.

Third, the organization and management of foreign R&D laboratories in the USA is shaped in large measure by the need to attract and retain high-level scientific and technical talent. The laboratories surveyed in the sample operate with a great deal of autonomy, are relatively "open," and allow their people to publish in the scientific and technical literatures. As we have seen, these laboratories make little apparent effort to transfer styles of management and organization associated with R&D laboratories in their home country. The reason for this is that scientists and engineers tend to demand the US form of loosely structured, university-like environment with the ability to generate new ideas and (in the case of doctoral staff) to publish the results of their work. Management needs to provide this kind of environment, as noted above, if it wants to attract and retain the best scientific and technical talent.

Fourth, a central task of R&D management involves balancing corporate coordination and autonomy. Generally speaking, foreign-affiliated R&D laboratories possess considerable autonomy in developing and managing their technical agendas, with in-house staff being principally responsible for initiating new projects and hiring new scientists and engineers. While foreign-affiliated laboratories regularly report to sister R&D facilities and to corporate headquarters in the home country, this communication is primarily concerned with administration and coordination and tends not to impinge upon in-house technical projects. A critical task of R&D management is to effectively connect these organizational units in a network of product development capabilities which can turn the ideas they generate into successful new commercial products. Balancing the loose control of the decentralized environment of innovation with the inevitable constraints of corporate funding and strategic relevance is a major challenge.

Finally, offshore R&D units must be innovative, and enable their staffs to engage in innovative activity and publish their work. The laboratories in this study are highly innovative, exhibiting rates of patenting and article production that exceed the norm in the USA. There are two reasons for this. The first is that they function as good corporate citizens, adding to the stock of new knowledge in science and technology. The second is that norms of the scientific and engineering professions require this kind of openness. Such organizational structures and practices are required for firms and managers to capture the top-level scientific and technical talent required to compete on a global basis.

Notes

1 Research funding was provided by grants from the Carnegie Bosch Institute, Japan Science and Technology Management Program, and the Alfred P. Sloan Foundation. The Center for Survey Research at the University of Massachusetts-Boston administered the survey research. Michael Massagli oversaw the collection and initial analysis of the survey data. Lewis Branscomb and Harvey Brooks provided helpful comment.

2 A revised and updated version of the Commerce Department study lists 645 foreign-affiliated R&D establishments (Dalton and Serapio, 1995). However, there are reasons to believe this may be an over-statement. It is likely that a substantial fraction of these establishments are not actually involved in research and development, particularly since the sample for this study and the Commerce Department list are drawn from largely the same sources.

3 This grouping system is similar, though not identical, to the standard industrial classification system and is based on the specific technology fields reported by respondents.

4 This estimate is an extrapolation which takes into account non-respondents to this question. The 186 foreign-affiliated R&D establishments that responded to the survey spent $4.1 billion on R&D in 1994.

5 The latter includes R&D spending by all corporate units, including manufacturing divisions and plants, and spending by foreign companies at US universities, and other third-party providers.

6 Survey respondents employed a total of 52,395 workers, including 19,904 scientists and engineers, and 5,875 doctoral-level researchers.

7 These data represent reported spending by respondents only and are not estimated to account for the total sample population.

8 Economists and other experts have long noted the difficulties associated with measuring innovation outputs, including difficulties in constructing reliable and consistent outcome measures, lags in the innovation process, and the complexity of the process of technological change (see Cohen, Florida, and Goe, 1994). It is particularly difficult to measure the more intangible aspects of innovation such as new ideas and techniques which lead to

improvements in products and processes. Still, there are a number of useful measures of the more direct and tangible outputs of the innovation process, such as patents and published articles, which can be measured. The survey collected data on four such classes of direct innovation outputs: patent applications, patents, copyrights, and articles published in the open scientific and technical literature. It is worth noting that the survey data can directly link innovation output to particular facilities. These data thus allow more systematic comparison than the available government statistics which do not allow for comparison or analysis at the establishment level.

9 The performance measures used here are modeled after those in Cohen, Florida, and Goe (1994) see also, Cohen and Florida, 1996; Randazzese (1996).

10 The US average is based on 36,074 patents and $76.9 billion in company-financed R&D (National Science Board, 1993: 455, 371).

11 The US figure is for 1989, the latest date for which data can be obtained – 35,734 industry patents and 726,000 scientists and engineers (National Science Board, 1993: 455, 309).

12 The US data are for 1991 – 12,660 articles, $76.9 billion in company-financed industrial R&D (National Science Board, 1993: 428, 371).

13 The US figure is for 1989 – 11,963 papers, 726,000 scientists and engineers (National Science Board, 1993: 428, 309).

14 There is some variation in reporting by technology area. Foreign-affiliated R&D laboratories in the automotive sector were more likely to be linked both to sister R&D facilities and corporate headquarters. Nine out of ten automotive laboratories were linked to sister R&D facilities compared to an average of seven or eight out of ten for the other sectors. More than 80 percent of automotive laboratories were linked to corporate headquarters compared to an average of four to seven out of ten for the other three sectors.

References

Abernathy, William and James Utterback (1978) "Patterns of innovation in technology," *Technology Review*, 80, 7 (June–July): 40–47.

Angel, David and Lydia Savage (1994) "Global localization? Japanese R&D laboratories in the USA," Worcester, MA: Clark University, Graduate School of Geography, unpublished paper.

Bartlett, Christopher and Sumantra Ghoshal (1989) *Managing Across Borders: The Transnational Solution*, Boston, MA: Harvard Business School Press.

Cantwell, John (1989) *Technological Innovation and Multinational Corporations*, Oxford: Basil Blackwell.

Casson, Mark (ed.) (1991) *Global Research Strategy and International Competitiveness*, Oxford: Basil Blackwell.

Cohen, Wesley and Richard Florida (1996) *For Knowledge and Profit: University–Industry Research Centers in the United States*, New York, NY: Oxford University Press.

Cohen, Wesley, Richard Florida and W. Richard Goe (1994) *University–Industry Research Centers in the United States*, Pittsburgh, PA: Carnegie Mellon University.

Dalton, Donald and Manuel Serapio (1993) *U.S. Research Facilities of Foreign Companies*, Washington, DC: US Department of Commerce, Technology Administration, Japan Technology Program, January.

Dalton, Donald and Manuel Serapio (1995) *Globalizing Industrial Research and Development*, Washington, DC: US Department of Commerce, Office of Technology Policy, Asia–Pacific Technology Program, October.

Dunning, John and Rajneesh Narula (1995) "The R&D activities of foreign firms in the United States," unpublished paper.

Florida, Richard (1996) *Foreign Direct Investment in Research and Development: Scope, Performance and Activities of Foreign-Affiliated Research Laboratories in the United States*, Pittsburgh, PA: Carnegie Mellon University.

Florida, Richard (1997) "The globalization of R&D: results of a survey of foreign-affiliated R&D laboratories in the USA," *Research Policy,* 26: 85–103.

Florida, Richard (1998) "Other countries' money," *Technology Review,* March–April: 29–37.

Florida, Richard and Martin Kenney (1991) "Transplanted Organizations: The Transfer of Japanese Industrial organization to the United States," *American Sociological Review,* 56, 3 (June): 381–398.

Florida, Richard and Martin Kenney (1994) "The globalization of innovation: the economic geography of Japanese R&D in the US," *Economic Geography,* October.

Gomory, Ralph (1989) "From the ladder of science to the product development cycle," *Harvard Business Review* (November–December): 99–105.

Graham, Edward (1992) "Japanese control of R&D activities in the United States: is there cause for concern?," in Arrison, Thomas and C. Fred Bergsten (eds) *Japan's Growing Technological Capability: Implications for the U.S. Economy,* Washington, DC: National Academy Press: pp. 191–206.

Herbert, Evan (1989) "Japanese R&D in the United States," *Research Technology Management* (November–December): 11–20.

Howells, Jeremy (1990) "The internationalization of R&D and the development of global research networks," *Research Policy,* 20: 472–476.

Howells, Jeremy and Michelle Wood (1993) *The Globalization of Production and Technology,* London: Belhaven Press.

Kenney, Martin and Richard Florida (1993) *Beyond Mass Production: The Japanese System and its Transfer to the US,* New York, NY: Oxford University Press.

Klevorick, Alvin, Richard Levin, Richard Nelson, and Sidney Winter (1993) "On the sources and significance of interindustry differences in technological opportunities," unpublished paper, March.

Levin, Richard, A.K. Klevorick, Richard Nelson, and Sidney Winter (1987) "Appropriating the returns from industrial R&D," *Brooking Papers on Economic Activity,* 783–820.

Mansfield, Edward, David Teece, and Anthony Romeo (1979) "Overseas research and development by U.S.-based firms," *Economica,* 46 (May): 187–196.

MIT Commission on Industrial Productivity (1989) *Made in America,* Cambridge, MA: MIT Press.

Mowery, David and David Teece (1992) "The changing place of Japan in the global scientific and technological enterprise," in Arrison, Thomas and C. Fred Bergsten (eds) *Japan's Growing Technological Capability: Implications for the U.S. Economy,* Washington, DC: National Academy Press, pp. 108–143.

Mowery, David and David Teece (1993) "Japan's growing capabilities in industrial technology: implications for U.S. managers and policymakers," *California Management Review,* (Winter): 9–33.

National Science Board, Science and Engineering Indicators, Washington, DC: US Government Printing Office, 1993.

Nelson, Richard (1986) "Institutions supporting technical advance in industry," *AEA Papers and Proceedings,* 76, 2: 186–189.

Nelson, Richard (1993) *National Systems of Innovation,* New York, NY: Oxford University Press.

Nonaka, Ikujiro and Hirotaka Takeuchi (1995) *The Knowledge Creating Company,* New York, NY: Oxford University Press.

Patel, Pari and Keith Pavitt (1991) "Large firms in the production of the world's technology: an important case of non-globalization," *Journal of International Business Studies,* 22, 1: 1–21.

Porter, Michael (ed.) (1986) *Competition in Global Industries,* Boston, MA: Harvard Business School Press.

Porter, Michael (1990) *The Competitive Advantage of Nations,* New York, NY: Free Press.

Randazzese, Lucien (1996) *Profit and the Academic Ethos: The Activity and Performance of Univer-*

sity–Industry Research Centers in the United States, Ph.D. dissertation, Department of Engineering and Public Policy, Carnegie Mellon University.

Roberts, Edward (1994) "Strategic benchmarking of technology," Cambridge, MA: MIT, Sloan School Working Paper.

Ronstadt, R. (1977) *Research and Development Abroad by U.S. Multinationals,* New York, NY: Praeger.

Ronstadt, R. (1978) "International R&D establishment and the evolution of research and development abroad by seven U.S. multinationals," *Journal of International Business Studies* (Spring–Summer): 7–23.

Rosenberg, Nathan (1982) "How exogenous is science?" in Rosenberg, Nathan (ed.) *Inside the Black Box,* New York, NY: Cambridge University Press, pp. 141–159.

Rosenberg, Nathan and Richard Nelson (1994) "American universities and technical advance in industry," *Research Policy,* 23: 323–348.

Utterback, James (1989) "Innovation and industrial evolution in manufacturing industries," in Guile, Bruce and Harvey Brooks (eds) *Technology and Global Industry,* Washington, DC: National Academy Press, pp. 16–48.

Vernon, Raymond (1966) "International investment and international trade in the product cycle," *Quarterly Journal of Economics,* 80: 190–207.

Vernon, Raymond (1977) *Storm over the Multinationals,* New York, NY: Basic Books.

Von Hippel, Eric (1988) *The Sources of Innovation,* New York, NY: Oxford University Press.

Westney, D. Eleanor (1992) "Cross-Pacific internationalization of R&D by U.S. and Japanese firms," *R&D Management,* 23, 3.

Part 2

STRATEGY, INTEGRATIVE PROCESSES, AND DIFFERENTIATION

6

INTERNATIONAL COMPETITION

How cognitive maps can help top management

Roland Calori

Introduction[1]

Increasing international competition creates more complex environments for managers to deal with. The diversity of countries, customer behavior, and management styles requires local adaptations combined with a global strategy.[2] New organizational structures and administrative mechanisms are designed to cope with this increased diversity. Multinational corporations have adapted various solutions, such as decentralization, divisionalization, and matrix structures to reduce the strategic variety that top managers have to cope with at the corporate level, but they are not sufficient. Top managers have to develop a "world view" or "mind-set."[3] Bartlett and Ghoshal (1989) argued that "the task is not to build a sophisticated structure, but to create a matrix in the minds of managers."[4] Moreover the executives in the top management team have the particular function to integrate strategies across business sectors and geographical zones. Consequently, the complexity of top managers' mental maps of their competition should match the complexity of their international strategic systems.[5]

Even in companies focused on their national markets, executives cannot neglect the turbulence created by new entrants coming from foreign countries. Organizational learning becomes a priority in order to counteract ethnocentric biases:[6] that is, the tendency to focus on and prefer one's own social group and country.

Ethnocentric bias leads to strategic myopia in a global economy. Catching up with globalization trends becomes extremely difficult for late movers unless they can create substantial competitive advantages. Ethnocentrism is a form of cognitive rigidity. It reduces the scope of events considered by managers and freezes the strategies learned in the home market. As a consequence, decision makers fail to adapt to different rules of the game. At the organizational level, international competition should stimulate knowledge flows across borders. At the individual level, international competition should stimulate managerial learning by:

- making explicit one's own schema of the competition;
- allowing comparison with others in order to elicit ethnocentric biases;
- preparing and improving the strategic debate within the firm and with external experts;
- developing one's own schema (before being forced to do so by a major crisis).

It is commonly argued that the creation and sharing of knowledge are critical strengths of successful international corporations. Sharing a variety of conceptions amongst top managers on critical issues is one of the processes that strengthens a firm's competitive potential.

Strategy is thinking, preparing, and interpreting action; thus, cognitive analysis methods should help managers to analyze their international environments and formulate international strategies. Some managers' biases are conscious, some are unconscious; the purpose of cognitive analysis (the analysis of knowledge) is to raise awareness and to stimulate the learning process.

This chapter demonstrates the ethnocentric biases of top managers toward international competition. Methods for mapping strategic thinking are presented and applied to the world car manufacturing industry and the European brewing industry. We discuss how managers can learn from the comparison of their cognitive maps with those of other experts, how they can improve strategic debates and strengthen scenario planning. It will be argued that such methods are helpful in developing managers' cognitive complexity[7] in order to match the complexity of international competition.

Cognitive maps

Traditionally, cognitive analysis methods have been used in education science to understand the learning process.[8] They have also been used by marketers who study the reasoning behind consumer behavior and are at the core of the development of expert systems (that is, codifying the reasoning of experts).

In the field of strategic management, the interest in these methods is more recent.[9] It is based on the premise that executives take decisions according to their understanding of the environment, and their understanding is biased and bounded by their past experience. Managers tend to select information that matches their cognitive structures, and they are unable to evaluate all variables relevant to a decision (Schwenk, 1984). Also, individuals make sense of information (that is, interpret it) in a way consistent with their cognitive structures (Weick, 1979).

The theory of bounded rationality is not new (Simon, 1957); what is new is the use of cognitive analysis methods to help managers analyze their environment. On the other hand, cognitive simplifications and heuristics are useful as they enable managers to cope with decision-making complexities (Kiesler and Sproull, 1982). Experts are known for their ability to select the relevant variables, and for the apparent simplicity of their analyses, based on their past experience (Schvanveldt *et al.*, 1982). The apparent paradox between bounded rationality and expertise is resolved when the expert (in this case, a manager) is aware of his or her own biases and is eager to learn from other experts (other managers).

Cognitive structures are often represented by schema which give a holistic simplified view of the elements considered by the decision-maker, and of the links between these elements (for instance, similarities versus differences, or cause–effect relationships), hence the term "cognitive schema." Schema are often drawn in two dimensions in order to capture multiple elements and links, hence the term "cognitive map." Some maps of the managers' environment represent categories (for instance, market segments or strategic groups of competitors: see Figures 6.1 and

6.2); other maps represent cause–effect relationships, for instance the diagnosis of a problem or a scenario of the dynamics of a competitive system (for example, Figures 6.3, 6.4, and 6.5).

Several stages in the strategy formulation process can benefit from cognitive analysis: the diagnosis of a problem; market segmentation; the identification of key success factors; the analysis of strategic groups of competitors; the evaluation of core competences; and scenario planning. Such issues involve the subjectivity of managers placed in ambiguous situations. Here we focus on two applications which have become common in a number of innovative companies: the analysis of competitors (strategic groups) and scenario planning.

Introspection, meditation, and self-questioning can provide the material for the manager to self-map his or her ideas. Most managers communicate simplified holistic representations of their thoughts. There are two problems with self-cognitive mapping. First, each individual has his or her own way to formalize thoughts, thus comparisons between individuals are difficult. Second, self-questioning may not be sufficient to force a deep analysis of the environment; in other words, the elicitation of the "whys?" may be incomplete. For these reasons the intervention of an analyst is preferred. Practically, the task can be achieved by an external consultant, by the firm's marketing department, or by its planning department.[10]

Researchers and consultants use a variety of methods to collect the material and construct cognitive maps. In-depth, open-ended interviews are commonly used. Such interviews typically last from one-and-a-half to three hours, and start with a broad question, such as: "Tell us your view of the future evolution of the [. . .] industry." Then the interviewer uses neutral conversational prompts to get the manager to express his or her understanding as fully as possible. The interview is tape-recorded. In spite of its apparent simplicity, this technique requires some know-how from the interviewer, who should avoid prompts which bias answers. In such interviews, the laddering technique (Fransella and Bannister, 1977) can be used to explore the factors which influence an event by asking the question "why?" several times. Also, successive questions about the consequences of events can be introduced when the objective is to map cause–effect relationships in a system.

The content of the transcripts is then analyzed and first-order concepts or elements are identified and weighted. (For instance, Figures 6.3, 6.4, and 6.5 are composed of first-order concepts weighted according to their importance by one to four asterisks.) Then, the links between concepts are identified, as explicitly mentioned by the interviewee. First-order concepts are clustered into second-order concepts, or dimensions, which are useful for organizing the map. (For instance, in Figures 6.3, 6.4, and 6.5, Key Success Factors, a second order concept, is placed at the center of the map.) The content analysis is made by two analysts working separately, then inter-coder reliability is checked. Finally, the map is presented to the interviewee to check if it is a reliable representation of his or her views. The application to scenario planning in the brewing industry, presented in the next section, followed such a protocol.

Prahalad and Bettis (1986) argue that the theoretical framework used by a person cannot be obtained simply by asking for it, and recommend the use of creative questionnaires and analysis procedures. The "Self-Q" technique developed by Bougon (1983) can substitute for open-ended interviews for studying the dynamics of a system. Repertory grid techniques[11] have been used to map competitors and elicit constructs for the understanding of competition (Reger and Huff, 1993), but several researchers report boredom from the interviewees (Brown, 1992). Competitor analysis, a key issue in understanding international competition, is the technique used here. The methodological challenge is to design a protocol that is both reliable and well accepted by managers.

The Visual Card Sort Technique developed by Daniels *et al.* (1994) is aimed at categorizing competitors and eliciting key constructs for the analysis of competition. It reduces the intervention of the interviewer to a strict minimum and leaves the managers free to build their own taxonomy and to draw their own maps. We used the Visual Card Sort Technique to analyze competition in the car industry. The protocol is presented in Appendix 6.1 and the results are presented in the next section (pp. 108–111).

Comparing one's own map to others is a crucial step in the learning process. When each individual receives the maps produced by the other respondents, he or she realizes the bounds of his or her knowledge of the industry, and the richness of the collective knowledge base of the group. In the final stage of the process, face-to-face interactions between the participants contribute to the exchange and sharing of new knowledge.

In order to stimulate reciprocal learning and benefit from cognitive complementarity, the group of participants in international scenario planning and competitive analysis should be as diverse as possible. Of course a variety of nations should be represented, but also a variety of functions. The group may include the members of the top management team when the main objective is to improve reciprocal learning and the quality of the strategy debate within the firm. The group may include a diversity of experts in the same industry (for instance, the heads of firms involved in the competition) when the main objective is to broaden the range of perspectives and correct organizational biases. The group may also be mixed (both internal and external experts).

In the following sections we report on the results of a competitive analysis of the car industry and a scenario planning exercise concerning the European brewing industry. The first was conducted with a mixed group of experts, while the second was conducted with a group of top managers from different firms.

A cognitive analysis of competition in the world car industry

As far as the understanding of international competition is concerned, top managers' cognitive biases can be threefold:

- omission of some key competitors;
- omission of, or excessive importance given to, some sources of competitive advantage;
- biased evaluation of some competitors.

Ethnocentric bias will lead managers to focus on their home markets and strategic plans although the competition may be global. For this reason the car industry, which is undergoing a process of globalization, is an interesting field of study.

The globalizing automobile industry

American car manufacturers took significant positions in the European market in the 1950s and 1960s, when the USA dominated the world both economically and technologically. Ford created an autonomous European division in 1967; General Motors developed its European brands (Vauxhall in the UK and Opel on the continent); Chrysler acquired Rootes (UK) and Simca (France).

During the high-growth 30-year period following World War II, European car manufacturers focused on their respective domestic markets. The other European countries and former colonies were viewed as territories for export. When growth slowed, European manufacturers started to target the North American market. In 1974, Volkswagen set up a manufacturing unit in Westmoreland (Pennsylvania); in 1979, Renault acquired American Motors, and in the same year Peugeot started to sell its 505 and 405 in the USA.

The Japanese car industry first grew under the protection of its home market, then Japanese competition emerged on the international scene in the mid-1970s. During the following period many companies experienced great difficulty in accomplishing their international strategies.

It took a long time for the Americans to produce compact or sporting cars in the European style. Chrysler had to sell its European operations (to PSA in 1978); Renault was not able to manage the recovery of American Motors; Peugeot had to withdraw from the USA in 1985; while Volkswagen could not maintain its position after the success of the "Beetle," and moved to Mexico in 1989. Experts believe that European competitors were not prepared to work in the highly competitive US environment, and that they failed to adapt their models to the American market in terms of design, comfort, and security. Moreover, both American and European car manufacturers misunderstood and were surprised by Japanese competition (Womack, Jones, and Roos, 1990). It took several years to catch up with Japanese quality, lean manufacturing, and rapid product development. As a consequence Toyota, Honda, and Nissan gained significant shares of both the North American and unprotected North European markets in the late 1980s.

In the mid-1990s, European car manufacturers still suffered from the consequences of their past ethnocentric biases, with significant positions in only a single region of the Triad (NAFTA, Japan, and the European Union, with three-quarters of the world's vehicle sales in 1993). European car makers had a 60 percent share of the European market and their sales outside Europe represented less than 20 per cent of their turnover. Mercedes, BMW, and Porsche were the only exceptions, with worldwide positions at the top end of the market. In 1995, American car makers had a 64 percent share of the North American market, Ford and GM had a 25 percent market share in Europe, and Chrysler was trying to strengthen its marginal position. GM had minority stakes in Isuzu and Suzuki, and Ford in Mazda, but their shares of the Japanese market were still very low (Das, 1997). Indeed Toyota, Nissan, and Honda were leading the global game. Japanese car manufacturers had significant operations and market shares in the three zones of the Triad (90 percent in Japan, 25 percent in North America, and 11 percent in Europe).

It took many years for top European managers to change their perspectives on the world car industry and adopt new frames of references in order to react to the Japanese moves. A new chief executive at Opel, the European continental operations of GM, stimulated the members of the executive committee by asking each of them to play the role of the CEO from a competitor, and to reconstruct the strategy of this competitor before their next meeting. This was seen as one way to reduce ethnocentrism.

Mapping the world car industry

A group of 13 managers from four car manufacturing companies participated in the exercise. The companies cover two French and two US firms, or more precisely the US headquarters of one American firm and the European division of another American firm. A wide range of functions was represented in the group.

The objectives were:

1   to analyze strategic groups of competitors;
2   to identify sources of competitive advantage (that is, criteria by which strategies could be grouped);
3   to give feedback to the participants; and
4   to evaluate each competitor on the full list of criteria.

For this purpose we used the protocol presented in Appendix 6.1 (the Visual Card Sort Technique).

A total of 22 firms were cited twice or more, but only one was cited by all the respondents, namely Toyota. Figures 6.1 and 6.2 show two maps of strategic groups constructed by two managers, among the 35 different maps produced by the participants in the group (an average of 2.7 maps per manager). Altogether the maps were constructed upon 47 different concepts; for simplicity the figures report the list of concepts elicited by two managers in the group. Each manager used seven concepts on average. These overall results show the high diversity of top managers' views of the international competition in the car industry.

The French managers considered a wider set of competitors than the Americans. They did not omit the smaller differentiated manufacturers (Volvo and Rover) and the smaller Asiatic competitors (Suzuki, Hyundai, Daewoo, and Proton). On the other hand, the American managers focused on a small number of large global competitors, and sometimes omitted some European generalists (Fiat) or specialists (Volvo, BMW, and Mercedes). Such differences may come from the relative simplicity of the North American market, where a small number of global firms compete, while the European market is still relatively fragmented and attracts a number of companies, of which European managers are more aware.

Table 6.1 summarizes the main sources of competitive advantage elicited by managers, classified according to their importance in understanding the competition. The columns (A, B, C, D) show the relative importance given to each factor by the subgroup of managers in each firm.

The top managers in the two American firms gave a great importance to global presence as a source of competitive advantage. They also emphasized profitability and financial strength as crucial to coping with increasing worldwide competition.

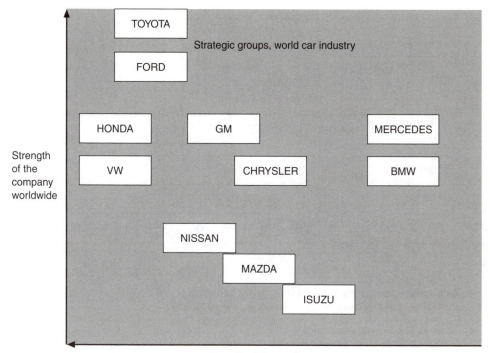

Figure 6.1 Cognitive schema of competition (V.P. Marketing, US car manufacturer).

French managers put less emphasis on these two dimensions, tending to think within the scope of the European market (13 million vehicles a year, or about one-third of the world market).

Such differences can be explained by the geographic scope of these companies. The two American firms already have positions in two continents, whereas the French make more than 80 percent of their sales within Europe. Also, as far as profits are concerned, American shareholders may be more demanding toward a global orientation than French shareholders (the state in the case of Renault, and the Peugeot family in the case of PSA).

The French respondents put more emphasis on the quality of services at the distribution level than their American counterparts. This difference may be explained by the vertical integration of European car makers who distribute their vehicles through exclusive sales networks, whereas multibrand "megadealers" are powerful in the United States. French managers also pointed out the importance of cooperation with the state and the EEC in order to define industrial and monetary policies,

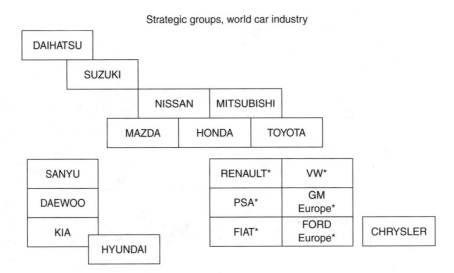

Strategic groups, world car industry

Key dimensions of the map
Significant positions in the European market (marked with an *)
Cultural groups (European, North American, Japanese, Korean)

Sources of competitive advantage
• State intervention, cultural community.
• Presence on the European market (single market, Japanese threat).
• Quality of management.
• Success of new models, intuition of market trends.
• Product coverage extent.
• Investments.
• Flexibility.
• New product development.

Figure 6.2 Cognitive schema of competition (Directeur des Relations Extérieures, French car manufacturer).

and protect the European market from "unfair" foreign competition (mainly Japanese). The Americans did not even mention this aspect. Such differences may be rooted in the gap between the "Anglo-Saxon capitalism" philosophy and the "social market economy" which is the rule in continental Europe. Table 6.1 also shows that the relative importance of certain concepts, such as style and design, is specific to managers in one firm. These are organizational biases corresponding to specific firm strategies.

These ethnocentric biases come from the influence of the "focal-home market" (national or regional). Such biases may hinder development in foreign regions. French car manufacturers may get into trouble in the long term if they maintain a defensive strategy and a European scope. Likewise, if European car manufacturers are tempted again by the American market, they should not underestimate the tough competition at the distribution level and the financial strength required to build a defendable position in a new continent. Conversely, American car manufacturers may be tempted to seek market share in an extended Europe. They should

Table 6.1 Criteria for understanding the competition in the car manufacturing industry

A	B	C	D	Sources of competitive advantage
**	*	***	**	Financial strength
**	*	***	***	Profitability
***	*	***	***	Competitiveness/low costs
***	***	***	***	Product quality
**	**	**	**	Brand image
***	***	***	**	Product coverage extent (niche versus full line)
*	**	***	***	Worldwide presence
***	***			Presence in Europe
	***		**	New products, differentiation
*		**		Adaptations to different segments
			***	Style, design
**	**			Quality of services (distribution)
***				Cost of manpower
	*	**		Production volume
***	**	**	*	Productivity
	**	*		Quality of management
**	***			Dependence toward state's industrial policies
**	**			Cooperation between state and industry
*	*			Cultural characteristics (American, European, Japanese)
		*		Potential for joint ventures
*				Human resources
			*	Training
		**		Technical skills
	*			Investments
	*			Flexibility
			**	Presence in growth segments
			**	Communication

Notes
Relative importance of the criteria, according to the top managers of the company:
***Crucial.
**Very important.
*Important.
A French company;
B French company;
C European division of American company;
D American company.

not underestimate the smaller competitors in this arena, the importance of the quality of services at the retail end in Western Europe, and the stakeholders' interests which are so important in social market economies.

At the individual level, each top manager has a partial view of the competition. The high diversity of individual cognitive maps results from the combination of ethnocentric, organizational, and individual biases, linked to personal experience and specific position. On the other hand, the integration of the 13 partial views gives a rich comprehensive picture of the competition in the industry: the sources of competitive advantage, and evaluations of the main competitors. Indeed, the assessment of competitors (not reported here), using the list of criteria in Table 6.1 provides a solid basis for benchmarking. Last but not least, in the process, each individual becomes aware of the relativity of his or her own understanding to the views of the others. Since a critical factor in the success of any strategy is shared understanding, this is a valuable benefit.

A cognitive approach to scenario planning in the European brewing industry

Scenario planning is a process by which managers imagine possible futures within a competitive system. The outputs are industry scenarios, which show the forces driving the dynamics of competition and the major uncertainties. The brewing industry, a multidomestic activity in the 1970s, has become a "mixed industry"[12] with increased international turbulence, which makes scenario planning a useful exercise.

The brewing industry

In the 1980s, the major North American brewers, Anheuser Bush, Miller, and Coors, seemed to be satisfied with their huge domestic market, and their export sales were marginal. Among Europeans, Heineken, Carlsberg, and Guinness were the first brewers to export to other continents. Given the small size of their respective home markets (the Netherlands, Denmark, and Ireland) these companies were forced to take an international view of their industry. However, in 1994, the European leader Heineken had only a 2 percent share of the North American market. Other major European competitors, BSN-Kronenbourg (France) and Interbrew (Belgium), limited their international ambitions to the Western European market. The Japanese, Asahi and Kirin, seemed to be satisfied with the Asian market. The common view in the industry was that beer could not be transported over long distances because of the high relative transport cost. Worldwide overcapacity limited direct investments abroad. Moreover, strong local brands and specific local consumer tastes appeared to restrain the potential for global products and global brewing companies (Jacobs and Steele, 1997). In this context, at the end of the 1980s, most managers in the industry thought that the strongest competitors would not be challenged by significant newcomers. Managers who focused on their continental arena were surprised by the global strategic move of the Australian group Elders.

In 1989, the Elders group sold $6 billion of its assets in order to focus on its brewing business, and became the Foster's Brewing Group. After the acquisition of Courage, a major British brewery (1986), and Carling O'Keefe, a major Canadian brewery (1987), Foster's strengthened its position in Canada with the acquisition of Molson (1989) to become the leader in that market. The split of the British brewing industry between brewing and retailing (pubs) offered new opportunities. Foster's strengthened its position in the UK by merging with GrandMet (1991), and became the co-leader in the British market, a springboard for continental Europe. In a few years' time, Foster's "came from nowhere" to become the number four brewing group in the world. This unique intercontinental position attracted the best foreign partners for brewing under licence (Carlsberg, Holsten, Coors, and so on). The Japanese firm Asahi took up 20 percent of the equity of the Australian group. The Foster's Group quickly diversified its portfolio of brands and could respond to the growing need for diversity (in foreign, exotic beers). At a 1991 conference, the CEO of Foster's declared: "We have only scratched the surface of the world market."

After this strategic surprise, some North American and European competitors started to react. Among others, Miller showed some interest in an alliance with Heineken, but Heineken preferred independence and invested in Eastern Europe and South East Asia. Interbrew acquired Labatt in Canada to create the world's fifth largest brewing group. Foster's had benefited, however, from the earlier ethnocentric bias of major competitors.

Foster's brewing group had difficulties in achieving their ambitious goals in continental Europe. Top management may have underestimated the reaction of continental European brewers. In 1995, the group sold its operations in the UK to Scottish & Newcastle and redirected its investments to the high-growth Asian markets. By the mid-1990s, the brewing industry had become a turbulent intercontinental battlefield where top managers had to develop a sophisticated worldview of markets and competition.

Mapping the brewing industry

Scenario planning is based on the consultation of experts. The scenario approach may be used for the elaboration of industrial policies (at the level of a sector or a region). More and more companies also use scenario planning in the strategy formulation process, as pioneered and extensively used at Shell (Wack, 1985). When scenario planning is considered as much a learning exercise for managers as a strategy formulation method, the emphasis is put on the variety of the set of scenarios and a broad range of uncertain future events. The number is later reduced to a simplified set of two or three.

The scenario planning method was applied to the European brewing industry. The study was conducted in 1990 with the participation of 22 top managers from 22 European breweries, most of whom were CEOs, while others were members of top management teams. The firms were drawn from seven European countries (Denmark, Germany, France, Great Britain, Italy, the Netherlands, and Spain) in order to represent the diversity of markets. The executives participated in open-ended interviews following the protocol presented in the first section (p. 108). The interview was guided by a broad opening question: "What main changes do you expect in the European brewing industry in the 1990s?" Most of the interviews were highly discursive in nature with managers ranging over issues they chose to emphasize. Where managers were less forthcoming, two forms of prompts were employed: first, neutral conversational prompts; and second, more specific prompts based on the conventional framework of industry analysis – competitors, customers, suppliers, new entrants, substitute technologies, state intervention, sources of competitive advantage, and industry segmentation.[13] However, prompts were always open-ended, for instance: "What about new entrants?" or "What about substitute technologies?" The interviews ended with the following question: "What changes are you thinking of for your company in the 1990s?" The transcript of each tape-recorded interview was analyzed and the content was represented in the form of a cognitive map of the future dynamics of the industry, according to each manager. The 22 cognitive maps represented a set of scenarios for the European brewing industry in the 1990s.

Altogether, the managers used 107 different concepts in total, on average each manager focused on ten concepts (a minimum of 6, a maximum of 17). Such results show the diversity of top managers' cognitive maps and scenarios. They also show the bounds of individual maps and the richness of the pooled answers. There was a consensus on a limited set of constructs: the increasing importance of brand image (20 citations); increasing importance of scale economies; increasing differences between big and small competitors; small competitors focusing on niches; a need to be involved in the few growth segments; further concentration of the industry; increasing pressure from retail chains; improvement in the quality of products and services; consumers caring more and more about health and pleasure; increasing marketing "investments" (five citations).

These issues can be considered as the common trunk from which 22 different scenarios emerge. Figures 6.3, 6.4, and 6.5 show three of the scenarios from a French, a Dutch, and a British top manager respectively. It is important to mention that the three firms are major European competitors, all pursuing an international strategy.

The comparison of these maps elicits several differences. The French manager emphasizes increasing investment in new process technology, while the others disregard this trend. Compared to his British and Dutch counterparts, he tends to underestimate the opportunities created by the restructuring of the British market, and the growth strategies of Australian and American brewers in Europe. The Dutch manager emphasizes the concentration of the German brewing industry while the others tend to neglect this evolution. On the other hand, he underestimates the risks of parallel international distribution channels and the reduction of price differentials (and, consequently, the reduction of profit margins) across Europe. The British manager emphasizes the future diversification of brand portfolios, through intercontinental alliances and reciprocal distribution agreements between major competitors. The consumers' demand for more diversity is related to this evolution. He seems to underestimate the future market growth for low-alcoholic beer and tends to focus his scenario on the British market.

These biases can be partly explained by different corporate strategies (that we cannot reveal here) as well as ethnocentric frames of reference. These cognitive differences provide a basis for differences in scenario planning which firms should take into account. The differences suggest scenario alternatives:

- new entries and growth strategies of major Australian and North American brewers in Europe particularly in the UK (significant versus insignificant);
- the concentration of the German brewing industry (quick versus slow);
- the reduction of price differentials across Europe (significant versus insignificant);
- the diversification of brand portfolios based on agreements between major competitors (significant versus insignificant);
- the market growth of non-alcoholic and low-alcoholic beer (high versus low);
- the rate and impact of new process technologies (significant versus insignificant).

Executives should consider these major uncertainties and should assess the resilience of their business strategies in the face of these alternative scenarios. Moreover, the identification of uncertainties can help design a selective business scanning system in order to sense weak signals announcing major trends.[14]

While some managers may not feel the need to use the results as inputs in formal strategy formulation processes or scanning systems, we have found that the compari-

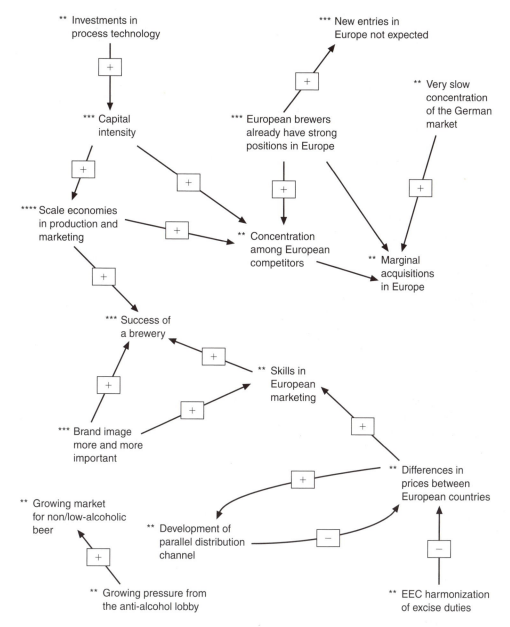

Figure 6.3 Scenario: the dynamics of the European industry (top manager, French).

son of their own maps with the maps of the other participants is perceived as a powerful learning exercise. Each manager receives the whole set of cognitive maps and comments from the analyst about:

- the specificity of the manager's map;
- the set of concepts common to most managers ("the industry recipe");

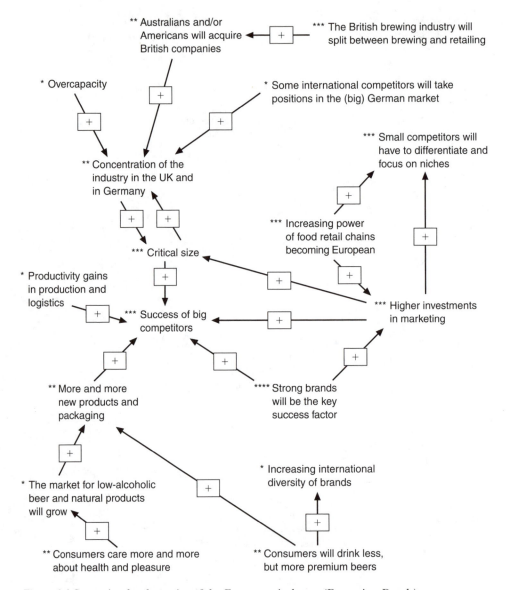

Figure 6.4 Scenario: the dynamics of the European industry (Executive, Dutch).

- the complementarity of concepts;
- the divergent views.

Such feedback raises individual awareness and stimulates the search for new information on the environment, both important dimensions of strategic thinking.

Some executives wish to go further and replicate the exercise within the company. The members of a top management team may improve the internal strategy debate by comparing their cognitive maps of the environment. At any level in the hierarchy, multifunctional or transnational teams may use the same method in

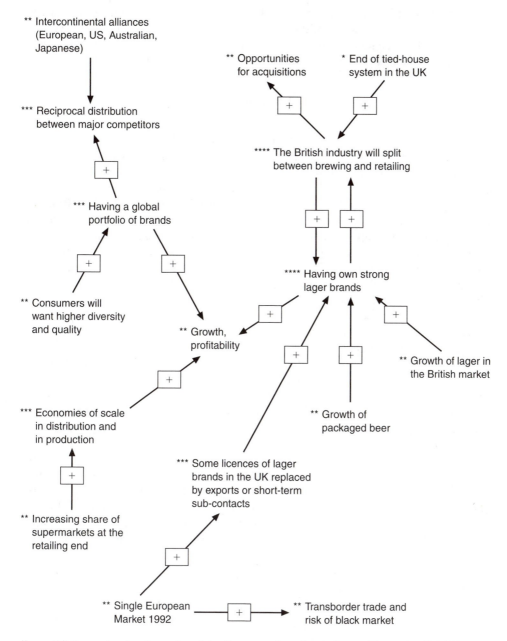

Figure 6.5 Scenario: the dynamics of the European brewing industry (Executive, British)

order to improve reciprocal learning. In this context the analysis of individual cognitive maps and the written feedback are provided in advance of a meeting, at which the cognitive differences are debated, and where interactions further stimulate learning. Computer software can help the groups integrate individual maps into a collective map summarizing the consensus view.[15]

Several applications have shown the relatively high diversity of individual environmental maps within a company, due to the diversity of individual experiences, professions, and management styles. Articulating this diversity and making tacit knowledge explicit is one of the benefits of cognitive mapping.

Conclusion

The applications reported here show that cognitive analysis methods can improve top managers' understanding of complex international environments in two key areas: competitive analysis (strategic groups, benchmarking) and scenario planning, including the design of scanning systems. These methods strengthen comparisons between managers' views, and also help managers in making more explicit judgments. Beyond the "tangible" outputs, such as grids for benchmarking or scanning systems, managers learn from the feedback they receive when they participate in such a process through exchanging cognitive maps and other written outputs. Learning comes from the high diversity of individual schemas. When comparing one's own map with others, an individual realizes the bounds of his or her cognitive structures and the richness of the whole set of maps. Indeed, revealing diversity stimulates further interactions with others.

Mixed panels of experts appear to be the most efficient solution. The experts and managers are first interviewed separately, then the members of the group within the company meet to interact with each other, discuss differences within the group, and between the group and external experts, so that individual biases and organizational biases are elicited and debated. Such a discussion is a good start for a strategy debate, marginal views can be expressed, tolerance to different views is generally enhanced, and the risk of forced consensus is lowered. Some of the negative effects of group dynamics are reduced, while preserving the positive effects of interactions.

International network corporations aim to achieve both local responsiveness and global integration. In these organizations the quantity and quality of transnational knowledge flows are paramount in order to reduce ethnocentric biases. The learning process in a network organization requires a basic condition: individual open-mindedness. It relies on interactions between individuals, which can be achieved over time through international training, job rotation and participation in international task forces and teams. Cognitive analysis methods support these interactions and, thus, improve the learning process and accelerate the personal development of managers coping with complex international competition.

Appendix 6.1: The Visual Card Sort Technique

The protocol involves four phases:

1 In a first interview the interviewee is asked to name the competitors in the industry; the interviewer writes the names on small cards and then asks the manager to map these cards according to similarities and differences between firms (placing similar firms close to each other in a group and dissimilar firms far from each other). The result looks like a map of strategic groups, but without revealing yet the

dimensions on which the clusters are based. A photograph of the map is taken. Then the manager is asked to explain the reasons why he or she clustered firms this way. In doing so he or she reveals the key concepts used to understand the competition. The interviewer writes the concepts on a new set of small cards. The interviewee is asked to map again the cards naming competitors according to any other important aspect of the competition, a photograph is taken, new concepts are revealed, and so on, until the manager does not see any other relevant way to map the competition.

2 The second phase of the first interview is focused on the concepts elicited during the first part. The manager is asked to group concepts which are closely linked to each other (for instance, he or she may cluster together concepts such as: size, volume, economies of scale). Having a view of the full set of clustered concepts, the interviewee is asked to order them according to their importance in the competition. A photograph of the arrangement is taken. From this description it should be clear that the intervention of the interviewer is kept to a minimum (he or she provides cards, a camera, makes sure that a desk is available to display the cards, and writes names and concepts on them). It is the manager who arranges the map, so that at any time during the interview he or she has a holistic view of the whole set of elements. Figures 6.1 and 6.2 give examples of strategic groups (phase one) and lists of clusters of concepts (phase two) which were considered by two managers in the study of the car industry.

3 In a second interview, the whole set of maps elicited by the managers and the external experts involved in the exercise are presented to the interviewee and discussed, and cognitive commonalities and differences are pointed out. This phase is useful for the manager to understand how his or her perceptions of the competition compares with those of colleagues.

4 In the fourth phase, the respondent is given a table with the full list of competitors identified by the group of experts (columns), and a full list of the key concepts identified in the first phase (rows). He or she is asked to characterize each competitor using the list of concepts. For instance, Table 6.1 (p. 111) gives a list of concepts elicited in the study of the car industry; each of the 22 competitors identified in this industry will be assessed on these 27 criteria. This is not an easy task, many points remain unanswered, and the manager realizes the bounds of his or her knowledge of the industry. On the other hand, when answers are received from the whole group of respondents each manager realizes how useful the collective knowledge of the group can be for understanding a complex international competitive system.

Notes

1 The author would like to thank Professors Kevin Daniels, Gerry Johnson, and Chuck Stubbart for their important contributions in the study of the automobile industry.
2 Prahalad and Doz (1987) defined the mission of multinationals as "balancing local demands and global vision."
3 In the terms used by Prahalad and Doz (1987).
4 This is a major trait of "transnational" organizations described by Bartlett and Ghoshal (1989: 212).
5 Calori *et al.* (1994) found relationships between the geographical scope of the organization and top managers' mental maps.

6 Perlmutter (1969) wrote about the ethnocentric mode of management in multinationals, Kogut (1991) showed the difficulty of adapting administrative practices to new foreign contexts.

7 Cognitive complexity is defined as the managerial capacity to simultaneously conceptualize different types of businesses. The ability to perceive several dimensions is referred to as "differentiation" or "comprehensiveness" and the development of connections among the differentiated characteristics is referred to as "integration" or "connectedness" (Bartunek, Gordon, and Weathersby, 1983).

8 Piaget (1937) was one of the pioneers, in his studies of the cognitive development of children.

9 The emergence of cognitive psychology in the field of strategic management started at the end of the 1980s. See, for instance, Huff (1990); Eden and Radford (1990).

10 Lenz and Engledow (1986: 341) argued that an essential function of planners "is to continually enrich and update the cause maps used by managers in key decision-making positions."

11 Repertory grid techniques are based on the Personal Construct Theory developed by Kelly (1955); Fransella and Bannister wrote a manual for repertory grid technique (1977).

12 According to Prahalad and Doz (1987), a "mixed industry" is characterized by significant forces driving global integration and significant forces driving local responsiveness. Mixed industries are between the global and multidomestic archetypes of international competition.

13 This framework is drawn from Porter (1980 and 1985).

14 A method for designing such a scanning system has been proposed by Calori (1989).

15 Several computer software packages are available. COPE (developed at the University of Strathclyde by Colin Eden) is one of the most widely used (Eden and Radford, 1990).

References

Bartlett, C.A. and S. Ghoshal (1989) *Managing Across Borders: The Transnational Solution*, Boston: Harvard Business School Press.

Bartunek, J.M., J.R. Gordon, and R.P. Weathersby (1983) "Developing complicated understanding in administrators," *Academy of Management Review*, 8, 2: 273–284.

Bougon, M. (1983) "Uncovering cognitive maps: The Self-Q Technique," in Morgan, G. (ed.) *Beyond Method: A Study of Organizational Research Strategies*, New York, NY: Sage, pp. 173–188.

Brown, S.M. (1992) "Cognitive mapping and repertory grids for qualitative survey research: some comparative observations," *Journal of Management Studies*, 29, 3: 287–307.

Calori, R. (1989) "Designing a business scanning system," *Long Range Planning*, 22, 1: 69–82.

Calori, R., G. Johnson, and P. Sarnin (1994) "CEOs' cognitive maps and the scope of the organization," *Strategic Management Journal*, 15: 437–457.

Daniels, K., L. de Chernatony, and G. Johnson (1994) "Differences in managerial cognitions of competition," *British Journal of Management*, 5, Special Issue: 521–529.

Das, R. (1997) "A note on the world automobile industry," in Johnson, G. and K. Scholes (eds) *Exploring Corporate Strategy*, London: Prentice Hall, pp. 637–653.

Eden, C. and J. Radford (eds) (1990) *Tackling Strategic Problems, The Role of Group Decision Support*, London: Sage.

Fransella, F. and D. Bannister (1977) *A Manual for Repertory Grid Technique*, New York, NY: Academic Press.

Huff, A.S. (ed.) (1990) *Mapping Strategic Thought*, Chichester: John Wiley.

Jacobs, T. and M. Steele (1997) "The European brewing industry," in Johnson, G. and K. Scholes (eds) *Exploring Corporate Strategy*, London: Prentice Hall, pp. 533–557.

Kelly, G.A. (1955) *The Psychology of Personal Constructs*, vols 1 and 2, New York, NY: Norton.

Kiesler, S. and L. Sproull (1982) "Managerial response to changing environments: perspectives on problem sensing from social cognition," *Administrative Science Quarterly*, 27: 548–570.

Kogut, B. (1991) "Country capabilities and the permeability of borders," *Strategic Management Journal*, 12, Special Issue: 33–48.

Lenz, R.T. and J.L. Engledow (1986) "Environmental analysis: the applicability of current theory," *Strategic Management Journal*, 7: 329–346.

Perlmutter, H. (1969) "The tortuous evolution of the multinational corporation," *Columbia Journal of World Business*, 4: 9–18.

Piaget, J. (1937) *La Construction du Réel chez l'Enfant*, Neuchatel and Paris: Delachaux et Niestle.

Porter, M.E. (1980) *Competitive Strategy, Techniques for Analyzing Industries and Competitors*, New York, NY: Free Press.

Porter, M.E. (1985) *Competitive Advantage*, New York, NY: Free Press.

Prahalad, C.K. and R. Bettis (1986) "The dominant logic: a new linkage between diversity and performance," *Strategic Management Journal*, 7, 6: 485–501.

Prahalad, C.K. and Y. Doz (1987) *The Multinational Mission, Balancing Local Demands and Global Vision*, New York, NY: Free Press.

Reger, R.K. and A.S. Huff (1993) "Strategic groups: a cognitive perspective," *Strategic Management Journal*, 14, 2: 103–124.

Schvanveldt, R.W. *et al.* (1982) *Structures of Memory for Critical Flight Information*, Air Force Human Resource Laboratory, Technical Report 81–46.

Schwenk, C.R. (1984) "Cognitive simplification processes in strategic decision-making," *Strategic Management Journal*, 5, 2: 111–128.

Simon, H.A. (1957) *Models of Man*, New York, NY: Wiley.

Wack, P. (1985) "Scenarios: uncharted waters ahead," *Harvard Business Review*, 63, 5: 73–89.

Weick, K.E. (1979) *The Social Psychology of Organizing*, 2nd edn, Reading, MA: Addison Wesley.

Womack, J.P., D.T. Jones, and D. Roos (1990) *The Machine that Changed the World*, New York: Macmillan.

7

MANAGING DIVERSITY ACROSS MODERN MARKETS

Jeffrey Williams

Introduction

The roots of modern competitive diversity originated 3,000 years ago with the development of the agricultural society and the craftsman's guild. Two hundred years ago saw the advent of the industrial revolution with its emphasis on economies of scale. Twenty years ago we witnessed the onset of a third type of management priorities associated with a still-shorter period of advantage; that of fast-moving industries associated with the information economy. As each new cluster of management styles was established, the previous management styles remained and were refined. Today, the result of these many and different management priorities is increasing business complexity, whereby managers face a range of sometimes complementary, and at other times conflicting, approaches to serving customers from market to market and from country to country.

Consider the increased diversity of rivalry as manifested in price competition. If we look at industries like healthcare, consulting, defense, and entertainment, we see that organizations in these industries avoid direct price competition. These industries are protected from competition in the traditional sense, in that firms in these industries are able to raise prices gradually over time. In the case of healthcare in the United States, real prices increased at a rate of 6 percent a year for two decades, whereas in Europe, healthcare price increases have been more gradual. In contrast, businesses like appliances, automobiles, and financial services see that the ability of any one organization to sustain price advantage is limited. Competitors enter and duplicate first mover advantage at lower costs or offer superior alternatives. Consequently, prices are more competitive, gradually declining over time. In still other, information-rich industries like personal computing, consumer electronics, and telecommunications devices, innovation is rapid, as products are copied quickly. Annual price reductions of 10 to 30 percent are common. Clearly, the competitive complexity from one industry to another is significant, and in particular, when seen in terms of what can be termed "sustainability conditions" (Williams, 1998), these industries reflect a range of management priorities, or ways of serving customers.

Management styles are the cluster of internal business processes, organization-wide control systems, and external competitive approaches that support a company's products, making the company distinctive to its customers. Management priorities for any organization reflect the alignment, or fit, between the central features of an internal organization and the demands of its external environment. In terms of dependencies, certain management priorities lend themselves to more success in some competitive environments than in others. Organizations that maintain a higher degree of organizational coherence, that is, greater corporate-wide tolerance for alignment among different management styles, should be more successful than corporations that have a less robust competitive capability. This should be true for domestic as well as for international corporations.

The traditional language of business as it prescribes styles of management assumes relatively uniform, extended rivalry between large, economies of scale-based organizations (Porter, 1980). Although useful, as we will see, the traditional language of business can limit the ability of managers to capitalize on modern competitive diversity. Against this backdrop, it is understandable that the international corporation is emerging as a network of market dependencies with more or less related priorities, which operate across diverse environments, under an international management structure that is struggling to adapt to the differing requirements of established and emerging industries. Our interest is in how industries are becoming more complex at the same time that modern organizations are seeking to improve organizational coherence. Diverse forces in competitive environments place demands on the diversified organization's internal control system, organization structure, and corporate culture, causing the poorly-prepared organization to under-perform compared with its less complex rivals. Of concern is to what point the increasing business complexity of international corporations like Bosch, Sony, Siemens, and 3M outstrips the abilities of their managers to exert effective international leadership across the modern economy.

Management styles and sustainability

As one gauge of competitive diversity, we can compare market forces and the critical success factors in them, based on the economic half-life of products; that is, the amount of time that passes until per-unit profit margins drop to one-half their highest amount. The economic half-life, or product half-life, varies according to the presence or absence of isolating mechanisms that slow down convergence toward perfectly-competitive markets (Williams, 1998). Differences in the duration of product advantage, which can be studied in terms of sustainability conditions, can be traced, in turn, to management priorities in various settings.

At one end of the spectrum of sustainability, some organizations stand out by relying on the specialized talents of skilled individuals, and they enjoy stable profitability over time. Software firms, book publishers, and consulting firms fit this description. Other profit-stable firms rely on long-term, complex relationships between themselves and their customers, as in defense, aerospace, accounting, and investment banking. In these businesses, organizational features and international strategy styles are dictated by specialized human processes or the highly specialized needs of a few customers.

Another set of strategy styles requires the co-ordination of large teams of workers involved in complex, large-scale production processes. We see such management styles in Daimler Benz's production of automobiles, McDonald's international mass-market, fast-food franchise, the international pharmaceutical firm Bayer, or international banking by American Express. These organizations are oriented toward providing a "no-surprises" experience in mass markets.

A third set of strategy styles can be associated with serving markets dominated by rapid product innovation and obsolescence. Here, uncertainty about the technologies of supply or the preferences of customers is high. Examples include the semiconductor and consumer electronics industries, as in the case of firms like Sony, Philips, and Motorola, and the toy and fashion goods industry, as with Hasbro and Benetton.

Ranging from slowly-converging to rapidly-converging markets, these styles of management can be grouped as: slow-cycle (local monopoly) situations, characterized by long-lived organizational advantage that is isolated from direct competition; standard-cycle (oligopolistic) situations, characterized by extended, economies-of-scale-based competition between a few large organizations; and fast-cycle (Schumpeterian) situations, characterized by a rapid rate of innovation accompanied by convergence to highly competitive markets (see Table 7.1).

The strategy style differences that we emphasize are neither inherently good nor bad. Each strategy style establishes a particular kind of relationship with customers in its environment, based on convergence pressures at work. As a result, these styles are based on factors that are simultaneously economic, technological, and cultural. Consequently, they are difficult to learn and hard to change, as should be the case for profitable advantage to endure. But this also means that it ought to be difficult for one organization to master and extend a diversity of styles across diverse global settings.

These distinctions are not unique to international business. As an illustration, differences in price competition are seen in domestic industries where, for example, in the personal computer industry, prices fall rapidly for computer hardware and hold steady for software like the Windows operating system. In applying these distinctions to questions of international management, managers can be responsive to international differences in competitive pressures resulting from:

- the stability of demand and how quickly customer purchase patterns are shifting.
- how quickly profit margins are being squeezed by the actions of competitors.
- the required speed of investment and how the payback period on investments is expected to differ between industries.

Sustainability conditions dictate performance criteria in areas such as market share, cost reduction, and productivity goals. These conditions also reflect differences in product design and marketing, human resource policies, staffing, and operational integration that are not easily accounted for by traditional models of management.

Herein lies the challenge to the global manager: an international firm will face challenges, of different types and to different degrees, when it attempts to extend successful practices learned in one market into another environment operating differently in economic time. The ability to meet these challenges as they arise distinguishes the leading international companies from their less successful counterparts.

Table 7.1 Competitive diversity across the modern economy

	Market analogy	*Dominant strategies*	*Organizational capabilities*
Schumpeterian (fast-cycle)	Schumpeterian: dynamic Temporary scale economies Gale of creative destruction Dynamic and unstable barriers Competitors enter/exit at stage of market evolution	Innovate and "eat your children" Ramp up–ramp down volume Access distribution quickly Be disloyal to products Reduce price rapidly	Entrepreneurial, risk seeking culture Fast learning, fast forgetting Rapidly changing relationships Capabilities renewed frequently Precise timing, entry and exit Selection efficiency
Oligopolistic (standard-cycle)	Oligopolistic: extended rivalry Scale-driven barriers to entry, mobility, and exit A few organizations dominate Competitors segment based on cost and differentiation	Gain and hold market share Standardize product and process Segment markets Emphasize brand loyalty Discipline competitors Price near costs to hold share	No surprises, zero-defects culture Command and control orientation Teamwork, improvement oriented Process, mass market oriented Uniform systems and measures
Monopolistic (slow-cycle)	Monopolistic: isolated rivalry Non-scale barriers to entry High mobility barriers Market ownership common Subject to tipping Winner-takes-all outcomes	Embrace and extend market lock-in Pursue ownership of market factors Use staircase strategies Stable long-run pricing	Superstar, artisan-like culture Specialization valued Scale economies limited Stable product support structure Organization flexible, informal Gardener-type leadership

Source: Adapted from Jeffrey R. Williams (1998).

In the section that follows, we turn to explaining the international strategy styles that are adopted by firms in each type of environment. We start with the standard-cycle environment (as it is a close cousin to traditional oligopolistic rivalry) with its emphasis on size and economies of scale. This will be a point of departure from which to discuss slow-cycle and fast-cycle environments and the differences in international strategy styles in these settings. We enter into discussions of examples of international companies, each of which is interesting and relevant in terms of helping to understand the adaptation of the company's style to its specific industry. We have chosen three different companies as each of them operates in relatively homogeneous sustainability conditions with strategy styles to match. Later, these distinctions will help us to understand the difficulty of mixing international strategy styles as a firm expands into different product areas that operate differently in economic time.

We consider three US-based organizations that operate internationally across this range of sustainability conditions. First, American Airlines, which offers (standard-cycle) international air travel in oligopolistic environments with an emphasis on market share and economies of scale. Then, we look at Compaq Computer,[1] which produces and sells personal computers internationally in fast-cycle industries where products have a short half-life and convergence pressures on profits are extreme. Lastly, we look at toy maker Mattel, which makes Barbie, a slow-cycle product that has achieved near market ownership on an international basis. Each of these organizations operates in over 100 countries internationally and, together, they reflect the increasing competitive diversity of modern markets.

Scale-orchestrator American Airlines

American Airlines is a contemporary example of the classic business model with its ability to orchestrate scale economies over global-scale, international markets. American Airlines operates in a standard-cycle environment and sustains scale economies through operational integration. Organizationally, the company's managers spend considerable time on process re-engineering, which is supported by extensive controls. Although growth is primarily through increasing internal scale economies, it is augmented with selective acquisitions so far as they enhance operational efficiencies. (Carriers like American also benefit from hub control that is not the focus of this analysis.)

In American Airlines we see management priorities that value the ability to manage large, complex operations with far-flung elements, and control them through procedures and training. Continual fine-tuning of market segmentation at many points across the globe (through their yield management system) reflects the necessity to control all aspects of operations in fine detail, balancing local and global needs with high precision. Success is measured by zero-defects, "no surprises" for customers, thousands of times daily across a complex, high-volume international infrastructure. This management priority is common in international, standard-cycle companies like Toyota, Ikea, General Electric, IBM, Wal-Mart, and Daimler-Benz.

Revenue at American Airlines is closely circumscribed by the actions of competitors. Due to increased competition, revenue per passenger mile has not been increasing as fast as cost per mile. For American Airlines, and for many of its competitors, this has put pressure on profit margins across the industry. Aircraft fuel prices are American's second-largest expense after capital costs and are higher for international than domestic operations. (Raw material is often a significant fraction of total costs for standard-cycle organizations.)

As for any scale orchestrator, there are four operational elements that are harmonized at high volume: growth, product design, process engineering, and organizational learning (Williams, 1998). The need for scale orchestration is seen in many ways, through an emphasis on reliable, numerous flight frequencies, the desire to sustain brand loyalty against attractive alternatives, and the importance of low operating costs.

Growth through access to international routes is achieved in concert with a process of optimization and harmonization with existing scale-based infrastructure.

Acquisitions play an important role in this regard to the degree that they enhance operational efficiencies and economies of scale. Toward this end, American purchased Eastern Airlines' routes to Central and South America, giving it 200 flights weekly to that region of the world and dominant carrier status in that market. In 1991, the company bought Trans World Airlines' routes from the USA to the UK that included 90 flights weekly to London Heathrow, Manchester, and Glasgow. Also in that year, American Airlines bought Continental Airlines' Seattle–Tokyo route and received approval for a San Jose–Tokyo route. The purchase of well-established routes provides a means to spread high fixed costs and extend operational efficiency gains over a stable, expanded revenue stream, a management priority common to standard-cycle organizations.

Frequent flyer programs in these markets are designed to build brand loyalty by encouraging customers to use the same vendor repeatedly in an environment which values transactions between company and customer that are frequent and extended. Also, as is typical of standard-cycle organizations, American Airlines benefits from large-scale investments in marketing and distribution that can be spread over large markets for extended periods of time. By combining frequent-flyer-based and marketing-based brand loyalty with route expansion and brand partnerships (a joint arrangement between American and Japan Airlines, for example), American pursues scale orchestration internationally.

Process engineering focuses on continual gains in efficiency. As new aircraft are added to the fleet, old aircraft are retired, and the use of computerized reservations systems improves capacity utilization across an expanding, worldwide network. American entered into code-sharing agreements with other airlines as a means of route acquisition because this further improved operational scale. For example, service to Amsterdam and the Netherlands was provided in cooperation with British Midland Airways. In Beijing, American opened an office and assigned full-time representatives there as part of a plan to extend service.

Organizational learning is expressed in the careful selection and training of flight crews, ongoing changes to corporate structure, and the careful crafting of corporate-wide procedures to ensure a "no-surprises" experience for customers throughout the American Airlines system worldwide.

Orchestration among scale, learning, product, and process is ongoing. American Airlines has been selective in its domestic operations by carefully employing market segmentation and organizational re-engineering with the goal of lowering costs and raising operating efficiency. A strategic framework known as the Transition Plan focused on making the core business bigger and stronger by shedding routes where the company could not compete profitably. American's ongoing organizational improvement and market re-segmentation focus is typical of priorities found in scale-co-ordinated, standard-cycle international operations.

Children-eating Compaq Computer

Traditional strategy models assume that competitive advantage, once achieved, is more or less sustainable. In contrast, competitive processes in fast-cycle industries operate along lines that are more Schumpeterian in nature (Schumpeter, 1942), in that advantage is defined by processes of innovation and imitation. Product advantage is short-lived because innovators lack ways of preventing imitation. As innovative products yield profits, they attract imitators and are quickly reverse-engineered and copied. Because imitators benefit from lower development costs, they are able to offer equivalent or superior products at lower prices.

In fast-cycle industries, consumer preferences are unstable. Brand loyalty plays a small part in consumers' buying decisions. Although brand loyalty is low, advertising is helpful when it creates brand awareness, allowing a large amount of product to be sold in a short amount of time. The ability to inform customers quickly of a new product, new features, and new performance alternatives across different regions of the world confers advantage. International brand strength is seen with products like the Sony Walkman and Intel microchips, where branding is designed to sell a large amount of product in different countries quickly, before price erosion sets in.

Schumpeterian management styles are evident in the case of Compaq Computer. Compaq's management priorities are predicated on the assumption that advantage is fleeting, in that products have a short economic half-life. Prices can be set high initially, as the marginal utility of early adopters is high. Entry barriers, however, fall with time as high prices and initial demand attract competitors with look-alike products. To gain the fullest profits possible, capacity at Compaq must be ramped up quickly, and then, as the product begins to mature (within a year), capacity must be taken off-line quickly. This process must be managed with a minimum of obsolete inventory, outdated plant and equipment, and distributor disruption. (This is why, irrespective of country, Compaq's operational priorities employ aggressive pricing and incentive programs that are designed to build sales quickly.) The fast-cycle demands of international competition faced by Compaq mean that its managers must develop skills at capitalizing on market opportunities that change rapidly, but at different rates in different countries.

As for many fast-cycle organizations, Compaq experienced hypergrowth. During the 1990s, the company expanded rapidly into Europe and Asia. By 1994, only 10 years after its founding, almost half of the company's $11 billion in revenues were from overseas (and in that year international sales growth outpaced US domestic sales increases by 54 percent to 48 percent). Part of the reason for the typically-rapid international expansion of fast-cycle organizations is that, in fast-cycle industries, customer preferences are often similar among countries (microchips, cell phones, innovative financial instruments). Similarly, there are few cultural, regulatory, or transportation entry barriers between countries.

International market share goals for organizations like Compaq have a dynamic character. As isolating mechanisms are weak, the goal is to distribute product quickly across as many markets as possible at the highest price points allowed, before price erosion sets in. Real-time data on inventory and as to how sales are changing are also required in order to facilitate dynamic pricing, a tactic of reducing price just fast enough to maximize production with no stock-outs or inventory build up.

Manufacturing makes use of flexible manufacturing systems that are designed to produce a variety of products using the same equipment so that changeovers can be done rapidly. The capacity of each line can be ramped up and down quickly to match changing demand without causing obsolescence of capacity itself. The reason

Compaq can do this is because its products are organizationally simple; that is, they do not require complex organizational procedures. (A typical personal computer has about 100 parts, compared to about 12,000 parts for a typical automobile.) Compaq also outsources a large number of these parts, which are standardized on an international basis, from vendors that are responsive and nimble.

Also common in these settings are finely-tuned exit strategies, pre-determined plans for removing products from the marketplace with the full knowledge that they will become obsolete. Central to making this insight operational is estimating when market erosion will cause product price to fall below production costs. By estimating this certain effect in advance, managers are better able to focus efforts on the next innovation rather than supporting products that are becoming obsolete. Part of this approach is ensuring compatibility, being careful that this strategy does not result in stranded investments for customers or suppliers.

The tactics used for the timing and introduction of new products are also distinctive to fast-cycle styles. Product pre-announcements are one example. Successful product rollovers from generation to generation entail capturing higher rents from newer products by sacrificing lower rents on older products. If pre-announcements are made too late, profits from existing products will turn negative. If they are premature, there will be an excessive time lag before new profits can be generated to replace those lost on predecessor products.

Like standard-cycle American Airlines, fast-cycle Compaq has a high degree of operational integration. But unlike American, operations at Compaq have a lower degree of operational complexity. The process of assembling a computer is relatively simple from an organizational standpoint. A few dozen subassemblies, supplied by vendors, come together in a plug-and-play environment. Instead of American's command and control priorities, the requirement is for speed, the ability to reduce time-to-market. Also needed is the ability to track and manage inventory levels worldwide, so as to minimize the amount of obsolete unsold product at any point in time. Because brand loyalty is low, local responsiveness requires knowledge of customers' changing preferences, of fluctuating inventory, of competitors' many offerings, and of rapidly-changing regional price points. Speed and responsiveness are more important than efficiency, and that is why, in international organizations like Compaq, enterprise-wide co-ordination requires less investment in complex, operational procedures than for counterparts like American Airlines.

Compaq managers require close co-ordination and communication between R&D, manufacturing, and marketing to achieve quick decision-response times. Geographical and cultural dispersion are a challenge to this kind of fast-cycle co-ordination. Similarly, marketing with speed requires co-ordination and swift feedback between sales activities, assembly, and manufacture. Thus, Compaq's international management priorities are uncomplicated, by design. The company has the ability to achieve economies of scale quickly, but it can also take capacity off-line quickly, altering production capacity rapidly as customer demands change.

In 1984, Compaq opened its first international subsidiary, its European headquarters in Germany. In 1991, the company added manufacturing facilities in Scotland and Singapore to increase responsiveness. Operations are centralized for the purpose of speed and responsiveness, not for the intention of cost reduction as in traditional industries. Compaq does not choose to locate large-scale production in countries like Thailand or Malaysia, even though labor costs are lower there.

This kind of industry structure makes sense when it is noted that, in fast-cycle industries, less efficient manufacturing processes can outperform more efficient manufacturing processes if it allows the company to get more product to market quickly, before price erosion sets in. Thus, a more flexible process, as long as it is time-responsive, can do better than traditional approaches that still rely on long production runs and spreading fixed costs over a limited number of product variations. Because a PC is a relatively simple product to make, with most components available from a variety of vendors, it can be duplicated quickly in many countries around the globe. In these environments, when time-to-market is critical, international operations stress responsiveness and flexibility over the traditional benefits of efficiency and bargaining power.

The lack of national differences in customer requirements is another part of the reason that Compaq can move quickly on an international scale. As there are few cultural or usage-based international barriers in the personal computer industry, domestic competitive advantage is both readily exportable, and at the same time, effective against fast-cycle competitors potentially operating anywhere in the world.

In this way we can understand why organizations that historically have dominated international industries find the international PC market a difficult one in which to compete. IBM in the USA, NEC in Japan, and Olivetti in Europe provide examples of international organizations that had traditional first-mover advantages and more experience in international industries than organizations like Compaq but have, nevertheless, fallen behind. The growth barrier for these traditional companies has been the difficulty in mastering the non-traditional management styles of fast-cycle organizations. Thus, the key to fast-cycle internationalization is not to be found in traditional measures of international strength like economies of scale and adaptability to local cultures, but rather in the ability to respond quickly to wide swings in regional differences in demand, dynamic pricing, rapid entry and exit, fast-paced innovation, and the ability to cannibalize one's own products. On this basis, it would seem reasonable to expect that historical dominance in international industries is a poor predictor of who will dominate future fast-cycle markets.

Global Monopolist Mattel's Barbie

Mattel, the international toy maker, was founded by Harold Mattson and Elliot Handler, who began by making doll furniture in a California garage. Mattel's Barbie was introduced at the New York Toy Fair in 1959, where it was said that the doll would never catch on. By 1994, Mattel's Barbie was Mattel's largest and most profitable product line, accounting for 34 percent of its business. Mattel's Barbie doll is an international cultural standard and has become the world's most popular toy, with production rates of over 55,000 per day.

Mattel's Barbie dominates the fashion doll market segment of the toy industry in over 100 countries and half of Mattel Barbie's sales are outside the United States. Worldwide sales in 1997 were $1.9 billion, with more than 600 million Barbies having been sold since its inception.[2] Mattel has offices and facilities in 36 countries and sells its products in 140 nations. In international toy markets, often characterized by rapid change and cultural preferences that prevent globalization, no product has even approached Mattel Barbie's overwhelming international dominance during its four-decade history.

Mattel Barbie's emergence as a global monopolist coincided with the post-war period in the United States, when the concept of a teenage lifestyle was emerging for the first time in history. Mattel's Barbie is forever 19 years old, and with her fashion consciousness, striking accessories, and affluent lifestyle, she represented the values of young, newly affluent, female Americans of the first suburban television generation. These values have changed little in the past 40 years. With exaggerated proportions (life-size she would be 39–18–32), blue eyes, and blonde hair, she has traces of American idols like Marilyn Monroe, Grace Kelly, and Jayne Mansfield.[3] As this Americanized image became the focus of millions of teenage girls in the United States, and as American movies, fashion, and culture spread worldwide, Mattel's Barbie image became the first worldwide teen fashion standard.

Establishing Mattel's Barbie as a world standard was a gradual process characterized by trial and error. When Barbie was introduced in Japan in the early 1980s, she was specifically designed for the Japanese market as "Moba Barbie" that resembled Japan's leading doll, Jenny, who had gentle features such as doe brown eyes, an upturned nose, and a girlish figure. Moba Barbie was not successful, only gaining 5 percent of the market against Jenny's 75 percent. Japan was the only market where Mattel's managers deviated from the standard Mattel Barbie, as they were not sure that Japan had accepted Western culture as embodied in Barbie's looks and appeal. After market tests showed that Japanese attitudes might be open to Western looks, Mattel launched traditional Barbie models into the Japanese market with greater success. They also learned through market research that Japanese girls did not know how to play with Barbie, so Mattel used commercials to show Japanese girls how to play with the dolls, an approach that proved particularly successful.

Competitors attempted to imitate the Mattel Barbie standard. Hasbro conceded to the Barbie standard when they created Maxie, who looked like Mattel's Barbie but was younger, and could fit into Barbie's clothes even though she had her own wardrobe. This strategy did not work, however, as mothers were adverse to buying a product that resembled Mattel's Barbie but was not the real thing. Hasbro's Jem doll was slightly bigger than Mattel's Barbie but only popular in her first year. Not only could she not wear Barbie's clothing, but she was too trendy, having a punk rock look that did not appeal across the world. In Great Britain, competitors revamped the Sindy doll to resemble her American counterpart. The former girlish, plain-looking doll parted with her sensible wardrobe and streaked her brown hair blonde and became fashionable. She ended up looking very similar to the American Barbie. Mattel responded with legal action, taking out injunctions across Europe until Sindy was forced to abandon her Mattel Barbie look.

Mattel continues to expand Barbie into a range of Barbie-related products across the world, from children's clothing to Christmas ornaments, thus capitalizing on the Mattel Barbie world standard. Mattel has been successful in using a "staircasing" strategy (Williams, 1998) to extend Mattel Barbie's market ownership to a wide range of applications. The central profit center for Mattel's Barbie is her accessories. A Mattel Barbie can be purchased for as little as $5, but her glamorous outfits, shoes, jewelry, and other fashion staples cost more than the doll itself. More than 20 million pairs of shoes are purchased for her each year, along with a comparable number of outfits. Her other props include dream homes, pink convertibles, shops, and offices. She has also held a wide assortment of jobs, from McDonald's worker to doctor, and has joined 19 universities as cheerleader, all of which provide additional revenue platforms.

By focusing on brand ownership and staircasing strategies, slow-cycle international organizations like Mattel do not sustain advantage through centralized control and economies of scale. Manufacturing is widely dispersed across relatively small facilities. Seventy-five percent of Mattel's total product volume is produced in 15 company-owned plants that are dispersed across seven countries: Malaysia, Indonesia, China, Italy, Mexico, the USA, and England. Its overseas production sites are not particularly large or capital intensive. Local sourcing provides shipping cost savings, and to some degree the flexibility to adjust the product for regional preferences. (For example, in Egypt, "Egyptian Queen" Barbie was a response to local preferences.) Although operations are geographically dispersed, Mattel requires far less operational integration of international operations as do faster-cycle counterparts American Airlines and Compaq Computer. Barriers to entry are sustained with relatively little emphasis on cost controls, speed, or manufacturing efficiency.

Europe is Mattel's largest international market, with its highest sales in Germany, France, and Italy. Mattel's international marketing network has been expanded to include organizations in Japan and Eastern Europe, and wholly-owned subsidiaries in Mexico and in most of the middle-to-high-income countries of the world. Products are marketed through distributors in certain parts of Latin America, the Middle East, and Southeast Asia.

Mattel's dispersed channels of distribution similarly require a low level of operational integration. Minimal requirements for speed associated with long-lived product inventory help to explain how organizations like Mattel expand into international markets through acquisitions and alliances that require a low degree of operational assimilation. Mattel acquired Fisher-Price in 1993, and the Kranso business and J.W. Spear & Sons plc a year later. Mattel has also concluded a strategic alliance with Disney, allowing Mattel to sell Disney-related toys worldwide.

With global market ownership, Mattel's level of international sustainable advantage is arguably among the highest of all international organizations. At the same time, in terms of management priorities, Mattel's level of operational integration is among the lowest of all international organizations. International organizations like Mattel operate as the international equivalent of modern-day "artisans."

Summary and conclusion

The management styles explored here are but a part of the emerging competitive landscape. They reflect factors that organizations face that are simultaneously economic, technological, and cultural, and thus, each management style is difficult to learn and hard to change. Consequently, together, they present a challenge for the international organization seeking to extend itself across diverse international settings. They raise questions as to how practices in the international organization can become mismatched when expanding into a new market if managers fail to adjust their practices to maintain alignment with the diverse sustainability conditions present in different countries. We know that conglomerates, for example, have recognized the need to simplify their management styles in the face of market complexities, even in a single national market. To take greater advantage of the competitive diversity in modern markets, international managers can ask the following questions.

How fast is advantage likely to be imitated in each of our markets? Is the speed of imitation and rate of convergence the same from country to country? The rate of innovation of the personal computer industry in America, for example, is faster than the rate of innovation in Japan, whereas the rate of innovation of the automobile industry is faster in Japan than in America. Japanese electronics organizations, like NEC in the early 1980s, which sought to gain and defend high market share, have experienced difficulties in fast-cycle industries where they have been reluctant to replace aging product lines fast enough. NEC's traditional priorities toward economies of scale and brand loyalty, rather than innovation, allowed faster-cycle organizations like Compaq to establish a foot-hold with traditionally loyal Japanese customers.

Are sustainability conditions changing in our markets? Airline deregulation led to the emergence of local monopolies in the United States, a development that was not foreseen by policy makers at the time of deregulation. Gate control, a strategy that requires a focus on capturing a geographical region through targeted routing and pricing practices, can turn a competitive market into a non-competitive market. Airline strategies leading to hub control were first ignored by regulators in the United States and Europe, only to become of great interest later, and in particular, to European air carriers concerned with the entry of American air carriers into European markets.

How much management diversity can our international organizations master? In multicycle rich organizations like Sony, Robert Bosch, and Hewlett Packard, managers are required to embrace a variety of management priorities and to govern across sophisticated, heterogeneous control systems. Consider the multicycle international organization, Sony. This company operates simultaneously in slow-cycle studio recording equipment, standard-cycle television receivers, and the fast-cycle handheld electronics market. This strategy has been described by company executives as a "one stop shopping" approach, in that the goal is to provide both content and delivery in the entertainment industry. Such an approach, however, even as it may offer opportunities, also presents an additional layer of complexity around the traditional question of how to "produce globally and sell locally." Multicycle management requires both the ability to master the range of competitive approaches required and, in terms of decision-making, the ability to recognize how businesses operating in different markets can reinforce each other.

Even with a multicycle tradition, organizations can face challenges when they seek to extend practices that are successful in one market into another market with different sustainability conditions. In the case of Sony, for example, managers may have set market share goals that were inappropriate in the case of its American entertainment subsidiary, Columbia Studios. The production of motion pictures is an artisan-like activity, not easily aided by economies of scale. When Sony took over Columbia Studios, Sony management set ambitious goals to build market share. After years of heavy investment in new film releases, high actor and manager salaries, and a volume-oriented approach, Columbia Studios management had turned in a mixed record. Similar performance problems were encountered when Matsushita imposed similar, volume-oriented goals on its American motion picture subsidiary, Universal Studios.

Still another international corporation, a large, medical products company, has had a difficult time implementing its international vision. Part of the reason is that the appropriate management styles are so different between its slow-cycle pharmaceuticals business and its standard-cycle consumer products operation. Performance goals and standards have been set in a uniform way. Although some differences are acknowledged between businesses, they must be defended rather than accepted as a basis for planning. Managers are struggling to achieve a "separate but equal" basis for each business as they seek to bring the diverse management styles of the company together. The problem of environmental complexity has been made more difficult by the success of still another type of business within the company that makes short-lived medical devices.

In summary, these examples of competitive diversity, based on sustainability conditions, illustrates how managers of international corporations face new challenges associated with crafting their company's international, multiproduct strategy. We have explored how an appreciation of competitive complexity can help managers adjust effectively to changes in the success drivers, required organizational capabilities, and the associated management practices required of businesses in the modern economy.

Notes

1 Compaq merged with Hewlitt-Packard in 2002.
2 If all the Mattel Barbies sold were placed end-to-end, they would circle the Earth three-and-a-half times.
3 In reality, Barbie's prototype was the less successful German Lili doll, which was inspired by a cartoon of the same name.

References

Porter, Michael E. (1980) *Competitive Strategy*, New York: Free Press.

Schumpeter, Joseph A. (1942) *Capitalism, Socialism, and Democracy*, New York, NY: Harper & Row.

Williams, Jeffrey R. (1998) *Renewable Advantage: Crafting Strategy Through Economic Time*, New York, NY: Free Press.

8

IMPLEMENTING LATERAL CENTRALIZATION AT THE FOREIGN SUBSIDIARY

The role of compensation and reward systems

Sharon Watson and Kendall Roth

Introduction

In recent years it has become evident that traditional organizational forms may no longer be sufficient for achieving or maintaining competitive advantage on a worldwide basis. Nowhere is this more evident than in the case of the multinational enterprise (MNE) operating in a global industry environment. Competing in a global industry requires extensive strategic co-ordination among the various subsidiaries of the MNE, resulting in a high level of interdependence between subsidiaries. This has led multinational firms to develop and implement strategies, structures, organizational processes, and systems that enable the firm to capitalize on the advantages of interdependencies that exist among its various sub-units, most clearly in differentiated network organizations.

Although there has been a great deal of attention paid to the organizational structure issues involved in implementing international strategies (Egelhoff, 1982; Stopford and Wells, 1972) it has become apparent that there is a need to focus on subsidiary managers and their role in the implementation process. This shift in focus has occurred because it is increasingly recognized that lower levels in the organization, such as the profit center or business unit, are the site of strategic renewal. Entrepreneurial processes at these levels operationally define the firm's competitive advantage. Extended to the foreign subsidiary or business unit, competitive advantage must be defined in such a manner that managers of these units respond simultaneously to local market conditions and act in accordance with a globally integrated corporate strategy (Bartlett and Ghoshal, 1989).

Prior to the recent dramatic globalization of many industries, the primary concern of the subsidiary manager was the performance of the subsidiary in the local market. Industry globalization has resulted in a redefined role for the subsidiary manager, wherein he or she is increasingly accountable for the contribution made by the subsidiary to the competitive position of the corporation as a whole. This is particularly true in multinational firms that exhibit an international network structure, in which the activities of any particular foreign subsidiary are highly interdependent with those of subsidiaries in other countries. In such international network corporations, managerial decisions and actions that take place in one location can have important ramifications for the operations and performance of other sub-units throughout the firm. Because of this major change, it has become increasingly important to focus on internal processes and human resources policies at the level of the foreign subsidiary.

If managers at the foreign subsidiary level are expected to contribute to the achievement of corporate level goals, then it is important for the MNE to have organizational systems and processes that encourage and facilitate subsidiary manager decisions that are consistent with such goals. One aspect of organizational design through which headquarters can greatly affect the subsidiary manager's perception and performance of his or her role is that of international human resources management practices (Edstrom and Galbraith, 1977; Kobrin, 1994; Rosenzweig and Nohria, 1994). In particular, it is increasingly recognized that the compensation and reward system is a key factor in the implementation of an organization's strategy and the accomplishment of its strategic objectives (Galbraith and Kazanjian, 1986; Schuler and MacMillan, 1984). Compensation and reward systems can be used to encourage the top management actions and behaviors necessary to meet the firm's objectives (Finkelstein and Hambrick, 1989). In the case of the foreign subsidiary manager, the compensation and reward system can be used to elicit or support those behaviors and decisions that are in accordance with the global strategic goals of the MNE as opposed to those that address only local market performance.

In this chapter we will discuss the results of a recent research study undertaken to better understand the role of compensation and reward systems in the implementation of different types of international strategies. First, we will examine the characteristics of foreign subsidiaries with two different strategic roles. The discussion will then focus on the elements of the compensation programs used to manage foreign subsidiaries with one of these two distinct strategic roles. Finally, we will present some of this study's implications for the management of foreign subsidiaries.

The research study

One way in which MNE managers have met the challenges of implementing a co-ordinated global strategy in the international network corporation is by differentiating the strategic roles and co-ordination mechanisms of the firm's various foreign subsidiaries (Ghoshal and Nohria, 1989; Gupta and Govindarajan, 1991). In this study, two distinct subsidiary roles are examined, global rationalization and lateral centralization. With global rationalization, the foreign subsidiary is a single part of a system rationalized worldwide, in which the responsibility for system co-ordination resides predominantly at headquarters. The foreign subsidiary performs only a subset of the value-adding activities of the MNE, producing a single component or product for further use or value addition by the other units of the multinational firm.

At the other extreme, with lateral centralization, the foreign subsidiary has worldwide responsibility for a complete set of value activities associated with a particular product or product line. The corporation's expertise for the product or product line resides in the subsidiary, with the subsidiary managing the research and development, production, and marketing activities on a global basis. Thus, strategic and operational activities are centralized and co-ordinated worldwide, but the critical point or focus of decision-making is at the subsidiary level, not at headquarters. Viewed at the corporate level, lateral centralization disperses the responsibilities for global decision-making throughout the organizational network, with responsibility for the value activities for different product lines being centralized at different subsidiary locations. Thus, one subsidiary can be a central node within the organizational network for a particular product line, while another subsidiary may be central for a different product. As is characteristic of network corporations with lateral centralization, corporate decision-making responsibility is dispersed throughout the organization at the subsidiary level.

In order to better understand the strategic and organizational implications of these two distinct foreign subsidiary roles, we obtained information from the senior managers of 100 different foreign subsidiaries operating in global industry environments. The subsidiaries were each competing in one of two industries – scientific measuring instruments and controls, or surgical and medical instruments – both of which are highly global industries, exhibiting extensive transnational integration (Kobrin, 1991). Subsidiaries from five different countries were used in this study: 40 foreign subsidiaries operating in the USA, 22 in the UK, 14 in Canada, 12 in Japan, and 12 in Germany. For each of the subsidiaries included in the study, the parent corporation had at least 51 percent ownership of the subsidiary and was domiciled in one of the other four countries. For example, subsidiaries in the USA were owned by either Japanese, German, Canadian, or British corporations.

To facilitate the comparison of subsidiaries based on their strategic role, the subsidiaries were classified into groups based on their responses to questions regarding subsidiary responsibilities. The following presentation of the study's findings first compares subsidiaries with a role of lateral centralization to those with a role of global rationalization. This section highlights the differences in the organizational characteristics of the two groups of subsidiaries as well as their relational attributes, or relationships with corporate headquarters. The next section details how the two groups of foreign subsidiaries differ in the compensation and reward systems that are used to motivate subsidiary management and employees. (A more detailed description of the methodology used in this research study can be found in Appendix 8.1.)

Characteristics of lateral centralization and global rationalization

As the foreign subsidiary's strategic role is increasingly characterized by lateral centralization, there are significant implications for several of the inter-relationships between the subsidiary and the rest of the multinational organization. Table 8.1 summarizes several of the distinctive differences in operating characteristics and headquarters–subsidiary relationships that were found between subsidiaries characterized by lateral centralization and those that are part of a system of global rationalization. The information in this table provides a useful starting point for a more complete description of these two types of international strategic roles.

Table 8.1 Characteristics of foreign subsidiaries: lateral centralization versus global rationalization

Variable	Lateral centralization	Global rationalization
Operating characteristics		
Percentage of subsidiary's purchases from entities within the corporation	Low (9.5)	High (67.6)
Percentage of subsidiary's products also produced by the parent	Low (4.7)	High (74.6)
Percentage of subsidiary sales that are international	High (36.5)	Low (20.8)
Subsidiary size (number of employees)	High (798)	Low (309)
Relational attributes		
Subsidiary decision-making autonomy	High	Low
Subsidiary–parent conflict	Low	High
Subsidiary manager's commitment to the parent organization	Low	High
Cultural distance between parent and subsidiary	Low	High

Differences in operating characteristics

As indicated by the operating characteristics in Table 8.1, subsidiaries that are characterized by lateral centralization were found to exhibit a greater degree of operational independence and autonomy than those that are part of a globally rationalized system. Those foreign subsidiaries that exhibit a high degree of lateral centralization make a significantly lower percentage of their purchases from entities within the MNE. As indicated by the scale used to measure international strategy (see Appendix 8.1), with lateral centralization, R&D, production, and marketing responsibilities for a given product or product line are centralized at the foreign subsidiary. Thus, lateral centralization results in fewer intra-firm product exchanges.

Conversely, global rationalization results in a high level of intra-firm purchases, as the foreign subsidiary performs only a subset of the value-adding activities of the system. In performing its function, such a subsidiary purchases a high percentage of its inputs from other corporate entities, completes its portion of the value-added, and, in turn, may then sell or transfer its outputs to still other corporate entities so that they may continue the value-adding process.

Additionally, as shown in Table 8.1, lateral centralization is characterized by fewer of the subsidiary's products also being produced by the parent. The parent headquarters is not directly involved in the operations or administration of that product, so it is less likely that it would be producing many of the same products as the subsidiary. Such is not the case with a globally rationalized system, where headquarters and several different subsidiaries may all be contributing to the same product or product line, albeit through different value-adding activities.

The finding that the laterally centralized subsidiaries have a higher percentage of international sales than their globally rationalized counterparts underscores the notion that, with lateral centralization, a subsidiary has worldwide responsibility for its product line. These subsidiaries develop, produce, and market their products for use on a global basis. They do not merely market internationally a product that was originally developed for the local market but, rather, they take the lead in developing a product intended for worldwide sale from its inception. With lateral centralization, the global market, not the home market of the subsidiary, is the primary focus throughout the development and production of the subsidiary's product. This type of global focus at the sub-unit level is characteristic of "transnational" organizations, in which particular sub-unit competencies are leveraged to reap worldwide benefits (Bartlett and Ghoshal, 1989).

It is interesting to note one additional organizational characteristic that was found to differ between the two groups of subsidiaries: size. On average, subsidiaries characterized by lateral centralization are much larger than their globally rationalized counterparts, with an average of 798 employees versus 309 employees in the other group. This size difference is likely due to the wide range of functional responsibilities that are centralized at the subsidiary level. A subsidiary with worldwide R&D, production, and marketing responsibilities for a product line must be large enough to perform all of those functions.

Differences in relational attributes

In addition to exhibiting different organizational characteristics, the two groups of foreign subsidiaries also differ in several attributes of the headquarters–subsidiary relationship. As indicated in Table 8.1, subsidiaries characterized by lateral centralization exhibit a high degree of decision-making authority, with decisions regarding R&D, production, and marketing being made independently by the subsidiary. Conversely, in a system of global rationalization, a greater amount of co-ordination is needed to ensure the smooth flow of parts, components, and products through the value-adding system. With global rationalization, decisions tend to be co-ordinated on a worldwide basis rather than being made independently by the subsidiary. It is quite likely that the difficulties inherent in such worldwide co-ordination of decisions result in the higher level of subsidiary–parent conflict exhibited by subsidiaries in a system of global rationalization. These subsidiaries play an important role in the value-adding process, yet they have little decision-making authority, as decisions are co-ordinated by headquarters on a worldwide basis. With lateral centralization, the focal subsidiary for a product has worldwide authority over decisions regarding its product or product line. Therefore, little conflict is experienced between the subsidiary and the parent corporation. In the case of lateral centralization, the subsidiary's role and domain of authority appear to be more clearly delineated, so fewer disagreements arise.

Although the level of subsidiary conflict is lower with lateral centralization, so, unfortunately, is the level of commitment that the subsidiary manager displays toward the parent company. Again, this is likely due to the autonomy and authority that the subsidiary has regarding its primary product line. The subsidiary manager's responsibility is to the worldwide success of the subsidiary's dominant product or product line. It is not surprising that he or she exhibits a low level of commitment to the parent organization as compared to managers of subsidiaries in a system of global rationalization. What is not clear is whether this lack of commitment to the parent organization has any detrimental effects on the performance of the MNE as a whole.

Finally, Table 8.1 indicates one additional attribute of the headquarters–

subsidiary relationship for subsidiaries in this study that are high in lateral central-ization. Subsidiaries that are given the worldwide responsibility for a product or product line tend to be those that are in countries that are culturally close to the home country of the parent. Countries are "culturally close" when they are similar along the four cultural dimensions of individualism, uncertainty avoidance, power distance, and masculinity/femininity (Hofstede, 1980). MNE top management seems to be less willing to give this kind of responsibility to a subsidiary in a cultur-ally distant country. In a truly "transnational" organization, nationality would not be a factor when giving a subsidiary a worldwide product mandate; such decisions would be made based on the market characteristics and the capabilities and distinc-tive competencies of the individual subsidiaries in the multinational network, regardless of national borders (Bartlett and Ghoshal, 1989). This study suggests that many MNE corporate managers have not yet developed a transnational mind-set or geocentric orientation, but remain to a large extent home-country oriented (Perl-mutter, 1969), confining worldwide product line responsibilities to subsidiaries located in markets culturally similar to their own.

As Table 8.1 clearly demonstrates, subsidiaries with a strategic role of lateral cen-tralization differ markedly on several characteristics from those that have a global rationalization role. Effectively implementing international strategies that incorpo-rate these two very different strategic roles will require different sets of organ-izational processes and designs. One aspect of organizational design that is now seen to be extremely important in the implementation of a firm's strategic object-ives is human resources management, an important dimension of which is the firm's compensation and reward system. Reward systems are pivotal in the motiva-tion, attraction, and retention of the human resources that are so vital to the suc-cessful attainment of a firm's goals (Lawler, 1981). Such systems are particularly important in the international context, as subsidiary managers are given a great deal of autonomy at dispersed geographic locations. This makes direct monitoring difficult, yet the desire is for their actions to support or represent both corporate and subsidiary objectives. The next section of this chapter examines several characteristics of foreign subsidiary compensation policy and how they are related to the subsidiary's international strategic role.

The role of compensation in implementing lateral centralization

Managers as well as researchers increasingly recognize that the compensation and reward system is a key factor in the implementation of an organization's strategy and the accomplishment of its strategic objectives. One of the objectives of human resources managers is to tie compensation and reward systems to the organization's operating objectives and strategies (Balkin and Gomez-Mejia, 1990). The previous discussion of the difference between lateral centralization and global rationalization demonstrates, as do several international management research studies (Ghoshal and Nohria, 1989; Gupta and Govindarajan, 1991), that different business units or subsidiaries within the MNE can and do have different strategic roles and objectives. It follows that the managers at the business unit level may need to be motivated to perform different tasks, depending on the strategic role of the subsidiary. Thus, compensation policies should differ at the subsidiary level, based on the desired managerial behaviors necessary to implement the strategy of the particular business unit (Roth and O'Donnell, 1996).

The behaviors and decisions that are required of the foreign subsidiary manager to effectively implement a lateral centralization strategy are quite different from those required for a strategy of global rationalization. Therefore, it is expected that the compensation and reward systems of these two types of subsidiaries should differ, in order to elicit the managerial behaviors required for each respective strategy. Our study demonstrates these differences. As indicated in Table 8.2, several elements of subsidiary compensation do, indeed, differ significantly between subsidiaries characterized by lateral centralization and those that are part of a system of global rationalization. These elements are divided into three categories, the structure of the compensation paid to the subsidiary top management team, the structure of the compensation paid to all subsidiary employees, and the criteria used to determine compensation for the top management team.

Compensation structure for subsidiary top management

Concerning the subsidiary top management team, one of the most evident differences between the two groups of subsidiaries is in the percentage of the top

Table 8.2 Characteristics of the foreign subsidiary compensation program: lateral centralization versus global rationalization

Compensation variable	Lateral centralization	Global rationalization
Subsidiary top management team compensation structure		
Salary as percentage of subsidiary TMT compensation[a]	Low (74.3)	High (82.3)
Incentives as percentage of subsidiary TMT compensation	High (24.4)	Low (17.7)
Bonus as percentage of subsidiary TMT compensation	High (22.2)	Low (15.5)
Short-term bonus	(19.5)	(14.7)
Long-term bonus	(2.7)	(0.9)
Equity incentives as percentage of subsidiary TMT compensation	Low (2.3)	Low (2.1)
Short-term equity	(0.1)	(1.5)
Long-term equity	(2.1)	(0.6)
Total subsidiary compensation structure		
Salary as percentage of total subsidiary compensation	High (91.5)	Low (87.5)
Incentives as percentage of total subsidiary employee compensation	Low (7.8)	High (12.4)
Subsidiary top management team compensation criteria		
Percentage of TMT total compensation based on regional or corporate performance	Low (5.7)	High (10.5)
Percentage of TMT incentive compensation based on regional or corporate performance	Low (13.4)	High (24.9)

Note

a In some cases the percentages do not add up to 100 due to an additional "other" category on the questionnaire.

management team compensation package that is made up of fixed salary versus incentive compensation. Both groups of subsidiaries emphasize salary over incentives; however, for subsidiaries that are part of a globally rationalized system, fixed salary is a substantially greater percentage of the top management team's compensation. Conversely, the percentage of subsidiary top management team compensation that is made up of incentives is greater for subsidiaries employing a strategy of lateral centralization. These differences in incentive pay between the two groups become clearer when the incentive portion of the top management team compensation package is broken down into its various components. Regardless of the subsidiary's strategic role, most of the top management's incentive pay is in the form of bonus, in particular short-term bonus. However, the subsidiaries with a lateral centralization role use more of both short- and long-term bonus than do those with a role of global rationalization. Equity incentives do not seem to be utilized at the subsidiary level, as the top management teams of both groups receive only about 2 percent of their compensation in equity form. Interestingly, the two groups differ in how that equity compensation is structured. For the lateral centralization role, the equity incentive is primarily long-term equity, while for the global rationalization role, it is more heavily weighted toward short-term equity.

The differences in compensation systems used in these two cases can be explained in terms of agency theory. The greater emphasis on incentive compensation for the top management team of subsidiaries with a lateral centralization strategy is consistent with the behavior desired to support this strategy, which must be more long-term and strategic in nature. The subsidiary top management team has broad responsibility for its product or product line and a high level of decision-making autonomy and managerial discretion. This is accompanied by a greater variety of increased decision options, resulting in less programmable managerial behavior. As managers are less constrained in their decision-making, the monitoring of managerial work is more difficult (Rajagopalan and Finkelstein, 1992) and the potential for opportunistic behavior and managerial shirking become greater.

Incentive compensation serves as a means through which to encourage the appropriate managerial decisions and behaviors in situations where direct monitoring is difficult or costly, and this fits the needs of foreign subsidiaries with lateral centralization strategies. Conversely, as part of a system of global rationalization, a subsidiary's specific role must be more clearly delineated, as will be the goals and tasks of the subsidiary management team. The subsidiary is interdependent with other entities within the firm, and its actions and outcomes are relatively visible within the globally linked system. Specialized strategic knowledge for managing the globally rationalized system is headquarters-based, with the responsibilities of subsidiary managers being more task-oriented or operational in nature. Because decisions and actions by managers of such subsidiaries can be monitored more easily, incentives are less valuable as motivators.

Although the laterally centralized subsidiaries use more long-term incentives in their top management team reward systems than do those that are globally rationalized, the percentage of the compensation package that is made up of long-term incentives is surprisingly low in both cases. Despite these subsidiaries' strategic emphasis on long-term issues such as worldwide product and market development, only 4.9 percent of the top management team's compensation comes from incentives based on long-term performance. This finding may be due to the fact that the percentage reflects the long-term incentives of the top management *team*, not just the subsidiary top manager. It may be that the president or managing director of the subsidiary receives a greater proportion of his or her compensation in the form of long-term incentives than do other members of the top management team. Or, it could be that long-term performance is not regarded by such corporations as a useful measure.

Compensation structure for all subsidiary employees

The findings concerning incentive compensation are somewhat different when the compensation structure for all subsidiary employees is examined, rather than just that of the top management team. Interestingly, the use of incentives in the subsidiary-wide compensation program also differs between the two strategy types, but in the *reverse* direction. In terms of the compensation paid to *all* subsidiary employees, the percentage paid in the form of incentives is greater for subsidiaries in a globally rationalized system than it is for those with a lateral centralization role. Within a global system, the use of incentive compensation extends to lower levels within the foreign subsidiary. Members of the top management team receive an average of 17.7 percent of their compensation in incentive form, while for all subsidiary employees the average drops only a few points to 12.4 percent. In subsidiaries with a role of lateral centralization, incentive pay is used primarily for the top management team. At this level, incentives comprise 24.4 percent of pay, but when all subsidiary employees are included, the percentage drops to 7.8 percent. Clearly, incentive compensation is not being used to a great extent for lower level employees in such subsidiaries.

These findings are probably due to the nature of the strategic interdependencies that exist with the two different strategic roles. With global rationalization, the foreign subsidiary is a single part of a system that is strategically planned and co-ordinated by headquarters. The foreign subsidiary is interdependent with other subsidiaries within the multinational network; however, these interdependencies result from the co-ordination that is necessary at the functional and task levels. It is not only subsidiary top management that is involved in the cooperative exchanges that occur between subsidiaries, but also individuals at the functional and task levels, who must understand and act in accordance with corporate-wide goals. A critical implementation issue in managing this type of global interdependence is the development of a "shared vision and personal commitment to integrate the organization at the fundamental level of individual members" (O'Donnell, 2000). The greater use of incentives throughout all levels of the subsidiary is a tool with which to facilitate the development of this shared vision at the functional and operational, as well as managerial, levels.

By contrast, the laterally centralized subsidiary is the central decision making point for worldwide strategic activities concerning the mandated product. It is senior subsidiary executives, rather than individuals at lower levels, who make important product line decisions that can affect the firm's worldwide operations. Thus, incentive compensation is directed at upper level management in laterally centralized subsidiaries. Additionally, because decisions and activities for a particular product are centralized at such subsidiaries, functional and operational tasks for that product are not necessarily interdependent with the activities of other subsidiaries. Therefore, incentive compensation may be less valuable at lower levels, where employee responsibilities are primarily operational in nature, rather than strategic.

Criteria for top management team compensation

Another interesting way in which the compensation programs of the two groups of subsidiaries differ is in the criteria used to determine the compensation for the top management team. Table 8.2 also indicates the percentage of top management team compensation that is based on regional or corporate performance, as opposed to individual or subsidiary performance. The subsidiaries that are part of a globally rationalized system use regional and/or corporate performance as evaluation criteria for both total compensation and incentive pay to a much greater extent than do subsidiaries characterized by lateral centralization. Regional and corporate performance are used to determine nearly 25 percent of the incentive compensation awarded to the top management team of foreign global subsidiaries of a globally rationalized system, whereas they are used as the criteria for only 13 percent of incentive pay in subsidiaries with a lateral centralization role. Correspondingly, the laterally centralized subsidiaries place a greater emphasis on the performance of the subsidiary or the individual manager in the determination of managerial incentive compensation.

These findings are in line with the distinctly different managerial responsibilities required for the two different strategic roles that the foreign subsidiaries play. As part of a globally rationalized system, a foreign subsidiary is often highly interconnected with other subsidiaries, with the performance of its specific role being affected by the performance of other subsidiaries that are upstream in the system. Likewise, its performance influences the performance of downstream subsidiaries. Because of the interlinked nature of the roles of different international subsidiaries in a globally rationalized network, it is important for subsidiary managers to realize the importance of their subsidiary's contribution to corporate goals, as system optimization is critical. Thus, making compensation at the subsidiary management level contingent on regional or corporate performance underscores the importance of the subsidiary's role in the overall system.

The performance of the subsidiary characterized by lateral centralization is equally important in the overall corporate strategy, but strategic responsibilities are now centralized at the foreign subsidiary. Compared to global rationalization, the performance of the subsidiary with a lateral centralization strategy is more self-determined, given the subsidiary's greater strategic autonomy. It contributes to corporate goals by being an innovator and by being the global leader in its particular product or product line. Subsidiary management is concerned primarily with the performance of its particular product, and because this responsibility is centralized at the subsidiary level, it is subsidiary-level performance that most directly reflects this responsibility. Thus, the incentive compensation of the top management team of such subsidiaries is based less on regional and corporate performance.

The actual percentage of subsidiary top management compensation that is determined by regional or corporate performance raises several questions. For the subsidiaries in this study, on average, only 7.5 percent of the total compensation paid to subsidiary top management (including salary and incentives), is based on regional or corporate performance, with the remainder being determined by individual or subsidiary performance. It appears that, despite all of the talk about the importance of global performance, international managers are still being rewarded primarily on a "multidomestic" basis. Little is being done to tie the decisions of foreign subsidiary managers to regional or corporate goals. This finding is particularly salient given that the study was conducted within industries that have been highly globalized for some time. Two of the possible explanations for the low usage of regional or corporate performance goals are the following:

1 it is not clear to headquarters managers that regional or corporate performance criteria have any impact on organizational outcomes; or
2 top managers believe that such performance criteria are important, but they have not yet implemented such a reward system because its implementation is difficult to accomplish.

Evidence from this research study can be used to explore each of these possible explanations.

Using regional and corporate performance as compensation criteria

To explore the effects of using regional or corporate performance as criteria in the determination of subsidiary management compensation, the 100 foreign subsidiaries were divided into two groups: those that did not use corporate or regional performance in the design of subsidiary compensation policies; and those that did rely on corporate or regional performance, however slightly. Table 8.3 presents some of the differences between these two groups of subsidiaries.

The two groups of subsidiaries differ significantly on several organizational characteristics. The subsidiaries in which corporate or regional performance is used in the determination of managerial compensation tend, on average, to be larger than those in which these criteria are not used. Additionally, the parent corporations of these subsidiaries tend to be somewhat smaller. The combination of these

Table 8.3 Characteristics of foreign subsidiaries: the use of regional and corporate performance criteria

Characteristic	Regional/corporate performance criteria	
	Are used	*Are not used*
Subsidiary size	High	Low
Parent size	Low	High
Subsidiary decision-making authority	High	Low
Subsidiary performance – ROI	High	Low
Subsidiary performance – increase in sales	High	Low
Parent–subsidiary conflict	High	Low

two factors indicates that corporate and regional performance criteria tend to be used in those foreign subsidiaries that have a more dominant or visible position within the MNE's network of subsidiaries. Larger subsidiaries have the ability to leverage their dominant position within the MNE to set and pursue their own goals, which may not be in the best interest of the corporation as a whole. It may be that regional and corporate performance criteria tend to be used by headquarters for managers in these relatively dominant subsidiaries to encourage them to work toward corporate goals rather than to only pursue the local interests of the sub-sidiary. It appears as though these criteria are used primarily in cases where there is a greater risk of the subsidiary pursuing its own local goals over those of the MNE as a whole. This line of reasoning is further supported by another entry in Table 8.3, which indicates that those subsidiaries in which corporate and regional perfor-mance criteria are used also have more decision-making autonomy. Again, corpor-ate or regional performance criteria may be perceived as being more important in cases where the subsidiary manager has a greater ability to shape subsidiary perfor-mance through such decision-making authority.

The use of regional and corporate performance criteria in the determination of subsidiary management compensation is also related to several organizational out-comes. Most importantly, the two groups of subsidiaries differ in performance. Those subsidiaries in which corporate or regional performance criteria are used perform better on two different measures: return on investment and increase in annual sales. The cross-sectional nature of this research study precludes any causal conclusion, so it is difficult to say whether these performance evaluation criteria are determining factors in the higher level of subsidiary performance. Table 8.3 also indicates that a higher level of subsidiary–parent conflict is experienced in those subsidiaries that utilize corporate or regional performance criteria. It is quite likely that much of this conflict is due to the dual pressures faced by foreign subsidiary managers – pressures to be locally responsive versus pressures to achieve corporate goals. Having a portion of the manager's compensation package determined by local performance and part by corporate performance highlights the dual nature of these pressures. These findings regarding subsidiary performance and parent–subsidiary conflict demonstrate that the use of corporate and regional performance criteria in the determination of subsidiary manager compensation *is* related to organizational outcomes, yet the precise nature of these relationships warrants further research.

It is also clear from comments by subsidiary and corporate managers that it is dif-ficult to implement a compensation program that incorporates corporate or regional performance. Several managers at both the subsidiary and corporate level commented on difficulties they had experienced in trying to design compensation systems that reward subsidiary managers based on corporate performance. One sub-sidiary human resources manager cited the most pressing problem as "difficulty in establishing a simple incentive program for manufacturing employees." Human resources managers at the corporate level stressed the importance of local input in the design of the reward system, with several managers indicating that it is import-ant to be aware of local norms and competitive practices. All of the managers who participated in this research study recognized the importance of a properly designed reward system, but several indicated that their current system had been in place for a long time and was unlikely to be changed in the near future. In one case, subsidiary compensation policies were the same as those at the parent, which had not changed in 50 years. These examples indicate that managers believe that compensation and reward systems can have an impact on the achievement of corporate and subsidiary goals, but that it is difficult to design and implement reward systems that are properly aligned with the strategic goals of both the subsidiary and the MNE as a whole.

Conclusion

Industry conditions have undergone dramatic changes in recent years, especially in global industries such as the scientific and medical instruments industries examined in this study. MNE managers and their foreign subsidiary managers appear to have recognized these industry changes, and some have made corresponding changes in their corporate and subsidiary level strategies. However, the results of this study suggest that the implementation of some of the organizational processes and systems to support these strategic changes has not yet reached down to the foreign subsidiary level. In particular, it is evident that many MNEs are having difficulty in designing appropriate compensation and reward systems for use at their foreign subsidiaries.

On the other hand, some companies have redesigned their compensation policies to better reflect their current worldwide strategies and goals. For example, a European pharmaceutical firm that dramatically reorganized after a series of international mergers in the late 1980s also redesigned its compensation system for international executives. Twenty-five percent of the compensation package for an international area manager consists of incentives based on corporate performance. Similarly, 25 percent of a country manager's compensation is based on regional performance as opposed to being based solely on local performance. This firm also has a specific measurement formula to determine international executives' performance and their related incentive bonus.

A large US high-tech manufacturing MNE has taken a different approach. This firm has a matrix structure in which international managers have dual reporting responsibilities. They report to both a country manager and a product line manager. The firm's compensation policies are structured such that a dual-reporting manager receives incentives tied to the performance of the product division as well as the geographic unit. Additionally, the incentive structure is not applied uniformly across all geographic regions or product lines. For example, in emerging markets, the incentives are tied more closely to geographic performance than in industrialized countries. Similarly, managers of product lines that tend to rely less on locally responsive marketing techniques and more on global standardization receive more incentives based on worldwide product division performance than on geographic performance. The same firm also has the strategic roles of its different foreign subsidiaries differentiated based on the unique competencies of select locations. Three of its subsidiaries with lateral centralization roles include a French subsidiary with worldwide responsibility for chemicals, a German subsidiary charged with mechanical R&D, and a Japanese subsidiary specializing in electronic imaging for a global market.

While most firms focus on financial incentives based on numeric performance targets to influence subsidiary management decisions and actions, we found several MNEs that use other types of incentives. For example, an American telecommunications firm has several explicitly stated corporate values which have been translated into the local language at each international subsidiary. Subsidiary managers can receive corporate rewards for demonstrating support of and adherence to these values. Some of the rewards are non-financial, such as recognition awards and inclusion in regional or worldwide management development activities. Although the current study focused on the use of financial incentives, it appears as though non-financial incentives may also be useful tools for motivating managers at foreign subsidiaries. This may be particularly true for international network corporations in which different foreign subsidiaries are highly dependent on one another and in which activities at one subsidiary can have a significant effect on the firm's worldwide operations.

As demonstrated by these examples and the results of this research study, internal organizational systems for motivating international subsidiary managers to make decisions that benefit the corporation as a whole can take a variety of forms. The primary concern for MNE headquarters executives should be to identify the strategic roles that different subsidiaries perform within the corporate network and to link compensation and reward policies for each subsidiary to specific outcomes. Given that strategic roles and performance outcomes often differ across subsidiaries, it may be necessary to design reward systems that are subsidiary-specific, with only certain elements that are common across locations.

Design of effective processes and systems at the subsidiary level is of utmost importance given the changes occurring in many complex multinational organizations. The need for attention to organizational processes at this level is increasing as the role of the foreign subsidiary manager evolves from that of the traditional implementer of headquarters-determined decisions to the primary initiator of new opportunities for the corporation (Bartlett and Ghoshal, 1993; Birkinshaw, Hood, and Jonsson, 1998). In organizations encompassing subsidiaries with the strategic role of lateral centralization, initiative and entrepreneurial activity flow from the subsidiary level. If entrepreneurial processes and organizational renewal are increasingly defined at lower levels within the organization and this renewal is consistent with and driven by corporate values, then corporations must begin to provide better alignment between the espoused values and the systems which support behaviors consistent with these values.

Appendix 8.1: research methodology

Data collection

The data for this research study were collected in two stages. In the first stage, we identified all of the foreign subsidiaries in the USA, Canada, the UK, Germany, and Japan in the scientific measuring instrument and medical instrument industries, whose parent corporations were headquartered in one of the other four countries. A mail questionnaire was then sent to the senior manager of each subsidiary for which a contact name could be identified. After verification of the names and addresses, the final sample consisted of 372 subsidiaries, from which we received 100 usable responses. This questionnaire requested information on the international strategy, compensation policies, and performance of the subsidiary.

To ensure the validity of the data collected from the subsidiary manager in the first stage, a second set of data was collected in which some of the same information was requested from additional respondents, also via mail questionnaire. To verify the information on subsidiary strategy and performance for each of the 100 responding subsidiaries, we sent a questionnaire to the headquarters manager responsible for operations at that subsidiary (in most cases this was the V.P. of International Operations). To verify the compensation information, a follow-up questionnaire was sent to the subsidiary human resources manager or the headquarters human resources manager. Tests for inter-rater reliability indicated that the information collected from the subsidiary manager on international strategy, compensation, and subsidiary performance was reliable.

Measures

Several of the variables in this study were measured using multi-item scales which are detailed below.

International strategy was measured with an eight-item index (Roth and Morrison, 1992). The higher the score on this index, the more the subsidiary exhibits a strategic role of lateral centralization. Respondents were asked to indicate on a scale of 1 to 5 how characteristic the following statements were in describing the responsibilities of the subsidiary:

1   the subsidiary is primarily an implementor of headquarters-developed strategy;
2   the subsidiary has worldwide responsibility for production activities of a product or product line;
3   product expertise within the corporation resides within this subsidiary;
4   the subsidiary maintains control over the export marketing of products;
5   production process innovations are developed by the subsidiary;
6   the subsidiary has worldwide responsibility for marketing activities of a product or product line;
7   the subsidiary controls product research and development activities;
8   international market development costs are incurred by the subsidiary.

To measure *subsidiary decision-making authority*, respondents were asked to indicate on a scale of 1 to 3, for 23 decisions activities, how the decision was co-ordinated within the corporation, with 1 = decision made by the subsidiary, and 3 = decision co-ordinated worldwide (Gates and Egelhoff, 1986). Lower scores on this index reflected higher subsidiary decision-making authority. Sample decision activities include the following: changes in product design, advertising, and promotion decisions, decisions regarding quality control, decision to significantly increase inventories, short-term borrowing, choice of suppliers, hiring top management in the subsidiary, and entering new markets outside the country.

Parent–subsidiary conflict was measured with an eight-item scale in which respondents were asked to indicate on a scale of 1 to 5, where 1 = never and 5 = often, how often disagreements between the subsidiary and the parent or regional head-quarters occurred on the following dimensions (Van de Ven and Ferry, 1980):

1   over the strategy of business;
2   regarding specific ways work is done or services are provided;
3   about specific terms of the relationship between the subsidiary and headquarters;
4   regarding investment/capital allocation decisions;
5   about cash flow repatriation levels;
6   regarding quality standards;
7   regarding innovation/product development priorities;
8   about the specific charter of the subsidiary.

The subsidiary manager's *commitment to the parent* was measured with a previously used scale (Gregerson and Black, 1992) and is based on prior measures of organizational commitment (Mowday, Porter, and Steers, 1982).

The *cultural distance* between the subsidiary and the parent countries was calculated for each country pair using an equation that incorporates Hofstede's (1980) four dimensions of culture: individualism, masculinity, uncertainty avoidance, and power distance (Kogut and Singh, 1988).

References

Balkin, D.B. and L.R. Gomez-Mejia (1990) "Matching compensation and organizational strategies," *Strategic Management Journal*, 11: 153–169.

Bartlett, C.A. and S. Ghoshal (1989) *Managing Across Borders: The Transnational Solution*, Boston, MA: Harvard Business School Press.

Bartlett, C.A. and S. Ghoshal (1993) "Beyond the M-form: toward a managerial theory of the firm," *Strategic Management Journal*, 14: 23–46.

Birkinshaw, J., N. Hood, and S. Jonsson (1998) "Building firm-specific advantages in multinational corporations: The role of subsidiary initiative," *Strategic Management Journal*, 19: 221–241.

Edstrom, A. and J.R. Galbraith (1977) "Transfer of managers as a coordination and control strategy in multinational organizations," *Administrative Science Quarterly*, 22: 248–263.

Egelhoff, W.G. (1982) "Strategy and structure in multinational corporations: an information processing approach," *Administrative Science Quarterly*, 27: 435–458.

Finkelstein, S. and D.C. Hambrick (1989) "Chief executive compensation: a study of the intersection of markets and political processes," *Strategic Management Journal*, 10: 121–135.

Galbraith, J.R. and R.K. Kazanjian (1986) *Strategy Implementation: Structures, Systems and Process*, St. Paul, MN: West.

Gates, S.R. and W.G. Egelhoff (1986) "Centralization in headquarters–subsidiary relationships," *Journal of International Business Studies*, 19, 2: 71–92.

Ghoshal, S. and N. Nohria (1989) "Internal differentiation within multinational corporations," *Strategic Management Journal*, 10: 323–337.

Gregersen, H.B. and J.S. Black (1992) "Antecedents to commitment to a parent company and a foreign operation," *Academy of Management Journal*, 35: 65–90.

Gupta, A.K. and V. Govindarajan (1991) "Knowledge flows and the structure of control within multinational corporations," *Academy of Management Review*, 16: 768–792.

Hofstede, G. (1980) *Culture's Consequences: International Differences in Work Related Values*, Beverly Hills, CA: Sage.

Kobrin, S.J. (1991) "An empirical analysis of the determinants of global integration," *Strategic Management Journal*, 12: 17–31.

Kobrin, S.J. (1994) "Is there a relationship between a geocentric mind-set and multinational strategy?," *Journal of International Business Studies*, 25: 493–511.

Kogut, B. and H. Singh (1988) "The effect of national culture on the choice of entry mode," *Journal of International Business Studies*, 19: 411–432.

Lawler, E.E. (1981) *Pay and Organizational Development*, Reading, MA: Addison-Wesley.

Mowday, R.T., L.W. Porter and R.M. Steers (1982) *Employee–organization linkages: The Psychology of Commitment, Absenteeism, and Turnover*, New York, NY: Academic Press.

O'Donnell, S.W. (2000) "Managing foreign subsidiaries: agents of headquarters or an interdependent network?," *Strategic Management Journal*, 21: 525–548.

Perlmutter, H.V. (1969) "The tortuous evolution of the multinational corporation," *Columbia Journal of World Business*, Jan.–Feb.: 9–18.

Rajagopalan, N. and S. Finkelstein (1992) "Effects of strategic orientation and environmental change on senior management reward systems," *Strategic Management Journal*, 13: 127–142.

Rosenzweig, P.M. and N. Nohria (1994) "Influences on human resource management practices in multinational corporations," *Journal of International Business Studies*, 25: 229–252.

Roth, K. and A.J. Morrison (1992) "Implementing global strategy: characteristics of global subsidiary mandates," *Journal of International Business Studies*, 23: 715–735.

Roth, K. and S. O'Donnell (1996) "Foreign subsidiary compensation strategy: an agency theory perspective," *Academy of Management Journal*, 39: 678–703.

Schuler, R.S. and I.C. MacMillan (1984) "Gaining competitive advantage through human resource management practices," *Human Resource Management*, 23: 241–255.

Stopford, J.M. and L.T. Wells, Jr. (1972) *Managing the Multinational Enterprise*, London: Longmans.

Van de Ven, A.H. and D.L. Ferry (1980) *Measuring and Assessing Organizations*, New York, NY: John Wiley & Sons.

9

BUSINESS PROCESS RE-ENGINEERING IN INTERNATIONAL NETWORK CORPORATIONS

Gary Katzenstein and Javier Lerch

Introduction

Hammer and Champy (1993) define business process re-engineering (BPR) as "the fundamental rethinking and radical redesign of business processes to achieve dramatic improvements in critical contemporary measures of performance, such as cost, quality, service, and speed." With the promise of quantum improvements in performance, many companies worldwide have embraced this new form of business transformation.

What are the basic ideas underlying BPR? A considerable literature emphasizes that organizations have traditionally been organized hierarchically, with specialization into functional areas. While this structure aids exception-based decision-making and the need for authority and control, it ignores the "white space" between the functional areas in the organization (Rummler and Brache, 1990). In other words, the operations of each functional area may work well by themselves, but the links between these functional areas may be less than satisfactory. When that happens, the output from one functional area may not mesh well with the needs of other functional areas downstream. Furthermore, the wait time between functional areas for any transaction may be significantly longer than the actual processing time within an area. In short, because no one owns, manages, and co-ordinates the various functional areas in a hierarchical organization, the co-ordination that yields smooth operations from beginning to end of the process is generally missing.

If co-ordination is important and challenging for corporations within a single nation, the stakes and difficulties are magnified in multinational companies. As Bartlett and Ghoshal (1989) point out, International Network Corporations (INCs) purposely establish distributed operations in various international locations to take advantage of the markets and specialized resources that each location offers. However, this distribution comes at a cost: an INC must reconcile the diversity of perspectives and interests it deliberately fosters, integrate the widespread assets and resources it deliberately disperses, and co-ordinate the roles and responsibilities it deliberately differentiates (Bartlett and Ghoshal, 1989). Furthermore, the strategies it uses to do so depend on whether what is to be co-ordinated are goods, resources, or information. Given these added complexities of transnational flows, having a good understanding of co-ordination becomes particularly critical for the successful operation and process and redesign of an international network corporation.

To solve co-ordination problems, whether domestic or international, many BPR experts advocate a *process* rather than a *structural* view of an organization. In a process orientation, the actions of many functional areas are co-ordinated to achieve the customer's goals. Problematic handoffs and communications between the traditional functional areas are eliminated or redesigned to allow those transitions to be done quickly and smoothly. Essentially, streamlining occurs by managing the "white space" that is ignored in traditional organization charts. To that end, Hammer and Champy (1993) recommend several heuristics for BPR:

- combine several jobs into one;
- let workers make decisions;
- refine processes into multiple versions;
- perform work where it makes the most sense;
- reduce checks and controls;
- minimize reconciliation.

These recommendations seem hard to argue with as techniques for creating lean, efficient organizations. And while BPR's annals do contain several glowing and oft-repeated success stories, these contrast sharply with reported failure rates of 40 to 70 percent. Why have these failures occurred, and how can managers learn from them? According to some surveys, poor change management strategies and implementation are one major reason (Reynolds, 1994). Given the magnitude of BPR-induced change, employees' fears and their resistance to organizational change are not unexpected barriers.

We believe that two additional factors contribute to BPR failures. One is the danger of radical change. Despite some practitioners' recommendations that one redesign from scratch, companies' histories cannot be ignored; while critical resources, such as expertise and power, cannot easily be altered or shifted. The other major culprit is the failure to consider the human issues involved in re-engineering. That is, many re-engineering projects focus on the more accessible daily operations, ignoring the critical social and political elements that comprise the organizational context in which the process operates. These elements are particularly critical in multinational firms, where social and political systems vary across the firm's operating entities, adding a level of complexity to the BPR task.

Given this understanding, this chapter's main goal is to develop a methodology and tools for BPR that are particularly useful for international network corporations. The main argument is that social context, a missing element in most BPR models and methods, can and should be gainfully included in process redesign tools and techniques. The chapter also argues that, while social context is useful in domestic process re-engineering, it is even more important in international network corporations. This heightened importance comes because social context varies across operating units of an INC, and must be made explicit and then co-ordinated for the corporation to work effectively and efficiently.

The chapter's central element and practical foundation is a manufacturing company's purchasing process. Using case study data from this process, as well as research on other existing BPR models, the chapter first assesses the limitations of existing models, noting problems that might be altered or exacerbated by an international setting. Using the purchasing process, the chapter then develops a framework for BPR that addresses the shortcomings of existing models. Key elements of this new framework are deep and surface structures. The chapter first describes three specific deep structure elements – expertise, goal conflict, and accountability – and illustrates their importance to the process through examples from the case study. The subsequent section provides a more formal representation of deep and surface structures by developing the Goal–Exception–Dependency (GED) model of organizational processes, with heuristics for process redesign that use the model's elements. Again, examples of the model and its heuristics draw on the case study. Having established a model of BPR for single-nation processes, the final section extends this model to international firms. The chapter details the particular differences between single nation and international BPR, and describes the utility of the GED model and accountability for understanding and redesigning processes in international network corporations.

Limitations of current methodologies

Why do the limitations of BPR methodologies exist, especially the relative ignorance of social context? Some deficits can be understood by tracing the history of re-engineering. That is, many common concepts and practices of re-engineering grew out of process analysis methods and tools used in computer science and systems analysis. Because they came from the "hard" sciences, these process models are good at capturing the visible or clearly described interactions between parts of the system. They help us to manage process logistics by identifying bottlenecks, communication breakdowns, and inefficiencies, often enabling the use of information technology to solve these problems.

Because social context is not an issue in modeling a computer system, no means for looking beneath the surface of a process at its supporting context was ever developed. However, social context is clearly important in understanding organizations and redesigning processes, so that when these limited models are applied in organizational settings, the results are not always satisfactory. Therein, perhaps, lie some of the seeds of BPR failure. The following section details elements of this fundamental limitation in most BPR modeling and redesign methodologies. These limitations are:

1   focus on surface-level activities only;
2   focus on a single operational routine only;
3   failure to show missing resource and information flows;
4   failure to capture process emergence;
5   reliance on quantitative methods;
6   lack of adequate heuristics for process redesign.

A focus on surface-level activities only

Most organizational process maps tell us what goes on in a process, but fail to tell us why those actions occur. Surface level representations do not convey the actor's goals and motivations behind the behaviors we observe. Yet, those goals and motivations actually drive the observed process, and must be clear to organizational process redesigners who wish to change behavior from its roots. For example, to receive their items as quickly as possible, people in a purchasing process might order items without filling out purchase orders and submitting them to the Purchasing Department. This also suggests conflicting goals between the purchasing process users and the Purchasing Department. An explicit understanding of those goals is critical to being able to resolve those goal conflicts.

In many ways, it's not surprising that most models capture surface level activities only. They are far easier to discover and represent than such abstract organizational elements as accountability or power. But that doesn't mean that these more difficult elements should be ignored. Unfortunately, most BPR methods do not consider these tough but critical issues, and provide no means for making these elements explicit.

The need to go beneath surface logistics is particularly important for international network organizations. Similar surface operations in different countries may belie very different goals and motivations among the network's organizational nodes in their respective countries.

A focus only on a single operational routine

Most process representations provide a single picture of what a process looks like. Yet research (Suchman, 1983) shows that processes can rarely be captured as a single process. Although there may be one idealized process that the organization would like its members to follow, or that *can* be followed a significant part of the time, single process representations rarely capture the varied realities in most organizations. Myriad transactions may be related to the core process but they do not fit the idealized process because of particular characteristics of the items, individuals, or timing involved. For example, the process needed to order services may differ from that used to order physical products because one may not be able to precisely determine the total number of hours, and therefore the price, of a service beforehand. Besides these natural variations, process players often improvise to meet local needs for which the single, idealized version of the process does not provide. An example would be the "order without purchase order" behavior of the previous section. Such variations seem more likely in international network corporations than in purely domestic companies, as different local circumstances may induce variety in operating procedures across the network's dispersed nodes. Despite the importance of these variations, most existing process representations do not convey their richness.

Again, this is not surprising. It would be impossible to simultaneously convey all variations in a single, sequential representation without overwhelming users, particularly in graphic process maps. Despite these problems, we argue that capturing those variations and exceptions to the baseline process representation is essential for effective process redesign.

A particularly crucial variation rarely provided in standard process maps is exceptions. Exceptions are those practices that deviate from standard operating procedure, providing rich information for understanding a process and its deficiencies. By presenting only standard operating procedures and not showing exceptions within the system explicitly, current representations fail to present much of the information needed to effectively analyze problems and generate new solutions.

Failure to show missing resource and information flows

Most process representations only show resource and information flows that knowingly and explicitly flow as part of the designed process, ignoring resources, and information that individuals need to achieve their goals, but which they are not receiving. An example of missing information would be an Accounts Payable clerk in a purchasing process who is not told the terms of payment from the Purchasing Department when Purchasing places an order, but who could use that information to achieve discounts for the company. Similarly, employees who need to know when an ordered item is expected in, but who do not receive such information, are another example of missing information flows not captured by conventional models. Such missing resource flows provide important clues to process designers about which individual and process-level goals are not being achieved satisfactorily. Making such information explicit can help meet individuals' needs, resulting in a more efficient process.

Missing information flows are relevant to international network corporations in that network structures imply looser control and more difficult co-ordination than in traditional organizational hierarchies. Furthermore, communication and monitoring may be more difficult given the physical and social distance among nodes of the network and the different languages used in each entity of the corporation. A consequence of these circumstances is an increased likelihood of unfilled information flows in INCs compared to those in purely domestic or hierarchical organizations.

Failure to capture process emergence

Most organizational processes evolve beyond their original and officially designed forms. These unplanned, *ad hoc* changes to processes, often done by individuals or groups without official approval or notification, represent process *emergence*. Processes often emerge because of co-ordination problems or individuals' motivations that are not being fulfilled; thus, the emerged process captures procedures more accurately and richly than the official version. Furthermore, given that emergent processes often arise because they help process members meet their goals, they can provide new ideas for the redesigned process. Despite the utility of process emergence, existing BPR models provide no means of capturing such information.

Process emergence seems more likely in international network corporations than in hierarchical, domestic firms, as network structures make it more difficult to monitor and control what other units in the organization are doing. Furthermore, the horizontal nature of such organizations makes it more difficult for one unit to hold other units accountable or to sanction those units when necessary. Consequently, the organization nodes in INCs may find it easier to act autonomously than those in more traditional organizational settings. As a result, the improvements that emerge may not be widely or rapidly shared.

Reliance on quantitative methods

BPR methods and tools extol the virtues of measurement. They advocate capturing process times, costs, and delay times as means of better understanding a process. While numbers can give process redesigners a sharper picture of a process, they only go so far, despite the lack of awareness of this limitation evidenced by many practitioners.

Simulations are an excellent example of the unrecognized, but potentially dangerous reliance on quantitative reasoning. Once, simulation was mostly a tool for production and operations specialists; now simulation is increasingly touted as "the" BPR tool. Indeed, simulations can help process redesigners gain a better sense of otherwise hard-to-see interactions in the system, but they are not the full answer. In fact, experience suggests that process re-engineers who rely on simulations may develop a false sense of precision.

This use of simulations, however, exemplifies a more general problem typical of BPR – a reliance on quantitative rather than qualitative reasoning. Just because something can be measured doesn't mean that it should be, or that such measures will be useful. While quantitative analysis can show redesigners where concrete, measurable problems exist, it cannot tell them about the softer organizational realities beneath the surface that contribute to or cause those visible bottlenecks. Given the language difficulties inherent in any international redesign situation, INCs may be more inclined to use quantitative analysis because it helps transcend language barriers. Thus, INCs may be particularly at risk for having a narrow analytic focus.

Given this limitation, we argue that qualitative reasoning is important to understanding a process at a deep level, and for generating fresh ideas for a new system. Most practical redesign sessions depend on qualitative, not quantitative, reasoning. Nevertheless, quantitative methods are continually touted, presumably because they are more easily done, they give their user some sense of control and precision, and they are easily packaged into tools that can be sold and learned.

Lack of adequate heuristics for process redesign

Regardless of the adequacy of process maps and representations, one glaring omission in the area of process redesign is the lack of heuristics or methods for using process representations. Very few process-modeling representations tell process designers how to use the representation to discover problems with the existing process, or how to generate and evaluate new solutions. Indeed, most practitioners' literature suggests that to formulate new solutions, redesigners should employ the vague, undirected technique of "brainstorming."

Again, this problem occurs with simulations. First, they provide no clear idea of how to generate new designs once the existing system has been modeled. For that reason, a second limitation may arise; that is, that redesigners who rely on simulation are more likely to tweak local parameters than to generate radically different designs. This is not to say that tweaked parameters cannot be more effective than wrenching and costly radical redesign. The point is simply that simulations don't seem to guide redesigners toward radical changes, and in some cases may actually inhibit such changes because they focus on local parameters.

In international network corporations, a lack of unified heuristics might mean that different nodes of the corporate network will propose or use redesign methods that make sense locally, but may not work well over the entire system, or be comparable with other methods being used. A single set of clearly stated, unifying heuristics for the entire network would help co-ordinate efforts in international settings.

A social context model for business process re-engineering

Given the shortcomings of existing BPR models, this study set out to develop a process model and heuristic methods that remedy some of these limitations. This was done through a detailed case study of a purchasing process in a medium-sized ($100 million in revenues and 450 employees) multinational manufacturing company (to be called the ABC Company). The purchasing process studied was used to procure non-production materials and services; that is, items needed to develop products and sustain everyday operations, but not materials actually used in the final products themselves. Because the company could generate a significant competitive advantage by producing high-quality products from assembled parts as quickly as possible, an effective and efficient purchasing process was strategically important for the company.

The standard operating procedure was typical of many purchasing processes, and ran as follows:

1   When requisition writers (often the company's engineers) need an item, they first source the item (i.e., decide on an appropriate supplier).
2   Next, they write up a Purchase Order (PO) on a four-part form, and depending on the cost of the item, get their supervisors' approval of the PO.
3   After approval is obtained, the requisition writer submits the PO in hard copy form to the Purchasing Department.
4   The Purchasing Department places the order with the supplier if there are no problems.
5   The supplier then ships the item to the company's Receiving Department.
6   The Receiving Department delivers the item to the requisition writer if all paperwork is in place.
7   Finally, the Accounts Payable department reconciles the PO, packing slip, and invoice when it arrives, and sends a check to the supplier to complete the process.

To provide some context, this company operates in a highly competitive and regulated industry. At the time of the study, the company had not produced a new product in two years. Thus, the employees were under great pressure to develop products as quickly as possible, leading requisition writers to constantly pressure the Purchasing Department to supply them with their ordered items quickly.

Based on a study of this purchasing process, the remainder of this chapter develops a framework for BPR that addresses the shortcomings of existing models and methodologies. The key elements of this framework are deep and surface structures. The next section describes three specific deep structure elements – expertise, goal conflict, and accountability – and illustrates their importance to the process through examples from the case study.

Surface versus deep structure

To remedy limitations of most existing BPR models, we propose that business processes should be viewed at both surface and deep levels. A process's surface or logistic level includes its daily operations, including visible activities and the flow of physical objects and information. Examples include product shipments, transmission of faxes, and the production of management reports. Deep-level structures are more abstract organizational context elements, such as goals, expertise, accountability, and power – elements that are social, political, or psychological, and therefore often intangible. Examples include individual and group goals, incentive structures, and the underlying corporate and national cultures (Figure 9.1).

Deep structures are also important because they determine and constrain the surface-level operations. For example, surface logistics that go against existing distributions of power in the organization may be resisted by those who currently hold power. Therefore, if someone redesigned a process so that individuals who held power by keeping valuable information were forced to give up or share that information, those people would resist the changes, as they would undercut their sources of (deep-structure) power. Thus, power and other deep structures constrain the surface logistics that are feasible for any redesigned process.

As this example suggests, to understand and design better at the surface level, one needs to understand the deep structure. From this information, successful BPR can be realized by co-ordinating deep-level structures, such as expertise, goals, and accountability, and then either purposefully generating suitable surface-level operations, or allowing desirable surface structures to emerge.

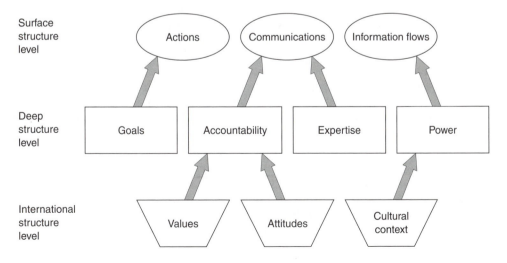

Figure 9.1 Multiple levels of organizational processes.

Elements of deep structure

Despite some general statements in the literature about the role of deep and surface structures in understanding organizational processes (Drazen and Sandelands, 1992; Giddens, 1979), little concrete work specifies what a deep structure is in terms that are explicit, concrete, and somewhat measurable. Based on our work, we have found three useful deep-structure elements that meet these three criteria:

- expertise;
- goal conflicts;
- accountability.

The next section explores the role of these deep-structure elements, providing examples that show how they influence process logistics and process emergence.

Expertise

Given that organizations rely on specialization of knowledge and skills to achieve complex tasks, expertise is necessarily distributed among process members. Since one reason for operating internationally is to take advantage of diverse expertise, particularly that tied to local knowledge, the distribution of expertise especially influences processes in INCs. The main implication of expertise for organizational processes is that process members need to establish dependencies with others to obtain needed expertise. Therefore, the distribution of expertise across the process, and the social relationships and information technology available in the process, help determine which dependencies are fulfilled and how easily this can be done.

For example, in the ABC Company's purchasing process, various splits between who had the needed expertise for a task, and who was designated to act on that expertise, created considerable logistic headaches and needs for surface co-ordination. The engineers, who had the technical expertise to order the products they needed, did not order the parts themselves. Rather, the Purchasing Department, which had the commercial expertise that the engineers did not have, was entrusted with that responsibility. Because each group needed expertise held by the other, a costly need for co-ordination between Purchasing and the engineers arose, resulting in numerous time-consuming phone interactions and delays. However, by re-engineering the system so that all the needed expertise was encapsulated in either the engineers or Purchasing (or at least was made more accessible to those who did not have it), the logistic nightmares of continual phone-tag could have been lessened or eliminated.

As this illustrates, by including expertise as a deep-structure element in the model, one can link surface logistics to deeper elements, thereby explaining the emergence of process improvement. The missing expertise that frustrated process members' abilities to do their jobs also helps to show what information flows were missing, helping analysts to understand the source of the exceptions (Table 9.1).

Table 9.1 How GED model elements address limitations of existing BPR models

	Goals	Exceptions	Dependencies	Influence arrows	Expertise	Goal conflict	Accountability
Surface level only	✗	✗			✗	✗	✗
Single operational routine		✗					
Missing information flows			✗		✗		
Fails to capture process emergence		✗	✗		✗	✗	✗
No qualitative reasoning	✗		✗	✗			
No heuristics or method for redesign		✗	✗				

Goals and goal conflicts

Goals represent a main driver of process emergence, helping to make explicit the motivations of process members. That is, by linking emergent logistics back to process members' goals, one can begin to understand why a process behaves as it does. Because of the importance of goals, more about their implications is provided later. This section focuses on goal conflict, whose influence on process logistics can be more observable and dramatic than the influence of goals alone.

Because organizations and organizational processes are sets of people pursuing individual interests, goal conflicts are inevitable, at least to some extent (March and Simon, 1958). Such conflicts are particularly likely in INCs which specifically rely on node organizations with different specialties and therefore different goals. Some of these conflicts may cause overt power struggles, which can be politically and logistically costly to the participants. Therefore, goal conflict provides strong motivation for one or both parties to change the process logistics to better enable them to meet their needs. An entity's ability to do so depends on various factors, including the accountability of that entity. Commonly, when emergence results from goal conflict, one party to the conflict is often better off, while the other party has more difficulty achieving their goals.

For example, at ABC, one of the engineers' goals was getting the items they needed as quickly as possible, while the Purchasing Department wanted to ensure that supervisors' signatures and confidentiality agreements were in place before the orders were placed. These conflicting goals motivated engineers to generate exceptions and problematic behavior at the surface level, such as having the engineers order items before a Purchase Order was approved by one's supervisor. The extra work that this non-standard behavior required for Purchasing shows clearly how deep-structure goal conflicts can generate and explain poor surface-level co-ordination (Table 9.1). Re-engineering that harmonized the two departments' goals would clearly lessen the tendency for counterproductive surface-level activities to emerge.

Accountability

Accountability is another important deep structure that strongly affects process emergence. We define accountability as "being answerable to audiences for performing up to certain prescribed standards, thereby fulfilling obligations, duties, expectations, and other charges" (Schlenker *et al.*, 1994). As a deep-structure element, process members' sense of accountability to other process members, and the associated sanctions, provide the social glue that motivates the following of standard operating procedures and fulfillment of obligations to other process members. Because it plays this role, accountability captures psychological and social sides of processes not represented in the models described above (Figure 9.1). In other words, accountability complements existing models, helping us to understand what motivations people have for carrying out the steps of a process by specifying the social relationships, obligations, and control mechanisms that underlie the logistics of co-ordination. Given these characteristics, different conceptions of accountability should generate correspondingly different logistic processes.

Semin and Manstead (1983) claim that, when people are accountable, the need arises for "an authority or other judge who requires information about some event to evaluate and sanction the actor's conduct." Based on this observation and its associated actions, accountability affects the emergence of process logistics in two ways. First, because judges often prefer adherence to the formal process, accountability helps constrain process members' abilities to deviate from the standard operating procedure, at least in ways that affect the accountability holder. Second, accountability itself requires logistic operations of information capture and transmission that become surface-level manifestations of the underlying accountability. Because such information capture slows down the process and impedes goal achievement, accountability induces those being held accountable to break the rules in ways for which they will not be held accountable.

As an illustration of the role of accountability in process emergence, in the ABC purchasing process, the Maintenance Department is responsible for buying and distributing to company employees both key product development components and tools, and stock items such as wastebaskets and computer surge protectors. Because no rigid accounts system was in place, employees in the company regularly took items from the stockroom without any sense of accountability. Not surprisingly, the Maintenance Department's budget skyrocketed as a result, as the Maintenance Buyer attempted to keep the stockroom well supplied. Ultimately, the Maintenance Department experienced significant budget overruns. The Maintenance Buyer was held accountable to his Department Manager for these overruns, even though the other employees' lack of accountability actually caused the problem. To hold the Maintenance Buyer accountable, his Department Manager changed the logistics of the process, asking him to submit all his purchase orders to the Department Manager for approval. This need for accountability on every purchase order in advance could have been eliminated, if only timely management information reports had been available on the buyer's actions to keep the Maintenance Buyer accountable. Unfortunately, the company's cost accounting reports had insufficient detail and arrived two months after the fact, both of which contributed to the Department Manager's inability to hold the Maintenance Buyer accountable during the year. Without a means of holding his buyer accountable, the Department Manager had chosen the costly logistic solution.

Taken together, an unhappy confluence of missing and overplayed accountabilities clearly influenced the poorly co-ordinated and dysfunctional surface activities that emerged. Re-engineering that changed the underlying accountability patterns could have helped alleviate these problems.

BPR as co-ordination at the deep-structure level

What can we learn from these demonstrations of the deep structure–surface structure link? First, these examples suggest that deep-structure elements can help explain process emergence by providing a clearer understanding of the psychological and social context that influences surface logistics. These descriptions of processes at the deep-structure level provide a depth missing in traditional, surface-level models. These examples also suggest that a more useful way of defining co-ordination in processes may include both surface-level and deep-structure co-ordination.

What does co-ordination at the deep-structure level mean? Using our three indicators of deep structure, we can redefine co-ordination in the following ways:

- *co-ordinated goals*
  - goals of the participants conflict to the minimum degree possible, so that process goals can be achieved.
- *co-ordination of expertise*
  - expertise is distributed so that it is accessible to those who need it; this eliminates the need for surface co-ordination of communication.
- *co-ordination of accountability*
  - the location of accountability points must be such that accountability is distributed evenly throughout the process, both physically and temporally.
  - accountability should also be distributed at appropriate levels (not too high or low) for the particular goals and risk associated with the process.

Together, this framework allows us to see re-engineering as achieving co-ordination at the deep structure level, which allows the surface-level operations to emerge.

A social context model for re-engineering

The Goal–Exception–Dependency (GED) model

The above discussions suggest that deep-structure elements can enhance a BPR model, but our brief discussion of expertise, goal conflicts, and accountability is not, in itself, a complete model and methodology. Rather, we need a more coherent framework for BPR that incorporates deep-structure elements such as expertise, goal conflicts, and accountability, and yet connects these elements with surface structures and activities. This section provides such a framework by integrating goals, exceptions, and dependencies into the Goal–Exception–Dependency (GED) model (Table 9.2).

Table 9.2 Elements of Goal/Exception Diagrams

1 *Entities*
- People or groups in the process.

2 *Goals*
- What the entities in the process hope to achieve.

3 *Exceptions*
- Deviations from standard operating procedures.

4 *Influence arrows*
- The influence of an exception or a goal on other goals in the process.

Goals

Goals are targets that a process, or individuals in the process, strive to achieve. Examples of process-level goals for a purchasing process might be "to build high quality products" or "keep overall costs low," while individual–level goals could include engineers wanting to "source items as easily as possible" or the Accounts Payable Department wanting to "take discount terms on invoices." Because they help determine many logistic actions that arise, goals are deep-structure components. For example, to source items as easily as possible, an engineer might establish dependencies with some of the more expert engineers in his or her department. Only by making goals explicit is it possible to co-ordinate them among the process members. This is a key to successfully redesigning a process.

Dependencies

A dependency occurs when the goals that one person or group has in a process must be satisfied by some action performed by, or item held by, another person or group in the process (Figure 9.2). For example, let's say a Purchasing Agent has the goal of ordering an item for an engineer from a supplier. To do so, the Agent will depend on the engineer to supply the needed technical information before he or she can place the order. The extent to which, and means by which, a dependency is fulfilled depend on the particular dependency. In the above example, to fulfill the

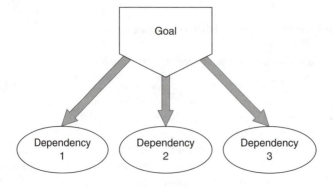

Figure 9.2 Goals achieved through dependencies.

Purchasing Agent's dependency satisfactorily, the engineer would need to supply information that is accurate, complete, understandable, and timely. Each goal may be supported by several dependencies, just as each dependency may support several goals.

Including dependencies in the model is not arbitrary. After all, seeing the relationships between organizational entities as dependencies has a considerable history. Organizations, by definition, exist because people form dependencies to accomplish tasks that no single person could achieve. The literature on co-ordination (Galbraith, 1973; Malone and Crowston, 1994; Thompson, 1967) addresses the need to understand and provide solutions to the dependency problems that result from organizational specialization.

Similarly, Role Theory (Thomas and Biddle, 1979) tells us that processes are systems of interdependent activities, so that process roles are interdependent with one another. Interdependence implies that one actor's activities will be influenced and perhaps strongly determined by the activities carried out by others. Because of these interdependencies, the demands of others in the process become an important set of constraints on the behavior of agents involved in the process, as evidenced by our discussion of accountability. This is particularly true in INCs, which are founded on the notion of strong global interdependencies among operating units. Thus, showing those dependency links will be critical.

In addition, a dependency means the dependent person must interact with someone whose goals may or may not mesh with his or her own. When agents have highly conflicting goals, the dependency may not function smoothly for the dependent person. Given these two effects of dependencies, the larger the number of dependencies in a process, and the larger the degree of goal conflict across the dependencies in the process, the more likely the process will have trouble achieving its goals.

From a practical perspective, one major gap that prevents progress in business process redesign is the lack of a universal language to describe business processes and the redesign operations that act on these representations. BPR experts have proposed various heuristics that can be used to transform and re-invent existing processes (Davenport, 1993; Hammer and Champy, 1993), yet there exists no common means for understanding the underlying logic of these seemingly varied transformations. We believe that many organizational processes and the transformations that BPR experts recommend can be concisely described through a language of dependencies.

Exceptions

Exceptions are deviations from standard operating procedures (either the officially designed process, or a stable process that has become the *de facto* standard operating procedure via the accumulation of emergent changes). They represent either shifts in the network of dependencies that people rely on to achieve goals, or simply sets of dependencies that are not being fulfilled to the dependents' satisfaction. An example of the former type of exception would be an employee buying from an unapproved supplier rather than from a company on the approved supplier list to meet his goal of low-cost purchases. In this case, the individual has shifted his dependency from one company to another. In doing so he has violated the standard operating procedure. Because this kind of exception is generated willfully by some agent in the process, it is termed an "active exception."

An example of an exception that represents a deviation from standard operating procedure would be "telephone-tag" between the Purchasing Department and requisition writers in a Purchasing process. In such a situation, the designed process may be such that a single phone call or Purchase Order from requisition writer to Purchasing Department should be enough to get the order placed. However, if the Purchasing Department depends on the requisition writer for technical information that is not usually adequately conveyed and the requisition writer depends on Purchasing for pricing information that is hard to obtain, the process may turn into telephone-tag, an exception or deviation from the intended process. Because no single entity willfully generates the exception, but rather it emerges as an unhappy confluence of design and circumstances, this kind of exception is termed as "passive exception." The accountability implications of passive exceptions are significantly different from those of active exceptions.

Exceptions are important to the framework for several reasons. First, they indicate the trouble spots that arise in the current process, providing a clearer picture of where to begin the redesign. In addition, exceptions provide access to people's goals that would not otherwise be accessible.

The dynamics of the GED model and process emergence

Having examined the individual elements of the Goal–Exception–Dependency (GED) model, the next task is to see the relationships among them. This is done via the GED model's dynamics, which predict that processes are generated or emerge via the following relationships among its three elements.

An organization and its members seek to achieve numerous goals and subgoals to help realize their strategy. To achieve those goals, individuals in the process establish networks of dependencies that are fulfilled to varied extents. When peoples' dependencies are fulfilled satisfactorily, allowing them to accomplish their goals, all is well. However, when important dependencies are not fulfilled, people will seek to alter their dependency networks to achieve their goals. When people do so, they create exceptions, deviations from standard operating procedures. Because a new set of dependencies for one entity may be problematic for another, exceptions often reflect and reveal conflicting goals among members.

Which goals people seek to achieve and how they seek to achieve them are influenced by accountability considerations. More specifically, whom people are accountable to and the extent to which they are accountable determine goal-seeking behavior in two ways. The more accountable a person is to another person, the more important achieving that second person's goal becomes. This is especially true if the relationship between the two individuals is formally important, such as that between a worker and his or her superior. Second, the less accountable an individual is to other process members, the more likely that person will be able to generate exceptions to achieve those goals that he or she deems most important.

Some examples of the Maintenance Department described above illustrate this emergence process. For example, when the Maintenance Department Manager from the previous section, who depended on the Management Information Systems (MIS) Department for information regarding his employees' spending activities, did not receive that information, he changed the nature of those dependencies. Thus, to compensate for a problematic dependency, the Maintenance Manager created an exception that unintentionally made the Purchasing Buyer's dependency on him also problematic. The increased accountability on the Purchasing Buyer was a burden to achieving his goals, but made him think of generating exceptions against process members to whom he was not accountable, including Purchasing, Receiving, and Accounts Payable. Other examples throughout this chapter can also be seen as instances of this basic process emergence dynamic.

As this discussion shows, exceptions play a key role in addressing limitations of other BPR models (Table 9.1). In particular, exceptions allow one to capture and even predict process emergence, based on goal conflicts and unfulfilled dependencies. Exceptions also connect deep-structure elements (goals) with surface-structure elements (dependencies), providing a key link that can be used to better analyze and understand a process.

Using goals, dependencies, and exceptions

This somewhat abstract discussion of goals, dependencies, and exceptions provides a foundation for understanding the elements of the GED model, but no clear means of using them. Thus, we need some means of representing these items that allows process redesigners to see the relationships between the elements, and to use heuristics for developing new processes. The method we have developed relies on two diagrams – Goal/Exception Diagrams and Dependency Diagrams – and a set of heuristics designed to take advantage of the information contained in these representations. The following describes these process maps and the means for using them.

Before explaining the diagrams, however, it is helpful to understand that, in the GED methodology, the goal of BPR is devising a system of dependencies that allow overall process goals to be achieved. This, in turn, is done by achieving process sub-goals, which then become individuals' local goals. By implication, processes become problems when they contain one or more key dependencies that are not being met. These often reflect goal conflicts and generate exceptions. Thus, one subtask of the BPR designer is to design a process that minimizes goal conflict and unfulfilled dependencies, with the hopes of minimizing the emergence of unproductive exceptions.

Goal/Exception Diagram (Figure 9. 3)

The Goal/Exception Diagram gives the manager a context for evaluating an existing process. It does so by highlighting both process-level and individual goals, the exceptions that have emerged in the process, and the goal conflicts that are reflected in those exceptions. Figure 9.3 shows a Goal/Exception Diagram for ABC's purchasing process, which involves engineers, their supervisors, and the Purchasing Department. Each of these entities is represented by a diamond on the diagram. The "home-plate" shaped symbols represent goals, with those above the

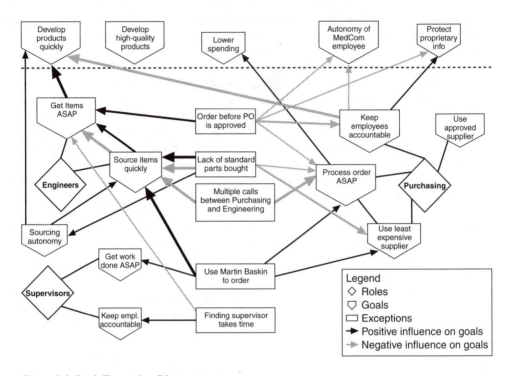

Figure 9.3 Goal/Exception Diagram.

dotted line representing process-level goals that the overall process strives to achieve, while individual-level goals that contribute to the process-level goals are shown as home plates below the dotted line, connected to the entity diamonds. For example (Figure 9.3), some of the process-level goals are to "Develop products quickly" and to "Develop high-quality products." At the individual level, the engineers want to "Get items as soon as possible," and to "Source items quickly," while the Purchasing Department wants to "Process orders as soon as possible" and to "Keep employees accountable."

The diagram also shows the exceptions that arise in the process as rectangles, and the influence of those exceptions on individual- and process-level goals by dark and light arrows that indicate positive or negative influence, respectively, of an exception on one or more goals. The exceptions shown on this diagram include "Order before Purchase Order is approved" and "Multiple calls between purchasing and engineering." "Order before Purchase Order is approved" is an exception because it indicates that engineers sometimes order items directly from the suppliers before they gain the approval signatures from their bosses. "Order before Purchase Order is approved" has positive effects in helping the goals of "Get items as soon as possible" and "Autonomy of the ABC employee," but a negative influence on "Protect proprietary information" and "Keep employees accountable." The exception is initiated by the engineers because it helps them to achieve their goals, even though it may hinder others' abilities to do so.

"Multiple calls between purchasing and engineering" reflects the need for engineers and the Purchasing Department to call each other to gain the technical or commercial expertise needed for an order that is not initially specified in the PO that engineers submit to the Purchasing Department. This kind of exception is not generated by anyone, but merely reflects an unhappy distribution of expertise in the process. The arrows show that "Multiple calls between purchasing and engineering" has strong negative effects on achieving the goals of "Get items as soon as possible," "Source items quickly," and "Process orders as soon as possible." Presenting exceptions as they are shown in the Goal/Exception Diagram allows us to see multiple versions of a process simultaneously, overcoming a limitation of other BPR methodologies (Table 9.1).

The Goal/Exception Diagram helps analysts to identify three critical problems that drive process redesign that are not easily seen through traditional BPR methods (Table 9.3):

- First, Goal/Exception Diagrams allow us to identify key process-level goals that are not being met and the reasons for this. By tracing back from process-level goals that are being impeded by local-level goals that are not being achieved, or by problematic exceptions, redesigners can target key problem areas that are not only logistic bottlenecks, but that are key to overall process goals. For example, the process-level goal "Develop products as quickly as possible" is not being achieved because the engineers' individual-level goal of "Get items as soon as possible" is not being achieved satisfactorily. The use of influence arrows from goals to goals, or from exceptions to actor- or process-level goals enables us to do qualitative reasoning, a feature not readily available in other process redesign methods.
- A second use of Goal/Exception Diagrams is to identify goal conflicts that may be impeding the process and causing frustration. A goal conflict arises when an exception helps one individual or group in the process, but hurts others. For example, "Order before purchase order is approved" helps the requisition writer get his or her item quickly, but impedes the Purchasing Department's goal of keeping employees accountable.
- Finally, Goal/Exception Diagrams help us to identify lose/lose situations, those exceptions in which no one affected by the exception gains from the inter-action. These situations are often passive exceptions that arise from an unhappy confluence of designed process and organizational situation. An example would be "Multiple calls between purchasing and engineering," which represents the telephone-tag between engineers and Purchasing needed to order a technically complex item.

Thus, the three situations analyzed, unfilled goals, goal conflicts, and lose/lose, give the redesigner a targeted view of where problems exist in the current process, and do so by showing not only logistic bottlenecks, but also the conflicting goals and

Table 9.3 Uses of Goal/Exception Diagrams to identify problems

1 Identify key process goals that are not being achieved.
2 Identify goal conflicts between people or groups in the process.
3 Identify lose/lose situations.

motivations that are causing the process to go awry. In our method, we advise business process re-engineers to use these three methods first to fully understand the context in which the current process operates. These techniques form the foundation of a methodology for analyzing and redesigning processes, an important advance over less-directive visual or analytic BPR tools.

Dependency Diagrams (Figure 9.4)

Dependency Diagrams show the interdependencies that exist between the individuals and objects that carry out the process. By showing more of the "nuts and bolts" of the process, the Dependency Diagram complements the Goal/Exception Diagram, which provides the context for understanding why the dependencies exist as they do, and what the implications of changing these dependencies are.

Dependency Diagrams consist of three elements (Table 9.4), the dependencies that exist between individuals, the extent to which those dependencies are being fulfilled, and the degree of balance or enforcement between the dependencies. Our model suggests that the extent to which dependencies (and therefore goals) are not being fulfilled is a good indicator of both process dysfunction, and of the number and severity of exceptions.

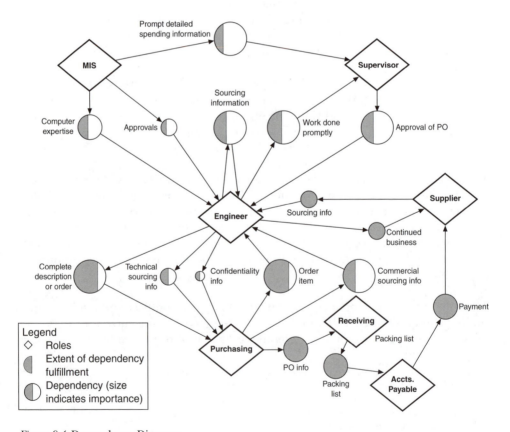

Figure 9.4 Dependency Diagram.

Table 9.4 Elements of Dependency Diagrams

1 Magnitude and direction of dependency.
2 Coverage of the dependency.
3 Balance of the dependency.

Returning to the three elements of the diagram, dependencies are represented by a circle between two arrows. The arrows in a Dependency Diagram point to the dependent entity. For example, the dependency labeled "Technical sourcing info" reflects the Purchasing Department's dependency on the engineers for technical information needed for an order. The magnitude of a dependency, which is represented by the size of the circle, is related to the importance of the dependent person's job or goals and the effect of not having that dependency fulfilled. For example, the dependency that engineers have on Purchasing for "Commercial sourcing info" is a major dependency, as designated by the size of the circle, because it is related to the engineer's major goal of "Get items as soon as possible."

The second element, fulfilling a dependency, has to do with supplying the actions, items, or information required by the dependency. Fulfillment can range from "not at all" to "complete," and may reflect not only quantity of resources fulfilled, but also quality, format, timing, and other considerations depending on the dependency. The degree to which a dependency is fulfilled is represented by the shading of the circle, with full shading representing complete fulfillment, and no shading representing no fulfillment. In the "Commercial sourcing info" dependency, the partial shading means that the engineers' dependence for that information is partially fulfilled; fulfillment is partial because the information is hard to obtain from Purchasing, requiring inconvenient phone calls. This feature of Dependency Diagrams addresses the issue of missing information flows mentioned at the outset. Such missing information flows usually represent process emergence, or alternatively, they can help one predict where process emergence is likely to occur somewhere else in the process.

Enforcement, the third element, describes the motivation and likelihood that the dependent person will get the dependency fulfilled by the other party (the "dependee"). This depends on the congruency of dependent and dependee's goals, the balance of dependency relationships between the two agents, and the network of dependencies associated with the dependee. The congruency of goals can be seen by goal conflicts between entities on the Goal/Exception Diagram. The balance of dependencies between entities can be seen on the Dependency Diagram by the number of dependencies between two entities and whether there are more dependencies in one direction than the other. Finally, the network of dependencies can be seen on the Dependency Diagram by the number of dependencies going into a particular entity's node.

Dependency Diagrams can be used to analyze the current process through "white space" analysis. Dependencies with considerable white space (lack of adequate fulfillment) indicate goals not being achieved on the Goal/Exception Diagram and may generate exceptions as people shift their dependencies. For example, the partially-fulfilled dependency that engineers have on Purchasing for "Commercial sourcing info" has motivated them to generate the exception "Order before PO is approved," meaning that they have shifted their dependencies away from the

171

Purchasing Department by calling the suppliers directly, creating a dependency between the supplier and the engineer.

One interesting aspect of processes that the Dependency Diagram makes clear is the interconnectivity of dependencies. That is, one person's exception and shifted dependencies can easily trigger other individuals to alter their dependencies, and those individuals' exceptions can likewise trigger others. This chain reaction suggests that dependencies form a network. Therefore, changing one dependency in the network can have effects on other dependencies, depending on the structure of the particular network. As far as process redesign is concerned, this suggests that solving the problems of a particularly influential dependency may solve the problems of many other dependencies. Conversely, one particularly problematic dependency can have disastrous effects for other dependencies in the network. This realization can be profitably employed during process redesign.

Thus, in addition to facilitating qualitative reasoning, the dependency network also enables viewers to view multiple versions of a process simultaneously. That is, the various paths that might be drawn across a network's dependencies represent different alternative means of achieving some goal within a process.

Generating and evaluating new processes

Goal/Exception and Dependency Diagrams are not only helpful for analyzing the current system, but for generating new process designs. Several heuristics based on these diagrams can help redesigners find workable, new-process solutions. These heuristics build on the problem-finding techniques mentioned previously, addressing a methodological shortcoming of many other BPR tool kits.

Using the Goal/Exception Diagram to generate new processes

To generate new process alternatives, one can take certain exceptions on the Goal/Exception Diagram, particularly those that help individuals and the overall process to achieve major goals, and make them the rule. After all, new procedures in organizations often start out as exceptions to the rule. Another valid way of challenging organizational assumptions and developing new and effective process redesigns is questioning the need for individual goals that are constraining the new solution. For example, the exception, "Order before Purchase Order is approved" could become an acceptable new process step by lessening the negative influences on Purchasing's goals of "Protect proprietary information" and "Process orders as soon as possible."

Using the Dependency Diagrams to generate new processes

Given the three components of a dependency described above, a process redesigner working with a Dependency Diagram has three alternatives for redesigning problematic dependencies (Table 9.5):

- alter the dependency;
- provide some means of satisfying the dependency by providing the action or resource needed;

Table 9.5 Methods for using the Dependency Diagram

---

1 Alter the dependency by:
  • shifting the dependency to another agent;
  • changing the nature of the dependency.

2 Make the action or resources needed for the dependence more available.

3 Make the dependency more likely to be fulfilled by:
  • balancing the dependencies;
  • lessening the number of dependencies on an individual;
  • aligning a person's goals with others.

• balance the relationships of dependencies among agents so that agents can and are motivated to fulfill the dependency.

To alter the dependency, redesigners can either shift the dependency to another agent or change the nature of the dependency. One example of the former would be to shift a dependency from the Accounts Payable Department to issue a payment check to suppliers by having the Receiving Department do so when an item is delivered. Another example would be to shift a dependency for sourcing information needed to buy products from a small number of relatively inaccessible engineers to a more accessible computer database. In shifting dependencies, however, the issue is often a tradeoff: one shifts a dependency to improve it, but the shift may adversely affect other dependencies or create a need for other dependencies in reaction to the primary shift. For example, shifting to the database creates new dependencies on the MIS department to create and maintain the database.

Some redesigners talk of completely eliminating dependencies. This, however, is more illusion than reality; often one has not really eliminated the dependency completely, but unknowingly shifted the dependency to others, or created other unrecognized dependencies.

The other option for reformulating the dependency is to change its nature. An example would be to make a dependency less urgent by moving a deadline three hours later. After making this adjustment, the same level of service would now represent a higher degree of dependency fulfillment because the demands have lessened.

Assuming that one chooses not to alter the dependency because it is not desirable or feasible to do so, another alternative is to make the action or resource needed for it more available. For example, giving an employee better access to his supervisor for PO approvals would better enable the dependent employee to get his dependency taken care of. Information technology is also a common solution to providing access to information resources that would help fulfill a dependency.

A third alternative is to balance dependencies so that those that exist are more likely to be fulfilled. One reason why dependencies go unfulfilled is a lack of resources on the part of the dependee (the entity who fulfills the dependency). A dependee who is overloaded is less likely to regularly fulfill the needs of any one dependency. Similarly, a dependee who in turn depends on many others, or who has key unfilled dependencies, is less likely to be able to fulfill his or her own dependee roles.

Resource Dependence Theory (Pfeffer and Salancik, 1978) tells us that a dependee is more likely to fulfill a dependent's needs to the extent that the dependee has a reciprocal need. Situations in which one party depends heavily on the other but no reciprocation exists are likely to cause the dependent's dependencies to go unfulfilled. Thus, one means of inducing compliance of dependencies is to establish sufficient reciprocal dependencies between agents in the process. For example, if the Maintenance Department depended on the Accounts Payable Department to the extent that the A/P clerk depended on accurate Purchase Orders from Maintenance, perhaps the Maintenance Department would not be willing to inconvenience A/P by not following standard purchasing procedures.

Finally, dependees are more likely to fulfill dependencies to the extent that the dependency aligns with his or her goals. Thus, goal re-alignments between dependent and dependee are also likely to better ensure that the dependent's dependencies get fulfilled. Again, the Dependency Diagram allows us to analyze a problematic situation and suggest new alternatives.

Evaluation of process alternatives

Once a process re-engineer has identified solutions, he or she needs some means of evaluating the effectiveness and desirability of those alternatives. At that stage, the redesigner can consider the new dependencies that have been created in terms of the goals and exceptions on the Goal/Exception Diagram. Certainly, one would want to know how the new solution affects the likelihood of achieving process-level and individual-level goals. Process-level goals become the ultimate criterion against which the new design can be measured. Estimating the achievement of process-level goals could be done by estimating the influence of the new solution on individual goals and then tracing those results through to process-level goals. One would also want to ask how the new solution alters the likelihood or severity of any related exceptions and how those alterations affect individual- and process-level goals. This sophisticated form of qualitative reasoning, drawing on both deep and surface structures, provides the user with a richness of critical social context, logistic information, and "what-if" capabilities not present in many BPR methods.

In addition, one can do a "white space" analysis using the Dependency Diagram. As part of this analysis, several estimates can be derived of how well the new process allows key dependencies to be fulfilled (for the overall process and for each process member), and what percentage of the dependencies are satisfied by the proposed solution. The percentage of "white space" showing for the relevant dependencies indicates the extent to which dependencies and thus associated goals are not being fulfilled. In addition to "white space" analysis for particular entities or groups of entities, the same analysis could be done for key dependencies in the process; that is, in determining whether key dependencies are well fulfilled by potential solutions. This "white space" analysis is possible because Dependency Diagrams provide the missing information flows not commonly found in other BPR tool kits.

While each diagram and its associated heuristics and metrics provide valuable information for process redesigners, each alone is insufficient for process analysis and redesign. Rather, only by looking at the complex inter-relationships of goals, dependencies, and exceptions across diagrams can one adequately understand the deep structure implications of a new process design. In other words, having a clear sense of the relationships between the elements in this framework is as important as having the elements themselves.

How does international BPR differ from domestic BPR?

Does BPR for international network corporations differ from the BPR context that we have described so far, and if so, in what ways? Can the deep structure/surface structure framework and the GED model augment our understanding of international BPR? These two questions guide the next section's exploration of international BPR.

In general, international BPR differs from single-nation BPR because the need for co-ordination at both the surface and deep levels becomes more complex and difficult when multiple locations and cultures are involved. Certainly logistic issues become more complex as communication and transportation must overcome barriers such as different languages, tariffs and taxes, and quality or safety regulations. But deep structures of the process will also differ greatly across cultures. For example, the distribution of expertise, conceptions of accountability, and the occurrence and means of managing goal conflict vary between processes in different cultures. This can be clearly seen by considering those elements in Japanese and American processes. One might expect that expertise would be more diffusely scattered in Japanese processes than in American, as Japanese career paths lead Japanese workers to be more generalist than their American counterparts, who tend toward job specialization (Katzenstein, 1989). Accountability would also differ greatly, given the strong sense of obligation that Japanese feel to others within their group (Benedict, 1946; Nakane, 1973). An American sense of accountability, on the other hand, would be more formal and less a cultural imperative. Finally, goal conflicts in Japan, when they exist, would be handled behind the scenes through negotiation, while American goal conflicts might be more overt and less likely to end in negotiated solutions (Vogel, 1975). Thus, the kinds of exceptions and the resulting process emergence may be expected to differ across cultures.

These examples show how deep structures are particularly useful for international BPR, largely because they can help explain differences in surface-level operations across countries in more meaningful terms than simply noting differences in observable activities and resource flows. In the following, we describe the utility of the GED model, and accountability as a specific deep-structure element, for BPR in an international context.

The GED model and process emergence in international networks

The GED model is particularly powerful for understanding multinational processes, given the higher probability of process emergence in INCs. Unplanned process emergence, that is, shifts of the process away from the designed standard operating procedure, is more likely across national boundaries given that the various INC operating units are inherently likely to have distinct goals, perspectives, and interests (Bartlett and Ghoshal, 1989). For example, one classic source of goal conflict arises in the relationship between the parent and subsidiary operating units. Add the logistic and social difficulties of monitoring and co-ordinating geographically dispersed units' actions, and the likelihood and feasibility increases that operating units will generate exceptions to meet their goals. Thus, process emergence seems inevitable in INCs, making the GED model an ideal means of capturing the associated goal conflicts, unfulfilled dependencies, and exceptions.

Creating shared appreciations

As McCann and Galbraith (1981) point out, whether interdependence is beneficial or dysfunctional depends on the extent to which shared appreciations of those interdependencies are created and maintained. The creation of shared appreciation is particularly critical to INCs as cultural differences across operating units foster tacit but divergent appreciations of interdependencies, goals, and activities. Despite its increased importance in international processes, the ability to share common appreciations is, ironically, hampered in INCs by geographic dispersion, language barriers, and divergent cultural expectations. The GED model, by helping to make explicit the tacit relationships among goals and dependencies, can aid the knowledge-sharing process needed for effective process redesign.

Shared appreciations provide a basis for agreement about the performance and merits of alternative strategies or designs for managing interdependency (McCann and Ferry, 1979). To achieve these shared appreciations, the particular knowledge of the process held by individual process members must be transferred to other process members. In other words, unless process members learn about other members' perspectives, goals, expertise, and problems, the redesign process may not succeed.

To share that knowledge, the process members' tacit knowledge of their goals and values must be made explicit, a process that Nonaka (1994) calls "externalization." In addition, this newly explicit knowledge, and the process members' previously explicit knowledge of their individual goals and dependencies, must also be transferred to other process members, effectively creating new knowledge throughout the process. This dissemination of knowledge allows the designers to create a set of interdependencies that best co-ordinates all members' goals and actions. The difficulties of knowledge transfer within a single nation are multiplied by the logistics and cultural obstacles in international processes.

Accountability

Accountability as a deep structure element is particularly useful in international BPR because it taps directly into a company's social context and culture. Because the nature of obligations, duties, and expectations varies across cultures, the probability of a single set of prescribed standards working across operating units becomes significantly lower in INCs. Unless these implicit and conflicting standards are made explicit and co-ordinated across cultures, the odds for deep-structure-driven co-ordination breakdowns increase significantly. For example, if, in a process spanning the USA and Japan, the standard in the Japanese operating unit is that people should do whatever is necessary to complete a project (Katzenstein, 1989), while the American operating unit's standard relies on explicit and constraining union rules, then a crisis arises involving both units may cause problems for co-ordinating acceptable logistics to resolve the situation.

Similarly, Prahalad and Doz (1987) point out that, because international interdependencies "muddy the accounting system" for shared resources, joint costs, and transfer costs, managers in INCs often develop confused perceptions of responsibility. No one feels accountable for overall business performance results, such as profitability or market share, even though they all feel responsible for selecting the scope of the business, such as picking market niches in which to compete. This analysis suggests that accountability is not only a natural concomitant of interdependency, but that issues of accountability are particularly complex and important in international processes, where differences in operating units' goals, combined with distance and language problems, amplify the accounting ambiguities of any interdependent system.

Accountability should also help distinguish among international processes because conceptions of accountability not only influence the logistic patterns that emerge, but are tied to deep-rooted cultural assumptions about characteristics of acceptable social relationships. For example, in Hofstede's (1980) study of international cultures, two of the four main cultural elements that he found to have organizational consequences (Power Distance, reflecting tendency toward social hierarchy; and Group/Individual orientation), probably link to a culture's conception of accountability and its characteristics in organizational processes. For example, countries with a high Power Distance may have more formal accountability mechanisms than those in low Power Distance countries, reflecting the heightened clarity or formality of authority–subordinate relationships. Similarly, in group-oriented countries, the group rather than any single individual is more likely to be held accountable for a given action. Also, the accountability of group members toward each other in group-oriented cultures may be stronger than that in individual-oriented cultures. Thus, watching the actions of someone else in one's group and sanctioning them might be more common and acceptable in group-oriented cultures.

Given this background, there are two implications of accountability for international BPR. One is that, because conceptions of accountability vary across cultures, redesigners doing international BPR will have to balance not only accountability among process members, as naturally occurs in any process, but also different conceptions of what constitutes accountability as the process moves from one culture to another. For example, where an international process jumps between Japan (a group-oriented culture) and the USA (an individualistic culture), neither the strict Japanese nor American conception of accountability will help manage the dependencies that span the Pacific. Thus, somehow, this accountability gap must be bridged through compromise or a negotiated version acceptable to both parties.

In addition, accountability helps us to track the influence of organizational and national culture on process logistics. Whereas connections between culture and observable logistics are difficult to trace because of the large number of intervening mediators and steps, accountability is more easily linked to both organizational cultures and to observable actions, as described previously. Thus, accountability provides an observable mediator between culture and actions, enabling us to trace the relationship between culture and logistics through accountability structures. In other words, because culturally-based conceptions of accountability are likely to differ across units of an INC, accountability, by acting as a link between culture and logistics, should provide considerable insights into why different logistic co-ordination patterns emerge in different countries.

Dependencies in an international context

Dependencies are particularly useful for describing processes in multinational corporate settings where they are more complex because of unseen, but critical, underlying cultural factors. Therefore, altering dependencies in which the two actors involved are in different countries will be more difficult because one must take into account not only the usual considerations, but also the cultural underpinnings.

To be more specific, an international context means that dependencies will change in two ways:

- the patterns of dependencies that arise in each country to accomplish the same task; and
- the degree to which, and mechanisms by which, those dependencies are fulfilled.

Patterns of dependencies should vary from country to country because they are partly generated by underlying cultural values and practices. For instance, processes that are carried out sequentially in some countries may be done concurrently in other countries. An example would be the largely sequential design processes that have been used in the USA, in contrast to the concurrent design preferences of the Japanese (Robb, 1992). The underlying cultures of group work in Japan and individual autonomy in the USA help determine why these patterns of dependencies emerge.

Given these different patterns of dependencies in different countries, international BPR projects must co-ordinate processes not only across different functional areas, as in a single-nation BPR project, but across functional areas varying because of culture. For example, if a largely sequential department in the USA interfaces with a concurrently organized department in Japan, specific attention needs to be given to co-ordinating the connection. Without a picture of these different dependencies provided by the Dependency Diagram, this critical issue may not be obvious.

Perhaps the most interesting question regarding a dependency representation scheme is whether it is equally applicable and useful in different national cultures. Hall's concept of low- and high-context cultures is helpful for this analysis (Hall, 1981). High-context cultures, such as those of Japan and Korea, are environments in which individuals need not spell everything out in their interactions with others. As a result, processes are created in which considerable on-the-spot adjustment between parties is required and expected. These cultures generate processes with few written procedures because the actual procedure may vary given the particular requirements of the individuals in the process at the time it is performed. Given this variability in who depends on whom, an interesting question is whether a Dependency Diagram can be meaningfully constructed for such processes. Similarly, with standard operating procedures so hard to pin down in high-context cultures, the concept of an exception – a deviation from the standard operating procedure – also becomes more difficult to define and observe.

On the other hand, in low-context cultures, such as Germany, individuals interact more often by spelling things out explicitly. In these cultures, the dependencies can be more easily seen, and are less likely to shift over time. Thus, Dependency Diagrams seem a natural and more easily derived tool in these cultures.

What is particularly interesting are those processes that contain dependencies that cross cultural boundaries between high- and low-context cultures, as suggested earlier. How a poorly defined, flexible process in a high-context culture can successfully interface with a cleanly-defined, stable process in a low-context culture is a question worth further investigation. Our research indicates that use of the framework presented here should help to expose the problem.

Finally, not only are patterns of dependencies likely to differ across cultures, but also the extent to which those dependencies are fulfilled and the organizational and psychological mechanisms that produce that fulfillment are also likely to change. Again, how and why dependencies are fulfilled is largely tied to the underlying culture. In some cultures, presumably low-context ones, people are likely to fulfill dependencies because they are established explicitly, with almost legalistic expectations of fulfillment. For example, union contracts in low-context cultures would clearly specify the requisite and proscribed dependencies for a process, and the acceptable means of fulfilling those dependencies. On the other hand, in high-context cultures such as Japan, the sense of obligation known as *giri* and *on* (Nakane, 1973; Reischauer, 1982) designate such strong implicit, socially-infused obligation to others, that few external means are needed to ensure that people fulfill obligations and dependencies. Again, processes that cross cultures and involve different psychological mechanisms of enforcement are likely to founder unless explicit attention is paid to those culturally-generated differences.

Exceptions in an international context

Exceptions provide useful insights into an organization's deep structure in domestic settings; this occurs by making explicit the relationships between the various process members' goals and dependencies. They give us a sense of how process members have altered their dependency networks to solve existing co-ordination problems and goal conflicts. Given this role, they are particularly helpful in international settings, where deep structure is quite likely to vary across cultures. In other words, exceptions provide a "window" into how dependencies and goal conflicts are managed differently in different countries. These exception "windows" can give analysts access to cultural assumptions that may differ across countries and patterns that are critical to the redesign, but which individuals in those cultures may not be able to articulate without exceptions.

For example, if a systems analyst asked individuals in a process involving Japanese and Americans what their concepts of time were regarding the process, they might both reply that they "want the process to be accomplished promptly." However, the Japanese conception of "prompt" may be two days, while the Americans may consider "prompt" to be a week. This distinction would most likely come up as a result of an exception, when one partner sees a deviation from what he or she considers a standard operating procedure. For instance, a product part that the Americans consistently deliver to the Japanese in a week, that the Japanese expect in two days, would be flagged an exception by the Japanese during process analysis. Given this concrete point around which discussion can begin, the implicit goals of each side can then be made explicit, and appropriate re-engineering of this goal conflict can then begin.

Conclusions

What, then, have we learned about BPR, both within a single nation and for international network corporations? First, we described the limitations of existing BPR methodologies for both types of processes, and developed the GED model and method to overcome those limitations.

The GED model and methodology has been shown to address each of the limitations of existing methodologies discussed in this chapter. That is, the GED model goes beyond surface-level activities by involving deep-structure elements such as goals, goal conflicts, and accountability. GED also allows representation of more than one routine for the process through the use of exceptions and Dependency Diagrams. Unlike other models, GED shows missing information and resources through "white space analysis" of dependencies, and details process emergence through exceptions. Finally, the GED model, through the causal relationships of Goal/Exception Diagrams, allows the qualitative reasoning needed for process redesign, and provides specific heuristics based on Goal/Exception and Dependency Diagrams.

Taken together, this chapter's findings suggest that BPR is fundamentally about managing dependencies to achieve process-level goals. Re-engineering, then, becomes the task of rearranging dependencies to allow individual and process level goals to be achieved most easily, while minimizing goal conflict among process members.

Our research also suggests that effective BPR requires that we understand people's motivations. The inclusion of goals and accountability in the model provides good barometers of those motivations. Finally, our research tells us that to fully analyze and understand a process we need to understand the underlying pressures in the system, as captured by exceptions.

The nature of INCs, with their three key characteristics of dispersion, specialization, and interdependence (Bartlett and Ghoshal, 1989), makes international BPR more challenging than BPR in a single-nation context. Dispersion and specialization of operating units in the network mean that each operating unit may have increased difficulties in understanding and tracking others' operations, environment, and concerns. These aspects also increase the likelihood of goal conflicts and process emergence. The GED model addresses this issue by providing operating units with the "big picture" of overall operations. This enables people and organizations to overcome local information restrictions and see the goals and constraints that other units have. This facilitates the negotiation and compromise that characterize organizational process redesign.

Another major characteristic of INCs is the reciprocal nature of their operating units' interdependencies. The GED model makes these interdependencies explicit and shows which of these links are not being adequately fulfilled. More importantly, by linking the "white space" on the Dependency Diagram to the goal conflicts and exceptions on the Goal/Exception Diagram, analysts can begin to understand why key interdependencies are not working adequately, and what can be done to remedy the situation at a social or political level, taking into account differences in culture, business practice, and regulation.

Further complications of specialization arise from the lack of shared appreciations of other process members' roles and values. At the same time, difficulties occur in assigning accountability to members in highly interdependent processes, in which language difficulties, cultural differences, and communication gaps are exacerbated by different physical locations. The GED model helps mitigate these problems by providing a common language for international BPR. By using common terminology across functional areas and cultures, the Goal/Exception and Dependency Diagrams can help integrate the disparate pieces of an international network corporation.

Finally, international BPR is complicated when dependencies bridge two or more cultures. The different patterns of how processes are organized, different conceptions and mechanisms of accountability, and different communication patterns, expectations, and assumptions reflecting underlying high- and low-context cultures, mean that bridging these culturally based differences will require particular attention by the process redesigner. Nevertheless, by making these elements explicit through the GED model, one has tools for finding common ground.

Although achieving both deep- and surface-level co-ordination under those conditions may be difficult, the payoff for international processes should be significant given the symbiosis gained from effectively harnessing a diversity of resources. The flexibility and generality of the GED model, and the ability of its elements to bring out those differences that international BPR practitioners must address, renders it an important research and practical tool for INCs engaged in business process redesign.

References

Bartlett, C. and S. Ghoshal (1989) *Managing Across Borders: The Transnational Solution*, Boston, MA: Harvard Business School Press.

Benedict, R. (1946) *The Chrysanthemum and the Sword*, Rutland, Boston: Houghton Mifflin.

Davenport, T. (1993) *Process Innovation*, Boston, MA: Harvard Business School Press.

Drazin, R. and L. Sandelands (1992) "Autogenesis: a perspective on the process of organizing," *Organization Science*, 3, 2: 230–249.

Galbraith, J. (1973) *Designing Complex Organizations*, Reading, MA: Addison-Wesley.

Giddens, A. (1979) *Central Problems in Social Theory: Action, Structure, and Contradiction in Social Analysis*, Berkeley, CA: University of California Press.

Hall, E.T. (1981) *Beyond Culture*, Garden City, NY: Anchor Press.

Hammer, M. and J. Champy (1993) *Reengineering the Corporation*, New York: HarperCollins.

Hofstede, G. (1980) *Culture's Consequences: International Differences in Work-Related Values*, Beverly Hills, CA: Sage Publications.

Katzenstein, G.J. (1989) *Funny Business: An Outsider's Year in Japan*, New York, NY: Soho Press.

McGann, J.E. and Ferry, D.L. (1979) "An approach for assessing and managing interdependence," *Academy of Management Review*, 4, 1: 113–119.

McCann, J.E. and J.R. Galbraith (1981) "Interdepartmental relations," in Nystrom, P.C. and W.H. Starbuck, *Handbook of Organization Design*, Vol. 2, New York, NY: Oxford University Press, pp. 60–84.

Malone, T.W. (1987) "Modeling coordination in organizations and markets," *Management Science*, 33, 10: 1317–1332.

Malone, T.W. and K. Crowston (1994) "The interdisciplinary study of coordination," *ACM Computing Surveys*, 26, 1: 87–119.

March, J.G. and H.A. Simon (1958) *Organizations*, New York, NY: Wiley.

Nakane, C. (1973) *Japanese Society*, New York, NY: Penguin Books.

Nonaka, I. (1994) "Dynamic theory of organizational knowledge creation," *Organization Science*, 5, 1: 14–37.

Pfeffer, J. and G. Salancik (1978) *The External Control of Organizations*, New York, NY: Harper and Row.

Prahalad, C.K. and Yves L. Doz (1987) *The Multinational Mission: Balancing Local Demands and Global Vision*, New York, NY: The Free Press.

Reischauer, E.O. (1982) *The Japanese*, Cambridge, MA: Harvard University Press.

Reynolds, B. (1994) "The rap on reengineering," *Computerworld*, 26 September.

Robb, W.L. (1992) "Don't change the engineers – change the process," *Research-Technology Management*, 35, 2: 8–9.

Rummler, G. and A. Brache (1990) *Improving Performance*, San Francisco, CA: Jossey-Bass.

Schlenker, B.R., T.W. Britt, J. Pennington, R. Murphy, and K. Doherty (1994) "The triangle model of responsibility," *Psychological Review*, 101, 4: 632–652.

Semin, G.R. and A.S.R. Manstead (1983) *The Accountability of Conduct: A Social Psychological Analysis*, San Diego, CA: Academic Press.

Suchman, L. (1983) "Office procedures as practical action: models of work and system design," *ACM Transactions on Office Information Systems*, 1, 4: 320–328.

Thomas, E.J. and B.J. Biddle (1979) *Role Theory: Concepts and Research*, New York, NY: Wiley.

Thompson, J. (1967) *Organizations in Action: Social Science Bases of Administrative Theory*, New York, NY: McGraw-Hill.

Vogel, E. (1975) *Modern Japanese Organization and Decision-Making*, Tokyo: Charles E. Tuttle Company.

Part 3

STRUCTURAL EVOLUTION, MANAGEMENT ROLES, AND COMPETENCES

10

AFTER FOREIGN MARKET ENTRY, THEN WHAT?

Managing the post-entry phase of foreign direct investment

Philip M. Rosenzweig and Sea Jin Chang

Introduction

In recent years, multinational corporations (MNCs) have increasingly been conceived as multicentered organizational forms, with foreign subsidiaries playing different roles within a larger network structure. By adopting an internally differentiated form, rather than insisting on identical roles for each foreign subsidiary, MNCs can tap the distinctive capabilities of each subsidiary and optimize their worldwide operations. Such MNCs are also better positioned to benefit from network flexibility, as they can shift production and sourcing among subsidiaries as various external conditions – competitive, financial, or regulatory – change. The chapters in this volume, many of which explicitly refer to MNCs as "networks," are testimony to the growing popularity of understanding MNCs in this way.

It is critical to note, however, that multinational networks are not born; they evolve. Aside from the few firms that are truly born multinational – that, from their moment of founding, might source inputs in one country, design products in another, manufacture in yet another country, and raise funds in still another – most MNCs begin in one country and evolve over time to become differentiated networks. This process of evolution is hardly automatic, but requires deliberate managerial action, often sustained over many years. The great number of MNCs that, despite their age, have never evolved into differentiated networks makes plain that the passage of time is not a sufficient condition for evolution. Furthermore, as firms which are able to navigate this evolutionary process more swiftly, more fully, and more efficiently are likely to achieve a superior competitive position, understanding the process by which MNCs evolve is of high importance.

Unfortunately, relatively little attention has been paid to the process by which MNCs evolve into differentiated networks. There has, of course, been a great deal of research about foreign direct investment. Numerous studies have examined factors that lead to FDI, including industry factors, currency effects, and competitive dynamics. Much of this research examines FDI as the dependent variable, and seeks to identify the associated independent variables. Although valuable, this research implicitly views FDI as a result, or an end point – yet by definition foreign market entry is also a beginning, and indeed is the beginning of a critical phase of the MNC's life. Explaining initial market entry is important, but understanding the process of building a strong and successful subsidiary after initial entry surely has important consequences for firm performance.

The Sony Corporation: a study in post-entry management

In this chapter, we examine the post-entry phase of foreign direct investment by presenting the experience of the Sony Corporation. Sony, the Japanese-based electronics and entertainment firm, is by any measure a mature and complex MNC. The Sony brand name ranks along with Coca-Cola and McDonald's among the most recognized in the world. Its worldwide sales in 1993 of $34 billion were almost equally distributed among North America (30.4 percent), Europe (26.0 percent), and Japan (25.8 percent). In the United States, Sony employed more than 20,000 people at many sites and in many distinct lines of business, including televisions, magnetic tape, semiconductors, and precision audio equipment. These lines of business varied widely in their importance and contribution to the corporation's worldwide activities: some performed only local manufacturing, others engaged in research and development, and others played a role of worldwide leadership. A partial listing of Sony's US activities is shown on Table 10.1.

Table 10.1 Sony Engineering and Manufacturing of America (1994)

1 *Administrative headquarters*, Park Ridge, NJ

2 *Product divisions*
   Picture tube, color television, and display products activities
San Diego, CA	Employees: 2,000	Est. 1972
Tijuana, Mexico	Employees: 2,200	Est. 1987
Pittsburgh, PA	Employees: 800	Est. 1990
   Audio Manufacturing Division, hi-fi speakers and audio racks
   Delano, PA   Est. 1975
   Sony Professional Products Company, professional audio and video equipment
   Boca Raton, FL   Est. 1982
   Sony Microelectronics, semiconductor manufacturing
   San Antonio, TX Est. 1990
   Factory Automation Division, factory automation solutions
   Orangeburg, NY   Est. 1989

3 *Research and development centers*
   Monterey, CA: Advanced Computer Architectures Research Laboratories
   San Jose, CA: Sony Microelectronics Design Center
                 Semiconductor and Systems Laboratory
                 Sony Intelligent Systems Research Laboratory
   San Diego, CA: Display Systems
                  Television Business Group of America
   Boulder, CO: Data Storage Laboratory
   Boca Raton, FL: Sony Professional Products Company
   Orangeburg, NY: Factory Automation Division

Source: Sony company documents.

Sony's activities in the United States are a vital part of its worldwide network, but they were not created overnight. Until 1972, Sony manufactured its products exclusively in Japan and exported them around the world. Its first direct investment in the United States was small, restricted to a single line of business – televisions – and a single operation – final assembly. Over the next 20 years, Sony's US activities evolved both in terms of the functions performed and in terms of the lines of business represented. A study of Sony in the United States can therefore shed light on many aspects of post-entry management.

Of course, Sony's experience in the United States is not representative of all MNCs. Its evolution took place over many years, consisted of many discrete steps, and involved many separate entries in distinct lines of business. We make no claim that Sony's experience is typical. Yet it is precisely the lengthy, gradual process of evolution which makes Sony an effective prototype, allowing us to think clearly about the dynamics of MNC evolution, and thereby providing a benchmark against which the post-entry management in other firms can be examined.

We conducted our case study of the Sony Corporation by gathering archival, documentary, and interview data. At first, we gathered and digested publicly available data, including company annual reports, press articles, books, and biographies. Once we had developed an understanding of the milestones in Sony's evolution in the United States, we conducted a series of interviews. First we met with senior managers at the Sony Engineering and Manufacturing America (SEMA) headquarters in New Jersey. We then visited Sony divisions in San Diego, California; Tijuana, Mexico; Pittsburgh, Pennsylvania; and San Antonio, Texas. A final series of interviews were conducted at SEMA headquarters in New Jersey and at the Sony Corporation headquarters in Tokyo.

In all, we interviewed more than 40 Sony managers, some more than once. They included a cross-section of managers: Americans and Japanese; senior executives, division managers, and technical professionals; and included functions including R&D, manufacturing, human resources, finance, and business planning.

The history of Sony in the United States

The Sony Corporation was founded in 1946 as Tokyo Tsushin Kogyo (TKK), a start-up in electronics that literally emerged from the ashes of Tokyo. The founding partners were Masaru Ibuka and Akio Morita. Among the earliest products were audio tape and tape recorders. In 1953 TKK licensed transistor technology from Bell Labs, and within a few years had developed the first transistor radio and the first pocket-sized radio.[1] In 1958 the company's name was changed to Sony – an easier name for Westerners to pronounce, which combined the Latin word for sound, "sonus," and the English term of endearment, "sonny."

During the 1950s and 1960s, the Sony Corporation designed and manufactured audio and electronic products in Japan, and exported them around the world. By 1960 it generated more than half of its sales outside Japan, with the largest share of sales in the United States. That same year, Sony established a US sales subsidiary, Sony Corporation of America, and in 1961 was the first Japanese company to offer stock on US financial markets.

The 1960s were boom years for Sony, thanks largely to its advanced color television, the Trinitron. With the increase in US revenues, however, came concerns about vulnerability to trade disputes. In the early 1970s, US television makers charged their Japanese rivals with dumping, prompting a Department of Commerce investigation. Akio Morita, by now Sony's CEO, successfully fought the charges, but was so shaken by the allegations that he decided to set up a manufacturing site in the United States. In strict economic terms, manufacturing in the USA did not yet make sense – at 360 yen to the dollar, it was more efficient to produce in Japan and export to the USA – but finding ways to reduce dependence on exports was seen as vital.

Entry into the United States

In August 1972, Sony became the first Japanese firm to undertake direct investment in the United States, establishing a small manufacturing operation at the Rancho Bernardo Industrial Park, north of San Diego. Thirty Americans were hired, none of whom had experience in appliance manufacturing, so that Sony could train them from scratch.[2] A team of Japanese expatriates supervised the fledgling venture, training the Americans and reproducing exactly the final television assembly layout in Japan.

At the outset, Sony's San Diego plant had a narrow focus: it performed final assembly for just one product – televisions. Strictly speaking, San Diego did not assemble televisions – it re-assembled televisions that had already been assembled, adjusted, then disassembled, in Japan. As one manager recalled, so concerned were Japanese managers about the quality of American workmanship that first they wanted to find out if Americans, working under the supervision of Japanese managers, could properly re-assemble a television. The quality of re-assembly at San Diego was carefully monitored by managers in Japan, and once they were satisfied that American workers could properly re-assemble televisions, prior assembly in Japan was discontinued.

Initial evolutionary steps, 1974–1977

As the San Diego operation proved that it could handle final assembly, Sony managers explored the possibility of adding functions. A logical next step was to manufacture television picture tubes (known as cathode ray tubes, or CRTs). Of all the parts in television assembly, CRTs were the heaviest and most expensive to ship, as well as the most brittle and prone to breakage. Local manufacture was therefore very attractive. Once again, Sony transferred manufacturing know-how from Japan, and in 1974 the San Diego plant began to manufacture CRTs, saving the cost of trans-Pacific shipping as well as reducing breakage. A few other items that were bulky and inexpensive were also sourced locally, including cartons, packaging materials, and cabinets, but all other inputs, including all key technology and electronic components, continued to be sourced from Japan.

The success of its initial experience in San Diego soon prompted Sony to establish a similar plant to serve the European market. In 1974 it opened a television assembly plant at Bridgend, Wales. Once again, the plant was set up by Japanese expatriates who transferred existing process and product technology, but this time experienced employees from San Diego were dispatched to assist in setting up the

Bridgend plant. Once again, only a limited amount of activity was performed in the new plant, with all inputs imported from Japan.

Sony also began to expand its US presence beyond televisions. In 1975, it opened a high-fidelity speaker plant in Delano, Pennsylvania, and in 1977 established a magnetic tape manufacturing plant in Dothan, Alabama. These were lines of business, like televisions, where Sony had a competitive superiority over local firms. As with the San Diego plant, Sony relied on Japanese expatriates to transfer product technology and manufacturing process technology to the USA and to train American workers.

By 1977, five years after it first began to re-assemble televisions in San Diego, Sony had already expanded its initial position along three dimensions. In terms of functional migration, it had gone beyond final assembly to add CRT manufacturing; in terms of geographic expansion it had replicated its television assembly operation in Wales; and in terms of lines of business it had added both audio equipment and magnetic tape in the USA. In each dimension, we note a small evolutionary step, based on the observed success of the initial position.

Gradual evolution: late 1970s to mid-1980s

Over the next decade, Sony continued to expand its position in the United States, although in a gradual manner. The television operation in San Diego grew steadily, with two new buildings added to accommodate greater capacity. Still, all inputs other than CRTs and packaging materials continued to be imported from Japan. The San Diego plant reported directly to the television line of business headquarters in Japan, which handled most functions, including product design and engineering, research and development, product strategy, and business planning. Whereas Sony's sales and marketing activities in the USA were managed out of New York by Sony North America (SONAM), the product divisions were organized separately and managed directly from Japan.

As Sony's confidence about managing in the United States grew, it began to add lines of business that were further removed from its core. It also expanded through acquisitions rather than solely through greenfield investment. In 1982, a business unit that specialized in professional audio equipment, Sony Professional Products, was created from the acquisition of Music Center Inc. in Boca Raton, Florida. In 1984, Sony opened a CD manufacturing plant in Terre Haute, Indiana.

Experience gained in many of these US plants, in turn, provided the basis to set up similar plants in Europe. Just as the San Diego television assembly plant had spawned an assembly plant in Wales, CRT manufacturing, established in San Diego in 1974, was followed by a CRT operation at Bridgend in 1982. The US magnetic tape plant, founded in Alabama in 1977, led to a similar plant in France in 1980. The 1984 CD manufacturing plant in Indiana led to a similar plant in Salzburg, Austria, in 1987. In each instance, the first plant was set up in the United States, with a European plant following just a few years later. Often, Japanese managers who had helped found US plants were sent to Europe where their experience could be applied. In addition, American managers were at times sent to Europe to apply their expertise about setting up new plants.

From the late 1970s to the mid-1980s, Sony's evolution continued along all three dimensions at a measured pace. No additional functions were added in televisions. New lines of business were added one at a time, not many at once. European plants were always set up a few years after their US counterparts, allowing the company to gain and transfer its experience after a level of performance had been achieved. In terms of organization structure, Sony's US activities continued to be split between its sales and marketing organization, SONAM, and its various manufacturing plants, each of which reported on a direct-line basis to its headquarters in Japan. Little coordination or sharing of expertise took place among the various US manufacturing plants.

"Global localization" in the late 1980s

Sony's evolution accelerated sharply in the late 1980s, largely stimulated by changes in relative currency values. Following the Plaza Accord of September 1985, the dollar fell from approximately 245 yen to 150 yen within a few months. The economic equation was suddenly transformed. Like many other Japanese firms, Sony determined it needed to incur more of its costs in local currencies rather than in Japan. Accordingly, Sony embarked on a policy of "global localization."[3] As Akio Morita stated:

> Global localization is a phrase coined by Sony which means that each region makes its own autonomous operational decisions while maintaining and reflecting the corporate policy at the global level. This is Sony's approach to meeting the challenges of an ever changing and increasingly complex world. With a multitude of countries with differing market needs, economic and political environments, "global localization" is the ideal approach for enhancing Sony's corporate direction, while responding more effectively to the needs of each country and region.[4]

Renewed functional migration in televisions

"Global localization" stimulated a major change in the management of Sony's US television business. Ever since its founding in 1972, all key decisions had been made in Japan; now the US operation was expected to take on "autonomous operational decisions" for everything from sourcing inputs to product design to business planning. Yet, as one manager told us: "We couldn't just say, 'Let's move everything at once to the US.'" There existed in the USA neither sufficient organizational infrastructure nor sufficiently trained managers to assume these responsibilities. In fact, as explained to us by veteran managers, the USA could not take on the business planning function unless it was also responsible for new product introduction; new product introduction could not be undertaken without responsibility for new product design; and new product design could not be undertaken in the United States as long as parts used in those designs were procured in Japan.

What followed, then, was a sequence of incremental functional migration. The first step was local procurement, which was not only essential for subsequent functional migration but also addressed directly the cost disadvantages associated with sourcing from Japan. Sony instituted a new program, called Procurement of Local Parts (PLP), under which Sony managers began to work actively with US vendors to determine the specifications, quality, and delivery of vital inputs. Over time, PLP was effective in reversing the sourcing of parts: until 1985, 83 percent of the dollar value of television inputs had been imported from Japan, versus 17 percent purchased locally; by the early 1990s, fully 80 percent was purchased locally.

As more and more inputs were procured in the USA, other functions, including product design, began to be shifted. These shifts raised a number of organizational complexities. Earlier functions, such as final assembly, had been replicated in the USA without diminishing the activities performed in Japan. Strictly speaking, these functions had been replicated rather than transferred. Product design was different – undertaking product design in the USA unavoidably called for a reduction of certain activities in Japan, and was therefore a more sensitive matter.

Transferring functions such as business planning proved to be even more difficult. At Sony, business planning involved an intricate set of procedures and interactions among managers, all of whom were Japanese, and all of whom shared an understanding of management procedures. Relocating this process to San Diego, where it would be undertaken by Japanese expatriates in conjunction with American managers, was unprecedented and, for some, difficult to imagine. Eventually, two top Japanese managers responsible for business planning were moved to San Diego and effectively brought with them the entire infrastructure for strategic planning. Key in this regard was the *seihan*[5] process, which matched marketing requirements and factory allocations for a line of business on a worldwide basis.

Management of the *seihan* process was critical because it established the operating capacities for factories around the world and therefore affected performance evaluation. As stated by several managers, shifting the *seihan* process to the USA was a profound event that signaled a clear shift in power from Japan to the USA.

Sony Engineering and Manufacturing of America

Along with increasing local functionality in many lines of business, an effort was made to strengthen Sony management in the USA at the national level. Until now, each line of business in the United States reported on a direct basis to its headquarters in Japan. No mechanism existed to co-ordinate activities or share expertise among the growing number of lines of business in the USA. In 1988, a new entity was formed: Sony Engineering and Manufacturing of America (SEMA). SEMA was headed by a country manager whose task was to optimize engineering and manufacturing activities at the national level.

New sites for televisions: Tijuana and Pittsburgh

When the San Diego plant had been established in 1972, the aim was merely to perform final assembly and thereby avoid potential import barriers. Cost efficiency was not a particular concern at that time, and indeed Sony's Trinitron was priced higher than most rival televisions. By the late 1980s, the television industry had been entirely transformed. Many other firms now offered televisions of similar quality but at substantially lower prices. In order to survive in an exceedingly competitive market, Sony recognized that it would have to compete on costs, which meant becoming a volume producer and also finding ways to lower transportation costs.

In 1988 Sony set up a plant in Tijuana, Mexico, to assemble smaller televisions, which were relatively labor intensive and price competitive. The San Diego plant gravitated increasingly toward the larger color televisions whose high profit margins could absorb higher US wages. More importantly, however, Sony managers questioned whether San Diego was the best place for a localized television operation. As long as Sony's US television operation sourced its inputs from Japan, being located in San Diego made economic sense. But once the company shifted toward greater local sourcing, San Diego was no longer as advantageous. Furthermore, as price competition in the television industry became more and more intense, concentrating television production in the southwest corner of the USA, far away from many of the most populated sections of the country, made less and less sense. At the end of the 1980s, therefore, Sony managers began to look for a "second site" in the USA. After a lengthy search, they settled on a large industrial site near Pittsburgh, Pennsylvania, that had previously housed a Volkswagen automobile plant. The Pittsburgh site offered inexpensive power and water, was close to transportation lines, and was closer to the US center of population. In setting up a new television plant, almost 20 years after the first TV plant in San Diego, Sony drew on managers both from San Diego and Bridgend.

Further line of business entry

The renewal of functional migration in the late 1980s, discussed above in relation to televisions, was matched by a fresh round of adding new lines of business. Initially, Sony had entered the USA only in lines of business where it enjoyed a superiority over local firms. It had leveraged that superiority by entering only with greenfield plants, so that it could design the factory layout, transfer key technology, and hire and train employees of its own choosing. These actions had been effective as a way to replicate successful manufacturing activities in Japan, leveraging its capabilities into a new country.

Now Sony began to undertake acquisitions. In 1989, Sony acquired Materials Research Corporation, a producer of thin metal film and etching equipment. In 1990, it acquired AMD's semiconductor equipment in San Antonio. In addition, Sony began to enter in lines of business where its objective was not to leverage existing capabilities into the USA, but to gain access to local capabilities and make use of it elsewhere in the firm. The motive was not one of exploitation, but exploration.

Several new lines of business were added at the San Diego site. In 1991, Sony established the Data Storage Systems Division, which manufactured floppy disk drives, CD-ROM drives, and computer mass storage systems. Although initially set up to assemble parts imported from Japan, thereby avoiding import duties, it was quickly recognized that the latest advances in data storage technology were taking place in the United States, not Japan. The Data Storage Division soon evolved into a center of advanced technology, setting up R&D labs in San Jose, California, and Boulder, Colorado, where other major computer and information systems firms were located. By 1994, just three years after its establishment, Sony's Data Storage System Division was responsible for R&D and product design, as well as manufacturing.

In 1991, Sony began to produce analog cellular phones in Japan and export them to the United States. Once again, it soon became clear that digital technology, not analog, was becoming dominant, and that the most advanced technology was in the United States, not Japan. Accordingly, the Personal Telecommunications Division was established in San Diego, not as the offshoot of a dominant Japanese business unit, but with the objective of spearheading Sony's worldwide personal telecommunications business. In an effort to jumpstart its digital cellular phone business, Sony established a joint venture with a local US company, Qualcomm. The expectation was that Sony could provide manufacturing and marketing, to combine with Qualcomm's advanced digital technology.

Completion of functional migration

In 1990, Sony's television sector was divided into three worldwide geographic units, one of which, Television of America (TVA) assumed business planning responsibility within the United States. The other two, TVJ and TVE, took responsibility for Japan and Europe, respectively. By 1994, TVA was responsible for all of the engineering of its models. Of the 25-plus new television models introduced each year, half were "productized" in the United States. A few key parts were still purchased from Japan, but more than 80 percent of the dollar value of inputs was purchased locally.[6] Furthermore, with the advent of electron gun manufacturing in Mexico, and the prospect of sourcing glass in Pittsburgh, the amount of local sourcing was likely to grow still further. By 1994, then, the process of functional migration in televisions was essentially complete, with all functions that had once been based in Japan now also performed in the United States.

Toward a model of post-entry management

The story of the Sony Corporation in the United States illustrates the process of post-entry management over a 20-year period, beginning with a small investment in television assembly and leading to a complex and varied position in numerous product lines. We observe, in addition, a geographic dimension, with entries in the USA leading to subsequent investment in Europe.

In many ways, Sony's experience is consistent with existing theory. Sony's migration of functions in televisions is consistent with models of internationalization based on progressive commitment. We observe a full range of functional migration, from final assembly, to manufacture of CRTs, to local procurement, to product design, and eventually to responsibility for business planning and strategic independence. The addition of new lines of business is also consistent with previous research, as Sony first entered the USA in core lines of business where it had a strong competitive advantage (televisions, audio equipment, and magnetic tape); later Sony entered in lines of business where superiority was less clear (semiconductors); and eventually entered in lines of business where it sought to tap US technological leadership (data storage systems and personal telecommunications). Related to entry by line of business is the choice of entry mode, where once again Sony's experience is consistent with existing theory. At first, Sony relied on small-scale greenfield investments as a way to ensure careful replication of its home country advantage; later, as it gained confidence in its ability to manage in the USA, and as it sought to capture host country capabilities, it began to make acquisitions.

Yet our study of Sony in the United States does much more than provide anecdotal support for previous research. We see Sony's evolution as the result of deliberate decisions undertaken by managers, in part responding to external factors, and in part facilitated by internal organizational dynamics. In this section we depict the process of post-entry management as a series of recurring loops, each involving a particular kind of organizational knowledge and capability development, and each facing particular impediments.

Post-entry evolution as a series of recurring loops: functional migration in televisions

The process of functional migration in televisions can be distilled into several steps, as shown on Figure 10.1. Until 1972, Sony managers decided that manufacturing should take place entirely in Japan; no functions were performed in the USA aside from sales and marketing. What triggered a change was an exogenous event, the charge of dumping, which led Akio Morita and Sony top management to consider direct investment in the USA. The combination of internal assessments and external forces led to the decision to invest in the USA, initially at a low level of functionality, performing only final assembly (Step 1). Based on this decision, technical knowledge, including both process know-how and product know-how, was transferred by expatriates from Sony's television division in Japan to San Diego, where an identical assembly process was built (Step 2). In addition to receiving financial resources and technical and managerial know-how from its Japanese parent, the new subsidiary secured resources locally (Step 3). It leased factory space at Rancho Bernardo, hired local employees, and purchased some inputs and equipment

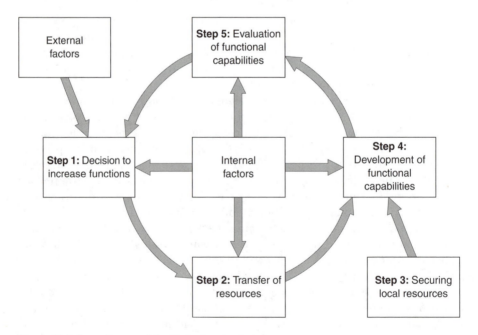

Figure 10.1 A process model of functional migration.

194

locally. By combining resources from its parent with resources secured locally, the San Diego plant began to perform its initial functions, assembling kits into working televisions (Step 4). The plant was carefully monitored by managers in Japan, who wanted to know whether American workers could achieve satisfactory performance. Once it was apparent that acceptable levels of quality could be achieved, the benefits of greater functionality were evaluated (Step 5).

The final step in the first loop is the first step in a second loop. Having successfully set up final assembly in San Diego, Sony's television managers contemplated additional functional migration (Step 1). The advantages of adding CRT manufacturing were clear given the costs of transportation and risks of tube breakage. No further exogenous factors were needed to decide on an increase in functionality. Additional knowledge was transferred from Japan, as engineers and technicians with expertise in CRT manufacturing were sent to San Diego (Step 2). Additional resources were secured locally (Step 3). By 1974 the San Diego plant was manufacturing CRTs (Step 4) and meeting expectations of performance (Step 5).

Impediments to the process of functional migration can be identified at each step. While these were not central to our analysis, we can at least enumerate the most important ones here. Inaccurate analysis or internal resistance may cause a firm to err at Step 1, either deciding not to add functionality or deciding to add too much. Ineffective or inappropriate mechanisms to transfer know-how may prevent a firm from achieving a success at Step 2. The inability to secure local resources – frequently human resources, often a challenge for foreign-based firms, or physical inputs, also a challenge given a frequent lack of knowledge concerning local vendors – may prevent success at Step 3. Either will present effective performance of the new function, Step 4.

After completing two loops, and successfully performing television assembly and CRT manufacturing at San Diego, Sony paused. In the absence of further external stimulus, no additional loops were undertaken. Relative factor input costs made it inefficient to undertake further functional migration. Ultimately it was an exogenous factor, the dollar's plunge against the yen in 1985, which renewed the process of functional migration. Over the next several years, a series of loops took place, first for local parts procurement, then local product design, eventually performance of the *seihan* process, and finally the creation of TVA, which conferred upon the USA equal status and strategic independence. Each can be understood as a discrete loop, with initial evaluation, decision to increase functionality, transfer, feedback, and evaluation of further functional migration.

Yet we also see that impediments changed with successive loops. For early loops, which sought to locate assembly or CRT manufacturing in the USA, the most important impediments were the effective transfer of technical know-how and the ability to secure resources locally. There was little resistance from television headquarters in Japan, only an initial concern that American workers could match Japanese levels of quality. As functional migration progressed, impediments changed. Some managers in Japan were opposed to local product design because they doubted the USA could achieve a sufficiently high level, but others were opposed for more parochial reasons, as such a shift actually diminished the power and scope of the Japanese activities.

195

Entry by additional lines of business

Entry by additional lines of business can also be depicted as a series of loops. Sony first entered in televisions, a core business which boasted a competitive advantage over local firms. Such an advantage was necessary to compensate for the intrinsic disadvantages that Sony faced as an inexperienced foreign firm in the United States, referred to as the "liability of foreignness."

The process of sequential LOB entry is depicted in Figure 10.2. Rather than a decision to increase functionality within a given line of business (as depicted in Figure 10.1), the process depicted here is that of entering a new line of business. Yet the sequence of evaluation, action, monitoring, and subsequent evaluation is the same. At the outset, the benefits of entering in a new line of business are evaluated in light of external factors such as technological change, competitors' actions, and relative costs, perhaps leading to entry in that line of business (Step 1). Resources are transferred (Step 2) and combined with local resources (Step 3) to develop country-specific knowledge and resources (Step 4). Based on the evaluation of this country-specific knowledge (Step 5), entry in a second LOB, audio equipment, was undertaken in 1975, and in 1977 a third entry was made in magnetic tape (Step 1).

With each additional entry, Sony added to its experience in the USA and accumulated resources that could be shared by subsequent entries. Sony developed a strong reputation as a good employer and as a good customer for local suppliers, learned about local regulations, and generally developed capabilities that were not specific only to televisions and magnetic tape, but could serve other lines of business as well.

Some additional lines of business, such as display systems, were related to the CRT business, and drew on Sony's existing capabilities. Other entries, however,

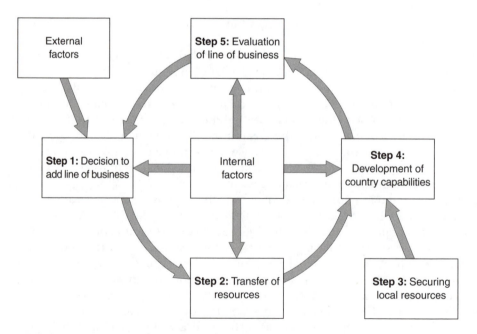

Figure 10.2 A process model of line of business addition.

were in LOBs where Sony did not have a strong advantage over US firms, but sought to tap local expertise, as with the Data Storage Division and Personal Telecommunications Division. These recently founded divisions would never have been attempted in the 1970s, when Sony concentrated on exploiting its competitive advantages; rather, they were possible only because of the existence of a strong country organization and the abundance of Sony capabilities – including management support, financial infrastructure, and engineering talent – that could be shared across units.

Lessons about post-entry management

Having presented the case of Sony Corporation in the United States, and having organized its experience into a process model consisting of a series of recurring loops, let us return to the questions identified at the outset of this chapter. We noted that MNCs are increasingly depicted as networks, yet the process by which these networks evolve is often overlooked. We pointed out that research about foreign direct investment has tended to explain initial entry only, without considering the process of managing foreign subsidiaries following entry. Based on the evidence presented here, what can we offer as lessons about post-entry management?

Separate dimensions of evolution

A first insight is that post-entry management, and by extension the development of a differentiated network, involves evolution along three discrete dimensions: functional migration, line of business addition, and geographic expansion. Sony's development from a Japanese-based firm to a differentiated network called for evolution along all three dimensions. These progressed concurrently but can be modeled separately. Each one involved a process of capability building, yet for each the nature of capabilities was different. Functional migration called for the successful development of function-specific capabilities, which provided the basis for further evolution. Adding new lines of business, by contrast, called for capabilities related to management in the host country.

Interaction among dimensions

These three dimensions of evolution were not entirely separate, but were linked in important ways. Most important is how function-specific capabilities in one line of business could be leveraged to stimulate further evolution along other lines of business. The creation of SEMA helped transfer engineering expertise among US lines of business. Similarly, shifting the *seihan* process in televisions made it easier to do the same for other lines of business, and vendor development at the San Diego site was leveraged to help vendor development in Pittsburgh. Thus, we find an active effort to manage MNC evolution as an integrated whole, with benefits from one dimension helping to stimulate continuing evolution along others.

Changing impediments

The Sony case also makes clear that impediments change over the course of discrete loops. In functional migration in televisions, for example, at first the challenges were mainly technical. They involved the replication of assembly layouts, the transfer of process know-how, and effective training of local employees. Later, as Sony sought to localize more functions in the USA, the most severe impediments involved vendor development, an added complexity because this step necessitated working with external entities. Finally, as product design and business planning functions were shifted to the USA, the strongest impediments were political, raising a new level of complexity and sensitivity.

The need for a variety of skills

Taking these points together, guiding the evolution of an MNC from initial foreign market entry to maturity as a differentiated network is complex and calls for a variety of managerial skills. First are skills related to transfer of technology. Second are skills in sourcing local resources, including not only supplies and materials inputs, which calls for the development of a supplier base, but human resources, often a difficult matter for a foreign-based firm. Third are political skills, needed to overcome resistance that may take place in the home country as activities are shifted, rather than merely replicated, to the host country. A final skill – or, perhaps more correctly, a virtue – is persistence. As we see with Sony, the process of post-entry management was lengthy and called for a steady approach over many years. Sony did not act precipitously, pushing functional migration in advance of economic prudence, but responded to exogenous variables with speed and effectiveness.

Limits of generalizability

The Sony Corporation's experience in the United States helps illuminate many of the challenges of post-entry management, but it is important that we do not assume Sony to be a typical company. In fact, what makes Sony an illuminating prototype is precisely its idiosyncratic nature. Sony was unusual for many reasons: it was an early entrant to the USA, it was a market leader, and a Japanese firm. Each of these factors may shape an MNC's evolution, as discussed here.

Early entrants versus late entrants

Sony was the first Japanese firm to set up manufacturing in the USA, and was therefore able to evolve slowly and deliberately over many years. Although its evolution was stimulated on a few occasions by external factors, notably threats of trade barriers in the early 1970s and the sharp rise of the yen in 1985, for the most part we observe Sony's evolution as driven by an internal logic. Nowhere did we learn of Sony needing to accelerate its evolution in order to respond to the initiatives of competing firms, as is often suggested in international competition.

Later entrants may not have the luxury of gradual evolution, but may need to compress the evolutionary process considerably. Sony undertook many loops, each of which involved a small increase in subsidiary functionality, and monitored the results of each loop carefully before beginning a next loop. Other MNCs may need to be more aggressive, expanding the activities of their subsidiaries by taking fewer large steps.

Mode of entry: greenfield and acquisition

Sony's first entries to the USA were efforts to exploit superior technology in a new market. Its choice of greenfield entry made sense as a way to control operations and ensure an exact replication of its successful Japanese operations. Only later, when Sony ventured into new lines of business and sought to capture superior US technology, did it undertake acquisitions.

Other firms may rely more heavily on acquisitions from the outset. Some operate in industries with substantial overcapacity and therefore cannot invest in new plants; others need a large scale in order to survive and therefore cannot begin small and grow slowly. Whatever the reason, many firms enter foreign markets through acquisitions, and inevitably face rather different dynamics of post-entry management than those encountered by Sony. In some ways, acquisitions may eliminate some major challenges, such as sourcing local resources. The existence of established contacts with suppliers and an established reputation for hiring talented employees may be of great value for the MNC. On the other hand, the set of recurring loops, denoting gradual and incremental evolution, will surely be different when an entire firm, often vertically integrated, is acquired in a single step.

National differences in MNC evolution

Although Sony is often regarded as an unusual Japanese firm – often thought to be more entrepreneurial and less formal than most – it nevertheless exhibited a typically Japanese approach in the management of its post-entry evolution. As noted by Kagono and colleagues (1985), Japanese firms often take an "inductive, gradual adjustment approach" to their development. Driving this process is the "continuous accumulation and development of in-house resources" through "learning and accumulated expertise," very much in keeping with the model set forth here. It is therefore not surprising that a Japanese-based firm has offered a clear example of an evolutionary approach to post-entry management.

Whether the approach we have seen in this case study can be generalized to firms from other parts of the world is therefore open to question. It has been suggested that European firms are more likely to evolve by taking a few bold steps, rather than a gradual approach. The large-scale acquisitions in the USA undertaken by European firms, including billion-dollar acquisitions of RCA by Thomson S.A., Rorer by Rhône Poulenc, and Merion Merrill Dow by Hoechst AG, all suggest an approach very different from Sony's, raising a very different set of post-entry issues than those exhibited in this case study.

Conclusions

Despite these limitations, Sony serves as an effective prototype, casting into sharp relief many challenges associated with managing an MNC from initial foreign-market entry to arrive at a mature and complex national position. As we have seen in this case, several distinct dimensions of evolution have been identified, each of which can be depicted as a series of recurring loops, and each of which builds distinctive capabilities that permit further evolution. We see, too, impediments at each stage of the processes, some of which change as evolution progresses.

We find, in sum, that effective management of the post-entry process calls on MNCs to be effective at evaluating opportunities for greater evolution, for effective transfer of know-how, for securing local resources, for recombining them to build local capabilities, and for effective monitoring to permit extended evolution. We note, in addition, that political resistance may grow over time, as continuing evolution involves not merely the replication of home-based activities, but a zero-sum transfer of activities. Building an effective multinational networks, therefore, calls not only for skills in technology transfer, but also skills in understanding and overcoming political obstacles within the organization.

Notes

1 This early history of Sony is drawn in part from Malnight (1990).
2 A number of Japanese firms did the same thing, including Honda Motor Company at its Marysville, Ohio plant. These firms were keen to train employees from scratch, and not struggle to change existing habits.
3 It is interesting to note how close is Sony's description of its policy of "local globalization" and the notion of transnational management as defined by Christopher Bartlett and Sumantra Ghoshal (1989). Both seek the benefits of global integration and national responsiveness.
4 Quoted in the Sony Company document, given to the authors on their visit to San Diego, June 1994.
5 *Seihan* literally means "make-sell," a term that captures nicely the two elements of the process: determining allocations of production and targets of sales.
6 "Global localization" did not imply that 100 percent of inputs would eventually be sourced locally. Some television inputs were most efficiently produced in low-wage countries of South East Asia, and were expected to be imported to the United States for the foreseeable future.

References

Bartlett, Christopher and Sumantra Ghoshal (1989) *Managing Across Borders: the Transnational Solution,* Boston, MA: Harvard Business School Press.
Kagono, Tadao, Ikujiro Nonaka, Kiyonori Sakakibara, and Akihiro Okumura (1985) *Strategic versus Evolutionary Management: a U.S.–Japan Comparison of Strategy and Organization,* Amsterdam: North Holland.
Malnight, Thomas W. (1990) "Sony Corporation: globalization," Case Study No. 9–391–071, Boston, MA: Harvard Business School.

11

MANAGING LEADING-EDGE MULTINATIONAL CORPORATIONS

Charles C. Snow, Raymond E. Miles, and Brent B. Allred

Introduction

Multinational corporations today face a variety of difficult organizational issues as they seek to build, extend, or renew their competitive advantage. Global strategies have become highly complex, sometimes requiring an international firm to achieve efficiency, responsiveness, innovation, and speed simultaneously. The organization structures needed to implement such strategies are similarly complex, and managers must upgrade their knowledge and skills in order to operate these leading-edge organizations.

The purpose of this chapter is to provide managers with a practical understanding of the full range of organizational approaches used to conduct international business. To accomplish this goal, we divide modern business history into three major periods: the Industrial Age, Information Age, and Knowledge Age. In each period, there is a dominant form of organizing: hierarchical (Industrial Age), network (Information Age), and cellular (Knowledge Age). In general, the increasingly dynamic nature of doing business globally is requiring more capability and flexibility in the structures of multinational companies. Although current organizational forms still serve the needs of many firms, we propose that a new form, the cellular organization, will provide leading-edge global companies with the means to conduct continuous innovation, the main source of competitive advantage in the twenty-first century.

The Industrial Age: an emphasis on specialization and efficiency

The US Industrial Revolution, which began in the 1860s, brought about major changes in the way people worked, lived, and consumed. The ability to mass produce certain products, such as steel and automobiles, led to the development of large, specialized firms. Relying on newly emerging transportation and communications technologies (for example, rail and telephone), those firms were able to offer standard products to increasingly larger markets (Chandler, 1986, 1990). Specialist firms were also the inventors of the first modern organizational form, the functional structure. The leading companies of the time were organized hierarchically by technical specialty, with top management exercising tight control over key business functions such as manufacturing, sales, and accounting.

After World War I, the emergence of several national product and service markets, coupled with growing consumer expectations, led to the invention of the divisional organization structure, most notably by General Motors and Sears-Roebuck (Chandler, 1962). Unlike the functional structure, the divisional form organized a firm into largely independent divisions, each with a full complement of functional resources focused on a specific product line or geographic area. By pursuing its own product and market opportunities, each division was able to customize its offerings to fit the needs and wants of its targeted customers.

By incorporating elements of both the functional and divisional structures, firms in the aerospace industry developed the matrix form of organizing in the late 1950s and early 1960s (Davis and Lawrence, 1977; Mee, 1964). At that time, pioneering companies such as TRW could produce differentiated but standard products for the civilian and military markets in one or more divisions, while simultaneously transferring some resources from those units into project groups that designed and built prototypical products for space exploration. In the 1970s and 1980s, many multinational companies developed global matrix structures.

During the period from the 1860s through the early 1970s, as the functional, divisional, and matrix organization structures successively appeared, each new structure built on and extended the capabilities offered by its predecessor. Generally speaking, the traditional structures associated with the Industrial Age were hierarchical in shape and heavily oriented toward efficiency, giving them a characteristic approach to competition and management (see Table 11.1).

Competitive mind-set

The competitive mind-set of Industrial Age companies centered on the belief of "Do it yourself." Vertical integration was frequently pursued, as companies brought needed resources under their own control both up and down the value chain. Moreover, firms seldom sought inputs or assistance from other firms in the pursuit of new ventures. By doing everything themselves, traditional firms minimized uncertainty and maximized control. And, of course, they grew quite large. Big companies were able to dominate their respective markets, and they developed a pervasive attitude among their managers that "bigger is better."

Table 11.1 Evolution of major organizational forms and managerial philosophies

	Industrial Age (1860–1970)	Information Age (1970–1995)	Knowledge Age (1995–)
Competitive mind-set	"Do it yourself"	"Focus on your core competencies, outsource other functions to partners"	"Be able to do anything, anytime, anywhere"
Organizational form	Hierarchical	Network	Cellular
Managerial philosophy	Human relations	Human resources	Human investment

Organization structure

Traditional organizations, whether functional, divisional, or matrix, were based on the concept of a pyramidal hierarchy of authority. The top management team resided at the apex of the pyramid, and its knowledge and skill base included not only technical abilities but commercial and governance abilities as well. Although divisional and matrix organizations pushed managerial capabilities farther down the pyramid than in the functional organization, all three hierarchical structures tended to be managed from the top.

Organizing in a hierarchical fashion typically resulted in a plethora of rules, policies, and standard operating procedures. Such organizations suited their purpose, however, because competition, both domestic and international, was much more stable and predictable than it is today.

Managerial philosophy

During the late 1800s and early 1900s, the notion of mass standardization was based on the belief that all factors of production must be utilized in the most efficient manner. Inputs, whether raw materials, machinery, or labor, were merely the means for producing goods. Combining these inputs in the most efficient sequence minimized costs. The activities of workers were reduced to the most economical motions that maximized productivity. The value of employees lay in their ability to complete a task quickly and efficiently, not in the knowledge or ideas they could contribute. Also, it was believed that as long as employees received a paycheck, their basic needs were met, and the company had no further obligation to them. The traditional philosophy held by managers was that few employees wanted or could handle work responsibilities that required creativity, self-direction, or self-control. Therefore, managers closely supervised employees who performed simple, repetitive tasks (Bendix, 1974; Taylor, 1911).

Between the two World Wars, and due largely to the results of the Hawthorne Studies (Roethlisberger, 1941; Roethlisberger and Dickson, 1939), managerial philosophies began to recognize that employees wanted to feel useful to the company and desired to belong to harmonious work groups. Managers were urged to make workers feel important and allow them some self-control in their jobs. In Industrial Age firms, however, the innovative and entrepreneurial tendencies of the individual were seldom unleashed, and control still resided at the top of the organizational pyramid.

International business in Industrial Age firms

The evolution of traditional organizational forms allowed companies to take advantage of various new technologies, advanced means of transportation, and mass production. With better transportation, products could be shipped to almost anywhere in the world. Less expensive products could now reach more customers and markets, providing additional economies of scale to the producer. As a result, product diversification that might have been targeted only for a domestic market began to find applications and demand internationally. As some US firms began to rely more heavily on foreign customers to sustain their growth and profitability, the presence of tariffs and other barriers to entry drove those companies to make direct investments into foreign countries more rapidly than they might have otherwise done (Vernon, 1966).

As Industrial Age companies began to enter the international business arena in a significant way, they needed to adopt strategies to facilitate growth and expansion, and to achieve their desired international presence. The international strategies that a firm adopts usually reflect the degree of risk they are willing to take, the knowledge and information they have regarding foreign markets, the amount of control they wish to retain over their products and operations, and the amount of resources they have available for global expansion. For Industrial Age companies, five major strategies were available to extend the firm's international reach. Each of these strategies involved varying degrees of investment, control, and managerial know-how.

Exporting

The most basic international strategy a firm can adopt is simply exporting current products to foreign customers or intermediaries, such as distributors. Typically, little or no product modification is performed to conform to local cultures and customs. Marketing responsibilities usually fall onto the distributors, since the producer is limiting its international involvement and has insufficient expertise and information about doing business in each foreign location. An export department facilitates and controls these activities. Exporting is beneficial to the producer since it increases revenues and production volumes, and little investment and resources are needed to manage the process. The largest hurdles for exporting firms are finding reputable intermediaries and dealing with international logistics such as transportation, tariffs, and customs issues. At the same time that exporting firms limit their involvement, they also limit their control. They have little control over what happens to the product once it leaves their hands. Also, dealing with foreign distributors on issues such as collections and the "gray market" for their products is difficult without having considerable knowledge about operations in each foreign location.

Licensing

Another basic means of gaining an international presence is to license product or service rights to other companies. The licensing arrangement can be an agreement by one company to give another firm the right to use specific trademarks, patents, copyrights, or product designs for a fee or royalty. A firm can benefit from licensing by obtaining additional revenues on already developed products and by having its products gain greater international exposure. Licensing, however, has certain limitations as well as benefits. For example, licensee firms may attempt to improve on the technology by developing their own products, not only making the licenser's product obsolete, but eliminating any further licensing fee obligations. The licenser should be very comfortable and knowledgeable with the terms and implications of the arrangement, especially in regard to future obligations. A special department or an international division might have the responsibility to oversee and manage an international licensing arrangement.

Franchising

Similar to a license, some firms will choose to franchise. This is usually found with establishments such as restaurants and retail outlets. The franchising firm, usually for an initial fee and subsequent royalties, gives another firm certain rights to use its name and/or sell its products. In doing so, it gives up some control, but is able to generate revenue with little expense on its part. A company such as McDonald's has a mixture of wholly owned and franchised restaurants, both domestically and internationally.

Acquisitions

Firms desiring quick access to foreign markets or know-how may wish to acquire companies in those markets. International acquisitions can be used to obtain technologies or products complementary to those of the acquiring firm. They may also be a means of gaining immediate market share and presence. An acquired firm in the target market will typically be better informed of the cultural, legal, and political issues associated with doing business in that country. An acquisition may also give legitimacy to the acquiring firm because of the acquiree's local reputation. Acquisitions, however, have some drawbacks as well. Purchasing a foreign company holds various hidden risks, since the acquiring firm may not be familiar with local laws regarding human resource management and technology transfers. In addition, the cultural differences between the two firms may cause friction and misunderstandings. The acquiring firm is able to establish legal control through the purchase, but it is not always clear to whom the foreign employees are loyal (Brooke, 1984). A firm following an acquisition strategy would usually organize its foreign operations under an international division or one of the global structures described below.

Creating a foreign subsidiary

Some firms may wish to avoid the challenges associated with acquiring other companies and maintain strong control over foreign operations. This can be done by creating a wholly owned subsidiary in the target market. By setting up its own subsidiary, the firm is able to align the operations of the foreign subsidiary with the strategy of the parent firm. Subsidiary creation is, however, usually fraught with high startup costs and uncertainty. In many countries being foreign has its costs, since people often prefer to "buy national." Recruiting, training, and retaining personnel is also a major challenge in countries such as Japan, since it is culturally important to work for the prestigious Japanese firms. In addition, there are political risks associated with wholly-owned subsidiaries. Certain countries require that foreign firms take on local partners. This arrangement may have some of the benefits of acquiring a firm, but it gives up ownership and control to another party. Also, the local partner may have little to offer in terms of financial or technical assistance.

Another political risk is that of the nationalization of industries. Although this risk has diminished in many countries, it may still appear in some form on occasion.

As a firm's international presence increases, so does the need to organize in such a way as to effectively satisfy foreign demand while retaining a desired amount of operational control (Stopford and Wells, 1972). The decision to expand internationally must be accompanied by a decision on how to organize foreign operations. The major organizational means used by Industrial Age companies to integrate an international strategy into their domestic business operations are discussed below (See Table 11.2 for a summary).

Export department

As a firm first enters the international marketplace, it is usually as an extension of its domestic operations. The needs of the local market take precedence, and international sales are incremental. To implement an export strategy, an export department – or even an individual employee – may be assigned the responsibility. Limited international marketing, logistics, administration, and distribution are provided by the organization. The influence of the export department is usually minimal, as are the attention and resources it receives from the company.

International division

An international division centralizes all of the firm's international operations and functions. With greater importance than an export department, the international division typically has more authority and resources available for its foreign activities. The international division can be organized by geographic area, product line, or function, usually in a similar fashion to how the firm's other divisions are organized. With an international division, greater attention is given to international activities, yet international operations may be seen as a peripheral or even competing unit of the organization. This structure is usually indicative of a firm that lacks a global mind-set.

Table 11.2 Evolution of international business approaches

Industrial Age (1860–1970)	Information Age (1970–1995)	Knowledge Age (1995–)
Exporting, licensing, and franchising through an International Division	Outsourcing	Simultaneous international competition and collaboration using multiple overlapping networks
Acquisition of foreign firms	International joint ventures	
Creation of foreign subsidiaries	Multi-firm networks	Boundaryless organizations (resources located geographically according to knowledge and expertise)
Global product, area, functional, and matrix structures		Self-governing resource clusters

Global product structure

As firms begin to incorporate a more global perspective in the way they do business, their international operations are no longer considered peripheral or competing. Instead, the strategy and structure of the firm will reflect the significance of being a true multinational corporation. Accordingly, a company organizes its international operations so as to be aligned with the firm's expanded strategic focus. Marketing-driven companies are especially likely to adopt a global product structure. In this form, the firm is organized around product lines. Although the headquarters will often retain overall R&D, marketing, and financial functions, each product division will have specific responsibilities for the development and marketing of its products throughout the world. With this structure, firms first focus on the development of core product lines and then adapt the products for regional or local markets as is deemed appropriate and as resources permit.

Global area structure

If a firm is most interested in serving local and regional markets effectively, it may adopt a global area structure. The company would be organized into regional divisions, such as Europe, Asia, North America, and South America. Each division is given the responsibility to take the company's existing products and then modify and market them according to specific regional or national tastes and preferences. Whereas the global product structure focuses primarily on the development of product lines and then on individual markets, the global area structure focuses primarily on geographic regions and develops products for those markets using existing technology and know-how.

Global functional structure

This structure organizes the firm's functional areas on a global basis. Functional executives who have worldwide responsibility for the use of their respective function's resources control production, finance, and sales. This structure allows for centralized control and minimizes duplication of resources and facilities, but makes co-ordination across product and geographic areas difficult.

Global mixed structure

Although each of the above global structures has advantages and disadvantages, some firms do not have strategies that clearly favor one structure over another. In such a case, a firm may wish to adopt a mixed structure to best organize its international operations. For example, a company may have one product line (A) that is central to its success. For the remaining product lines (B, C, and D), it uses a regional approach. In this case, the firm may organize into a global area structure, with divisions for North America, Asia, and Europe, except for product line A, which is organized separately into its own division with global responsibilities.

Global matrix structure

Other firms may desire to incorporate a reporting and organizing structure that blends more than one organizational responsibility. Unlike the mixed structure that organizes different responsibilities separately, the matrix structure organizes the firm in such a way that individuals or project teams report to different managers simultaneously. For example, a product development team might have a headquarters-based R&D manager, but the team also reports to geographic managers to ensure that the development of the product will meet local needs. Global matrix organizations have the potential to achieve a balance among product, functional, and regional concerns.

Industrial Age companies focused primarily on domestic production and competition. To the extent that they engaged in international business, the emphasis was on exporting "our" products and "our" ways to foreign markets. The dynamic internationalization of business over the last several decades, however, brought about a shift in the way business was conducted and a need for a new means of organizing people and other resources.

The Information Age: an emphasis on speed and responsiveness

Beginning in the 1970s, increasingly intense domestic and international competition left many large, hierarchical companies slow to respond to global threats and opportunities. The planning and co-ordination efficiencies achieved during the Industrial Age were frequently being offset by the unyielding bureaucracies that had been created. Although the extensive vertical integration of the previous decade increased the market clout of many firms, traditional structures became onerous when flexibility and speed were needed to remain competitive.

Mass production and standardization had made the products of Industrial Age companies affordable and available to the general populace. Consumers who enjoyed the fruits of mass production began to demand differentiated products and services, and power shifted from the manufacturer to the customer. Firms found it increasingly important to be responsive to the customer's needs and wants.

If a firm was not responsive, it could quickly fall behind other firms that were. Companies began to realize that differentiating their products could help them capture segmented markets. Consumers were often willing to pay a premium for these customized products, whether in price or loyalty (or both). Further, customization did not preclude companies from capitalizing on the many benefits of mass standardization, since economies of scale could still be generated at lower volumes through the use of advanced manufacturing technologies. Companies that did not conform to these new practices struggled to succeed. In addition to the transformation of local markets, the increasing internationalization of consumer awareness and tastes led to a similar need for company responsiveness on a global scale. The different cultures, laws, and customs that existed between (and sometimes within) countries, as well as increasingly sophisticated customers, meant that standardized products often held less value and sold poorly against those of differentiated competitors.

To become more competitive, corporations downsized, delayered, consolidated, and outsourced many functions throughout the 1980s. In innovative companies such as Nike, ABB, and Logitech, a new form of organizing called the "network" emerged (Miles and Snow, 1986; Thorelli, 1986). Significant developments in information technology allowed geographically far-flung organizations to be quickly assembled, deployed, and reassembled if necessary – and the virtual organization was born (Byrne, 1993; Davidow and Malone, 1992). By the end of the 1980s, the Information Age was in full bloom (see Table 11.1).

Competitive mind-set

Unlike Industrial Age firms, which attempted to do everything themselves, the competitive mind-set of Information Age firms is to "focus on core competencies and outsource non-essential functions to highly competent partners." Firms today realize that they cannot be the best at everything. The lack of capable partners, which was generally the case during the Industrial Age, is no longer a problem as many new and existing firms are willing to form partnerships to pursue international ventures. Greater accessibility to education and experience has provided more people with broad managerial skills to complement their technical competencies. Entrepreneurial individuals leverage these abilities inside companies to create fast-moving organizations that can collaborate in a variety of ways. Often such firms can provide valuable abilities more affordably and responsively than larger, hierarchical organizations can develop in-house.

Companies that focus on their core competencies and search outside for partners with complementary resources end up forming or joining multi-firm network organizations (Miles and Snow, 1994). Such organizations do not rely on rules and hierarchies to get things done. Rather, they use market mechanisms to make decisions and allocate resources. Thus, Information Age managers are comfortable working in market-driven companies which are responsive to customers', suppliers', and partners' needs.

Organization structure

Similar to a computer network, a network organization links independent firms to provide the critical expertise needed for specific projects or products. Rather than perform the entire sequence of researching, designing, manufacturing, and marketing of a product, various complementary firms are linked to provide high-quality services at each of these stages. Small network firms can use this structure to behave in a manner much larger than their actual size would normally permit. For example, a small software developer can use the network structure to outsource financial, personnel, and manufacturing functions, allowing it to focus its limited resources on product and technology development. The time and capital required to manage these non-critical functions can distract the firm from its core activities. Large network firms, on the other hand, can become more nimble by joining forces with smaller specialist partners. Nike, the sports apparel giant, no longer manufactures the shoes that bear the classic "Swoosh" logo. Upstream, the production function has been outsourced to manufacturing partners in Thailand, Vietnam, China,

Korea, Taiwan, and other countries with lower labor costs. In this network, the independent manufacturers benefit from the stability and expertise of Nike, while Nike benefits from the lower costs of not building and managing its own manufacturing facilities. Downstream, Nike utilizes competent distribution partners and major retailing chains to outfit its customers in Nike gear.

Even while companies adopted available network structures, other firms developed this organizational form even further. Led by the Dell Computer Corporation, companies are not only utilizing the competencies and skills of their suppliers; they are making them full partners in the process of "supply chain management." Trust is replacing formal control mechanisms as technical and market information passes freely among network firms (Miles and Creed, 1995). Such developments not only help to establish long-term relationships that promote responsiveness, but also result in the realization by all network member firms that what is in the best interest of the network as a whole is also in the best interest of the individual firms. The most advanced network organizations are characterized by continuous investment in training and education for all of their member firms.

Managerial philosophy

As firms adopted Information Age structures and attitudes, there was greater recognition of the value of individual employees. For example, the human resources model of management acknowledges that employees are more than just factors of production; they are important resources available to the organization for the attainment of objectives (Miles, 1975). If the success of a network organization is heavily based on trust and collaboration, human resources must be utilized to their fullest extent.

Although the inherent nature of people has not changed dramatically over the last 20–30 years, the realization of their potential and value has markedly improved. In many companies, employees want to make meaningful contributions to the organization in creative, responsible, and self-directed ways. Managers should therefore create an environment that allows all employees the opportunity to reach their full potential by understanding their developmental needs and providing appropriate opportunities. In network organizations, this requires more emphasis to be placed on inter-firm collaboration and project management skills (Allred, Snow, and Miles, 1996).

International business in Information Age companies

The advanced international strategies in the Industrial Age took on a more global outlook, and such strategies were typically implemented with global area, product, or matrix structures. However, those structures still retained all of the disadvantages of traditional hierarchies and bureaucracies. With the advent of network organizations, a truly global perspective could begin to develop. The need for international responsiveness required that firms became adaptable as well as efficient. By capitalizing on core competencies and outsourcing other functions throughout the world, the integrated network became globally competitive in ways that each individual firm could not. Thus, the traditional global organization structures were heavily augmented with two other arrangements for conducting international business: outsourcing and joint ventures.

Outsourcing

By outsourcing certain functions, firms are better able to focus on their core capabilities. There are often many qualified external partners to whom services and components can be outsourced. Outsourcing often provides a firm with more resources to concentrate on core competencies and can be used to reduce costs and improve quality. At the same time, outsourcing gives up some control to external parties and still requires a certain level of management, especially when the relationships are new. The best outsourcing relationships occur when lead firms and their suppliers view themselves as part of the same organization and treat each other accordingly (Miles and Snow, 1994).

International joint ventures

Joint ventures are a popular means of gaining the knowledge and expertise of other firms. In using a joint venture, a firm reduces its risk and exposure by sharing the venture with a partner. When entering foreign markets, a joint venture with local partners provides a firm with instant access to the market and knowledge about distribution, technologies, and so on. Although a firm may gain knowledge and market presence, it also gives up some control and may provide others access to its proprietary technologies (Bleeke and Ernst, 1995). However, in places such as Japan, joint ventures may be the only way to gain access to distribution channels and thus inroads into that market. The best joint ventures tend to be those that are based on complementary resources, have a clear business focus, and are staffed with the respective companies' best managers and technical specialists.

The network organization has provided significant benefits in today's dynamic global business environment. By focusing on the activities that it does best, a firm is able to become more innovative and competitive in those areas. By outsourcing selected functions to more competent external partners, a firm is better poised to take advantage of the best technologies and markets available. In the future, an even more advanced form of the network organization will be necessary for leading-edge companies to succeed in the global marketplace.

The Knowledge Age: an emphasis on entrepreneurship and innovation

At the beginning of the twenty-first century, the increasing sophistication of industrial and individual customers requires constant innovation in many business sectors. In a growing number of businesses, product life cycles are becoming alarmingly short. Moreover, many companies have adopted a continuous improvement philosophy throughout their operations. By doing so, they are creating learning organizations that are continuously innovative and adaptive. As a result, competition in many global industries is intense.

Because of the widespread desire for constant improvement, the main challenges of the next organizational wave will be those of entrepreneurship and innovation. Many organizations that are burdened by traditional hierarchies and attitudes will find it difficult to compete in the business environment of the twenty-first century. Many of today's stable network organizations may also struggle with the pace and demands that will be necessary to remain competitive in the future. The organizational form of the future will have to build on the unique advantages and characteristics of earlier forms: the specialization and efficiency of hierarchical organizations, and the speed and responsiveness of network organizations.

Competitive mind-set

By incorporating the best attributes of the previous organizational forms to position themselves to compete in the twenty-first century, Knowledge Age companies will be able to do "anything, anytime, anywhere." The requisite flexibility and innovation will mean that leading-edge companies – particularly in professional services and other knowledge-based businesses – will have thin, changeable boundaries and will be organized to act effectively and quickly. The responsibility to discover opportunities, and then manage the response, will exist throughout the organization. Managers in such organizations must be able to compete and cooperate simultaneously, an ability that has been referred to as "co-opetition" (Brandenburger and Nalebuff, 1996).

Organization structure

Some companies in the twenty-first century will use minimalist organization structures that serve primarily to facilitate the activities of entrepreneurial professionals. We call this type of structure the "cellular" organization (Miles *et al.*, 1997). The cellular metaphor suggests a living, adaptive organization. Cells in living organisms possess fundamental functions of life and can act alone to meet a particular need. However, by acting in concert, cells can perform more complex functions. Evolving characteristics, or learning, if shared across all cells, can create a higher-order organism. Similarly, a cellular organization is made up of cells (self-managing teams, autonomous business units or firms, and so on) that can operate alone but that can interact with other cells to produce a more potent and competent business mechanism. It is this combination of independence and interdependence that allows the cellular organizational form to generate and share the know-how that produces continuous innovation.

Building blocks of the cellular form

In the future, completely cellular firms will achieve a level of know-how well beyond that of earlier organizational forms by combining entrepreneurship, self-organization, and member ownership in mutually reinforcing ways. Each cell (team, business unit, firm) will have an entrepreneurial responsibility to the larger organization. The customers of a particular cell can be outside clients or other cells in the organization. In either case, the purpose is to spread an entrepreneurial mind-set throughout the organization so that every cell is concerned with improvement and growth. Indeed, giving each cell entrepreneurial responsibility is essential to the full utilization of the firm's constantly growing know-how. Of course, each cell must also have the entrepreneurial skills required to generate business for itself and the overall organization.

Each cell must be able to continually reorganize in order to make its expected contribution to the overall organization. Of particular value here are the technical skills needed to perform its function, the collaborative skills necessary to make appropriate linkages with other organizational units and external partner firms, and the governance skills required to manage its own activities. Application of this cellular principle may require the company to strip away most of the bureaucracy that is currently in place and replace it with jointly defined protocols that guide internal and external collaboration.

Each cell must be rewarded for acting entrepreneurially and operating in a business-like manner. If the cellular units are teams or strategic business units instead of complete firms, psychological ownership can be achieved by organizing cells as profit centers, allowing them to participate in company stock-purchase plans, and so on. However, the ultimate cellular solution is actual member ownership of those cell assets and resources that they have created and that they voluntarily invest with the firm in expectation of a joint return.

TCG: a cellular organization

Technical Computing and Graphics (TCG), a privately held information-technology company based in Sydney, Australia, is perhaps the best example of the cellular approach to organizing. TCG develops a wide variety of products and services, including portable and hand-held data terminals and loggers, computer graphics systems, bar-coding systems, electronic data interchange systems, and other information-technology products and services. The 13 individual small firms at TCG are the focus of its cellular approach. Like a cell in a large organism, each firm has its own purpose and ability to function independently, but it shares common features and purpose with all of its sister firms. Some TCG member firms specialize in one or more product categories, while others specialize in hardware or software.

At TCG, the various firms have come into the group with existing high levels of technical and business competence. However, the operating protocol at TCG assures that system-wide competence will continue to grow. The process is called triangulation, and it is the means by which TCG continually develops new products and services (Mathews, 1993). Triangulation is a three-cornered partnership among (a) one or more TCG firms, (b) an external joint-venture partner (e.g. Hitachi) that also provides equity capital to the venture, and (c) a principal customer (e.g. Telstra, an Australian telephone company) whose large advance order wins it contractual rights as well as provides additional cash to the venture (see Figure 11.1).

Each TCG firm is expected to search continually for new product and service opportunities. When a particular venture shows concrete promise, the initiating firm acts as project leader for the remainder of the venture. The first step in the triangulation process is to identify and collaborate with a joint-venture partner, a firm with expertise in the proposed technology. TCG receives partial funding for the project from the joint-venture partner, and it also gains access to technical ideas

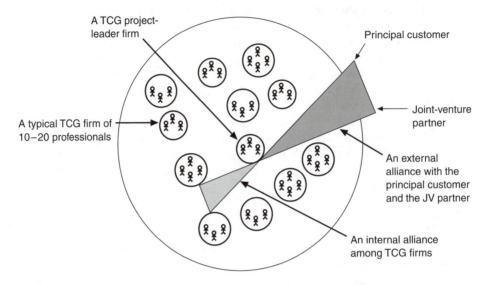

A TCG project-leader firm

Principal customer

A typical TCG firm of 10–20 professionals

Joint-venture partner

An external alliance with the principal customer and the JV partner

An internal alliance among TCG firms

Figure 11.1 TCG's cellular organization.

Source: adapted from Miles *et al.* (1997) "Organizing in the knowledge age: anticipating the cellular form," *Academy of Management Executive*, 11: 7–20. Republished with permission of *Academy of Management Executive*.

and distribution channels. Next, the project-leader firm identifies an initial large customer for the new product. TCG also collaborates with the customer in the sense that it agrees to custom-design a product for that client. By working together with the joint-venture partner and the principal customer, TCG is able to efficiently develop a state-of-the-art product that is tailor-made to the principal customer's specifications.

According to TCG's governance principles, the project-leader firm is also expected to search among the other TCG companies for additional partners – not only because they are needed for their technical contribution, but also because the collaboration itself is expected to enhance overall organizational know-how. The process of internal triangulation thus serves a dual purpose. It produces direct input to the project, and it helps to diffuse competence in areas such as business development, partnering, and project management. The three cellular principles are tightly interconnected at TCG, mutually reinforcing each other and producing a strong overall organization. First, acceptance of entrepreneurial responsibility is required for admission to the group and is increasingly enhanced by the triangulation process. Second, self-organization gives the individual firm both the ability and the freedom to reach deeply into its own know-how to create responses to a continuously evolving set of customer and partner needs. Third, each firm's profit responsibility, as well as its opportunity to hold stock in other TCG firms, provides an ongoing stimulus for the growth and utilization of know-how.

Adding value by using the cellular form

A close examination of cellular-organized firms such as TCG indicates that they also share some of the features of earlier organizational forms. Indeed, each new form, as noted earlier, incorporates the major value-adding characteristics of the previous forms and adds new capabilities to them. Thus, the cellular form includes the dispersed entrepreneurship of the divisional form, customer responsiveness of the matrix form, and self-organizing knowledge and asset sharing of the network form.

The cellular organizational form, however, offers the potential to add value even beyond asset and know-how sharing. In its fully developed state, the cellular organization adds value through its unique ability to create and utilize knowledge. For example, knowledge sharing occurs in networks as a by-product of asset sharing rather than as a specific focus of such activity. Similarly, matrix and divisional firms recognize the value that may be added when knowledge is shared across projects or divisions, but they must create special-purpose mechanisms (for example, task forces) in order to generate and share new knowledge. By contrast, as illustrated at TCG, the cellular form lends itself to sharing not only the explicit know-how that cells have accumulated and articulated, but also the tacit know-how that emerges when cells combine to design unique new customer solutions (Nonaka and Takeuchi, 1995). Such learning focuses not on the output of the innovation process, but on the innovation process itself: it is know-how that can be achieved and shared only by doing.

Beyond knowledge creation and sharing, the cellular form has the potential to add value through its related ability to keep the firm's total knowledge assets more fully invested than the other organizational forms are able to achieve. Because each cell has entrepreneurial responsibility, and is empowered to draw on any of the firm's resources for each new business opportunity, high levels of knowledge utilization across cells should be expected. Network organizations aspire to high utilization of know-how and assets, but upstream firms are ultimately dependent on downstream partners to find new product or service uses. In the cellular firm, the product or service innovation process is continuous and fully shared.

The tradeoffs one must make in order to obtain the benefits of a cellular organization are not, at this point, fully evident. However, two potential drawbacks of the cellular form can be postulated. The first involves the high-caliber human resources needed to staff a cellular organization. Finding people who possess a combination of technical, entrepreneurial, leadership, and self-governing skills will be, in most cases, difficult. Second, the approach required to "manage" such people has not been clearly defined. If cells (teams, small firms, and so on) are expected essentially to be self-directing and self-governing, then "management" becomes a service provided only on request. Both the form managerial services should take, and how they should be provided, are not yet clearly understood.

Managerial philosophy

Many organizational variations using some or all of the cellular principles are likely to emerge in the years ahead. While the direction of the evolution is clear, however, companies that attempt implementation of the complete cellular form face several significant challenges. It is certain that cellular-organized firms will not just happen – they are the product of a bold managerial vision and, even more importantly, of a unique managerial philosophy. The ability to envision and build the entrepreneurial, self-organizing, and ownership components of cellular organizations must be under-girded with a philosophy that emphasizes investment in human capabilities and the willingness to take substantial risks to maximize their utilization. Accordingly, we call this philosophy the "human investment" model (Miles and Snow, 1994).

The first requirement is a willingness to invest in human capability that goes well beyond simply providing for current education and training. The concept of investment calls for expenditures to build the capabilities needed to respond to the future demands that will be placed on the organization, even those that cannot be easily forecast. Training to meet current needs is not an investment, because the requirement is clear, and the costs and benefits can be calculated. Building competencies for future needs is an investment because risk is involved – not every return can be predicted and, moreover, not everyone whose skills are enhanced will remain with the firm.

The concept of investment always involves risk, which is usually proportional to the level of possible return. The biggest challenge facing most firms that are considering the use of a cellular form of organization is not just the investment required to build key competencies; it is the willingness to allow the levels of self-governance necessary to fully utilize that competence. For example, TCG takes what many managers would view as an extraordinary risk by allowing each firm (cell) in the group to initiate its own business, including forming joint ventures with other companies, and to voluntarily co-ordinate its activities with other TCG firms using agreed-upon protocols instead of hierarchical controls.

Perhaps even more challenging than making investments and taking risks, however, is the long-term requirement for sharing with organization members the returns of their knowledge utilization. If organization members are to accept professional levels of responsibility, traditional reward schemes such as bonus plans are not likely to be sufficient. The long-run pursuit of an increasingly competent organization may require innovative mechanisms providing real ownership and profit-sharing, mechanisms that give members' intellectual capital the same rights as the financial capital supplied by stockholders.

International business in Knowledge Age companies

The conduct of international business for leading-edge companies will change significantly in the twenty-first century. True Knowledge Age companies – those operating in hyper-competitive environments such as computers, biotechnology, design and engineering services, consulting, and so on – will make heavy use of the cellular organization form. In addition, the most innovative portion of a global network organization may benefit from the use of the cellular form no matter how mature its industry. The key is to use the cellular design principles in those organizational units that are pursuing a strategy of continuous innovation.

An attempt to build a large-scale cellular organization is evident at The Acer Group, where co-founder Stan Shih has created a vision of a global personal computer company (Mathews, 2002; Mathews and Snow, 1998). Shih's design, like that at TCG, calls for a federation of self-managing firms held together by mutual interest rather than hierarchical control. Although each firm has a core task to perform, new product concepts can and do originate anywhere in the federation.

Shih's vision for the Acer federation of companies, however, appears to go one step beyond that of TCG in terms of reinforcing both the responsibility of the individual firm for its own destiny and the responsibility of all firms for the long-term success of the total organization. At TCG, the value of each of the member firms is calculated by means of an internal stock market, and firms are free to leave the group if they so choose. At Acer, the firms are each jointly owned by their own management and home-country investors, with a (usually) minority ownership position held by Acer, Inc., the parent firm. Shih intends that Acer firms around the world will be listed on local stock exchanges and be free to seek capital for their own expansion. He believes that local ownership unleashes the motivation to run each business prudently.

With all Acer firms enjoying the freedom to both operate and expand, the value of their membership in the federation is the capacity of the "cells" to continue to serve one another in an increasingly competitive global marketplace. Acer has developed the competence to efficiently produce all its products for just-in-time assembly and distribution. With minimal inventories, the latest models are available at all times at every sales site. At the same time that Acer has developed its personal computer business to be globally efficient, some of the cells in the federation have gravitated toward the formation of Internet-based businesses.

As yet, Acer's operating protocols are not as explicitly geared to the diffusion of know-how as they are at TCG. Nevertheless, Acer's business model provides the opportunity for each firm to draw on federation partners as preferred providers or clients. Currently, Acer's worldwide training programs are being used to translate Shih's global vision into action programs at the local firm level.

Conclusion

The process of globalization will continue to change the shape of business strategies, organization structures, and managerial philosophies. The impact of globalization on a given firm, however, will vary considerably depending on that firm's industry, geographic location, and its position in the value chain (Snow and Mathews, 2002). For example, some firms in the advanced economies of North America, Western Europe, and parts of Asia will be challenged to adopt features of the cellular organization in order to compete on the basis of continuous innovation. Alternatively, many companies in less developed countries must learn how to become good partners in multi-firm network organizations where their role is to provide specialized products and services to a lead firm located elsewhere in the world. Lastly, many companies in emerging and underdeveloped nations will still need to learn how to achieve the basic abilities of traditional organizations, such as efficiency and standardization.

The framework offered in this chapter, in which the organizational forms of each major period in business history are described, allows managers to diagnose the organizational needs of their own companies and learn about the approaches used by other companies. Firms at the very leading edge of international business practice will continue to develop the human investment managerial philosophy to pursue "anything, anytime, anywhere" strategies, and they will increasingly rely on cellular forms of organizing that are characterized by widespread entrepreneurship, the ability to self-organize and self-govern, and by member ownership of company assets and resources.

Note

1 We are grateful for financial support from the Carnegie Bosch Institute for Applied Studies in International Management.

References

Allred, Brent B., Charles C. Snow, and Raymond E. Miles (1996) "Characteristics of managerial careers in the twenty-first century," *Academy of Management Executive*, 10: 17–27.

Bendix, Reinhard (1974) *Work and Authority in Industry*, 2nd edn, Berkeley, CA: University of California Press.

Bleeke, Joel and David Ernst (1995) "Is your strategic alliance really a sale?," *Harvard Business Review*, Jan.–Feb.: 97–105.

Brandenburger, Adam M. and Barry T. Nalebuff (1996) *Co-opetition*, New York, NY: Doubleday.

Brooke, Michael Z. (1984) "Autonomy and centralization in multinational firms," *International Studies of Management and Organization*, 14: 3–22.

Byrne, John A. (1993) "The virtual corporation," *Business Week*, Feb. 8: 98–102.

Chandler, Alfred D., Jr. (1962) *Strategy and Structure: Chapters in the History of the American Industrial Enterprise*, New York, NY: Doubleday.

Chandler, Alfred D., Jr. (1986) "The evolution of the modern corporation," in Michael Porter (ed.), *Competition in Global Industries*, Boston, MA: Harvard Business School Press, pp. 405–448.

Chandler, Alfred D., Jr. (1990) *Scale and Scope: The Dynamics of Industrial Capitalism*, Cambridge, MA: Belknap Press.

Davidow, William H. and Michael S. Malone (1992) *The Virtual Corporation: Structuring and Revitalizing the Corporation for the 21st Century*, New York, NY: Harper Business.

Davis, Stanley M. and Paul R. Lawrence (1977) *Matrix*, Reading, MA: Addison-Wesley.

Mathews, John A. (1993) "TCG R&D networks: the triangulation strategy," *Journal of Industry Studies*, 1: 65–74.

Mathews, John A. (2002) *Dragon Multinational*, New York, NY: Oxford University Press.

Mathews, John A. and Charles C. Snow (1998) "A conversation with Taiwan-based Acer group's Stan Shih on global strategy and management," *Organizational Dynamics*, Summer: 65–74.

Mee, John F. (1964) "Matrix organization," *Business Horizons*, 7: 70–72.

Miles, Raymond E. (1975) *Theories of Management*, New York, NY: McGraw-Hill.

Miles, Raymond E. and W.E. Douglas Creed (1995) "Organizational forms and managerial philosophies: a descriptive and analytical review," in Cummings, Larry L. and Barry M. Staw (eds), *Research in Organizational Behavior*, Vol. 17, Greenwich, CT: JAI Press, pp. 333–372.

Miles, Raymond E. and Charles C. Snow (1986) "Network organizations: new concepts for new forms," *California Management Review*, 28: 62–73.

Miles, Raymond E. and Charles C. Snow (1994) *Fit, Failure, and the Hall of Fame: How Companies Succeed or Fail*, New York, NY: Free Press.

Miles, Raymond E., Charles C. Snow, John A. Mathews, Grant Miles, and Henry J. Coleman, Jr. (1997) "Organizing in the knowledge age: anticipating the cellular form," *Academy of Management Executive*, 11: 7–20.

Nonaka, Ikujiro and Hirotaka Takeuchi (1995) *The Knowledge-Creating Company: How Japanese Companies Create the Dynamics of Innovation*, New York, NY: Oxford University Press.

Roethlisberger, Fritz J. (1941) *Management and Morale*, Cambridge, MA: Harvard University Press.

Roethlisberger, Fritz J. and William Dickson (1939) *Management and the Worker*, Cambridge, MA: Harvard University Press.

Snow, Charles C. and John A. Mathews (2002) "The new zoology of global business: strategic issues for managers," Working Paper, The Pennsylvania State University.

Stopford, John M. and Louis T. Wells, Jr. (1972) *Managing the Multinational Enterprise*, New York, NY: Basic Books.

Taylor, Frederick W. (1911) *The Principles of Scientific Management*, New York, NY: Harper & Brothers.

Thorelli, Hans (1986) "Networks: between markets and hierarchies," *Strategic Management Journal*, 7: 37–52.

Vernon, Raymond (1966) "International investment and international trade in the product life cycle," *Quarterly Journal of Economics*, 80: 190–207.

12

THE ROLE OF THE CORPORATE CENTER IN DIVERSIFIED INTERNATIONAL CORPORATIONS

Bruce McKern and John Naman

Introduction

Under the pressures of global competition, diversified international corporations have increasingly adopted global strategic business unit structures to focus resources on providing value to customers worldwide.

Firms have adopted a variety of organizational structures to reconcile the conflicting objectives of worldwide efficiency, nationally differentiated customer responsiveness, and the development and deployment of the firm's pool of knowledge (Bartlett and Ghoshal, 1989). According to the Bartlett and Ghoshal taxonomy, corporations with limited business diversification but substantial geographic spread initially adopted "multidomestic" strategies, characterized by dispersed, nationally focused units operating with great autonomy and little central co-ordination, the classic example being Unilever until the mid-1980s. In a handful of industries, mainly concerned with natural resources, the commodity nature of markets, coupled with opportunities for economies of scale in production, impelled firms to take a "global" approach, in which the worldwide scope of each business was co-ordinated and controlled centrally. In the 1980s, this strategy became much more widespread. In manufacturing, and later in services, firms began to address similarities in businesses across countries by adopting global strategies. In the interests of global economies of scale, each business unit headquarters controlled resource allocation and key decisions, allowing limited autonomy to local managers. Relatively undiversified corporations, such as Boeing, Coca Cola, the Swatch Group (previously SMH), and several multinational mining companies, were early examples.

Today, diversified corporations that have adopted global strategies and structures include many of the most prominent multinational enterprises, such as Emerson Electric, PPG, Bosch, Samsung, Hoechst, and ABB (subjects of this study). In such companies, each of the SBUs employs a global strategy, although the degree of centralization within each SBU varies according to the extent to which each business can be managed globally.

Global centralization is effective where the nature of customer demand is globally homogeneous and where economies of asset scale or scope exist. Global homogeneity of customer preferences is a separate dimension from global economies of scale

(Porter, 1987). The former is the key variable in the demand function, the latter a variable in the supply function, and the pressures of globalization are not necessarily the same for both.

The opportunities to gain global efficiencies vary along the chain of activities that create product value, being greater at the R&D and production ends of the chain and lesser for sales and service activities, which with few exceptions must be delivered locally and be responsive to local needs (Bartlett and Ghoshal, 1989). Also, while most industries exhibit positive economies of scale up to some point, the potential for concentration of assets is limited by risk aversion and other factors such as transport cost.

Despite the international convergence of markets that has taken place over the last couple of decades, the "moment of truth"[1] when a customer buys a consumer product or service remains an intensely local matter (although Internet commerce can now provide that function for some products and services from a central source). Some consumer products and services businesses, particularly those based on new technologies or those less subject to local idiosyncrasies of regulation or use (personal computers, soft drinks, credit cards) can be organized centrally at the upstream parts of the value chain. However, local adaptation is usually required at the sales and distribution end. Likewise, global products sold to industrial customers often demand finely tuned, localized marketing and product design specifications. In most businesses, some customization is required to meet the varying demands of different markets across a global network. The ability to be sensitive and responsive to local tasks and requirements remains an important competitive differentiator.

We should be cautious in assuming that local adaptation will be such a critical characteristic of international businesses in the future. The growth of Internet retailers suggests that it is possible to centralize sales and distribution functions while supplying to a worldwide market. The success of this approach probably depends less on the homogeneity of consumer demand across cultures than reliable transaction processing and prompt delivery, the retailer's reputation for product quality, coupled with the scale economies of a high volume of purchases and deliveries needed to amortize investments in information technology. If this is so, such an approach to sales and service may be able to cope with consumer demand fragmented across cultures, provided that the retailer's intelligence network can recognize and respond to such differences economically. This is a challenge yet to be conquered by Internet commerce.

Balancing the forces of global centralization, local operational autonomy, and optimal development and use of knowledge capital depends for its effectiveness not on a structural solution, but on organizational processes (Lorange *et al.*, 1993). These processes can be grouped into three groups: firm culture, performance measurement, and reward systems; personnel policies for selection, development, and promotion of personnel; and the sharing of responsibilities between headquarters and business units.

In this chapter, we focus on the third issue, the role of the corporate headquarters, which is the key determinant of the diversified firm's organizational response. We focus on a set of arenas of activity that must be managed in respect of any business. We hypothesize that increasing environmental complexity forces corporate headquarters to allocate greater responsibility for these arenas to the management of the business units. However, the degree of delegation has limits; corporate head-quarters reserves to itself certain functions over which it exercises responsibility. We argue that the rationale for corporate headquarters intervention is to compensate for "market failure" at the SBU level. We view market failure more broadly than does Williamson (1975), who saw the role of corporate headquarters in diversified firms primarily as providing an internal market for capital, for which SBUs compete. We argue that the center's role is to consider all the resources that can be exploited across the corporation and to intervene wherever market failures exist. By examining a sample of international corporations pursuing global strategies, we draw conclusions regarding the optimal set of activities that should be controlled centrally.

In the next section, we consider the impact of complexity on the internal gover-nance of the diversified multinational corporation. We then discuss the arenas in which the competences of the firm can be exercised and describe our investigation of these questions in a group of multinational companies. The findings and conclu-sions follow.

Complexity and the control of diversified corporations

As corporations diversify in terms of both lines of business and geographical loca-tions, management is faced with increasing difficulties in managing the diversity of the corporation's broadened strategic scope. Increasing diversity is accompanied by two dimensions of environmental complexity: the increasing pace of change (in technology, tastes, product innovation, and competition); and the increasing density of communication linkages within SBUs, between SBUs, and between corpo-rations (with suppliers, customers, and alliance partners).

The pace of change is certainly a concern for every large international firm. Williams (1992) argues that industries can be classified and analyzed according to the pace of change of their environment. He groups industries into slow, standard, and "fast cycle" categories. For firms in slow-cycle industries (such as the airline business), the pace of change is not a major force, but for the other two categories it increases managerial complexity. Williams concludes that strategies and structures must be aligned to the dynamics of the industry. For a multi-business corporation, this implies a range of different strategy "styles" suited to the dynamic pace of each SBU's business, each requiring specific strategic assets that may be difficult to share across the corporation.

The increased density of communication linkages arises from contemporary approaches to organization. The traditional pyramidal hierarchical structure has been, if not abandoned, greatly flattened through the compression of reporting levels and the elimination of middle managers and corporate staff functions. To cope with growing speed of change and diversity, authoritarian bureaucratic decision-making processes have been replaced by participative, consultative ones. Advances in communications and information technology have established addi-tional paths for information flows both inside and outside the firm. As a con-sequence, managers have to deal with more numerous chains of communication.

Managers no longer participate in mainly vertical information flows, but are con-

cerned with linkages across functions within the SBU, across SBUs within a function, and with opposite numbers in other corporations. They are less able than in
the past to rely on staff functions to provide information on issues such as economic
trends or conditions in product, capital, and labor markets. Information technology
puts more of these data at the fingertips of managers, literally so, as they are now
expected to use their keyboards to search for it.

These three forces of complexity: diversity, pace of change, and density of linkages, are powerful constraints on the ability of corporate headquarters to control
the far-flung operations of the typical multinational network.

In coping with complexity, many international corporations are today moving
toward structures like the differentiated networks described by Nohria and Ghoshal
(1997). Nohria and Ghoshal view the modern international corporation as a
network of related affiliates rather than a hierarchical structure. They adopt a contingency perspective, emphasizing the importance of fit between the structure of
the corporation and the environmental forces each company faces. Fit between the
environmental demands and the choice of corporate structure, they demonstrate,
has a strong impact on firm performance.

Nohria and Ghoshal provide a more comprehensive description of the structure
of multinational corporations than the traditional view that focuses on structures
organized by product line, geography, or function. They discern four structural
forms, based on the degree of differentiation and integration of subsidiary roles.
Differentiation of roles among subsidiaries and between headquarters and SBUs is a
response to environmental complexity, but integration is needed to capture potential economies of scale and scope. This model leads to four structural archetypes:

- structural uniformity (in which there is high integration and low differentiation
  of subsidiary roles);
- the differentiated network (high integration with high differentiation);
- differentiated fit (low integration and high differentiation); and
- *ad hoc* variation (low integration and low differentiation).

All of the companies studied in our research operated in environments characterized by demands for high integration and high differentiation, and they had
adopted many of the structures and processes typified as the differentiated network.

In the view of Nohria and Ghoshal, the appropriateness of the fit in a differentiated network needs to be considered in terms of four major features.

First, in most companies, there is a differentiated distribution of resources and
roles among the various subsidiaries in the network. Subsidiaries differ considerably
in size, internal structure, and managerial competencies.

Second, network organizations employ a variety of socialization mechanisms
designed to ensure a degree of normative integration. In addition to the intellectual
capital of individual managers, each possesses social capital, which can be directed
by the policies of the company toward integration. Socialization is more commonly
employed in differentiated networks than the alternatives of centralization, which
achieves integration by fiat, or formalization, which achieves it by bureaucratic
procedure.

Third, communication flows between and within subsidiaries, and between them and the headquarters, as well as outside the corporation, are an important feature of the modern international firm. Managers are more concerned today with communications laterally, across functions and across national boundaries, than with the vertical flows associated with the traditional hierarchy. Managers have to deal with far greater complexity in the management of the business than in the past, arising from the more rapid pace of change, the density of communication linkages, and greater diversity in business lines, geography, people, and business partners.

Finally, there are different forms of relationship between the headquarters and the subsidiary (the focus of this chapter). In our view, it is important to consider all the arenas of decision making that are important to a business and the allocation of responsibilities between headquarters and subsidiaries, which can differ among subsidiaries and between corporations.

Arenas of responsibility

There are many arenas of activity that need to be controlled by any corporation. Our study was concerned with six externally focused arenas and six internally focused ones, which we identified in preliminary discussions with executives.

Externally focused arenas

Relations with:

- shareholders (share value, accountability, governance);
- the capital market (other than equity: debt funding, bond rating, etc.);
- governments (local, state, and federal, in multiple countries);
- community and social stakeholders (local interests; NGOs, environmental and other interest groups; often in multiple countries);
- customers;
- suppliers.

Internally focused arenas

- Strategic process (vision, mission, values, strategies, and business plans).
- Performance motivation and incentives, measurement, and control.
- Human resources management (personnel policies, management selection, and development, and their linkages to strategy and performance).
- Technology (product innovation, R&D).
- Introduction of innovative management practices (quality management, re-engineering, supply chain management, etc.).
- Internal transfers of components, products, and services.

These arenas of responsibility are illustrated in Figure 12.1.

In a single-business firm, all of these functions are centralized. The first four external arenas are the responsibility of the CEO and the Board; customers are the concern of the marketing function, and for suppliers, the purchasing department, and all of these are centralized. Most of the internal arenas are also controlled cen-

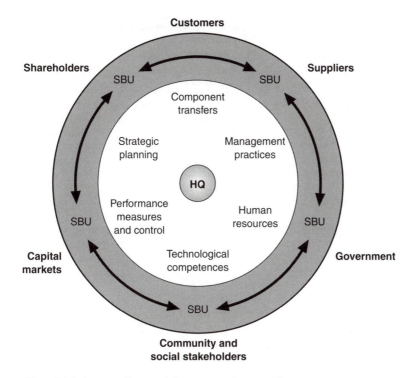

Figure 12.1 Arenas of potential corporate intervention.

trally. Internal transfers are simple and are governed by a costing formula, reference to market prices, or by edict.

In a complex diversified firm, the control of these 12 arenas is impossible to direct centrally. The classic response, indeed the traditional nature of the diversified firm, is the M-form structure or divisional organization, in which major functions are decentralized to product-based or geographic divisions. When the firm is diversified both geographically and by product line, central responsibility is doubly difficult. One possible response is to delegate all responsibilities to the divisions, so that the firm becomes no more than a portfolio or "mutual fund" of separate units, either geographic (a multidomestic structure) or product-centered (a global structure). Figure 12.2 illustrates increasing devolution of responsibility with increasing complexity toward the hypothetical extreme outlined above, in which the divisions have responsibility for all 12 functions.

The closest corporate approximation to this position is the pure conglomerate, where the firm is a collection of independent businesses under a common ownership, with the center acting as little more than a holding company. In terms of the 12 arenas of responsibility, the center controls only two: relations with shareholders and the capital markets. Since the cost of a central holding function is positive, we would expect such a corporation to be less valuable than a portfolio of independent companies covering the same range of businesses. This view is supported by financial literature on the performance of mutual funds versus index portfolios.

In recent years, some firms have adopted network structures approximating the

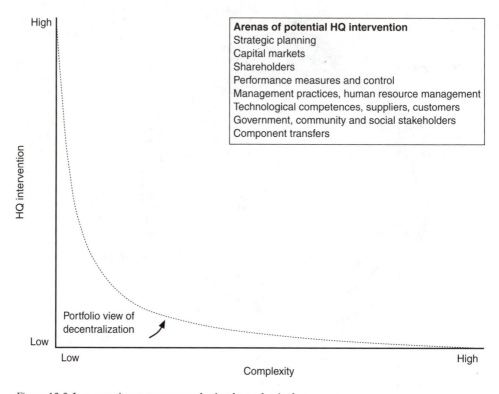

High

Arenas of potential HQ intervention
Strategic planning
Capital markets
Shareholders
Performance measures and control
Management practices, human resource management
Technological competences, suppliers, customers
Government, community and social stakeholders
Component transfers

HQ intervention

Portfolio view of
decentralization

Low

Low   High

Complexity

Figure 12.2 Intervention versus complexity: hypothetical response.

"transnational" organization structure and processes described by Nohria and Ghoshal (1997) and Bartlett and Ghoshal (1989, and Chapter 13 of this volume). Their "transnational" is a network of global SBUs with strong knowledge-sharing linkages between and within the SBUs, deploying significant managerial discretion at the local level. The network aims to effect a compromise between local and global pressures, partly by varying the extent of delegated local authority by function (with the greatest degree of latitude at the sales interface with the marketplace) and partly by facilitating lateral transfers of knowledge between managers globally.

These networks are, in essence, matrix structures, but cannot depend solely on structure to function. Most managers in the transnational network end up with two or three reporting lines: to a global business unit; to a local country or regional manager; and often to a functional head that may have a central co-ordinating role (marketing, distribution, and production being the most common cases). But there are important additional characteristics. Within SBUs there are denser communication links than the twin lines of responsibility traditionally associated with a matrix, and these are recognized and encouraged. Information flows within and across functional lines and also between SBUs help to share and sustain competences. Responsibilities for strategic assets and key knowledge resources are focused at centers of excellence, wherever they may be located.

Clearly then, the multiple aims of the transnational require attention to processes as well as structure. As Campbell, Goold, and Alexander argue (1995), corporate forms of organization may contribute to the destruction of shareholder value. In order to justify a degree of centralized responsibility over the 12 key arenas, the corporate center must be able to add shareholder value beyond what could be achieved by a passively held portfolio of commonly-owned businesses. This criterion goes to the heart of the issues of corporate governance and the current debate about the motivation, performance, and remuneration of managers and directors. It is a principal concern of portfolio investment managers and is reflected in the market for corporate control. It is therefore useful to explore the question of which arenas are most likely to benefit from centralized management, and under what circumstances. This is the central question of the research project summarized in this chapter.

Diversification and corporate competences

The extensive literature on diversification is skeptical of its value to the firm.[2] For example, Porter (1987) studied the diversification records of 33 large US firms over the period 1950–1986, finding that each company entered an average of 107 new industries, that is, approximately three business units per annum, of which 70 percent were by acquisition. Roughly half of these subsidiaries were subsequently divested or shut down. Thus, improving the capability of headquarters to manage the integration of new businesses would alone be of great economic value to firms, their shareholders, and stakeholders.

Following Rumelt's work in developing a measure of diversification types (Rumelt, 1974), a number of studies sharpened the focus by distinguishing between two alternative diversification strategies: related versus unrelated product diversification. Although the results have been mixed, there is some evidence that related diversification is superior to unrelated diversification in terms of performance measures such as return on sales or assets.

According to Markides and Williamson (1994), the inconclusiveness of the body of diversification studies is a result of inadequate specification of the relatedness variable. This variable is usually estimated by the extent to which the products of different business units share the same SIC categories. It is thus concerned with similarity at the market or industry level. The rationale for using a market-related measure is that businesses that produce products classified in the same SIC category are expected to share similarities in underlying assets such as production technologies, marketing processes, or distribution networks. The firm gains economies of scope through diversification by exploiting assets that are common to more than one SBU.

Markides and Williamson argue that this view is inadequate on two counts. First, while SBUs might share certain assets, these constitute a basis for sustainable competitive advantage across business sectors only to the extent that they are *strategic* assets, that is, assets that cannot readily be imitated by a competitor. Second, they argue that the usual measures are inherently static indicators of economies of scope, whereas a firm's ability to benefit from diversification depends on extending existing competences over time to create strategic assets in other business sectors. These two concerns are not addressed in the usual measures. The authors make a strong argument for a dynamic strategic-relatedness measure, proposing that this should be based on relatedness in five arenas in which firms deploy strategic assets:

- customers;
- channels;
- inputs (suppliers, factor markets, financial capacity);
- process assets (including technology, organization systems, and market-specific functional knowledge);
- market knowledge.

Markides and Williamson combined proxies for three of these strategic assets into a single measure of relatedness and showed that this measure was a more successful predictor of performance than the traditional measures.

These arenas are similar to five of the arenas of decision-making responsibility defined earlier in this chapter. The findings of Markides and Williamson lend support to the argument that managing a diversified corporation depends on competences that are applied across sectors to develop new strategic assets or to manage acquired ones.[3] When a firm diversifies into lines of business based on competences that are strategically related to its existing businesses, there is a greater likelihood of value creation than when the new businesses are not so related. A similar argument applies when a firm makes an acquisition in a strategically related product line.

In an earlier paper, Grant (1988) had stressed the concept of strategic relatedness, noting that most empirical research focused on operational-level relatedness, primarily in terms of market, technological, and vertical linkages. In his view, determinants of strategic similarity include similar sizes of capital projects, similar general management skills, similar key success factors, and goals defined in terms of similar performance variables. These factors are more generic and also capture aspects of the arenas of interest to this research.

Since multinational enterprises are doubly diversified, the value of international diversification has been the subject of a number of studies.[4] Geringer, Beamish, and daCosta (1989) investigated the relationship between performance, product diversification, and degree of internationalization for a group of US and European multinationals. They found that for those that pursued a strategy of related diversification, profitability increased with the degree of internationalization. However, firms that were very highly international (with foreign subsidiary sales to total sales in excess of 80 percent) did not perform better than those in the 60 percent to 80 percent range. They speculated, as did Grant (1987) and Siddhartan and Lal (1982), that substantial complexity imposes strains on management.

Kim, Hwang, and Burgers (1993) showed that internationally diversified firms can achieve significantly higher returns on assets, and at lower risk, depending on their degree of global market diversification combined with the extent of related product diversification. In contrast, less geographically diversified firms with high unrelated product diversity show below-average returns.[5] Their study also noted the importance of global industry profitability on the returns to participating firms, an industry effect observed in industrial organization and foreign direct investment studies.

The evidence from diversification research is consistent with the resource-based view of the firm.[6] The basis for competitive differentiation in firms is their assets and competences, the latter existing in the form of operating routines and the accumulated experience and knowledge of their employees. The special forms of knowledge needed to develop, produce, and market products are relatively specific to each particular market. Extending that knowledge to other products and markets is easier if the new ventures are similar in their knowledge requirements or competences, be it in technology, suppliers, customers, operational systems, or organization.

It seems obvious that the *management* of the process of diversification, to exploit and develop corporate competences over time, is critical to above-average performance.[7] Sharing competences does not happen easily, so developing and managing the process can be a differentiator between successful and unsuccessful companies. An important element of this process is how the tasks of management are allocated between headquarters and SBUs. Campbell, Goold, and Alexander (1995) see the task of the corporate headquarters as "parenting," or providing support and discipline for the SBUs.

Since each SBU is shielded from the shareholders and the capital markets by the corporate form, the parent's role is beneficial only to the extent that it can provide value superior to that achieved by competitor corporations or by a stand-alone business. The parent's role, in their view, is to provide structures, systems and processes, functions, central services and resources, and people and skills for the SBUs. The research presented here is complementary to their work in that it focuses on the specific arenas in which the corporate headquarters adds value, and proposes general principles to justify intervention.

Among the 12 identified arenas of responsibility it is obvious that some are less generic and more product-specific than others. Knowledge (or competence) about customers, suppliers, technology, and internal transfers of components or services is primarily product-specific and less easy to generalize across different businesses. It is to be expected that these arenas will be largely devolved to SBUs in a multi-business corporation.

On the other hand, knowledge about capital markets, the requirements of stockholders, strategic management, and the measurement and motivation of performance is generic, is applicable to any business line, and adaptable to differing national environments. Such generic corporate competences, if captured centrally, may constitute a competitive advantage that can be applied by headquarters across diversified businesses.

Arenas such as human resources management, the introduction of innovative management practices, technology development, and relations with community and special stakeholders have mixed attributes and it is not obvious what might be centralized or devolved.

While the classification of competences or arenas as described above may appear plausible, it is not clear what conditions drive the outcome adopted by a company or what guidance can be given to top management in making such decisions.

Our research suggests that corporate intervention on the basis of generic competences is needed because SBUs are not completely subjected to the market forces that would promote efficiency. Top management can use the concept of "market failure" as a rationale for centralized intervention. As will be explained later, we use "market failure" not in the macroeconomic sense of public choice, but in a microeconomic sense relevant to the mix of business environments found within an individual firm.

A diversified firm is a collection of businesses that, although under common ownership, are not directly exposed to all of the market forces that operate on a single-business firm. An obvious example is the absence of direct shareholder market pressure, which is exercised indirectly by a hierarchical substitute, the corporate management. There is "failure" of financial market pressure at the level of the business unit. On the other hand, most SBUs are fully exposed to customers and competitors, so that there is less likelihood of "market failure" in this arena, and less benefit to be gained from a hierarchical response. The headquarters intervenes when market pressures are inadequate to ensure efficient performance in any of the 12 arenas. Where do these failures occur and how does headquarters deal with them? To answer these questions, we studied a sample of international corporations.

Corporate competences and the headquarters' role in eight multinational corporations

The eight multinational corporations we studied differed from each other in size, product and geographic diversity, and the two other dimensions of complexity. Since only eight were researched, and they are not a random sample, they cannot be said to be representative of all MNEs. Nevertheless, we believe that their experience of dealing with the central issue of devolution is instructive and relevant to other companies. The companies included in our study are summarized in Table 12.1 below.

The sample included four companies from Europe, two from the USA, and two

Table 12.1 Indicators of size (1994) and degree of diversification of sample companies

Company and headquarters country	Sales ($US M)	Assets ($US M)	Net income ($US M)	No. of employees	Geographical diversity[a]	Product diversity[b]	No. of SBUs
ABB (Switzerland-Sweden)	29,718	29,055	165.9	207,557	0.53	0.77	5[c]
Acer (Taiwan)	731	727	40.7	1,994	0.68	0	1
Emerson Electric (USA)	10,013	9,399	929.0	78,900	0.46	0.49	2
Hoechst (Germany)	32,024	26,801	571.0	165,671	0.54	0.84	6[d]
PPG (USA)	6,331	5,894	514.6	30,800	0.48	0.64	3[e]
Robert Bosch (Germany)	22,244	17,941	286.5	156,464	0.66	0.65	4
Samsung Electronics (Korea)	14,939	12,196	1.3	51,926	0.44	0.67	4
Sulzer (Switzerland)	4,613	5,233	149.0	27,449	0.78	0.80	6

Sources: Worldscope 2/96 and company annual reports.

Notes
a Geographical diversity measured as Geographical Herfindahl Index based on sales by operating regions.
b Product diversity measured as Product Herfindahl Index, based on reported SBU sales.
c ABB operated in five "sectors" comprising 46 business areas.
d In 1994, Hoechst operated in six major broad areas or fields, comprising ten SBUs plus a number of joint ventures. In 1995, these were consolidated into broad areas comprising ten global divisions and some 35 business units, plus several joint ventures.
e In 1994, PPG operated in three major groups, comprising 16 business units.

from Asia. They ranged in annual sales revenue in 1994 from $US32 billion (Hoechst) to under $US1 billion (Acer). The least diversified in product terms was Acer, whose businesses were closely related: personal computers, computer memory, components, and technical publishing. In terms of major industry sectors, Hoechst was the most diversified, with six industry sectors, within which were grouped ten major SBUs as well as a number of joint ventures. Several of the firms were more diversified than Table 12.1 implies, including a broad range of businesses within each division. For example, ABB was reported by *Worldscope* as having only five divisions. However, the company described itself in 1994 as operating in five major business segments, containing 46 business areas (or SBUs), with over 120 major subsidiaries and some 1,300 companies, comprising 5,000 profit centers in 140 countries.[8] In 1999, after the disposal of some businesses and consolidation of a major business into a joint venture[9] ABB consisted of some 1,000 companies in six segments comprising 33 business activities.[10]

Although more consistent indicators of product diversity could be calculated from SIC data in the conventional way, the SBU groupings as reported by the companies are sufficient to gain an impression of their diversity. Likewise, with more detailed data from the companies regarding county-by-country sales, a better measure of geographical diversity could have been developed,[11] but these measures were not central to our concerns. Our objective was to understand how managers in each firm perceived complexity, which we believed would be likely to influence their behavior.

In the course of the study we interviewed senior managers in each company, some with headquarters' responsibilities, others with SBU responsibilities. Generally, we talked to heads of SBUs and the corporate CEO or senior staff, with the aim of understanding how the center and the operating units viewed both the degree of complexity of the company and the sharing of responsibilities for each of the 12 arenas.

Diversification

Most of the companies in our sample had diversified into related businesses. This was broadly true for Acer, PPG, Samsung Electronics, and Emerson Electric. A large part of Robert Bosch's business was automobile related, but the packaging machinery, power tools, and telecommunications businesses were more distant diversifications. In PPG the common thread among its paint, glass, and fiberglass businesses appeared to be process industry technologies and a number of major customers common to the first two business sectors. Sulzer, in weaving machines, industrial air conditioning, and climate control, medical devices such as replacement heart valves, and a miscellaneous group of industrial products, was diversified in a less related manner. However, there were some commonalities at the technological level, such as in fluid flow technology.

Some of the firms (Hoechst, for example) were in the process of reducing diversification by divesting themselves of non-core businesses and at the same time deepening their commitment to specific business fields. For example, the printing products business of Hoechst was sold to Agfa, a subsidiary of Bayer, because it was considered there was insufficient synergy with the rest of the company's business.

Hoechst's $7.1 billion acquisition of Marion Merrell Dow is an example of deepening commitment, in this case to the pharmaceuticals sector. Having acquired the French company, Roussel Uclaf, Hoechst needed an acquisition in North America and it so happened that Marion Merrell Dow was also looking for a partner. The new grouping made Hoechst the number three amongst global pharmaceutical companies, at a time when other drug manufacturers were consolidating worldwide.[12]

Structure

All of the eight companies had adopted a business unit structure, with each business unit responsible for a particular line of products worldwide. However, the extent of global penetration in each SBU differed across and within the companies. One company, Acer, had established several SBUs that would be considered small by comparison with the other firms, and which would probably be classified by them into a single business segment. In addition to the SBUs, Acer had adopted a unique regional business (RBU) structure, with the RBUs having responsibility for regional marketing, product configuration, and local assembly. The rationale for Acer's unusual mixed structure is discussed later (pp. 236, 237–238).

At Hoechst, major changes were made in the way the company managed its businesses. The principle was that all businesses would be managed as global strategic business units and the company undertook a regrouping of businesses in order to achieve appropriate business unit structures. A further aspect of the organizational change was that, consequent upon the creation of global business units, these business units were held fully accountable for the profitability of their businesses. Central Services, which was formerly a very powerful part of the Hoechst organization, was reduced, decentralized, and required to operate on a cost-of-service basis for the units that used its services. These major changes in strategy and operational philosophy were under way at the time of the research and, since that time, Hoechst has taken the more radical step of moving its legal base to France and changing its name to Aventis, reflecting its deep focus on the pharmaceutical industry. Over a few years, one of the original companies of the great German I.G. Farben chemicals group was transformed into a European pharmaceuticals enterprise, headquartered in France.

Although business units were adopted earlier than 1994, Hoechst had been organized with very strong functions at the corporate level, the divisional level, and the business unit level, with vertical reporting lines by functions up the chain of command. This meant that the corporate functions exercised a great deal of power and, as a consequence, decision making was slow. Furthermore, every major site was a profit center, often with several business units or divisions operating within a particular site. This meant that it was difficult for the business units to control the costs of the functions within their businesses. A major change was implemented on 1 January 1995, when the business units were made fully responsible for their worldwide businesses. Businesses that were not 100 percent owned by Hoechst (joint ventures and public companies) became separate operations with much more autonomy than before.

ABB, at the time of our study, placed great emphasis on balancing global product divisions with regional or country-based units, professing to operate in a truly matrix fashion in the manner of the transnational described by Bartlett and Ghoshal. ABB has since downplayed the regional dimension of its matrix and tilted the balance firmly toward global product divisions with full accountability for each worldwide business, as discussed more fully below (pp. 234–235).

Responsibilities of the center

The issue of what should be the role of the center, and how it could add value, was an important concern to each of the companies. In the mid-90s, several of them had considered the issue carefully and had re-organized quite explicitly as a result. An instructive example is Sulzer, which Dr. Fritz Fahrni had restructured, regrouping its businesses under an SBU structure and devolving most functions to the SBUs. Sulzer's organization structure (Figure 12.3) reflected Fahrni's conviction that only those functions that could clearly add value should be centralized. The strategic process, performance measurement, capital market relations, and statutory reporting were centralized. HR functions were devolved to each SBU, except for the selection, development, and succession of top management for the company. Most of the R&D was decentralized, except for some projects in which the technology was common to several SBUs (fluid flow research, for example), or where SBUs were not willing to invest enough in an emerging technology (such as electronics applications). In these

Figure 12.3 Alignment of corporate role and strategy at Sulzer (1995).

cases, headquarters provided the funding, although the work was performed in one of the business unit laboratories. Sulzer's reorganization under Dr. Fahrni not only focused businesses into distinct SBUs, but also focused sharply the role of the corporate center on where it could add value. The organization structure (Figure 12.3) fitted this view of the appropriate arenas of responsibility.

Since the time of the research, Sulzer has fundamentally changed its business mix, divesting itself of several businesses and entering new fields. In 2002 it was organized into five strategic business units, in the fields of:

- surface-coating technologies;
- turbomachinery services;
- pumps;
- chemical process technologies; and
- fuel cells systems.

In effecting this transformation, Sulzer has been consistent in retaining only a few functions at the center. These include the secretariate, corporate finance, corporate development, and "markets and technology."

ABB, likewise, is well known for devolution of important arena responsibilities to the SBUs. The main tasks of the center are strategic management, performance measurement and evaluation, appointment and development of top managers, and relations with shareholders and capital markets. In this respect, ABB's view of the center's role was similar to that of Sulzer.

There are differing views on how ABB managed the complexity of its global businesses. Bartlett and Ghoshal (1989) saw ABB as the archetypal "transnational." Yet one of its senior managers interviewed during the study described the company as a "grouping of national companies," that is, a multidomestic enterprise.[13] ABB pushed profit responsibility down to the level of a single business within a single country, so that its 5,000 profit centers had average sales revenues of as little as $10 million.

Certainly each profit center was focused at the country level, but ABB also tried to achieve strong co-ordination within each SBU across countries. The purpose was to enable ABB to gain global economies and transfer of knowledge, while maintaining a strong local focus in each operating unit. The company's ABACUS financial reporting system enabled profit center data to be aggregated and reported globally by SBU or by country, which is an essential requirement of a transnational approach.

Despite the undoubted success of ABB in integrating major acquisitions and devising an unusual matrix structure, its profitability has not been exceptional. As Berggren noted, as early as 1994, by comparison with General Electric, Siemens, and GEC-Alsthom, ABB's performance was weaker, suffering declines in earnings in 1992 and 1993 (Berggren, 1994). Since the time of this study, Göran Lindahl succeeded Percy Barnevik as CEO and tilted the decision-making focus in ABB firmly toward global product divisions with full accountability for each worldwide business. At the same time, Lindahl engineered a radical shift in the company's business mix, away from its traditional sectors and toward high technology and services sectors. The company's traditional locomotive and turbine businesses were sold or spun off and it entered into robotics, automation, and financial services. Stronger emphasis on the SBUs was no doubt a necessary accompaniment to a new strategy involving sales, spin-offs, and acquisition.

ABB's performance declined further and, in 2002, it faced a number of challenges, including the need to improve operational efficiency, restructure a debt-heavy balance sheet, and deal with criticism of its governance processes and inherited legal liabilities concerning asbestos.[14] Göran Lindahl was replaced by Jürgen Centerman as CEO and Percy Barnevik was replaced as Chairman by Jürgen Dormann, Chairman of Aventis (formerly Hoechst). The new leadership accelerated the reorganization of the company, reducing the power of the country-based organizations, which had developed considerable duplications of support services.

Central to restoring the company's performance was a further significant change in organization structure. The product divisions were replaced by four customer-centric divisions (dealing with four broad industry groups) and two product divisions, which both supply the customer divisions and sell indirectly to end users through channel partners. A sixth division, Financial Services, is both product-based and a customer-centric group. These divisions are supported by Group Services, which includes local corporate support, shared services, and a new entity called Group Processes, whose function is to streamline and improve organizational processes across the company. These include supply chain management, e-business, information services infrastructure, and other shared services.

A related, radical change was implemented in the country-based organizations, which no longer have responsibility for businesses within their region. Country organizations were simplified to holding companies comprising just four people: a country "ambassador" or senior liaison representative, a senior financial officer, a head of legal affairs, and a head of human resources.

Thus, ABB appears to have abandoned the matrix structure, at least formally. This shift by ABB, regarded hitherto by many observers as the archetype transnational, is evidence that effective control of global operations may require a shift in the balance of forces in the transnational matrix toward globally centered SBUs. But organizational structure cannot reconcile the conflicting pressures for global efficiency and local responsiveness with which international corporations have to live. ABB has the advantage of a large cadre of experienced executives and it does not appear to have abandoned its belief in the importance of their "transnational" attributes.[15]

Emerson Electric (now Emerson), under its Chairman, Charles Knight (also its long-serving CEO at the time of the study) had a clear view about the role of the center. Knight placed great emphasis on setting challenging goals for the corporation as a whole and expecting each SBU to achieve its expected contribution. Knight presided over a rigorous strategic planning and performance management system but left the running of the businesses to the SBU leaders. This process is discussed in more detail below (pp. 233–234).

At Hoechst, a major shift of activities toward the SBUs had been influenced by practices at Hoechst Celanese, a US company acquired by Hoechst in the 1990s. Celanese, under its CEO, Dr. Ernest Drew, had previously undertaken a review of the role of the corporate center and, as a result, had devolved many activities to its SBUs. The success of this transformation at Celanese had an important influence on the Board of Management of Hoechst, of which Dr. Drew became a member. It enabled Hoechst to use the experience of Celanese to implement a similar change in the parent company more quickly and more easily than would otherwise have been possible.

At Acer, the Chairman, Stan Shih, believed in a limited role for the center. Acer had been through a difficult period in the early 1990s and Shih, concerned about the necessity for speed, market responsiveness, and accountability, had reorganized to place more responsibility in the hands of SBU managers. In fact, at Acer, devolution of responsibility had gone much further than in the other companies studied.

Robert Bosch is a major German company with a strong reputation for innovation and technology, originally focused on the automotive industry, but later diversified into other businesses with a technological base. The company is unusual in that 92 percent of the capital stock is owned by the Robert Bosch Foundation, set up by the company's founder. Funds received from the income of the operating company, Robert Bosch GmbH, are disbursed for charitable causes by the Foundation. The governance of the company is exercised by the traditional German bodies, a Supervisory Board and a Management Board.

At Robert Bosch, profit responsibility had been delegated to 20 business units or divisions, which operate in four broad sectors:

- automotive equipment (comprising ten divisions such as gasoline and diesel engine management systems, ABS, chassis, and safety systems);
- communications technology (12 product groups, including GSM telephony infrastructure, public switching systems, private systems, satellite systems, and traffic control);
- consumer goods (power tools, heating and hot water equipment, household appliances, and electronics); and
- capital goods (packaging equipment, industrial equipment, and hydraulics and pneumatics).

The business units had worldwide profit responsibility, reflecting the global scope of the company's operations, covering all European countries and many other parts of the world. For the important US market, Bosch had established Robert Bosch USA as a separate legal entity to sell its products in the automotive aftermarket and to assist in promoting original equipment sales to US manufacturers.

Although some 54 percent of the company's sales were overseas in 1994, 75 percent of its production was based in Germany. Co-ordination between the worldwide business units and some 30 regional operations was achieved partly by a division of responsibilities between regional management and business unit management, and partly by having members of the Board of Management with oversight responsibilities both for divisions and for regions. In addition, the company had established a principle that managers one and two levels below the Board of Management were to have three- to five-years' experience outside Germany, and cross-functional rotation was also encouraged.

Samsung Electronics Company is a part of the Samsung Group, one of the largest chaebols in South Korea, with 1993 Group sales of $51.5 billion. The group as a whole in 1994 was implementing a "new management philosophy" under the Chairman Mr. Lee Kun-Hee, also the current Chairman of Samsung Electronics. Amongst a number of initiatives, the Chairman had announced that his office would become less involved in operating matters in order to focus on strategic issues.

Samsung Electronics operated as a separate company, with several closely affiliated joint ventures. It consisted of four strategic business units or divisions, which were:

- consumer electronics;
- information systems (computers and related products);
- telecommunications systems;
- semiconductors.

In addition, there were two regionally oriented sales units, one focusing on domestic sales and the other on global business. The global business organization included regional headquarters for North America (New Jersey), Europe (London), and Southeast Asia (Singapore), and smaller regional headquarters for Latin America, Eastern Europe, China and the Middle East, and Africa. The company also participated in four major joint ventures with partners that included Corning, Hewlett-Packard, and GE. More recently, the company has restructured again into four major business areas, to take account of the importance of the Internet and electronic commerce. Its divisions in 2002 included:

- home networks;
- mobile networks;
- office networks;
- core components, supporting network products.

Although in the past there had been a significant degree of intervention by head-quarters in the operations of the business units, by 1994 each of the divisions was a large business, operating with considerable autonomy and led by a managing director or vice-president. The company saw the role of headquarters as defining the broad scope of business for each of the divisions, as well as setting sales and profit targets and assisting in the development of their strategies. Corporate headquarters included corporate staff in the areas of personnel, finance, marketing, and technology. The company viewed the arenas of responsibilities shared between head office and business units as similar to those presented in Figure 12.1.

In discussions about Acer, the Chairman, Stan Shih, described the headquarters as a holding company for the corporation that provided services for the subsidiaries in return for payment of its costs. Because the Acer headquarters group was small (about 80 people) the "tax" on the subsidiaries was not excessive.

Shih made the point (consistent with the market pressure argument made in this chapter) that the business units faced market risk and therefore needed autonomy to operate effectively. He described the functions of headquarters as:

1 legal: however, SBUs were allowed to have their own legal functions to deal with local issues;
2 corporate consolidation and accounting, monitoring and auditing;
3 treasury: he intended to let subsidiaries have more local autonomy in this respect as well;

4   corporate purchasing, including company-wide negotiations and securing of preferred vendors;
5   global logistics, to achieve materials co-ordination and economies of scale. This was also important for the company to achieve its speedy "assemble to order" philosophy.

Shih said that the marketing role at Acer's headquarters was confined primarily to the corporate image and communications about the company.

It is clear from these discussions that there was a great deal of commonality amongst the sample companies regarding the arenas in which corporate intervention and responsibility were essential. Although several of the companies were going through major changes in organization, the common objective was to place responsibility for operations, as far as possible, in the hands of the leaders of worldwide strategic business units. They had carefully considered the arenas in which corporate headquarters could add value and had focused headquarters' intervention on these arenas. As we will confirm in the next section from our interview responses, of primary importance to each of them were relationships with shareholders and the capital markets, the strategic planning process, and performance measurement and control. Each of these was an arena in which the SBU was not directly exposed to pressures from the marketplace because of the corporate form, and headquarters acted to provide that pressure based on its generic competences. The leaders of these companies had also recognized that the SBUs were best able to deal with pressures arising in their markets, for which headquarters lacked market-specific competences.

There were differences of view between the companies on the relative importance of the headquarters' role in a number of other arenas, and these were driven by differences in the nature of the industries in which each firm operated. In subsequent sections of this chapter, we detail these differences and explain the reasoning behind the division of responsibilities.

Responses to environmental complexity

Before discussing the companies' solutions to the division of HQ–SBU responsibilities in depth, we summarize their views on the environment in which each operated. We asked managers in each company to describe their business environment in terms of the three dimensions of complexity described earlier. We believed that their perceptions of complexity would drive the roles adopted by their corporate headquarters. The means of these responses (gathered on a scale of 1 to 5 for each respondent) were calculated to give an indicator of environmental complexity perception for each company. We observed a good degree of agreement between headquarters and SBUs on the level of complexity for the company as a whole, despite some differences between SBUs.

The responses are summarized in Table 12.2 and the means for the sample are shown in Figure 12.4.

While most of the executives reported an increase in complexity over the preceding three to five years, they appeared (contrary to our expectations) to see diversity and pace of change as more important contributors to complexity than density of

Table 12.2 Perceptions of complexity in sample companies (mean responses, scale 1–5)

Company	Pace of change	Diversity	Density of linkages	Overall
A	4.5	4.0	1.0	3.17
B	2.75	2.5	2.25	2.5
C	3.0	4.0	3.0	3.3
D	4.0	4.5	2.0	3.5
E	5.0	3.0	2.0	3.3
F	2.0	5.0	2.5	3.2
G	2.2	2.4	1.2	1.93
H	2.5	3.5	2.0	2.67
Sample mean	3.24	3.61	1.99	2.95

Source: interview data.

Note
Companies are disguised to preserve confidentiality.

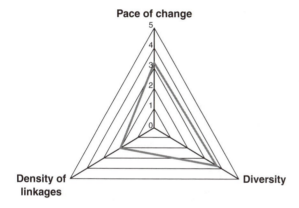

Figure 12.4 Managers' perceptions of environmental complexity: sample mean.

Source: interview data.

Note
Mean of environmental complexity values for eight sample companies. Scale measures 1 to 5 radially from center. 1 = low complexity; 5 = high. (Zero point is included for presentation clarity.)

linkages. As multinational enterprises expand by entering new countries and new markets (often involving high technologies and intense competition with a premium on rapid change) the perception of increased complexity is not surprising. However, managers also report that flatter structures and wider relationships within their companies and with external parties have heightened complexity and created greater pressures to perform. From our small sample, this is clearly an issue, but not as important as the other forces driving complexity.

Given the common view that complexity was increasing, we might have expected the division of responsibilities between headquarters and SBUs to be resolved by a high degree of decentralization (the null hypothesis outlined earlier). The responses to this question are presented in Table 12.3 and Figure 12.5, which show

Table 12.3 Degree of corporate intervention: sample mean (scale 1–5)

Arena	Sample mean	Standard deviation
Customers	2.2	1.2
Suppliers	2.6	1.3
Government	2.6	1.1
Community and social stakeholders	2.2	1.1
Capital market	4.4	0.8
Shareholders	5.0	0.0
Internal transfers	1.8	0.9
Management practices	3.5	1.3
HR	3.2	1.5
Technology	2.4	0.9
Performance measures	4.1	0.7
Strategic planning	4.7	0.4

Source: interview data.

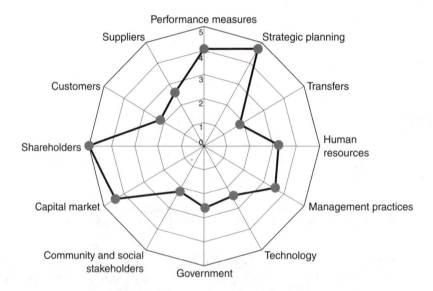

Figure 12.5 Degree of corporate responsibility: sample mean.

Source: interview data.

Notes

Mean of corporate intervention values for eight sample companies. Scale measures 1 to 5 radially from center. 1 = low corporate intervention; 5 = high. (Zero point is included for presentation clarity.)

Corporate intervention values for shareholders, strategic planning and capital markets showed low variance across the sample. For shareholders, the mean was 5.0 with no variance; for strategic planning, mean was 4.7, range from 4.0 to 5 and SD 0.4; for capital markets mean was 4.4, range from 3.5 to 5 and SD 0.8.

the means of the interview responses across the sample for the degree of HQ responsibility or intervention in each of the arenas. Figures 12.6 and 12.7 show the responses on each arena for two extreme cases (not identified to preserve confidentiality): a high-intervention case and a low-intervention case.

It is clear that there was a high degree of devolution of key responsibilities to the SBUs in all of the companies. The main arenas where HQ exercises significant influence were in shareholder relations, strategic planning, dealing with the capital market and internal performance measurement and control. The introduction of innovative management practices and human resources management were to a considerable extent delegated to the SBUs with some headquarters' role. Responsibility for arenas such as relations with customers and suppliers, inter-SBU transfers of materials, components or services, technology, and relations with social and community stakeholders, were placed primarily in the hands of SBU management.

Figures 12.6 and 12.7 are examples of two companies that showed a low and high degree of corporate intervention respectively. The company in Figure 12.6 confined its headquarters' responsibilities to shareholder relations, strategic planning, the capital market and performance management and control. As noted earlier, all of the companies in the sample showed a high degree of headquarters' intervention in these key arenas. For the company in Figure 12.6, the only other arena in which headquarters took a significant role was innovative management practices, which it drove from the center.

The high-intervention company (Figure 12.7) regarded headquarters' intervention in many arenas as important. In addition to the key arenas common to all of the companies, headquarters in this company also put great emphasis on the

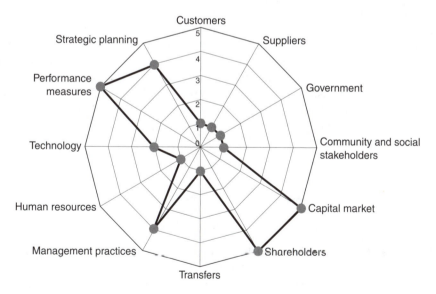

Figure 12.6 Degree of corporate responsibility: low-intervention profile.

Source: interview data.

Note
Corporate intervention values for a sample company: scale 1–5.

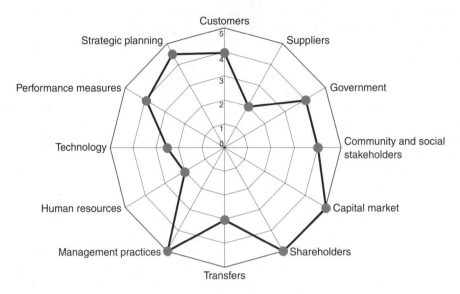

Figure 12.7 Degree of corporate responsibility: high-intervention profile.

Source: interview data.

Note
Corporate intervention values for a sample company: scale 1–5.

introduction of innovative management practices, dealing with customers, government, and other stakeholders. The reasons for these differing degrees of intervention amongst the companies are discussed in later sections.

Because of the small sample, it was not possible to correlate the degree of the headquarters' intervention with performance. It happened that the high-intervention case was the poorest performing company in the sample over the five-year period and, conversely, the low-intervention case was a relatively high performer. However, although this is consistent with a view of the limited ability of corporate headquarters to intervene successfully in a complex environment, it is not possible to generalize from these two cases.

To explain the differences in practices among the companies, we turn to each of the arenas in more detail.

The role of corporate headquarters in each arena

Relationships with shareholders and capital markets

All of the sample companies centralized these relationships. The explanation is straightforward. In a corporate structure, the entity responsible to the shareholders is the corporation, represented by its Board, which takes responsibility through the corporate center for statutory reporting, dealing with directors and shareholders, and the governance of the corporation. The SBUs, due to the corporate structure, are shielded from direct relationships with the shareholders and this is also a strong reason for centralization of the strategic planning and performance review arenas.

There was rather more flexibility in dealing with the other markets for capital, but this function was mainly centralized. The argument for centralizing this arena is pooling of financial needs across subsidiaries in order to gain economies of scale. At ABB, each legal entity had to take balance sheet responsibility for its own debt, but the debt was usually raised centrally. It was argued that, along with centralized exchange rate hedging, centralized debt management achieved greater efficiencies than would be possible if the SBUs had responsibility.

At PPG, capital allocation was a headquarters' function, decided by the Office of the Chief Executive consistent with the strategic plan. Headquarters raised capital centrally, including funds borrowed overseas to support foreign operations. Within each business unit, operating exposures were pooled, while the corporation hedged net exposures and such items as dividend payments from overseas subsidiaries. Policies for dealing with the capital markets were centralized in a similar fashion across nearly all the sample companies.

The chief exception was Acer, which delegated some of the fund-raising activity to SBUs or regional business units. Acer's argument for decentralization was partly to match assets and liabilities in common currencies but primarily to gain access to equity funding. It believed that local ownership would give "natural control" because of common interest on the part of local shareholders in the destiny of a local subsidiary, a belief in market pressure consistent with the argument of this chapter.

Strategic planning, performance measurement, and control

Strategic planning and performance measurement and control were focused centrally in each company, and provided the discipline for decentralization in other arenas. However, the manner in which this was done differed by company. The two US corporations (Emerson and PPG) and three of the European firms (ABB, Hoechst, and Sulzer), had developed strategic planning processes that, while driven from the center, depended on the SBUs for almost all of the input. Headquarters set indicative growth and profit targets for the SBUs and established a schedule for preparation and discussion of their strategic plans. However, SBUs were expected to formulate their strategies themselves. SBU plans were then reviewed by top management in intense face-to-face meetings designed to test the assumptions and the logic. Plans were often modified as a result of this process before being agreed by top management and committed to by the SBU management. Headquarters did not formulate the strategy proposals, but subjected them to a rigorous discipline of evaluation and review similar to that provided by a venture capital firm or an investment bank, effectively substituting for market pressure.

A prime example of this approach is Emerson Electric, which has had an enviable record of profit growth over many years. The strategic planning process at Emerson was driven by the Chairman, Charles Knight, who, for most of its recent history, was also CEO. Knight set the planning process, the timetable, and his expectations for performance for the SBUs (divisions), and conducted meetings to review strategic plans with their management. The division managers were expected to understand the strategic issues in their businesses and were responsible for preparing their strategic plans on a "5-back-5-forward" basis, which was a five-year rolling forecast, based on five years of prior data. As Knight said:

Once we fix our goals, we do not consider it acceptable to miss them. These targets drive our strategy and determine what we have to do: the kinds of businesses we're in, how we organize and manage them, and how we pay management. At Emerson this means planning.[16]

In detailed planning and review meetings, Knight explored each division's plans, testing assumptions, questioning forecasts, assessing resource needs, and setting stretching targets. This process culminated in a set of agreed objectives and operational plans for each business, with clear milestones and performance criteria.

The Emerson planning process proceeded at three levels: divisional, business, and corporate. Divisional-level planning began with financial targets for growth and profitability set by the CEO, followed by a detailed review session at which each division's proposals were challenged. Following this discussion, there was a post-planning conference for each division at which action programs were agreed. At the business level, the planning emphasis was to review trends in broad business groups, without discussing the details of divisional plans. There were three major phases: technology conferences in each business, a strategy session, and a business planning conference. Emerson claimed that this review was helpful in identifying broad trends and possible areas for diversification or acquisition.

Corporate-level planning involved meetings toward the end of the planning cycle, culminating in the corporate planning conference, which reviewed the previous year's performance for the corporation, discussed the plans consolidated from the divisions, and debated the one-year outlook.

Once the strategy for a division was agreed, milestones were set and annual budgets prepared. These became the criteria for divisional performance and were developed into performance indicators for each manager, to which remuneration (including a significant bonus element) was tied. If a division was meeting its strategic milestones and annual budget targets, it was left to operate autonomously. If, however, strategic goals were not achieved, reviews were held to determine what must be changed.

The Emerson culture is strongly performance-oriented. Executives are expected to achieve strategic objectives and annual budget goals, while managers within the divisions are held to annual and shorter-term goals. An important element of the process is measurement, to which remuneration is closely linked. Every Emerson executive receives regular performance data according to the established criteria, and is able to estimate the bonus element of his or her remuneration progressively.

There is limited tolerance in the Emerson culture for failure to meet targets, whether short-term or long-term. This "performance culture" is credited with the unbroken growth of the company's revenue and profit over the long term, and it is driven by the demanding process that establishes divisional goals and action plans. It is the decentralized strategy-making process, combined with a rigorous discipline that tests the coherence of each division's strategy and monitors performance, which has produced the remarkable consistency of achievement for which the company is renowned. The corporate headquarters' role in respect of each division is to provide the strategic discipline that the stock market and a board of directors would apply to a stand-alone business, while devolving fully the conduct of the business to SBU management.

At PPG, the approach had changed over time but, in 1994, had many similarities to the approach described above. Each business unit had a planning group, which prepared its strategic plans on a five-year horizon, but the timetable, and reviews of the SBU strategic plans were driven by headquarters. There were three elements to the strategic process:

- Strategic Reviews of each business;
- the Corporate Long-Range Plan; and
- the Annual Profit Plan.

Strategic Reviews of the SBUs were conducted every three years, unless a major change was being proposed. PPG had developed a scheme for categorizing businesses, depending, for example, on whether they were cash generators or growth opportunities. This categorization (similar to that at Hoechst) was important in assessing expected returns and placing constraints on capital spending.

The Long-Range Plan was developed from the SBU Strategic Reviews, and summarized primarily in financial terms. The Annual Profit Plan was the first year of the Long-Range Plan and was the main instrument for measuring performance on a monthly basis. PPG's Management Committee, which consisted of the heads of the major SBUs, the Head of Human Resources, the Chief Financial Officer, and the Office of the Chief Executive, met monthly to review performance relative to the profit plan. PPG claimed that its strategic planning process provided a strong discipline to assess performance and to achieve objectives. One executive said the role of the Office of the Chief Executive in dealing with the SBUs was much like that of the Board of a corporation. It needed to rely on the specialized knowledge within each SBU on market conditions and the operational aspects of the business, but the headquarters was important in setting expectations and making major decisions, such as allocation of capital to the SBUs, or exiting from a business.

In some of the sample companies, we saw a more centralized approach to the formulation and execution of strategy. In Robert Bosch, for example, most members of the Board of Management had significant experience in the mainstream of the company's business, the manufacture and supply of key components to the automotive industry. Because of the importance of the major automobile companies as clients, there was a high degree of common understanding of those customers and recognition that co-ordination between the different units of the automotive business was important. This meant that there was a tendency for the Board of Management to make strategic decisions for these SBUs centrally and consensually. Strategy formulation was more centralized than in the Emerson case and there was a greater degree of top management responsibility for strategy implementation.

In this respect, the Robert Bosch approach to strategic management of the automotive segments of its businesses was more like that of a single business company. The commonalities between many of the business units, based on technology or knowledge of customers, were powerful centralizing forces. On the other hand, several businesses, such as packaging, power tools, and telecommunications, are significantly different businesses from the company's traditional core, and in these businesses there appeared to be more devolution of strategic issues to the management of each SBU. Nevertheless, discussion and agreement on strategic matters at the Board of Management were considered important for these businesses too, reflecting the more centralized approach to strategic responsibility that has been traditional in many European corporations. It was noted that, because Bosch is not a public company, and is not able to raise equity capital, there was a strong emphasis on internal cash generation.

Three levels of planning were observed at Robert Bosch:

- the plant level, where the main objective was to operate efficiently and achieve targets set by the division;
- the divisions, which were worldwide strategic business units operating as profit centers (with the exception that they did not have separate balance sheets);
- the corporate level, which was the Board of Management, charged with achieving the goals of the corporation in conjunction with the Supervisory Board and the Robert Bosch Foundation.

Bosch operated on a one-year budget coupled with a two-year forecast. The Board of Management set out key objectives, especially profitability and cash flow, as well as common economic assumptions for the strategic process. These were the basis for the preparation of the divisional operating and strategic plans, which were presented and reviewed by the Board of Management in September each year. The Board Reviews focused on the divisional objectives and the strengths and weaknesses of the SBU likely to affect its ability to achieve the plan.

The packaging machinery division of Robert Bosch is an SBU whose business differed considerably from the company's core business. Nevertheless, strategic planning conformed to the Bosch system, with a strong headquarters input. The Board set targets including objectives such as head count, productivity, and profit, as well as cash flow, and the division presented its business plan at a general planning meeting. Clearly, the strategic planning process was led from the Board (with considerable SBU involvement) and corporate targets were set from above.

Hoechst had greatly adapted its strategic planning process to its new SBU structure. The corporate center at Hoechst consisted of the Board of Management, the Corporate Center, and Central Services. The Board of Management had nine Board members, each of whom had broad strategic responsibilities for one or more parts of the business, a geographical region and sometimes a function. For example, the Deputy Chairman at the time, Dr. Metz, was responsible for the Fibers Business, and the Plastics and Films Divisions, and also had geographic responsibility for the Americas. Another director had responsibility for Europe and Africa as well as materials management. The intention was not for directors to intervene in day-to-day operating matters but rather to focus on strategic issues. However, there was a concern that this span of responsibilities was too broad and this was, in part, a reason for the increasing devolution to the SBUs.

The Corporate Center was essentially the Office of the Chairman of the Board of Management and his staff, while Central Services included a number of service functions that were available at cost to the SBUs. These services include patents and legal services, pension fund, and vocational training; central R&D; internal management accounting; and procurement and logistics.

ABB and Sulzer placed primary responsibility on the SBUs to develop strategy. Nevertheless, in both companies, the Chairman or Chief Executive had strong views about direction and was a major influence on the process of strategy development. ABB is well known for the small size of its headquarters, so there are limited resources at the disposal of the CEO to engage in second-guessing the ideas of SBU management. His role was rather one of providing vision for the company as a whole, providing broad perspectives and contexts for the SBUs, and discipline in reviewing, questioning, and approving strategic plans (as at Emerson).

We saw a similar approach in Sulzer, where Dr. Fahrni had few central staff to assist in the strategic process, but provided vision and goals for the SBU general managers. This is not to play down the CEOs' understanding of the various businesses in each company, where detailed knowledge enhanced their credibility, but to underscore their preoccupation with vision, strategic process, accountability, and culture, which we believe should be the key concerns of leaders.

At Acer, the view of the Chairman, Stan Shih, was that it was his role to provide the company vision and philosophy, of which an important characteristic was a decentralized risk-sharing and profit-sharing organization with good planning, but decentralized implementation. Strategy formulation was done mostly in the business units and agreed on by consensus, but the Chairman also took an important role in ensuring that the strategies of the business units were consistent with the vision. The business unit heads held their own strategy meetings and talked to the Chairman by phone once a month. Every six months there was a summit meeting of the SBU heads in which the Chairman's focus was a reaffirmation of the global vision.

Technology management

In discussing practices with the executives interviewed, it was apparent that, in the arena of technology, there was a clear division of responsibilities. Technology management, which in many of the companies had previously been centralized, had been largely decentralized to SBUs, with typically 10 percent or less of R&D decided by headquarters. The principle followed by these companies was of aligning responsibility for R&D spending and funding with the product development strategy of each SBU.

The rationale was that SBUs were in touch with market needs and could best decide what technology investment was most beneficial. They would be more likely to invest in projects aligned to customer needs, and would also be more likely to invest efficiently. Proximity of R&D decisions to the marketplace was considered essential, as pressures from the market provided the signals for each SBU to allocate its R&D investment appropriately. There was no market failure in these arenas: SBUs were considered to be well exposed to market forces, so that they would allocate R&D resources efficiently without centralized intervention.

The negative aspect of this approach was that SBUs, driven by headquarters to achieve short-term financial targets, might under-invest in technology with long-term payoffs, given that the tenure of top management in any SBU was not permanent. Because of managerial opportunism, market signals might be ignored. This was not seen to be a problem in companies where managers expected to have long tenure within the corporation. In those firms, performance in one SBU would be a key part of the person's reputation and could be observed over a long period. Longevity of tenure was more apparent in the European companies (although even there cultures were changing). In several of the sample companies, however, the moral hazard associated with under-investment in long-payoff activities was one reason that had led them to fund a proportion of R&D centrally. This work was typically longer term and higher risk, and often had implications for more than one SBU; SBUs saw no incentive to invest when the direct benefits were uncertain and might be appropriated by another SBU. In some cases, the corporate headquarters took a view on an emerging technology, which none of the SBUs yet saw as important to their markets in the short term, and it funded projects in that field. The work was not necessarily performed by a central R&D laboratory, as these had been largely dispersed to the SBUs. Such projects were often funded by headquarters and performed within the appropriate SBU laboratory.

An example was Sulzer, in which basic work on fluid flow that was potentially valuable to several SBUs was funded centrally. Likewise, Sulzer had centrally promoted an electronics project that top management considered important because none of the SBUs was willing to devote its own resources to that field.

In the case of ABB, technology was the responsibility of a Senior Vice-President, Göran Lindahl (who later succeeded Percy Barnevik as CEO). Lindahl acknowledged that, with a staff of two people, he could not second-guess decisions about specific R&D projects. Instead, he had formed a committee of R&D and other senior managers from each of the SBUs, which reviewed R&D plans and decided priorities for the company as a whole. In his view, a group of peers with strong research expertise, coupled with SBU managers concerned with customer-focused innovation, was best able to make sensible judgments about research priorities without intruding too far into the domain of SBU management. This process had provided an internal pseudo-market for R&D funds, for which SBUs had to compete. This approach had proved efficient in allocating R&D funds and using shared R&D resources effectively, avoiding overlap and maintaining a commercial focus. ABB's approach kept the initiative for R&D and its execution in the market-driven SBUs, while providing an internal market-oriented funding process and a forum for communication among the SBUs on technical issues.

At Hoechst, a major decentralization of arenas, including technology, had taken place under the leadership of the Chairman, Mr. Jürgen Dormann. The large central research laboratory located at Hoechst outside Frankfurt had been reduced in size and many of its activities shifted to divisional labs. The Hoechst lab continued to work on chemicals research relevant to the business at this location, as well as process control and improvement activities for the plants on site. But many R&D activities relevant to other SBUs had been shifted out, such as work on pharmaceuticals, which was relocated to the new pharmaceutical business created with Marion Merril Dow. The very different nature of this market (despite its common roots in chemicals) and the long time-cycles for therapeutic drug development, made it important to devolve R&D funding to this SBU. Again, the strong market pressures in this business environment made decentralization a necessity.

Another strategic shift at Hoechst was a change in mentality from doing all innovation in-house to greater reliance on licencing from outside where appropriate. There had been over-reliance on in-house product development. An example quoted was the company's internal development of a process for producing resorcinol from benzene, which had led Hoechst to neglect an alternative process based on beta-naphthol, developed by Cyanamid. It had been difficult to get interest in the new process because of the committed investment in the Hoechst technology, with the result that Cyanamid sold the technology to Japanese companies that became significant competitors.

These were examples of a company being too strongly oriented toward in-house research (the familiar "NIH" syndrome) and being fixated on a particular technology without the flexibility to abandon it and move to others as times changed. The shift to placing most development expenditure in the divisions made sense from the viewpoint of relevance to the market, but it did mean that R&D could be constrained by the profitability of the division. For example, in pharmaceuticals, it was necessary to spend heavily on R&D to strengthen that business and this would have to be supported by cash flows from other divisions by corporate intervention.

Hoechst was clearly defining its corporate competences in the field of technology and had become more open to alternative technologies as a means of creating products. Nevertheless, at Hoechst, some long-term research work was supported by Corporate headquarters, and the central laboratory also performed work on behalf of the SBUs that required specialized, costly equipment, or that depended on scientists in narrow fields of specialization that the SBUs could not afford. The latter rationale, the scale economies of centralizing specialized and costly resources, was an explanation given by other companies for centralization of a proportion of R&D expenditure. However, the proportion of R&D funded centrally in the sample companies overall was small, and ranged from 5 percent to 10 percent of their total.

Human resources management

In the human resources management arena, Hoechst had also shifted away from a large, central HR department that had played a key role in the careers of a large number of the company's managers. Instead, a small unit was now concerned with the top 150 executives who were considered potential leaders for the SBUs and for the corporation as a whole. The Management Board was concerned directly with appointments of Level One personnel worldwide (approximately 40 persons who were leaders of divisions or SBUs). For the next two levels down, a Development Committee of the Board had an oversight responsibility. The Board Committee had two-year rotating memberships so as to include a variety of functional and business experience.

As these processes indicate, succession and development planning for senior and high-potential executives was still seen as an important headquarters function, with a key role in strengthening corporate competences, but most of the other HR activities had been decentralized to SBU management. This had become a necessity for Hoechst as the company had diversified, particularly as a result of the pharmaceuticals acquisition. Each SBU was considered better able to match HR practices to its strategy and industry environment.

In the case of Sulzer, Dr. Fahrni had decided on a limited HR role for the corporate center. He believed that this role should be only concerned with developing the leadership of the company, which he regarded as a key resource. Motivation and development of the executives leading each SBU and their direct reports was a central concern on which he personally focused, leaving the SBUs to manage HR policy for their other employees. Fahrni also believed that development of the whole person was important for effective leadership and he encouraged his senior managers to set at least one personal goal, unrelated to the business, each year. He had set himself the goal of climbing Mount McKinley, and his success inspired others to attempt similar feats. These actions helped create unity among the top management group and reinforced a culture of personal achievement.

A similar view on HR was held by Emerson Electric, which delegated most HR functions to its divisions. However, senior appointments in the divisions made use of a process resembling an internal personnel market. Key attributes of the top managers in Emerson were displayed along with their photos on whiteboards in a room at its St. Louis headquarters, showing the current organization charts for the managerial positions in every division of the company. When a manager was needed for a vacant position, the senior manager concerned consulted the histories of individuals with the assistance of this display and an HR manager who maintained the database and had a good knowledge of the individuals. Possible candidates were discussed and the manager then entered into negotiation with the desired candidate's manager to determine if a reassignment could be made. Although there was no bidding for the "market price" at which a person was reassigned, there was a good assessment of the competences and qualifications of each candidate, and this "trading" process resulted in reciprocal obligations between managers. It is interesting that, even in an arena so influenced by idiosyncratic factors, Emerson had developed the elements of a market process for the optimum allocation of its human resources.

At Acer, Stan Shih's main role with regard to human-resources management was establishing principles reinforcing the culture on such issues as ownership, motivation and incentives, and selecting people for top positions. There was a small human resources group for development of the higher levels of management and there was some rotation of managers to achieve common cultural awareness.

Innovative management practices

The evidence we gathered on the roles of headquarters and SBUs on the introduction of innovative management practices was surprising. It might be expected that, given that new ways of managing could be profoundly important to a company, the introduction of such ideas would originate uniquely at headquarters. Management practices are a more generic form of competence, not dependent on specific product knowledge, and thus more likely to be held centrally.

While the executives we met acknowledged this point of view, there was considerable decentralization within a variety of approaches. In some companies, a new practice had originated in one of the SBUs, and its success there had prompted headquarters to encourage other SBUs to adopt it. One CEO commented that trying out a new approach in a single SBU was low risk, as there was always a need to adopt and modify any new idea to other SBUs' circumstances. Having a new approach (in this case, quality management) spring up in one of its SBUs had been a good experiment, as the SBU's managers had gained experience that they later shared with other SBUs. The practices had been transferred to other divisions with little difficulty.

In terms of the market failure analogy, SBUs are placed under pressure by headquarters to perform efficiently and achieve strategic goals. With this incentive, SBU managers are probably more likely than headquarters managers to seek out new approaches to management and test their potential. Ideas such as customer focus, quality management, empowerment, and transformational leadership appeal to SBU managers as potentially useful in achieving divisional objectives.

On the other hand, innovative concepts such as Economic Value Added or tapping a firm's cultural diversity are generic in their application and more likely to arise at the center. SBUs vary in the competences and managerial slack they have available for such initiatives, and a challenge for headquarters is to encourage these initiatives, to avoid judging them prematurely, and yet to be ready to disseminate successful innovations quickly to other SBUs. We see its role here as both initiator and facilitator, by encouraging a climate in which experiments in managerial innovation can flourish.

Hoechst is an example of a company in which substantial changes in management practices were led by an SBU, in this case an acquisition. As mentioned previously, Celanese had been led through a significant transformation in management practices by its CEO. After the acquisition of Celanese, Hoechst saw it as a model on which the parent company's management changes could be based. Under a new Chairman, Hoechst resolved to transform itself along a number of dimensions. Businesses were re-evaluated and grouped into a new set of SBUs. The strategic prospects for each SBU were assessed and they were classified according to expectations for growth. This process was intended to provide guidance for SBU management on corporate intentions regarding the allocation of capital, new investment, cash harvesting, and so on.

At the same time, Hoechst examined a number of functions that had previously been strongly centralized, such as R&D and human resources management. Following the Celanese model, these were substantially devolved to the new SBUs. This led, for example, to a shift of focus in HR away from company-wide practices toward senior management appointments and succession. There was a major reduction in the size and role of the central R&D laboratories. A proportion of R&D funds (3 percent) was allocated centrally, but the majority was devolved to the SBUs to fund and perform themselves. An additional stimulus to this process was Hoechst's acquisition of two major pharmaceutical companies, Roussel and Marion Merril Dow, as part of a major strategic push into the pharmaceutical sector.

A contrary example, of an innovation initiated by headquarters, is Acer's organizational structure, which was modified by the Chairman, Stan Shih, to fit the firm's new strategy in the mid-1990s. Knowing that the pace of technological change affected different parts of its PC value chain differently, Acer adopted its famous "fast-food" strategy to deliver the most up-to-date product to its customers at the lowest possible price. This meant separating the production process into two parts: assembly of "slow-cycle" components such as power supplies and disk drives into PC boxes in Asia for shipment to markets worldwide; and installation of fast-cycle[17] or time-sensitive components such as microprocessors and random-access memory at the last minute in regional centers close to the customer.[18]

This new strategy necessitated a new organization structure to manage these operations. Acer adopted a "client–server" model, in which the slow-cycle production and assembly are organized in SBUs (which include other businesses such as technical publishing and a DRAM joint venture), while the sales, marketing, and final assembly operations in each market are managed by Regional Business Units ("RBUs"). A mixed SBU–RBU structure is not unique, but Acer's was different from conventional mixed structures in that there are strong product flows from SBUs to RBUs. Also, the role of RBUs in adapting products to meet last-minute customer specifications has led them into a stronger role in product innovation, which was formerly the province solely of the SBUs.

Mr. Shih saw this new structure as a step toward even greater devolution of headquarters' functions. The RBUs were already responsible for their own policies in human resources, customer relations, supplier relations, and dealing with local stakeholders. They had a limited technical role, although this was changing because of their proximity to the market. Shih intended that RBUs would become regional companies with local shareholding and fund-raising responsibilities, effectively transferring to them all the functions currently reserved to the headquarters. The RBUs would be subject to the market forces arising from local shareholders, capital markets, and regulatory authorities, as well as customers. Acer is less diversified in products than the other companies in our sample, so that the headquarters manages in a less complex environment. It could take more control of the activities of the RBUs, but it appeared not to do so by deliberate choice. It seems clear, from the decisions that Acer had made on organization structure, that it saw its environment as "transnational" in the terms of Nohria and Ghoshal (1997), with high requirements for both global integration and local responsiveness. The best organizational fit was a structure combining differentiation at the SBU level and structural integration across the corporation, or a "differentiated network." In terms of the Nohria and Ghoshal model, Acer appears to employ neither centralization nor excessive formalization in the face of a complex environment. Rather, it appears to rely more on socialization, in which executives share a common culture and expectations about performance, to achieve its corporate goals.

In the future, Acer might retain a non-controlling interest in the RBUs, but it is not clear how much influence the parent company would expect to exert and to what extent parent company competences would be enhanced. Firms' traditional preferences for international ownership structures (over arm's length contractual relations) have traditionally been explained in terms of transaction cost theory: the transaction costs of exploiting intangible assets across borders without control, which push the firm toward internalization of activities within the corporate boundary. Acer's intention to open up its regional companies to local investment is not counter to that view, but it raises questions of how the parent's intangible assets could be extended and exploited. Mr. Shih's expectation was that pressures on the regional companies in their markets would stimulate them to develop competences that would flow back to the parent company. In other words, foreign direct *divestment* could trigger a reverse flow of intangible benefits to the parent company. It is not clear how effective Acer's structural approach will be in transferring innovation throughout its network, but it is clear that the new structure was initiated from the center, not the SBUs, with that purpose in mind.

In the case of Robert Bosch, the impetus for new management practices tended to be from the Management Board. An example of this was the introduction of Continuous Improvement, which was initiated at Board level and gradually introduced to the business units. Given that Robert Bosch appeared to be more strongly centralized and formalized than Acer, it is understandable that this initiative came from the headquarters.

Customer relations

The companies in our sample had devolved responsibility for customer relations (the arena most directly influenced by market forces) to each SBU. None of the companies had a centralized marketing function, and corporate intervention was used only sparingly.

A couple of the companies had introduced structures to take account of important industrial customers or suppliers that were common to more than one SBU. This was the case where the company had diversified into closely related sectors. An example is PPG, where the automobile companies were customers for both paint and glass. Likewise, one of its major suppliers of pigment was a competitor in the end-product market. The company's executives believed that there was a need to co-ordinate relationships with such important customers or suppliers across the divisions. Headquarters had not taken direct responsibility for this role, but had created an inter-SBU team for the task – a use of formalization rather than centralization, which seemed characteristic of PPG.

For Robert Bosch, the global motor vehicle manufacturers were customers for brakes, lighting, engine ignition systems, and other components, and co-ordination of marketing relationships was considered essential. Completely independent marketing by each SBU could preclude opportunities to "package" products to major customers and probably forego some economies of scale. Maintaining a co-ordinated relationship with such customers also allowed the company to participate with the customer at an early stage in design decisions, by offering a service that covered several key components as a system, with the potential to "lock in" the customer to a broad portfolio of products and thus enhance differentiation.

For major customers, Bosch had located liaison personnel inside the customers' offices. For example, both the gasoline engine and diesel engine systems divisions had representatives within Volkswagen. Also, a member of the Board had responsibility for co-ordination with the major customers and for a unit within Volkswagen. The objective was to make sure that all the divisions' products were represented to the customer and, at the same time, serve the customer's interests from the perspective of the company as a whole.

At Sulzer, headquarters was concerned that the market for weaving machines was shifting rapidly to Asia, along with the textile industry. China was a growing market, but none of the SBUs had a strong marketing presence there. Fahrni believed that Sulzer needed to develop Asian marketing expertise by becoming active in this market. To create such a competence, headquarters established an Asian marketing operation and encouraged the SBUs to use it. Although not required to use the operation, SBUs were expected to do so unless an independent trading company could offer a better price.

Likewise, corporate headquarters at Hoechst had taken the initiative to set up an investment company in China to act as a vehicle for providing sales advice and assistance to all of the SBUs entering the Chinese market. Partly as a consequence of this approach, Hoechst had some 30 projects underway in China in 1995, involving an investment of approximately $600 million.

The Hoechst and Sulzer cases are examples of the headquarters taking a role when, despite the existence of market forces, SBUs were not reacting quickly enough because each could not separately justify the investment to set up in a risky region. Corporate intervention pooled the risk, provided the necessary investment and stimulated its usage. The SBUs gained the benefit of the marketing service and the growing expertise was retained inside the company.

Headquarters at ABB had decentralized the marketing role jointly to its matrix of SBUs and the country-based organizations. It placed great emphasis on the local knowledge of its country-based companies and their knowledge was intended to be shared across each SBU. ABB depended largely on socialization rather than formalization or centralization to effect knowledge transfer, but this became too cumbersome and costly, necessitating the shift to a global SBU structure and a greater reliance on formalization. Retaining and tapping the company's carefully nurtured pool of country-based knowledge will be a significant challenge for ABB under the new structure.

For companies directly serving consumer markets, co-ordination between SBUs was less relevant and headquarters had little potential to add value, so that marketing and sales functions were substantially decentralized. However, in some cases, firms had established regional organizations to provide marketing services for several SBUs. This was the case at Samsung Electronics, which had set up regional marketing units in the most important geographic regions to help the SBUs market their products. In the USA, for example, a regional headquarters provided a central point for dealing with government, expatriate employee policy, and corporate marketing. It did not, however, direct the US operations of its global SBUs, which were centered in Seoul. A good example of this policy was seen in consumer electrical appliances, where the Korean-based SBU had developed sophisticated, stylish appliances, equipped with fuzzy logic, for the Korean market. On the advice of the US regional group these had not been released on the US market, as the US office didn't consider them appropriate for US tastes. This advice was accepted by the global SBU.

As noted in the previous section, Acer has devolved marketing totally to its regional business units, also encouraging them to take on local assembly to ensure customer responsiveness. The decision as to which country market to enter was centrally made, in keeping with a strategy of growth in peripheral markets that attempted to avoid direct confrontation with other computer manufacturers.

Internal transfers of components, materials, and services

For the most part, these functions were decentralized by the sample companies to their SBUs. ABB, for example, had a "sell and buy" approach, where there was a presumption of an advantage to purchasing within the group but only when the market price externally was less favorable by an agreed percentage. There was a philosophy that each SBU would have the right of "first refusal and last call" for internal sourcing. There was also a view that business should not lightly be given away to competitors when ABB itself could provide supply. Otherwise, local autonomy was the rule.

Samsung Electronics took a more centralized approach to this arena, with headquarters deciding transfer prices between divisions and even, on some occasions, within divisions. The argument given for this was that there were strategic reasons for ensuring optimal use of company resources. However, it was acknowledged that the culture was changing after 1993 and there would likely be less intervention in the future.

The preceding sections have outlined the practices of the companies surveyed in managing the centralization–devolution challenge in each arena. We believe that, despite the diversity of the markets in which they operated, a pattern is clear. We summarize this in the following Conclusion.

Conclusion

Deciding the role of the corporate headquarters relative to the other administrative units in a corporation is an important task for top management. In the past, the decision has often been made by trial and error, based on prevailing views about suitable decision-making structures. The bureaucratic model common to the age of the large industrial corporation placed top management at the apex of a chain of information with little devolution to staff at lower levels. As the single-product company evolved into the M-form corporation, responsibilities were devolved to SBUs according to top management's preferences for power and control, but without a clear logic. At the opposite extreme, conglomerates devolved most arenas of responsibility except for shareholder and capital market relations, with positive short-term impact on share price, but negative long-term results.

The environment of global business today is far more complex than it has been in the past. At the same time, the competitive advantages of firms are now based far more than in the past on their competences, captured in operating routines and human knowledge, and expressed in competitive positioning. In seeking to manage this precious and intangible resource, corporate managers are forced to be more reliant on the knowledge, skills, and initiative of executives throughout their enterprises, through a greater reliance on decentralization. This wave of interest in tapping the individual well-springs of knowledge is, in our view, not transient. It reflects both a rational response to the management of complexity and a more enlightened, if self-interested, view of human nature and the potential of motivated people.

Enterprises are dealing with the complexity of their environments by looking for solutions that are based primarily on socialization and to a lesser extent on formalization. There is considerably less emphasis on the high degree of centralization that was common in the past. However, it is clear from this research that international firms see the issue of headquarters–subsidiary relationships not as a unitary issue but as involving a complex set of variables. They have decomposed the relationship into these key variables and considered each one in terms of its fit to the environment of each business. Important as these trends are in promoting the shift toward greater devolution, in the past there has been little evidence to guide mana-gers on the question of which functions should be devolved, and to what degree. The market failure approach outlined here provides, we believe, needed guidance on this issue.

Our null hypothesis was that corporations would devolve activities to the SBUs in order to cope with high levels of complexity. The hypothesis in this extreme form was not supported by the sample evidence. Arenas of activity close to the market-place that appeared to be subject to market pressures were devolved to the manage-ment of SBUs, but in arenas where market discipline was absent, the center intervened to place pressure for performance on SBU leadership. The observed pattern of intervention is illustrated schematically in Figure 12.8.

Of course, corporations do not deliberately seek competitive pressures on their businesses and this research does not imply that they do. What it does imply is that, when an arena of activity in a business unit is subject to competitive market pres-sures, corporate headquarters intervention is unlikely to add value to that activity. Where direct market pressures are absent, headquarters steps in to act as a surro-gate for market discipline to stimulate performance. This is most obviously the case where the corporate structure shields the SBU from shareholder or capital market pressures. It is also the case where the market signals perceived by individual SBUs are insufficiently strong to stimulate action in the presence of externalities, as was true of R&D development in several of the sample companies. Headquarters may

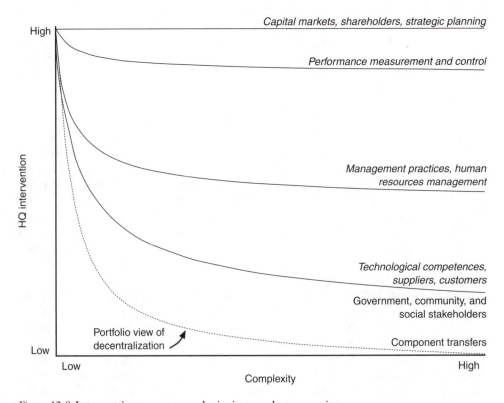

Figure 12.8 Intervention versus complexity in sample companies.

256

act directly by centralizing the activity, or it may establish a unit to provide services to the SBUs on an agreed pricing basis, which may be market-based or administered. In other cases, headquarters may attempt to create a mechanism approximating to an internal market, as in the case of R&D resource allocation at ABB and human resources management at Emerson.

Our conclusion is that top management should devolve to SBUs those arenas of responsibility where market forces are likely to promote efficiency. These are predominantly in customer and supplier relations, relations with government, the community and local stakeholders, and internal transfers of components, products, or services. As Stan Shih said: "One of Acer's core competences is that it knows how to decentralize."

Where there is "market failure," because of externalities such as customer or government relationships that are common to more than one SBU, or moral hazard issues in ensuring performance or investment, there are benefits in co-ordinating administratively.

In the arenas of shareholder relations and the capital markets, the role of the headquarters, as the only interface under market pressure, is clear. But the experience of Acer, where RBUs are exposed to some of these pressures, shows that it is sensible to question even this assumption over time.

Likewise, control of the strategic process – the format, timetable, and scrutiny of SBU plans, but not their preparation – is a key role for the center. The performance measurement system with its link to incentives and sanctions, equally, is a central responsibility in creating performance pressure. These two processes, and the systems, values, and discipline by which they are implemented, are top managements' main levers for the achievement of the corporate vision. They are corporate competences, as important for the success of the company as the product–market competences of the SBUs.

In the arenas of technology and human resources management, the research indicates that, for the most part, competitive pressures on SBUs favor devolution of responsibility. However, there are possibilities of externalities across SBUs, weak market signals, and moral hazard where pay-offs are long-term, that can justify a measure of corporate intervention. This can be done by central directive or by consultation between SBUs. While our sample suggests that the need for this is limited, each case should be considered on its merits. The presumption of market failure should not be made lightly and should be evaluated carefully before opting for an administrative solution.

Our research is not conclusive on the financial benefits of adopting the approach advocated above, as the sample is too small to provide reliable conclusions. A contingency view of strategy and organization leads us to expect that a good fit between the headquarters–subsidiary relationship and the demands of the environment would promote above-average performance. Nohria and Ghoshal (1997) found that the fit between the structure of a sample of companies and their environmental context was correlated with self-reported performance. An analysis of a larger sample, controlling for other factors, could shed light on this question. On the basis of our observations, we argue that an administrative solution should be adopted only when there is evidence of "market failure" within the corporate network. Corporate headquarters cannot centrally manage the enormous complexity of the modern multinational corporation, that is clear. In devolving arenas of responsibility to SBUs, the concept of market pressure provides workable guidance.

Notes

1 As described by the President of SAS, Jan Carlzon (1987).
2 For an extensive survey of research on diversification, see Ramanujam and Varadarajan (1989).
3 Some evidence for this conclusion was provided by an earlier study, confined to the pulp and paper industry (Davis *et al.*, 1992).
4 A comprehensive listing of these studies is provided by Sullivan (1994). He notes that most of these use foreign sales to total sales as the indicator of internationalization. He proposes a composite five-variable measure and demonstrates for a sample of major multinationals that it is a more reliable measure.
5 This finding is consistent with the quadratic relationship found by Tallman and Li (1996) for product diversification.
6 For a summary and comparison with traditional theories of the firm, see Conner (1991).
7 As concluded by Ramanujam and Varadarajan (1989)
8 Percy Barnevik, Chairman, quoted by M. Kets de Vries in *Across the Board*, October 1994.
9 ABB-Alsthom Power NV, which absorbed the company's power generation operations.
10 ABB Annual Report, 1999.
11 A sophisticated entropy measure of global diversification was developed by Vachani (1991) which incorporates both related and unrelated product and geographical diversification.
12 American Home Products acquired American Cyanamid in November 1994 ($9.7 billion) and Glaxo made a bid of $14.9 billion for Wellcome Plc. Earlier, Ciba-Geigy bought 49.9 percent of Chiron Corporation ($2.1 billion) and Roche acquired Syntex ($5.3 billion).
13 An indicator of future integration difficulties
14 An up-to-date account of the operating and financial issues facing ABB and the outlook is provided in Lehman Brothers (2002).
15 *The Economist*, 20 January 2001.
16 A good discussion of the Emerson approach to planning and strategy by Charles Knight is provided in Knight (1992).
17 See Williams (1998) for a detailed discussion of cycle time in business strategy.
18 For a detailed account of Acer's strategy and organization, see Mathews (2002).

References

Bartlett, C. and S. Ghoshal (1989) *Managing Across Borders: the Transnational Solution*, Boston, MA: Harvard Business School Press.
Berggren, C. (1994) "Building a truly global organization? The case of ABB and the hard task of integrating a multi-domestic enterprise," paper presented at International Research Conference on Corporate Change, Sydney, 22–24 August.
Campbell, A., M. Goold, and M. Alexander (1995) "The value of the parent company," *California Management Review*, 38, 1: 79–97.
Carlzon, J. (1987) *Moments of Truth*, Cambridge, MA: Ballinger Publishing Co.
Conner, K.R. (1991) "A historical comparison of resource-based theory with five schools of thought within industrial organization economics: do we have a new theory of the firm?," *Journal of Management*, 17, 1: 121–154.
Davis, P.S., R.B. Robinson Jr., J.A. Pearce II and S.H. Park (1992) "Business unit relatedness and performance: a look at the pulp and paper industry," *Strategic Management Journal*, 13, 5: 349–361.
Geringer, J.M., P.W. Beamish, and R.C. daCosta (1989) "Diversification strategy and inter-

nationalization: implications for MNE performance," *Strategic Management Journal*, 10, 2: 109–119.

Goold, Michael, Andrew Campbell, and Marcus Alexander (1994) *Corporate Level Strategy*, New York, NY: John Wiley.

Grant, R.M. (1987) "Multinationality and performance among British manufacturing companies," *Journal of International Business Studies*, 18, 3: 79–89.

Grant, R.M. (1988) "On 'dominant logic,' relatedness and the link between diversity and performance," *Strategic Management Journal*, 9: 639–642.

Kim, W. Chan, P. Hwang, and W.P. Burgers (1993) "Multinationals' diversification and the risk–return trade-off," *Strategic Management Journal*, 14: 275–286.

Knight, C.F. (1992) "Emerson Electric: consistent profits, consistently," *Harvard Business Review*, Jan.–Feb.: 57–70.

Lehman Brothers (2002) *ABB Ltd. Company Update*, London: Lehman Brothers, 13 March.

Lorange, P., B. Chakravarthy, J. Roos, and A. Van de Ven (1993) *Implementing Strategic Processes: Change, Learning and Co-operation*, Oxford: Basil Blackwell Ltd.

Markides, C.C. and P.J. Williamson (1994) "Related diversification, core competences and corporate performance," *Strategic Management Journal*, 15 (Special Issue), Summer: 149–165.

Mathews, J.A. (2002) *Dragon Multinational*, Oxford: Oxford University Press.

Nohria, N. and S. Ghoshal (1997) *The Differentiated Network*, San Francisco, CA: Jossey-Bass.

Porter, M.E. (1987) "From competitive advantage to corporate strategy," *Harvard Business Review*, 65, 3: 43–59.

Ramanujam V. and P. Varadarajan (1989) "Research on corporate diversification: a synthesis," *Strategic Management Journal*, 10: 523–551.

Rumelt, R. (1974) *Strategy, Structure and Economic Performance*, Boston, MA: Division of Research, Harvard Business School.

Siddhartan, N.S. and S. Lal (1982) "Recent growth of the largest U.S. multinationals," *Oxford Bulletin of Economics and Statistics*, 44: 1–13.

Sullivan, D. (1994) "Measuring the degree of internationalization of a firm," *Journal of International Business Studies*, 25, 2: 325–342.

Tallman, S. and J. Li (1996) "Effects of international diversity and product diversity on the performance of multinational firms," *Academy of Management Journal*, 39, 1: 179–196.

Vachani, S. (1991) "Distinguishing between related and unrelated international geographic diversification: a comprehensive measure of total global diversification," *Journal of International Business Studies*, 22, 2: 307–322.

Williams, J.R. (1992) "How sustainable is your competitive advantage?" *California Management Review*, 34, 3: 29–51.

Williams, J.R. (1998) *Renewable Advantage*, New York, NY: Free Press.

Williamson, O. (1975) *Markets and Hierarchies: Analysis and Antitrust Implications: A Study in the Economics of Internal Organization*, New York, NY: Free Press.

13

MANAGING IN A TRANSNATIONAL NETWORK

New management roles, new personal competencies

Christopher A. Bartlett and Sumantra Ghoshal

Introduction

After a decade of globalizing markets, restructuring industries, transforming technologies, and intensifying competition, there must be precious few managers who have been unaffected by the subsequent waves of downsizing, delayering, restructuring, and re-engineering that have reconfigured the form and redefined the functioning of the modern transnational organization. More important to the surviving managers is the impact that these transformational changes have had on their individual roles and responsibilities – and, by implication, on the personal competencies required of those who must implement the new management tasks.

In this chapter, we will report on part of the findings of a decade-long study, focused on what we have come to believe is the biggest change in the corporate form and the accompanying management model in three-quarters of a century.[1] In the first phase of the project, we examined the worldwide operations of a group of American, European, and Japanese companies that were responding to the globalizing forces that were forcing major organizational adjustment in the mid- and late 1980s. Our findings, presented in our book, *Managing Across Borders: The Transnational Solution* (Bartlett and Ghoshal, 1989), cannot be summarized here, but in the first part of the chapter, we highlight one central conclusion about the emergence of a new organizational form based on an integrated network model.

Even as we were concluding this phase of the study, however, we became acutely aware that, as companies developed their new networked structures to meet the intensifying globalization imperatives, they were all facing the same constraint. Managers who had spent their whole careers learning how to manage in the classic dependent relationships defined by traditional hierarchic organizations were stumbling to develop the more flexible interdependent relationships that characterized the new transnational organization model. As part of a broader follow-on research project reported in detail in *The Individualized Corporation: A Fundamentally New Approach to Management*, we examined how companies that had developed the new organizational forms were radically redefining their management roles and relationships (Ghoshal and Bartlett, 1997). And, from this understanding, we developed some hypotheses about the new personal competencies – the attitudes, knowledge, and skills – required of those who could succeed in the new management tasks.

In the first part of this chapter, we will show how the emerging integrated network model of organization is redefining the roles and responsibilities of managers from the top levels to the front line. Building on this understanding, we will then examine the implications these roles have for the personal competencies of those who must fill them. And we will conclude by showing how these changes in roles and competencies are part of a broad, fundamental change in management philosophy that is redefining the way the modern corporation works.

A new organization model: new management roles

In the wake of the explosion in global competition during the 1980s, most companies were forced to recognize that they could no longer succeed on the basis of their historic narrow sources of competitive advantage. In an earlier study, we showed that the most successful worldwide companies were those that had been able to build three potentially conflicting strategic capabilities: global-scale efficiency, local flexibility and responsiveness, and an integrated process of cross-border innovation and learning. It was the need to develop this multilayered strategic capability that led companies to build what we described as a truly transnational organization with three distinctive characteristics:

- *Multidimensional perspectives* To be able to sense and analyze the numerous and often conflicting opportunities, pressures, and demands it faces worldwide, the transnational organization must be built around three strong management groups, each with access to the company's decision-making process. Capable national subsidiary management is needed to sense and represent the changing needs of local customers and the aspirations of host governments; influential global or regional business management is needed to track the strategy of cross-border competitors and to rationalize the company's assets, products, and strategies worldwide; and effective functional management is needed to enhance and consolidate corporate knowledge and expertise, and facilitate its transfer and use among dispersed national units.
- *Distributed, interdependent capabilities* Having sensed the diverse opportunities and demands it faces, the transnational company must then be able to respond to them in a timely and effective manner. To do so, the company neither centralizes its capabilities in the home country nor fragments them on a local-for-local basis among different subsidiaries. Rather, it distributes its resources and capabilities around the world, typically building organizational assets in major markets, in key competitive centers, and in locations providing access to scarce expertise, such as technology. In any case, resources are specialized and linked regionally or globally to achieve economies of scale and skill. One major consequence of such a configuration of distributed, specialized capabilities is a high level of interdependence among worldwide units. The transnational manages these interdependencies by creating processes and mechanisms for

261

extensive cross-unit flow of resources, products, and knowledge. As a result, the transnational company builds a structure that can be described as an integrated network.

- *Flexible, integrative processes* Having established management groups represent- ing multiple perspectives and a network of distributed and interdependent assets and capabilities, the transnational requires a management process that can resolve the diversity of interests and perspectives and integrate the dis- persed responsibilities. This requires a sophisticated and subtle decision-making machinery based on three different but interdependent management mechan- isms. The first is a supportive but constrained escalation process that allows top management to intervene directly in the content of certain decisions – a care- fully managed form of centralization. The second is to define individual roles and supportive systems to influence specific key decisions through formaliza- tion. The third is socialization, built through shared norms and values and rela- tionships that create a context for delegated decisions. It is only by developing and selectively managing this portfolio of processes that a company can in- tegrate the multidimensional management perspectives and co-ordinate the dispersed resources and capabilities that characterize the transnational organ- ization. (The core characteristics of the transnational's integrated network are illustrated in Figure 13.1.)

In the second stage of our research project, we observed numerous companies that were converging on this organizational model despite wide differences in their core business, national origin, and corporate histories. Some, like AT&T, Komatsu, ABB, and Corning, were forced to shed traditional authority-based hierarchies to adopt the newer form, while others, like 3M, Kao, ISS, and Intel, had built their organ- izations in networked form over many decades and, as a result, had avoided the worst pathologies of the classic bureaucracies. In many ways this latter group pro- vided both the example and the inspiration for companies in the first group that were undergoing painful transformations to the integrated networked model.

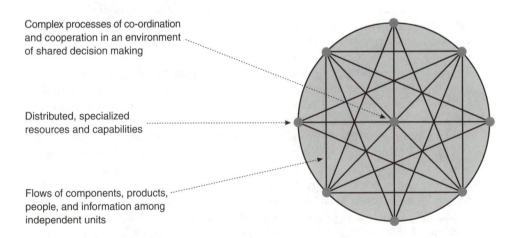

Complex processes of co-ordination and cooperation in an environment of shared decision making

Distributed, specialized resources and capabilities

Flows of components, products, people, and information among independent units

Figure 13.1 The integrated network.

As we refined our understanding of the operations of this emerging corporate form, we noted three additional characteristics common to companies making the transformational change. The first and most widespread trend we observed was that companies were rethinking their old approach of dividing the organization from the top-down into groups, sectors, and divisions. Instead, they were building from the bottom-up on a foundation of small front-line operating units. For example, the $30 billion Swiss-based electro-technical giant, ABB, divided its operations into 1,300 local operating companies, each of which is structured as a separate legal entity with its own balance sheet and P&L responsibilities. 3M's $15 billion of sales are generated by a portfolio of over 60,000 products, managed by 3,900 profit centers that are at the heart of the company's entrepreneurial process. And ISS, the Danish-based cleaning services organization attributes its growth into a $2 billion multinational corporation to its policy of forming not one national subsidiary, but four or five small autonomous businesses in each of the 17 countries it has expanded into, allowing each of them to grow by serving a particular client group.

The second common characteristic in the emerging organization model is the portfolio of cross-unit integrative processes designed to break down the insulated vertically oriented relationships that have dominated the classic authority-based hierarchy. In ABB, we found that the tensions embodied in the company's global matrix were resolved through a proliferation of business boards, functional councils, and project teams designed to play a primary role in ABB's management process at every level of the organization. At 3M, the R&D community's carefully developed network of communications channels and decision-making forums became the model for similar relationships that were fostered to link marketing and manufacturing resources across the company's portfolio of innovative front-line units. And ISS made extensive use of both training and development as well as regional cross-unit meetings and committees to ensure that knowledge and expertise developed in one part of the company were rapidly transferred system-wide.

Finally, in the emerging organization, these changes to the old structure and processes were supported by a strong commitment to genuine empowerment, a philosophy that represented a powerful challenge to the authority-based culture in most classic hierarchies. In ABB, CEO Percy Barnevik based the company's management practice on the twin principles of radically decentralized responsibility and tightly held individual accountability. 3M was known for its core principles that espoused a commitment to entrepreneurship and a belief in the individual, and had long worked to translate those beliefs into a culture that "stimulates ordinary people to produce extraordinary performance." And in his 30 years at the head of ISS, Poul Andreassen had developed a set of guiding principles, central to which was a genuine respect for his workers and a delegation of responsibility as close to the individual cleaning contract as possible.

This radically decentralized yet horizontally linked network organizational model with a strong culture of empowerment required companies to break with what we termed the "Russian doll" model of management, that assumed a neatly nested hierarchy of responsibilities and a set of management roles that were miniature replicas of the job at the next level. In these and other companies we studied, operating-level managers had to evolve from their traditional role as front-line implementers to become innovative entrepreneurs; senior-level managers had to redefine their primary role from administrative controllers to developmental coaches; and top-level executives were forced to see themselves less as their company's strategic architects and more as their organizational leaders. The implications of such role changes on the distribution of key tasks and responsibilities are profound.

The operating-level entrepreneurial role

In identifying the new roles and responsibilities of those running national subsidiaries, business units or other such front-line units, we studied the activities of scores of operating-level managers as they struggled to adjust to the demands of the new corporate model. We will focus on a select group of managers at ABB, 3M, and ISS, not as definitive role models, but as illustrations of the framework of management tasks we have developed.

Don Jans headed the relays business unit that was part of Westinghouse's troubled power transmission and distribution business, which it sold to ABB in 1989. Westinghouse had long regarded relays as a mature business, and Jans and his team had been encouraged to milk their slowly declining, modestly profitable operation. Yet, when exposed to ABB's decentralized entrepreneurial environment, the same management group turned their mature business into one with the performance profile of a young growth company. Within three years of the ownership change, export sales skyrocketed, new products were introduced, and operating profits doubled. Equally important, the revitalized US relays unit began developing an electronic capability to supplement its traditional electro-mechanical expertise, thus laying the foundation for long-term expansion into a major new growth area.

In 3M we saw a similar example of front-line entrepreneurship when, in 1989, Andy Wong became the leader of a project team that had been struggling for over a decade to commercialize a portfolio of the company's optical technologies that had never found market applications. Over the next four years, Wong redeployed the unit's resources, refocused its energy and attention, protected the operations from several threats to shut them down, and remotivated the discouraged team. By 1994, Wong's unit had become a showcase within 3M by introducing two new products, both of which proved to be highly successful in the marketplace.

And at ISS we observed Theo Buitendijk take over the company's small Dutch commercial cleaning business and double revenues within two years. He took the company into the specialized higher-margin segment of slaughterhouse cleaning, eventually becoming the company's center of expertise in this sector and supporting its expansion throughout Europe. Like Jans, Buitendijk had previously been a traditional line manager in a classic authoritarian hierarchy (in his case, Exxon), but found that the different organizational context in ISS not only allowed, but also encouraged him, to redefine his role and change his behavior.

In each of these companies, a similar framework of organizational structure, processes, and culture supported the entrepreneurial activities of front-line managers like Jans, Wong, and Buitendijk, as they took the initiative to drive the performance and enhance the capabilities of their units. Among the many tasks and responsibilities they undertook, we identified three that were central to their role as entrepreneurs rather than just implementers (see also Table 13.1):

Table 13.1 Management roles and tasks

	Operating-level managers	Senior-level managers	Top-level managers
Changing role	From operational implementers to aggressive entrepreneurs	From administrative controllers to supportive coaches	From resource allocators to institutional leaders
Primary value added	Driving business performance by focusing on productivity, innovation, and growth within front-line units	Providing the support and co-ordination to bring large company advantages to the independent front-line units	Creating and embedding a sense of direction, commitment, and challenge to people throughout the organization
Key activities and tasks	Creating and pursuing new growth opportunities for the business	Developing individuals and supporting their activities	Challenging embedded assumptions while establishing a stretching opportunity horizon and performance standards
	Attracting and developing resources and competencies	Linking dispersed knowledge, skills, and best practices across units	Institutionalizing a set of norms and values to support cooperation and trust
	Managing continuous performance improvement within the unit	Managing the tension between short-term performance and long-term ambition	Creating an overarching corporate purpose and ambition

- they took the lead in creating and pursuing new growth opportunities;
- they worked to attract and retain the scarce resources and skills necessary to pursue growth;
- they constantly drove their business to ensure ongoing performance improvement.

The most striking set of activities and achievements common to the operating-level entrepreneurs we studied were those related to their shared successes in taking the initiative to create and pursue new business opportunities. In contrast to the role they once played as implementers of programs and priorities pushed down from above, managers like Jans and Buitendijk found that in their new situations they were not only free to initiate new activities, but were also expected to do so. Jans rose to the challenge by expanding into export markets in Mexico, Canada, and the Far East, and committing to the development of microprocessor-based relays, despite the substantial up-front investment involved. Buitendijk's abattoir cleaning caused a sharp drop in his company's profitability before finally proving to be a much more attractive segment than the highly competitive core office cleaning business.

Beyond developing new products and markets, these front-line entrepreneurs had all expanded the assets, resources, and capabilities of their operating units. Rather than playing the more traditional passive–dependent role defined by corporate processes such as head count authorization, capital budget allocation, and management development procedures, these individuals saw it as their responsibility to develop the limited resources they had and "to do more with less," as one of them described it. Andy Wong's actions in upgrading his unit's existing technological and manufacturing resources were impressive enough, but his creation of an entirely new marketing capability in a resource-constrained operation was truly entrepreneurial. Through persistent negotiations with senior management, creative internal resource reallocations, and persuasive recruiting within the company, he was able to reinforce his small struggling unit with an experienced marketing manager and to back him with the distribution support of two other 3M divisions that agreed to help bring his unproven product to market. Don Jans's ability to develop a microprocessor-based product line, and his unit's recognition as the benchmark in cycle-time management exhibited the same commitment to build on and leverage existing capabilities. This capability led Jans to be recognized as a "giver" rather than a "receiver," as ABB terminology referred to managers who became net developers rather than consumers of the organization's scarce resources.

The third basic responsibility of front-line managers was the one with which they were most familiar: to ensure continuous performance improvement of their operating units. In the new organizational context, however, they were given considerably more freedom, incentive, and support to find ways to do so. Thus, despite the fact that he had long been driven to maximize operating performance in Westinghouse, Don Jans was able to achieve substantial additional expense cuts, inventory and receivables reductions, and operating efficiency improvements within the ABB organization, largely because he was given what Barnevik described as "maximum degree of freedom to execute."

Achieving current performance also became a priority for Andy Wong, who knew that by leveraging the unit's existing assets and resources, he could build the credibility and confidence he would need to obtain additional investment and support. It was for this reason that Wong initially invested a large part of his energy in focusing development attention on only two technologies and reducing manufacturing costs by 50 percent. It was only after building organizational confidence with his operating effectiveness that he won the freedom to engage the resources necessary to implement his unit's entrepreneurial new product launch.

If these three entrepreneurial tasks do not yet describe the actual practice of most front-line managers, it only shows the untapped potential for performance improvement available to most companies. The dramatically changed behavior of managers like Jans and Buitendijk, and Wong's rapid transition from engineer to project team leader, suggest that inside every hierarchy, even the most authoritarian, there are entrepreneurial hostages waiting to be unleashed. But the new entrepreneurial tasks can only be accomplished after the historical structures, processes, and cultural norms are replaced by a new organizational framework that not only allows front-line managers to abandon their old implementation role, but also demands they do so.

Senior-level development role

The risk of redefining the role of operating-level managers as entrepreneurs rather than implementers is that it will fragment the company's resources and capabilities and lead to the kind of undisciplined, localized expansion that conglomerates experienced in the 1960s. To prevent this, the senior-level managers – those between the front-line units and the corporate-level management typically responsible for the organization's divisions, regions, or key functions – must redefine their role from the historic preoccupation with authority-based control to a focus on support-based management and organization development.

Traditionally, senior managers' power came from their pivotal position in large and complex hierarchies. They played a vital intermediary role, disaggregating corporate objectives into business unit targets and aggregating business unit plans for corporate review. They were the linch-pins in the resource allocation process due to corporate management's reliance on their input in capital budgeting and personnel appointment decisions. And they stood at the crossroads of internal communication, interpreting and broadcasting management's priorities, then channeling and translating front-line feedback.

These classic senior management tasks have been challenged by the creation of small independent front-line units, the radical decentralization of assets and resources to support them, and the empowerment of the operating managers in charge. They have been further undermined by the delayering of middle levels of the organization and the impact of new information technologies on internal communication. Left to fulfill their traditional role, senior managers find themselves increasingly frustrated by the irrelevance and powerlessness of their position. Unless there is a radical realignment of their role, this group can become the silent subverters of change whose invisible, yet persistent resistance can derail even the most carefully planned transformation program.

Some companies have succeeded in this necessary redesign of the senior-management role to the extent that this group plays a key role in supporting the front-line units by co-ordinating their activities and coaching their operating-level entrepreneurs. Ulf Gundemark, Don Jans's boss and the head of ABB's worldwide relays business area, played a central role in managing the tension inherent in the company's ambition "to be global and local, big and small, radically decentralized with central reporting and control." Similarly, Paul Guehler, vice-president of 3M's Safety and Security Systems Division to which Andy Wong's unit belonged, challenged Wong to define the focus and priorities in his business, while simultaneously helping him build the support and obtain the resources necessary to make it succeed. And at ISS, Waldemar Schmidt, head of the European region, supported Theo Buitendijk's new business initiative despite its short-term profit impact, and led the effort to leverage the expertise his unit developed into a European business capability.

In none of these cases did these managers see their roles in the traditional terms of strategic spanbreakers, administrative controllers, and information relays. Instead of dominating their front-line managers, usurping their authority, or compromising their sense of responsibility for their operations, this new generation of senior managers added value to that activity through three core tasks:

- they became a vital source of support and guidance for the front-line entrepreneurs;
- they took primary responsibility for linking and leveraging the resources and competencies developed in the front-line units;
- they played a key role in ensuring resolution of the numerous tensions and conflicts built into the management process.

When a company decides to change its dominant management model from one driven by authority to one built on empowerment, the basic orientation of the senior manager's task is turned 180 degrees from direction and control to development and support. ABB not only reflected this change in its cultural norms; it institutionalized it in the way key senior-level jobs were structured. For example, although Ulf Gundemark was the relays business area head, he had a staff of only four to help him run the $250 million worldwide business. As a result, he routinely asked managers in operating units to take on broader responsibilities, stretching their abilities and developing their contacts and support as they did so. To develop the worldwide relays strategy, he assembled a nine-person team of managers drawn from the front lines of his operating companies; and to guide the ongoing business operations, he created a business area board that included his staff members and four key company presidents, including Don Jans. As Jans put it, "I'm a much broader manager today than I was at Westinghouse. . . . We feel we are rediscovering management."

Paul Guehler described his primary job as "to help develop the people to develop the business." He worked intensively with Wong and his team, challenging them to refine their plans, forcing them to commit them to paper, and, most important, encouraging them to communicate and defend them in multiple forums in order to build their struggling unit's thin support within 3M. And at ISS, Waldemar Schmidt had a similar philosophy about his role, stating "the most important thing I can do is to show an interest, to show that I care about them and their performance." He backed his words with actions, developing a strongly supportive relationship with his front-line managers that manifested itself in frequent telephone calls to say "Well done," or "How can I help?"

The second of the common development roles we observed was focused more at the level of organization development, as senior-level managers took on the task of linking the knowledge and expertise developed in their front-line units and embedding them as organizational capabilities to be leveraged company-wide. Gundemark's actions in forcing his front-line relays companies to rationalize and specialize in overlapping structures and responsibilities was a first step in integrating the portfolio of independent relays operations. He then appointed key specialists in each of the companies to Functional Councils, whose primary purpose was to identify best practices and capture other benefits of co-ordination in R&D, quality, purchasing, and other functional areas. Waldemar Schmidt achieved similar cross-unit linkages through his regular meetings specifically devoted to leveraging the expertise of particular country units. When Theo Buitendijk's unit in Holland was shown to have superior performance in customer retention, for example, Schmidt gave him a day at his next European Presidents Conference to discuss his approach.

Beyond these important developmental tasks, however, those in senior management positions must still accept responsibility for the performance of the front-line units they supervise. The common bottom line contribution of the three managers we described is that they all played the pivotal role in ensuring that those reporting to them kept the strategic objectives and operating priorities in balance. In ABB this task was framed by a global matrix, which was designed to legitimize rather than minimize the tensions and paradoxes inherent in most management decisions. To manage the conflict resolution vital to the organization's smooth operation, senior-level managers like Ulf Gundemark developed and managed a portfolio of supplemental communications channels and decision forums, such as the worldwide business board and the Functional Councils we described. These and other forums, such as the steering committees that act as local boards for each of the front-line companies, not only serve a development and integration role, but they also become the place where differences are aired and resolution obtained on the conflicting perspectives and interests created by the matrix.

In 3M, this critical balancing role is so ingrained in the culture that senior-level managers like Paul Guehler have integrated it into their ongoing management approach. For example, in what he terms his "give-and-take management style," Guehler tightened the screws on Wong's operations by requiring them to make the cuts necessary to meet their financial objectives, while behind the scenes, he was defending against attempts to close the unit down and was lining up resources and support to back their proposed development initiatives.

Senior-level managers are often the forgotten and forsaken group in the organizational transformation process. Amid rounds of delayering, destaffing, and downsizing, many corporate executives have overlooked the fact that the success of small, empowered front-line units depends on a company's ability to bring the benefits of a large company to those units. Organizations that dismantle their vertical integration mechanisms without simultaneously creating horizontal co-ordination processes quickly lose potential scale economies and, even more important, the benefits that come from leveraging each unit's assets, knowledge, and capabilities company-wide. At the same time, such intense horizontal flows can also paralyze the organization by distracting or overburdening front-line managers. It is the middle managers who can make "inverting the pyramid" operational, not only by developing and supporting the front-line entrepreneurs, but also by absorbing most of the demands of the cross-business, cross-functional, and cross-geographic integration needs. In this way, they can prevent those at the operating level from becoming overwhelmed by the ambiguity, complexity, and potential conflicts that often accompany such horizontal networked organizations, and allow them instead to focus on their vital entrepreneurial tasks.

The top-management leadership role

Those at the apex of many of today's large, complex organizations find themselves playing out a role that they have inherited from their corporate forebears: to be the formulators of strategy, the builders of structure, and the controllers of the systems. As these three tools became increasingly sophisticated, there was a growing assumption that they could allow organizations to drive purposefully toward their clearly defined goals, largely free from the idiosyncrasies of individual employees and the occasional eccentricities and pathologies of their behavior. To some extent, the objective was achieved: under the "strategy, structure, systems" doctrine of management, most large companies eventually became highly standardized and efficient operations, with individual employees being managed as inputs in the predicable but depersonalized system.

To free these entrepreneurial hostages requires a rollback of this dehumanizing management paradigm and thus a rethinking of top management's role from one grounded in the old doctrine of strategy, structure, and systems to one based on a new philosophy focusing on purpose, process, and people. From being the formulators of corporate strategy, those at the top of the most entrepreneurial companies in our study had evolved to become the shapers of a broader corporate purpose with which individual employees could identify and feel commitment. Instead of focusing on formal structures that gave them control over the firm's financial resources, they devoted much of their efforts to building processes that added value by having the organization work together more effectively. And rather than becoming overly dependent on the management systems that isolated them from the organization and treated employees as factors of production, they created a challenging organization context that put them back in touch with people and focused them on affecting individual inputs rather than just monitoring collective outputs.

In implementing this fundamental change in management philosophy, we saw top management focusing on three core activities:

- they developed stretching objectives and high standards, while constantly challenging the status quo;
- they built a trust-based environment that supported both risk taking and cross-unit collaboration;
- they provided a clear sense of corporate purpose that gave the system its stabilizing center.

The first task facing those at the top was to create a work environment that fostered entrepreneurial initiative rather than compliant implementation. Poul Andreassen was not someone who readily accepted the status quo, and like many of the CEOs we observed, he was constantly questioning the past and challenging his organization to achieve more. To overcome the constrained potential of continuing to operate ISS as a Danish office-cleaning business, Andreassen began to conceive of and define the company as a more broadly defined professional service organization. His explicit objective was to create a world-class company "to make ISS and service as synonymous as Xerox and photocopying." By raising the opportunity horizon, he legitimized the entrepreneurial initiatives of his management team as they expanded into new markets and unexplored business segments. And the stretching and challenging environment that he developed continued to support the entrepreneurial initiatives of operating-level managers like Theo Buitendijk, as he developed the abattoirs cleaning business in Holland, or the ISS manager in Germany, who saw an opportunity to expand into the former East Germany to start a business in the removal of building rubble.

The second key task common to the top managers we studied was to shape the organizational context necessary to support the radically decentralized structure and the management philosophy of empowerment. To ensure that the organization did not fragment its efforts or dissipate its scarce resources in this more decentralized form, traditional control-based values had to be replaced with norms of trust and support. Over the years, 3M's top managers have created an organization with such values, allowing resources and expertise to move freely across its 3,900 profit centers located in 47 divisions and 57 country operations. From the earliest days, they developed clear integrating norms such as the recognition that while products belong to the division, technologies belong to the company. They reinforced such beliefs by carefully developing a framework for collaboration and support. For example, the strong mutually supportive relationships within 3M's scientific community were formed and reinforced through institutionalized grassroots forums, internal technology fairs, cross-unit transfer practices, and many other elements that their company's leaders had built over the years. But over-arching all of this was a sense of trust embedded in the respect those at the top had for individuals and their ideas. As current CEO, Livio "Desi" DeSimone reminds his managers, they must listen carefully to subordinates and continually ask, "What do you see that I am missing?" It was this respectful, supportive, and trusting environment that allowed entrepreneurs like Andy Wong to take risks, and encouraged middle managers like Paul Guehler to back them.

Finally, in addition to providing a sense of stretch and challenge and an integrating context of collaboration and trust, the top-level managers we observed also played the vital role of providing the organization with a stabilizing and motivating sense of purpose. As chief executive of ABB, Percy Barnevik believed that he had to develop more than just a clear strategy for his newly merged worldwide entity; he had to create an organizational environment that made people proud to belong to and motivated to work for the company. He articulated ABB's overall mission not in terms of market share, competitive position, or profit objectives, but as ways in which ABB could contribute to sustainable economic growth and world development. He emphasized a sensitivity to environmental protection and a commitment to contributing to improved living standards worldwide, reflecting those beliefs not only in the company's formal mission statement, but also in the major strategic decisions he took. The company's pioneering investments in Eastern Europe, its transfer of technology to China and India, and its innovations in environmentally sensitive processes gave substance to its articulated purpose. This allowed ABB's employees to feel that they were contributing to changing the world for the better. As corporate executive VP Göran Lindahl explained, "In the end, managers are loyal not to a particular boss or even to a company, but to a set of values they believe in and find satisfying."

The approach taken by Barnevik and Lindahl and their counterparts in companies like 3M and ISS reflected the simple belief that their job as top-level leaders was not only to manage an economic entity whose activities could be directed through strategic plans, resource allocation processes, and management control systems. Equally important was their role as the principal architects of a social institution able to capture the energy, commitment, and creativity of those within it by treating them as valued organizational members, not just contracted company employees. In addition to managing the strategy and structure, they took the time to develop a corporate purpose and shape the integrating organizational processes. And rather than simply monitoring the performance of divisions or subsidiaries through abstract systems, they focused their attention on the people within the organizations – those whose motivations and actions would drive its performance.

In part, it was this new focus on the individual rather than the organizational entity as the primary unit of analysis that led to the current fascination with identifying and developing management competencies. But it was also spurred by the fact that companies had made fundamental changes in the roles of managers at all levels and some individuals were having difficulty in making the adjustment. Understandably, this, too, raised questions about the individual competencies required to succeed in the new roles.

The new management roles: the new personal competencies

Over the past few years, companies as diverse as AT&T, British Airways, BP, Siemens, and The World Bank have invested enormous amounts of management time and effort to define the ideal profile of their future corporate leaders. Siemens, for example, has defined 22 desirable management characteristics, listing them under its five basic competencies of understanding, drive, trust, social competence, and what they call a "sixth sense." The World Bank's ideal profile identifies 20 attributes and groups them into seven quite different categories: intellectual leadership, team leadership, staff development, work program management, communication, interpersonal impact, and client orientation. And Pepsico's desired competency profile for its executives of the future has 18 key dimensions defining how individuals see the world, how they think, and the way they act.

This focus on personal characteristics is understandable given the widespread problems that so many individuals have had in adjusting to the transformed organizational environment and performing the redefined management tasks. Indeed, this emerging interest in individual competencies has created a cottage industry among consultants eager to promote their expertise in identifying, measuring, and developing the desired personal capabilities to lead in the new corporate environment. Yet, despite prodigious efforts in designing questionnaires, conducting interviews, and running seminars to define this profile of leadership competencies, few of these programs have won the kind of credibility and support necessary for widespread adoption and application.

One problem is that, because there is rarely any clarity about what is meant by management competencies, the profiles that have been generated often include an inventory of personality traits, individual beliefs, acquired skills, and other personal attributes and behaviors assembled on the basis of unclear selection criteria and with little logical linkage to bind them. Furthermore, these profiles are often developed based on surveys of current managers or analyses of the most successful individual performers in the existing context. As such, they risk defining future leadership needs in terms of historical organizational roles, and the capabilities required to succeed in old organizational forms.

However, in our view, the most important limitation of these management competency exercises is that they are almost always defined as a single ideal profile. While such an assumption may not have been entirely irrational in the more symmetrical roles typical of the traditional authority-based hierarchy, this extension of the Russian doll model is far less viable in the emerging delayered organization built on a much more differentiated set of management roles and tasks.

As part of our research into post-transformation organizations, we studied the adaptation of managers to their redefined responsibilities. However, instead of asking managers to describe the personal characteristics they felt were most important, we preferred to observe those who had demonstrated their effectiveness in performing the key tasks that we had identified at the core of the redefined management roles. And rather than trying to develop a list of generic competencies with universal application, we were able to differentiate the profiles of managers who succeeded in adding value in very different ways at each level of the organization.

Yet, despite the fact that we were developing more differentiated profiles based on performance rather than opinion, the notion of individual competencies still seemed too vague and unfocused to be of great practical value. To be more useful to managers, the concept had to be more sharply defined and more clearly applicable to human resource discussions and activities. This led us to develop a simple classification model that helped us allocate the broadly defined competencies identified for each role into three categories:

- deeply embedded personal characteristics like attitudes, traits, and values that had become intrinsic parts of the individual's character and personality;
- attributes like knowledge, experience, and understanding that generally could be acquired through training and career path development;
- specialized skills and abilities that were directly linked to the job's specific task requirements and were built on the individual's intrinsic capabilities as applied to his or her acquired knowledge (see Table 13.2).

In categorizing management competencies in this way, we not only gave the concept a sharper definitional meaning, but were also able to identify much more clearly how managers focused attention on different attributes of the profile in various important human resource decisions. In particular, our observations led us to develop some hypotheses about the role different attributes play in the vital management responsibilities for selecting, developing, and supporting people in their particular job responsibilities. In the following sections we will outline those hypotheses and elaborate on their implications.

Selecting for embedded traits

The high rate of failure among managers attempting to adapt from their historic roles in traditional companies to their newly defined tasks in transformed and re-engineered organizations underscores the importance of identifying selection criteria that can help predict success in radically redefined roles. In ABB, for example, despite the careful selection of those appointed to 300 top- and senior-management positions when the merged company was created in 1988, over 40 percent of that group were no longer with the company six years later. As the company's leadership recognized at the time, the central problem was that there was a scarcity of candidates who had already developed the quite different set of skills they needed to

Table 13.2 Management competencies for new roles

Role/task	Attitudes/traits	Knowledge/experience	Skills/abilities
Operating-level entrepreneurs • Creating and pursuing opportunities	*Results-oriented competitor* • Creative, intuitive	*Detailed operating knowledge* • Knowledge of the business's technical, competitive, and customer characteristics	*Focuses energy on opportunities* • Ability to recognize potential and make commitments
• Attracting and utilizing scarce skills and resources	• Persuasive, engaging	• Knowledge of internal and external resources	• Ability to motivate and drive people
• Managing continuous performance improvement	• Competitive, persistent	• Detailed understanding of the business operations	• Ability to sustain organizational energy around demanding objectives
Senior-management developers • Reviewing, developing, supporting individuals and their initiatives	*People-oriented integrator* • Supportive, patient	*Broad organizational experience* • Knowledge of people as individuals and understanding how to influence them	*Develops people and relationships* • Ability to delegate, develop, empower
• Linking dispersed knowledge, skills, and practices	• Integrative, flexible	• Understanding of the interpersonal dynamics among diverse groups	• Ability to develop relationships and build teams
• Managing the short-term and long-term pressures	• Perceptive, demanding	• Understanding the means–ends relationships linking short-term priorities and long-term goals	• Ability to reconcile differences while maintaining tension
Top-level leaders • Challenging embedded assumptions while setting stretching opportunity horizons and performance standards	*Institution-minded visionary* • Challenging, stretching	*Understanding company in its context* • Grounded understanding of the company, its businesses, and operations	*Balances alignment and challenge* • Ability to create an exciting, demanding work environment
• Building a context of cooperation and trust	• Open-minded, fair	• Understanding of the organization as a system of structures, processes, and cultures	• Ability to inspire confidence and belief in the institution and its management
• Creating an overarching sense of corporate purpose and ambition	• Insightful, inspiring	• Broad knowledge of different companies, industries, and societies	• Ability to combine conceptual insight with motivational challenges

succeed in the radically different organizational and managerial context Percy Barnevik had defined.

When faced with such a situation, most companies we observed tended to select primarily on the basis of an individual's accumulated knowledge and job experience. These were, after all, the most visible and stable qualifications in an otherwise tumultuous situation. Furthermore, selecting on this basis was a decision that could be made by default, simply by requiring existing managers to take on totally redefined job responsibilities. In such situations, however, past experience did not prove to be a good predictor of future success. The most obvious problem was that much of the acquired organizational expertise was likely to reflect old management models and behavioral norms. Equally problematic were the personal characteristics of those who had succeeded in the old organizational environment. As many companies discovered, the highly task-oriented senior managers who were both comfortable and successful in the well-structured work environment of their traditional company often found great personal difficulty in adjusting to the coaching and integrating roles that became an important part of their redefined responsibilities.

As a result, many companies are coming to believe that it is much more difficult to convince an authoritarian industry expert to adopt a more people-sensitive style than to develop industry expertise in a strong people manager. It is a recognition that is leading them to conclude that innate personal characteristics – an individual's deeply embedded attitudes, traits, and values – should dominate acquired knowledge and experience as the key selection criteria. And equally importantly, they are recognizing that because the management roles and tasks differ widely at each level of the organization, so, too, will the attitudes, traits, and values of those most likely to succeed in each position. Recruitment and succession planning in such an environment becomes a much more sophisticated exercise of identifying the very different kinds of individuals who can succeed as operating-level entrepreneurs, senior-level developers, and top management leaders.

In ISS, for example, the company had long recognized the vital importance of recruiting individuals who were results-oriented competitors to run their front-line operating units. Although a country manager's job at ISS could be regarded as a low status position, (managing front-line supervisors in the mature and menial office cleaning business), ISS knew that by structuring the role to give managers status and autonomy, they could attract the kind of energetic, independent, and creative individuals they wanted. Like many of ISS's operating-level entrepreneurs, Theo Buitendijk had spent his early career in a traditional hierarchical company, but had been frustrated by the constraints, controls, and lack of independence. Status elements like the "managing director" title and the prestige company car signaled the importance ISS attached to this position, but entrepreneurial individuals like Buitendijk were even more attracted by the independence offered by operating their own business behind what ISS managers called "Chinese walls" to prevent unwanted interference. By creating an environment that self-starters found stimulating, ISS had found little difficulty in training them in industry knowledge and in helping them to develop the specific job skills they required to succeed.

The personal profile required to move to the next level of management was quite different, however, and few of the operating-level entrepreneurs were expected or indeed had an ambition to move up to the divisional-management level. One who did was Waldemar Schmidt, an operating-level entrepreneur, who had turned around the company's Brazilian business before being appointed head of the European division. Despite his lack of knowledge of the European market or his experience in that part of the organization, Schmidt impressed Poul Andreassen as a people-oriented individual who had a genuine interest in developing and supporting others. Indeed, the company's Five Star Development Program had originated in Brazil as part of Schmidt's commitment to continually upgrade his employees. Furthermore, he was recognized as being a very balanced individual, who tended to operate by influence more than authority, yet was demanding of himself and others. These were qualities that Andreassen regarded as vital in his senior managers and felt they far outweighed Schmidt's more limited European knowledge or experience.

At the top level of the organization, another set of personal qualities was felt to be important. When Poul Andreassen became the president of ISS in 1962, he, too, was selected primarily on the basis of his personal traits and values rather than his experience in the company or his proven leadership skills. As a young engineer in his mid-30s, he was frustrated in his job with a traditional large company and was looking for the opportunity to build a very different kind of organization. Despite his lack of industry background or ISS-specific management skills, he was attractive because he was much less interested in merely running an ongoing company than he was in building a more ambitious organization. His most appealing characteristic was his willingness to question and challenge everything, and even after 30 years in the job, he still felt that his best days were when he could go into the field and confront his division or business unit managers to help "stir up new things."

There are very few individuals who have the breadth of personal traits and the temperamental range to adapt to the very different roles and tasks demanded of them at different organizational levels, but Waldemar Schmidt was one such person. At ISS, he progressed from successful operating-level entrepreneur to effective senior-management developer, and, after Poul Andreassen's retirement, was asked to succeed him as top-level corporate leader. One of management's most important challenges is to identify the personal characteristics that will allow an individual to succeed in a new and often quite different role and, equally important, to recognize when someone who is successful at one level lacks the individual traits to succeed at the next. For those with the perceived potential, however, the next key challenge is to develop the knowledge and expertise that can support and leverage their embedded personal traits.

Developing for knowledge acquisition

While training and development activities are rarely very effective in changing the deeply embedded personal traits, attitudes, and values that we described as the foundation stone of recruitment and selection criteria, they are extremely appropriate means of developing the kind of knowledge and experience that allows an individual to build on and apply those embedded individual attributes. As a person who is naturally creative, engaging, and competitive learns more about a particular business, its customers and technologies, for example, he or she becomes a much more effective and focused operating-level entrepreneur. Poul Andreassen understood this well and made training and development one of the few functions that he controlled directly from ISS's small corporate office. Under the ISS philosophy of ensuring that all employees had the opportunity to use their abilities to the full, the Five Star Development Program defined five levels of training that allowed front-line supervisors with the appropriate profile to gain the knowledge and experience they would need in a broader management job.

Because of its strong promote-from-within culture, 3M also had a long-standing commitment to develop its people to their potential. Soon after a new employee enters the company (within six months for a clerical employee or three years for a laboratory scientist), a formal Early Career Assessment Process is initiated to ensure that the individual is a proper fit with the company, and to define a program to prepare those who are identified as such for their next career opportunity. For example, a promising accounting clerk might be set the personal education goal of becoming a Certified Public Accountant within three years, while being given an internal development assignment to provide experience in preparing financial statements and participating in audits. This process continues, albeit in a somewhat less structured format, throughout an individual's career in 3M, with the company providing internal business courses and technical seminars, and supporting partici-pation in external education programs.

On-the-job training is still the primary emphasis, and those with the will and the perceived personal potential are given every opportunity to develop that promise. For example, Andy Wong, the young engineer who turned the struggling Optical Systems project from a loss generator, facing shutdown, into a showcase of entrepre-neurial success, was carefully prepared for that role over five years. This quiet engi-neer first caught the eye of Ron Mitsch, a senior R&D executive who was impressed by the young man's tenacious, self-motivated, competitive personal qualities that 3M looked for in its front-line entrepreneurs. Wanting to give him the opportunity to prove that potential, the mentor told Wong about an opportunity to lead a small technical development team in the OS unit. While demonstrating his energy and persuasive persistence, Wong began to expand his knowledge about the unit's optical technologies, as he struggled to develop the understanding he needed to focus his team's rather fragmented efforts. After a couple of years in the OS labora-tory, Wong was asked to take on the additional responsibility for the unit's ineffi-cient manufacturing operations. Although he had no prior production or logistics experience, his initiatives (in rationalizing the complex sourcing arrangements, sim-plifying the manufacturing process, and consolidating production in a single plant) resulted in a 50 percent cost reduction and simultaneous improvement in product quality. It was through these experiences that Wong was able to broaden his know-ledge of the business beyond his focused understanding of the technology, and expand his familiarity with the organization's resources beyond his scientific con-tacts. Through careful career path development, he developed the kind of know-ledge and experience he needed to allow him to use his naturally competitive traits effectively as the newly appointed project team leader for optical systems.

While the developmental path for operating-level entrepreneurs focused on enhancing knowledge and expertise in a particular business, market, or function, the track to the next level of management usually required a much richer understanding of the organization and how it operated. Wong's boss, Paul Guehler, also began his 3M career in the R&D laboratory and also looked beyond the technologies he was developing to the businesses they represented. It was this budding entrepreneurial attitude that led to his transfer to 3M's New Business Ventures Division where his natural curiosity and intuitiveness were leveraged by focusing him on the task of exploring market opportunities and business applications for high-potential ideas and innovations. After a decade in this division, Guehler was transferred to the Occupational Health and Safety Products Division where his experience as R&D manager gave him the opportunity to broaden his understanding of the mainstream organizational processes and how to manage them. A subsequent move to the Disposable Products Division helped him to build on that experience, particularly when he was appointed Business Director for disposable products in Europe. This responsibility for a highly competitive product in a fast-changing market greatly expanded his experience in assessing the capabilities and limitations of a diverse group of individuals and organizational units and further expanded his understanding of the organizational dynamics and strategic tensions of having them work together.

By the time he was appointed as general manager and later vice-president of the Safety and Security Systems Division of which Wong's Optical Systems unit was a part, he brought not only hard-headed business knowledge but some sensitive organizational insights into his new role, as his diagnosis of the OS unit's situation indicates:

> You have to have people in these positions who recognize other people's talents and support their ideals for building a business. My job is to create an environment where people come forward with ideas and are supported to succeed ... So while the OS group probably thought I was being too tough, my objective was to get them to recognize their opportunities, to hold them accountable for their actions, to help them build their credibility, and ultimately to support them so they could succeed ... One of my most important roles is not only to develop business but to develop the people who can develop the businesses.

At the top level of 3M management, the need for a breadth of knowledge and experience was even greater. In 1991, when the company was in the process of selecting a new chief executive, ex-CEO Lou Lehr predicted that the successful candidate was likely to be a career 3M executive, five to ten years from retirement. He believed this for no other reason than that it usually took 30 to 35 years to accumulate the breadth of experience to be effective in the top job in this diversified global company. Desi DeSimone, the CEO elected in 1991, was described in one newspaper as "a textbook example of the quintessential 3M CEO." Having moved up through technical, engineering, and manufacturing management positions to assume general management roles as managing director of the Brazilian subsidiary and, eventually, area vice-president of 3M's Latin American operations, he was recognized as a senior manager with top management potential. "There were always people taking an interest in my development," DeSimone said on assuming the CEO job. In classic 3M fashion, he was brought back to corporate headquarters where he could be given experiences that would provide him with the background and knowledge to help him succeed in top-level positions.

Through the 1980s, he was assigned to head up each of 3M's three business sectors in succession, broadening his knowledge of their markets and technologies, while simultaneously allowing him to apply that understanding as he refined the skills necessary to have an impact on their performance. After spending most of his career focused on the company's far-flung units in Canada, Australia, and Latin America, it was also important for him to get a better sense of the organization's core structure, processes, and culture. By immersing him in corporate-level activities for more than a decade, 3M's top management and the board's appraisal committee wanted to ensure that he had the organizational understanding that was vital for maintaining and adapting the behavioral context that was so central in supporting innovation and entrepreneurship. Finally, DeSimone's promotion to the board in 1986 was important not only in bringing his expertise to board-level decisions, but also in broadening him as an executive by exposing him to the perspectives and experiences of top-level executives from other companies in different industries.

In companies like 3M, where an understanding of the strongly held organizational values and cultural norms is central to the source of competitive advantage, the importance of a career-long development process must not be underestimated. Sometimes, however, a manager's strong links to the company's existing policies and practices become disadvantageous, particularly when the embedded beliefs have deteriorated into reality-defying, blinding assumptions or outmoded conventional wisdom. In such cases, selection of an outsider with the desired personal characteristics can break the pathological cycle of inwardly-focused indoctrination. While such a radical remedy can succeed where knowledge and experience accumulated by the candidate in prior work is directly relevant in the new situation, too great an industry or business stretch risks stranding the new leader without the relevant knowledge required to develop the appropriate top management skills for the new company. So, while Larry Bossidy was able to make a relatively smooth transition from his top management job at GE to the leadership of Allied Signal, another traditionally structured diversified industrial goods company, merged with Honeywell in 1999, John Sculley's move from Pepsico to Apple became more problematic, due to his lack of computer industry background and his inexperience in managing the more informal network culture of Silicon Valley.

Coaching for skills mastery

Of all the elements in the competencies profile, the particular skills and abilities an individual develops are probably the best indicators of job success since these are the personal capabilities that are the most directly linked to a position's key roles and tasks. Not everyone becomes effective in these highly specific yet critical personal skills, and management's challenge is to identify those who will succeed and help them develop the skills. The reason is that most of these skills rely heavily on tacit knowledge and capabilities that often grow out of the interaction between an individual's embedded traits and accumulated experience. So, for example, the critical entrepreneurial ability to recognize potential in people and situations is not an easily trainable skill, but one that often develops naturally in individuals who are curious and intuitive by nature and who have developed a richly textured understanding of their particular business and organizational environment.

Thus, while some broader skills can be selected for and other simpler ones can be trained for, most of the critical skills are largely self-developed through on-the-job experience as individuals apply their natural talents and accumulated experience to the particular challenges of the job. In this process, the most effective role management can play is to coach and support those they have selected and prepared for the job, by providing the resources, reinforcement, and guidance to encourage the self-development process.

Göran Lindahl, the ABB executive vice-president, clearly articulated the notion that an individual's natural characteristics should be the dominant factor in selection: "I will always pick a person with tenacity over one with just experience," he said. He also spent a substantial amount of his time planning developmental job experiences for the individuals he selected. However, he saw his principal and most difficult management role as acting as a teacher and a coach to help those in the organization leverage their experiences and fulfill their natural potential. It was this commitment "to help engineers become managers, and managers grow into leaders" that was vital to the development of the skills required to meet the demanding new job requirements.

Don Jans was surprised when he was asked to continue to head the relays company that ABB took over as part of the acquired Westinghouse power transmission and distribution business. "The prevailing view was that we had lost the war . . . [and] that the occupying troops would just move in," he said. Yet Lindahl and Ulf Gundemark, his worldwide relays business managers, were impressed that Jans, like most of the Westinghouse managers, was a very capable individual with long industry experience, and felt that, with proper coaching, his natural energy, persistence, and competitiveness could be channeled toward the new skills he would need to manage in a very different way within ABB.

Jans met their expectations, and with his bosses' encouragement, support and coaching, was able to develop a whole range of new skills that not only helped him turn around his relays company, but also on a personal level made him feel as if he had "rediscovered management." By redefining Jans's company as part of an interdependent global network, ABB's senior level management was able to refocus his attention on export markets, thereby helping him re-ignite his latent ability to identify and exploit opportunities. Through their own highly motivating and inspiring management approach, Barnevik, Lindahl, Gundemark, and others provided Jans with role models that encouraged him to tap into his own engaging personality and develop a more motivating approach to drive his people to higher levels of performance. And ABB's cultural norm of high interest and involvement in the operations (what Lindahl called the "fingers in the pie" approach) led Jans to expand on his natural results-orientated competitiveness and develop a skill for creating and sustaining energy around the demanding objectives he set for his organization.

Meanwhile, Lindahl was helping to support a very different set of new skills in the select few of the operating-level entrepreneurs who had been chosen to take on senior-level business or regional responsibilities. One such individual was Ulf Gundemark, the young manager running the Swedish relays company. Lindahl had promoted Gundemark to worldwide relays manager due to the fact that, in addition to his 12 years of experience in various parts of the organization, he demonstrated the vital personality characteristics that Lindahl described as "generous, flexible, and statesman-like." Driven by his boss's urging to become a "giver" rather than a "receiver" of management resources, and constrained by his organizationally-designed lack of division-level staff, Gundemark leveraged his naturally supportive disposition into a sophisticated skill of developing the operating-level managers reporting to him. He did this by delegating responsibilities and empowering them to take decisions. Lindahl also encouraged Gundemark to establish formal and informal management forums at all levels of his organization and, by applying his flexible and integrative personality to his growing understanding of the organizational dynamics, the younger manager gradually acquired a strong ability to develop interpersonal relationships and team behavior. Finally, largely by following the role modeling example of his boss, Gundemark had developed the vital senior-management skill of maintaining the pressure for both long- and short-term objectives while helping the organization to deal with the conflicts that were implied. Although many were unwilling or unable to manage the very different task requirements of a senior manager's job (indeed, Lindahl estimated that even after careful selection, half the candidates for these positions either stepped aside or were moved out of the role), managers like Gundemark, who were able to develop their people and relationship-building skills, usually succeeded in these roles.

At the top levels of management, an even more subtle and sophisticated set of skills and abilities was necessary. More than just driving the company's ongoing operations or developing its resources and capabilities, these individuals had to be able to lead the company toward becoming what Lindahl described as "a self-driven, self-renewing organization." The most fundamental skill was one that CEO Percy Barnevik had encouraged in all of his top team: to create an exciting and demanding work environment. Harnessing his own innate restlessness, Lindahl focused his naturally striving and questioning personal style on his broad knowledge of the company and its businesses to develop a finely honed ability to challenge managers' assumptions while stretching them to reach for new objectives. His bi-monthly business meetings were far from traditional review sessions, as Lindahl led his senior managers through scenario exercises that forced them to think beyond straight-line projections and consider how they could respond to new trade barriers, political realignments, or environmental legislation. He also recognized that it was top management's role to develop the organization's values. He said, "In the end, managers are not really loyal to a particular boss or even to a company, but to the values they represent," and that one of the most vital was to create an environment of mutual cooperation and trust. By consistently applying his own natural forthright and open personal approach to a sophisticated understanding of the organization and its processes, he was able to create a belief in the institution and in the fairness of its management processes that was a prior condition for both entrepreneurial risk taking and shared organizational learning. Finally, Lindahl's sharp mind and inspiring personal manner were supported by a broad exposure to ABB's operating context to help develop the vital top management skill of being able to articulate messages that provided the organization with conceptual insight about the business, while simultaneously providing them with concrete motivational challenges. He routinely demonstrated this ability in his far-sighted views about ABB's role in helping develop the industrial infrastructure in a realigned global political economy, and in his translation of those insights into challenges to his management to find ways for the company to radically rebalance its own value chain from the developed world to the emerging giants such as China, India, and Eastern Europe.

The reason this set of top-management skills is so difficult to develop is that it both reflects and reinforces the conflicts, dilemmas, and paradoxes framed by the post-transformational organization. Unlike the classic top-management task that focused on managing "alignment" and ensuring "fit," the role we describe here involves at least as much energy being devoted to questioning, challenging, and even defying the company's traditional strategic assumptions and embedded organizational practices. Beyond building on the tension between the operating-level ability to drive ongoing performance and the senior-management skill of developing long-term capabilities, the required competencies involve an even greater level of subtlety and sophistication to maintain a balance between challenging embedded beliefs and creating a unifying sense of purpose and ambition. Not surprisingly, only a handful of people have the potential to develop these scarce leadership skills, and it is, perhaps, the most critical task of top management to identify these individuals and provide them with the necessary development opportunities and the coaching support to allow them to fulfill that potential.

From organization man to individualized corporation

The development of new integrated network organization models in response to new global strategic imperatives has been one of the major forces that are redefining management roles at every level of today's large transnational corporation. In turn, this is redefining the individual attributes and personal competencies of a new generation of front-line, senior-level, and top-echelon managers.

It is important to note, however, that these changes are just part of a much broader and deeper revolution that is fundamentally changing the face of the modern corporation and radically redefining the nature of contemporary management practice. It is a transformation born out of the convergence of the globalization of the economy and the maturing of the information age – forces which, together, are redefining the nature of competition.

In earlier decades, when capital was the scarce resource, top management's primary role was to use its control over investments to determine strategy, and to create the structures and systems to shape employees' behavior in ways that would support those capital allocation decisions. This strategy–structure–systems doctrine of management led to the development of what William Whyte (1956) termed "the organization men" – employees whose behavior was molded to suit the needs of the corporation and to support its strategic investments.

As the industrial era evolves into the Information Age, and as the relevant arena of competition shifts to the global stage, the scarce resource is shifting from capital to knowledge. Because of their old hierarchical structures and Russian doll management roles, however, most companies have neither fully comprehended nor appropriately responded to this profound change. Because the organization's vital knowledge, expertise, and strategic information exist at the operating-levels rather than at the top, as scarce capital did, the whole authoritarian hierarchy has had to be dismantled and the roles and tasks of each management level radically redefined. Far from wanting to subjugate individual differences by requiring conformity to a standardized organizational model (as the "organization man" philosophy implied), companies are recognizing that, in a knowledge-based environment, diversity of employee perspectives, experience, and capabilities can be an important organizational asset.

This realization implies a fundamental reconceptualization of the organization model and the management philosophy that supports it. Instead of forcing the individual to conform to the company's policies and practices, management's overall objective must be to capture and leverage the knowledge and expertise that each organizational member brings to the company, no matter where in the company he or she may be located. Thus the notion of the "organization man," and the Russian doll model of nested roles that it reflected and supported, is giving way to a concept we describe as the "Individualized Corporation" that is based on the need for companies to capitalize on the idiosyncrasies and even the eccentricities of exceptional people by recognizing, developing, and applying their unique capabilities.

The implication for global companies is profound. No longer can internationalization be regarded as simply a quest for incremental markets. Today, it is a battle to identify, capture, and leverage the critical information, the leading-edge knowledge, and the scarce expertise that are becoming the real strategic resources that ensure sustainable advantage. Companies can no longer assume that those increasingly scarce and valuable resources reside in their head office or are accessible in their home market. They must create true networking organizations that give them access to worldwide resources and capabilities and they must redefine the management roles to develop and deploy the scarce knowledge and expertise they access.

For most companies, the constraint they face in implementing this change is not lack of strategic insight, since most of them understand the new competitive imperatives. For many, it is not even a lack of organizational capability, since an increasing number have developed the integrated networks to frame their worldwide operations. But very few have mastered the new managerial challenges implied by the radically redefined roles and relationships called for by the new strategic tasks and organization models. The challenge for most companies is, as one manager succinctly put it, to learn how to fix the problems caused by "implementing third-generation strategies in a second-generation organization run by first-generation managers."

Note

1 The last major change in corporate form and management model came in the 1920s, when the adoption of the divisionalized organization gave rise to a model of professional management based on the delegation of responsibility counteracted by sophisticated planning and control systems. The birth of this corporate form is described in detail in Chandler (1962).

References

Bartlett, Christopher A. and Sumantra Ghoshal (1989) *Managing Across Borders: The Transnational Solution*, Boston, MA: HBS Press.

Chandler, Alfred D. Jr. (1962) *Strategy and Structure: Chapters in the History of American Industrial Enterprise*, Cambridge, MA: MIT Press.

Ghoshal, Sumantra and Christopher A. Bartlett (1997) *The Individualized Corporation: A Fundamentally New Approach to Management*, New York, NY: HarperBusiness Books.

Whyte, William (1956) *The Organization Man*, New York: Simon & Schuster.

INDEX

ABB: annual sales revenue 231; customer relations 254–5; differentiated networking organization 17; diversification 230; international innovation projects 41; leadership 235, 273, 275; managers 266, 271, 280; matrix form 234–5, 263, 269; network organization 209, 262, 263; R&D 6, 257; socialization 254; strategic business units 220, 232–3; strategic planning processes 243, 247; technology management 248
Abernathy, W. 82
accountability 69, 154, 162–3, 176–8
Acer Inc.: annual sales revenue 231; cellular organization 14–15, 216–17; decentralization 257; diversification 230, 231; human resources management 250; innovation in management 251–2; regional business units 16; strategic business units 232, 243; strategic planning processes 247; *see also* Shih
acquisitions 132, 192, 199, 205
aerospace industry 202
agency theory 142
airline regulations 133
Alexander, M. 226–7, 229
Allred, B. 13–14, 15, 210
American Airlines 9, 126–7
American Motors 107
Andreassen, Poul 263, 270, 276–7
Angel, D. 82
annual sales revenue 231
Arrow, K.J. 25
AT&T 17, 262, 272
Australian brewing industry 112, 114
automobile industry: *see* car industry
automotive manufacturing 86, 88, 89, 92

Balkin, D.B. 140
Bannister, D. 105
Barbie dolls 126, 130–2
Barnevik, Percy 235, 263, 266, 271, 275, 281
Barney, J.B. 23
Bartlett, C.A. 13, 14, 15, 17, 18, 40, 60, 78, 83, 86, 93, 103, 135, 139, 140, 148, 152, 175, 180, 200n3, 220, 221, 226, 233, 234, 260–1
Beamish, P.W. 228
Becerra, M. 5, 34
Belgian brewing industry 112
Bendix, R. 203
Benedict, R. 175

Berggren, C. 234
Bettis, R. 105
Biddle, B.J. 165
biotechnology 85, 86, 92
Birkinshaw, J. 148
Black, J.S. 150
Bleeke, J. 211
BMW 81, 107, 108
Boeing 220
Bosch 123, 133; customer relations 253; diversification 220, 230, 231; innovation in management 253; strategic business units 236; strategic planning processes 245–6
Bossidy, Larry 279
Bougon, M. 105–6
Boyer, R. 61
Brache, A. 152
brand image 114, 132
brand loyalty 128, 129, 133
brewing industry 112, 113–14; cognitive analysis 112–18; cognitive mapping 115–17
Britain 7, 112, 114
Brooke, M.Z. 205
Brown, S.M. 106
Buitendijk, Theo 264, 265, 268, 270, 275
Burgers, W.P. 228
business environment 2, 238–9, 255
business process re-engineering 153–4, 157, 174–5; accountability 176–8; co-ordination 152–3, 163; dependencies 164–5; exceptions 165–6; failures 4, 11, 153; Goal–Exception–Dependency model 11–12, 161, 163–7; international network corporations 157–8, 180–1; multinational corporations 11–13; purchasing process 158–63; social context model 158–63; surface/deep structure 159–60, 163, 181
Byrne, J.A. 209

Calori, R. 8–9
Campbell, A. 226–7, 229
Canadian brewing industry 112, 113
Canon 7, 81, 88
Cantwell, J. 81, 82, 86
car industry 107–8, 110–11, 123–4; cognitive analysis 106–12; competition 111–12; competitive advantages 108–9; ethnocentric biases 106–7; globalization 107–12; innovation 81, 133

284